330.9   2162044
B97e
Butler, Joseph H.
Economic geography

Economic Geography

Strictly speaking all locations are interdependent. No one location or location factor can be called leading and the others dependent. The location system, like the solar system, hangs free in space, so to speak, nowhere suspended and held together only within itself. In practice, however, those natural factors to whose sources production is necessarily bound have special weight as a rule: arable land, natural resources, valleys, harbors, and climate. . . . in many cases the proximity and superior quality of several natural factors is so strikingly combined that such regions may be regarded with high probability from the first as cardinal points in the location system.

August Lösch

Economic Geography
Spatial and Environmental Aspects
of Economic Activity

Joseph H. Butler

Harpur College

State University of New York at Binghamton

John Wiley & Sons

New York · Chichester · Brisbane · Toronto

Library of Congress Cataloging in Publication Data:

Butler, Joseph H.
  Economic geography.

  Includes index.
  1. Geography, Economic. I. Title.
HF1025.B86   330.9   80-14542
ISBN 0-471-12681-0

Printed in the United States of America

10 9 8 7 6 5 4 3 2 1

To my mother and father

Preface

This book is based on the conviction that economic geography can contribute in an important way to an understanding of economic phenomena and is relevant to a wide range of contemporary problems. This conviction began to form many years ago when, as a young engineer working for an international company based in Manhattan, I took my first course in economic geography at Columbia University. The subject proved so interesting and so useful in my work that it led, ultimately, to my conversion to full time academic geography.

When concern over the environment grew and began to find expression in public policy in the 1960s, it seemed logical that economic geography would become more relevant than ever. However, although economics, anthropology, and other disciplines treated the environment as an intellectual frontier, an influential group within economic geography tended to ignore it, concentrating almost exclusively on abstract spatial models, until economic geography came to resemble in some places a surrogate regional science.

The swing of the pendulum away from the real world and toward spatial abstraction, at first an essential move, has carried too far, resulting in texts that do not meet the needs of a large proportion of students and instructors. A concomitant trend has been the narrowing of economic geography's focus to location, with the neglect of other aspects of economic activity, such as the interaction of natural resources, production, and waste.

An approach that incorporates, rather than ignores, the real-world environment restores economic geography to its traditional, broader role—a role recognized in their works by Erich Zimmermann, Gunnar Myrdal, August Lösch, Paul Samuelson, Walter Isard, and other influential economists, as well as by economic geographers.

This book is designed as an introductory text in economic geography; it combines both spatial and environmental explanatory approaches and emphasizes that the location and character of economic activity are interdependent aspects of the economic landscape. The distinctive but complementary rent doctrines of Ricardo and von Thünen are used to formalize the environmental and spatial explanatory approaches. The use of the two rent doctrines as organizing concepts is consistent with modern efforts to give economic geography a more unified theoretical base.

The combining of environmental and spatial influences in the study of economic activity is anything but a regression toward environmental determinism. On the contrary, it helps reveal more fully the nondeterministic nature of economic processes, and the roles of human judgment and environmental perception in decisions shaping the economic landscape. Even Robinson Crusoe in his spatial economy is shown to have choices between nearby, lower grade resources, and more distant, higher grade resources, illustrating the universal principle of substitution between variable transport and production costs—a principle that would be meaningless under the assumption of a uniform environment. The consideration of a spatially variable natural environment is also essential to such fundamental concepts as economic rent, resource depletion, the Law of Diminishing Returns, conservation, waste assimilation, and many others—including even the Weberian Industrial Location Model.

The dual explanatory approach has other advantages. It permits traditional topics in economic geography, such as primary production, to be treated in a more systematic manner. In addition, it allows frontier topics, such as the economic effects of environmental impact, to be handled more effectively.

Finally, the combined treatment of spatial and environmental aspects of economic activity makes modern economic geography more relevant to many contemporary problems, and more applicable to such applied areas as regional and urban planning, resource management, land-use analysis, and environmental management.

This book was created for use in a one-semester or one-quarter course in economic geography or as a supplementary reading for other courses in geography, business, environmental studies, economics, planning, or resource management. No preparation in mathematics or other subjects beyond the academic high school level is required. The book has been extensively used in draft form in the classroom, and has benefited from feedback from students and former students. I will be grateful to readers for comments, suggestions, and corrections.

Many people over the years have inspired and helped me professionally, and have thus indirectly contributed to this book. Courses and seminars with the late John Orchard, and with Herman Otte and William Hance at Columbia provided a foundation in economic geography that still sustains me, while work under Arthur Strahler gave me a lasting appreciation for environmental systems as they interrelate with human activities. Wesley J. Hennessy, a geographer and former Dean of Engineering at Columbia, arranged for me to work as his assistant, enabling me to support my family while completing my last two years of graduate work.

In more recent years, I have benefited from a close and supportive relationship with Joseph Van Riper and other colleagues in the Department of Geography at S.U.N.Y. Binghamton.

A number of people have helped me directly in the book's preparation. Daniel Loetterle gave me advice and creative assistance with a number of maps. Ms. Suzanne Snyder and Ms. Jean Sircovitch expertly typed the bulk of several drafts and the final manuscript. The staff at John Wiley and Sons were generous with their patience and untiring assistance. And, lastly, in addition to countless typing, editing, and other chores—often of an emergency nature—my wife, Janet, along with my children, provided the continuing encouragement and support essential for the book's completion.

Joseph H. Butler

Contents

xii

1

INTRODUCTION

"For naturally economic geography sets the stage."

Gunnar Myrdal*

In many ways the 1970s was a decade of reexamination and redirection. New attitudes, policies, and planning objectives evolved to meet the growing problems of food and energy supply, resource depletion, pollution, environmental deterioration, urban blight, and the overall need for wiser land use for a growing population. The long range challenge is a formidable one: how to raise incomes and improve the quality of life throughout the world and still protect the planet for future generations.

Industrialization is no longer considered the cure-all for less-developed countries. The emphasis of Western social scientists on economic growth as a general solution to national problems has been modified by longer-range ecological goals. A growing belief exists that per capita money income is an inadequate measure of a people's total welfare; life-styles among many in the industrialized world reflect a retreat from extravagant materialism. The assumption of limitless, low-cost energy supplies was shattered in 1973. Much of the "conventional wisdom" concerning acute urban problems has been challenged. And there is a sharper realization that the high income. high resource-using, high energy-consuming nations are expanding the gul' between them and other nations of the world.

* *Rich Lands and Poor,* Harper and Brothers, New York, 1957, p. 26.

1

In the past, economic development has provided an unprecedented abundance of goods and services in industrial nations. However, the growth of population and wealth in these countries has also created an intensification of land use.

In Great Britain, Canada, Israel, Sweden and other countries, geographers play important roles in government planning. In the Soviet Union, economic geographers contribute to regional and national development programs. France's National Urban Growth Strategy, developed in the late 1960s, was the creation of a group of geographers. In the United States, although geographers are making important contributions within the private

---

THE NEED FOR A "SECOND AMERICA" BY 2000 A.D.

A study by the federal government* has predicted the need for the construction of a "Second America" by the end of the century. The following quote from the report shows the magnitude of that need:

Our intensive and consumptive use of the land is expected to escalate dramatically . . . In fact, all that has been built in the history of this Nation may have to be duplicated. That is, the equivalent of every school, pipeline, power-plant, office building, airport, shopping center, factory, home and highway that has been built during our first 200 years may have to be matched to accommodate population and market demands projected for the year 2000.

Here are some conservative projections for land use in the U.S. over the next generation.

19.7 million acres may be consumed by urban sprawl by 2000—an area equivalent to the states of New Hampshire, Vermont, Massachusetts, and Rhode Island.

3.5 million acres may be paved over for highways and airports by 2000.

7 million acres may be taken from agricultural use for recreation and wildlife areas by 2000.

5 million acres may be lost to agriculture for public facilities, second home development, and waste control projects by 2000.

492 power stations may be built by 1990, many of them requiring cooling ponds of 2,000 acres or more.

2 million acres of right-of-way may be required by 1990 for 200,000 additional miles of power lines.

* United States Environmental Protection Agency, "Environmental Facts," Washington, D.C., July, 1973.

2

as well as the public sector, their involvement in applied fields has by no means approached its full potential.

SOME TYPICAL QUESTIONS IN ECONOMIC GEOGRAPHY

The study of geography emphasizes spatial distributions. Geographers are concerned not only with *where* things are, but *why* they are located where they are, and the nature of the processes that affect location. *Economics* can be defined simply as the study of choice necessitated by scarcity. There are different ways of defining *economic geography*. However, a good way to get to the heart of an academic discipline is to consider the kinds of questions it seeks to answer. Here is a broad sample of the questions economic geography deals with:

What accounts for the patterns of land use we see all around us? Why is one plot of land a farm, another a used-car lot, and another the site of a skyscraper?

Why does land vary so much in price from place to place? Why does an acre of land cost millions of dollars in Peachtree Center in downtown Atlanta, Georgia, and only a few hundred dollars in other parts of the state not far away?

Why can you obtain certain goods and services (for example, gasoline and haircuts) in virtually every small town in America, while some other goods and services are found only in a few very large cities?

What accounts for the great difference in the location of world petroleum and coal production?

How are increased energy prices likely to influence the spatial economy of the United States? Of Canada? Of Brazil?

How has the depletion of high grade iron ores influenced the location of iron and steel production in the United States? In the world?

Why must the Soviet Union, with four times as many farm workers, buy millions of tons of grain from the United States?

In what ways have water and air pollution become important plant location factors?

Why does the State of Wyoming, with an area larger than Great Britain, have only 400,000 persons?

These questions relate to some of the most basic concerns of humanity, including where and how people earn their living, and where and how they spend their income. All the questions have both *spatial* and *environmental* aspects, and all can be viewed within the organizing framework of a *spatial economy.*

THE CONCEPT OF A SPATIAL ECONOMY

The concept of a *spatial economy* or, in more formal language, a *spatial economic system,*[1] is a fundamental one in economic geography. The simplified model of a spatial economy suggested here consists of a set of *consumers* and a set of *production establishments* within some defined space. The elements making up the set of consumers—all living persons within the space—are mobile (or movable), while the elements making up the set of production establishments—such as factories, farms, shops, schools, mines, amusement parks, and so on—are spatially fixed, at least in the short-run period.

Within the model spatial economy the two sets of elements, consumers and production establishments, obviously have different spatial patterns. To overcome this discrepancy, the consumers move about to purchase goods and services; or, conversely, goods and services, such as delivered milk and television repairs, "move to" the consumer. In addition to *consumption* and *production,* a third activity that takes place is *exchange,* the process by which supply and demand are matched up in space. Exchange involves movement of people, goods, and information (Chapter 12). In many cases both the consumer and the product move to a mutually accessible place—a *market place*—to minimize total transport costs. Food items grown on farms move through a series of processing stages to the supermarket, to which the consumer travels to shop for many of these items.

Ideally, in a free market economy, the supply and demand for individual goods and services are reflected in their prices. In an ideal spatial economy

---

STOLPER'S GENERALIZATION OF THE LOCATIONAL PROBLEM

In an article written in 1954, economist Wolfgang Stolper posed the locational problem in its full generality: "What is the optimum distribution of the production of all goods and the location of all people if all goods and all factors (except perhaps land and certain natural resources) are mobile at a cost"?*

*"Spatial Order and The Economic Growth of Cities: A Comment on Eric Lampard's Paper," *Economic Development and Cultural Change,* University of Chicago, Vol. 3, 1954-55, p. 138.

---

[1] These two terms are used synonymously in this book.

prices adjust over time to keep supply and demand at just those levels that will enable all consumers and all producers to benefit most.

A source of confusion exists about *value* and *price*. The price of something essential (in the sense that we cannot be without it) may be very low. Municipal water supply is an example. On the other hand, the price of gold is very high, despite the fact that its possession is not critical or even necessary. This seeming paradox is resolved when it is understood that the price reflects only the last (*marginal*) unit of a good or service placed on the market. Thus, water is relatively abundant with respect to our needs and commands a low price, while the opposite is true of gold.

All living persons, as mentioned above, are consumers; this is true whether they are producers or not. The person lying unconscious in a hospital is, of course, consuming services at a high rate. The production establishment, whether producing goods (bread) or services (auto repairs), is normally a physical unit of capital investment, consisting of land and structures

---

A CLASSIFICATION OF INDUSTRIES

The most detailed classification of industries in this country is the *Standard Industrial Classification* (SIC)*. In the SIC Manual, there are ten *Divisions:*

A. Agriculture, forestry, and fishing

B. Mining

C. Contract construction

D. Manufacturing

E. Transportation, communication, etc.

F. Wholesale and retail trade

G. Finance, insurance, and real estate

H. Services

I. Government

J. Nonclassifiable establishments

Each Division is subdivided into *Major Groups;* each Major Group is subdivided into *Groups;* each Group is subdivided into *Industries;* and, within each Industry are many individual *Production Establishments.*

* Published by the Technical Committee on Industrial Classification, Office of Statistical Standards, United States Bureau of the Budget.

---

and operating with an organized labor force. Production establishments are therefore entities that can be mapped. Production establishments producing similar goods and services are classified into *industries.*

Even the thousand or so industries listed in the *Standard Industrial Classification* do not include all forms of production. Housekeeping services done in one's home, for example, represent work that is not included in production or employment statistics. (If people would do each other's housework for wages, this would magically transform their "noneconomic" activity into "economic" activity with respect to social security regulations).

An important term associated with the production process is that of the *firm.* A firm is a unit of business ownership such as a proprietorship, partnership, or corporation. One firm may own many production establishments (plants) in one or more industries. The question of what are a firm's objectives is not easily answered. It is most frequently assumed in economic analysis that the firm attempts to maximize profits. However, many business proprietors, particularly those with small enterprises, are motivated by other objectives as well. For example, some firms are operated by the owner to provide personal satisfaction, subject to some minimum income constraint. This is called *satisficing behavior* in contrast to *maximizing behavior.*

So far we have been dealing with a general model, and therefore one that is highly idealized. In reality, economic space is also environmental space, which is anything but uniform or homogeneous. In the real world, too, consumers do not all think or behave alike. Communities and nations, as well as individuals, have different tastes, perceptions, and life-styles. To make things more complex, spatial economic systems change over time. Populations increase or decrease and change in age structure; technologies often change rapidly; new resources are discovered or developed as others become depleted. All these factors, together with others of a noneconomic nature, can influence the location and character of economic activity.

In view of the complexities of real-world spatial economies, their fundamental nature can best be grasped by examining a primitive example. The simplest illustration that meets the model criteria, described above, was created for us by the novelist Daniel Defoe in his classic *Robinson Crusoe.* Here, the spatial economy is clearly defined as Crusoe's island home of 28 years. This space contained a set of one consumer, Crusoe himself—at least until the advent of his companion Friday.

Although this example seems simple in the extreme, it is not necessarily a trivial one because it expresses some very fundamental relationships in economic geography. Even with a single consumer, a structured spatial economy develops. To survive, Crusoe must journey to sources of fresh water; he searches the beach for shellfish and the island for fruit, berries, nuts, and

6

other food. Resources for constructing his buildings and fences and clothing must be gotten from various places in his environment. Such a resourceful castaway as Crusoe might even be expected to furnish himself with certain "services" as well as goods by moving about in his resource space: perhaps to a waterfall for a bath, or to the top of a hill to view a beautiful sunset.

Robinson Crusoe was fictional, but a number of real-life castaways have been found, including Japanese military personnel lost on Pacific islands during World War II. For all we know, as yet undiscovered individuals or groups may still exist on remote islands, within totally isolated and self-sufficient spatial economies.

The cases of individuals or communities existing as independent economic systems are, of course, very rare in today's world. With the exceptions mentioned above, virtually all the world's over 4.5 billion people now live in local economies that are linked in some way to regional, national, and even international economic systems. The degree of interaction between local economies and the outside world varies greatly. Some local economies still remain nearly self-sufficient. An example would be the Hanunóo people of southeastern Mindoro Island in the Philippines (Fig. 1.1). Despite their isolation, however, even these groups have some economic links to the outside world.

Much of the Third World population lives in rural farm villages, where most inhabitants are born, live out their lives, and die without ever journeying far from home. Even so, a part of their economic life is inevitably linked in some way to outside markets and suppliers. An example of an illegal economic linkage is the international black market trade in gold, which reaches down to rural hoarders in villages in many parts of South Asia.

A very different situation exists in the industrialized regions and nations of the world. Here, the people in local communities are highly integrated into national and even global economic systems. In such nations as Canada and the United States, the degree of local self-sufficiency is very low and the consuming public is highly dependent on products and services sold in national or world markets. Consider, for example, the origins of a typical American breakfast: orange juice from Florida or California, wheat from Kansas in the cereal or toast, bacon from Iowa, cheese from Wisconsin, salt from Michigan, coffee from Brazil, sugar from the Philippines, pepper from Malagasy. Even perishable milk and eggs may be shipped several hundred miles to the local supermarket.

The extent to which consumers in industrialized nations depend on a worldwide system of supply is not always realized. For example, here are typical sources of the raw materials used in a standard desk telephone in the United States: aluminum (bauxite) from Surinam; beryllium from Brazil;

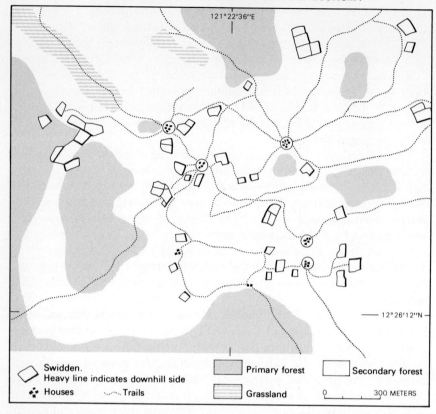

Figure 1.1   A community of shifting "slash and burn" cultivators on Mindoro Island, the Philippines. A total of 128 Hanunóo people lived in this area when studied by anthropologist Harold Conklin in 1954. Nearly all production, exchange, and consumption takes place in an area of about two square miles. The seemingly haphazard locations of house clusters, swiddens (agricultural clearings), and connecting trails through the hilly forest actually represent a highly efficient response to the need for conserving energy and time. The economic landscape undergoes yearly change, as the soil rapidly loses fertility and new clearings must be made. It is doubtful that a modern systems analyst, using a large computer, could match the dynamic network design created by these illiterate people. (Source: Adapted from Harold C. Conklin, "An Ethnoecological Approach to Shifting Agriculture," Transactions of the New York Academy of Sciences, 2d ser., Vol. 17, 1954, pp. 133-42, by permission of the author and publisher.)

8

chromium from Turkey; cobalt from Republic of Congo; gold from Australia; lead from Mexico; nickel from Norway; paper from Sweden; rubber and tin from Indonesia; silver from Peru; palladium from Canada.

A close relationship exists between incomes and the degree to which the local economy is integrated within the global economic system. Average real incomes are much higher in industrialized nations than in Third World nations because, among other things, people in industrialized nations have access to relatively low-cost goods and services from remote suppliers. An assumption exists in economic theory that every consumer lies within the market area of each good. This assumption is approached only in highly developed countries, which are sometimes called *exchange economies*. Nevertheless, perhaps half of the consumers in the world live as farmers or farm workers in agricultural villages.

THE ECONOMIC LANDSCAPE: THE SPATIAL PATTERN OF LAND USE

Unlike the spatial economy model, which can be viewed in the abstract, the *economic landscape* refers to real world patterns of land use. Simply expressed, the economic landscape is what can be seen by an observer on or above the land, or what can be perceived from maps, aerial photographs, or other remote sensing techniques about the spatial pattern and other features of economic activity. The economic landscape reveals a combination of both natural and artificial features, and results from economic decision making. It

---

BERRY ON THE SUBJECT OF MARKETS

Markets exist where a number of buyers and sellers communicate, and the price offered and paid by each is affected by the decisions of the others. A market, then, is a system which produces self-regulating prices; the prices in turn, are the mechanisms connecting individual actions of choice. In this general sense there are world markets *for wheat or copper. Most types of exchange, however, involve a specific* market place. . . . *The Chicago wheat pit and the London metals exchange are dramatic examples of market places of international significance, yet equally important are the hundreds of thousands of small* market centers *that dot the globe. Although they are seldom imposing, it is in these market centers that the daily process of exchange takes place.**

* Brian J. L. Berry, *Geography of Market Centers and Retail Distribution*, Prentice-Hall, Inc., Englewood Cliffs, N.J., 1967, p. 1.

---

often appears as a mosaic of different land uses, resulting from human modification of the land through the application of labor and capital.

Elements of the economic landscape viewed on a large scale can be buildings, highway intersections, parking lots, or individual sections of a single farm. Viewed at smaller scales such detail is obscured, but much larger areas can be shown; here, the recognizable features can be shopping centers, industrial districts, and towns. At even smaller scales, entire urban agglomerations can be shown as viewed from space (Fig. 1.2). The economic land-

Figure 1.2   The Dallas-Fort Worth, Texas, urban region, taken during NASA's Apollo 6 Mission, April 4, 1968. In addition to the built-up areas, major highways, reservoirs, and other features of the economic landscape are recognizable. (Source: National Aeronautics and Space Administration.)

10

scape may appear as largely natural, as in a national park, or as almost entirely created by humans, as in a city's *Central Business District* (CBD).

The economic landscape we see today, regardless of place or scale of observation, is not the same as it was at some point in the past. Certain economic landscapes change very slowly, while others undergo rapid change (Fig. 1.3). Parts of North America, Japan, and Europe have changed from forest cover to fertile cropland and then to urban regions in little more than a century. In some places the economic landscape contains features from different cultures and historical periods. Some economic landscapes support very few people (Fig. 1.4), while others support thousands of persons per square mile (Fig. 1.5).

Examples of economic landscape evolution can be drawn from widely different space-time scales of observation. On the one hand, there are the radical changes in the map of an entire nation, The Netherlands, which have taken place over many centuries. At the other end of the scale we can

Figure 1.3 Encroachment of suburban housing on agricultural land in San Mateo, California. Three years before the photograph was taken, the entire area was producing artichokes (foreground). (Source: USDA—Soil Conservation Service.)

personally observe, year by year, changes in land use in our home communities.

Economic landscapes, like the spatial economies they physically reflect, contain elements representing the three forms of economic activity: production, exchange (including transportation), and consumption. Common examples would be, respectively, a factory, a shopping center or a railroad terminal, and an amusement park. Economic landscapes sometimes reveal evidence of past economic activity, such as an exhausted open pit mine, an abandoned railway line, or a ghost town, even though these are no longer productive.

Where an element in the economic landscape is the source of a social cost or inconvenience of some kind instead of an economic benefit, this element can be considered *counterproductive*. Examples would be an abandoned warehouse or a slag heap, which are perceived as public dangers or eyesores. Counterproductive phenomena can be unintentional results of economic production (Fig. 1.6). These are called *negative externalities* and will be discussed in Chapter 5.

Figure 1.4   A sheepherder and wagon on the spring range in Wyoming. Because of limited rainfall and long distance to markets, sheep grazing is the only profitable land use over large regions of the U.S. West. Sheep grazing requires very little labor and very little capital (horse, wagon, and dog, primarily), but needs vast amounts of semi-arid land, and therefore supports only a very sparse population. (Source: USDA—Soil Conservation Service.)

12

Figure 1.5   A view of Hudson River piers and mid-town Manhattan. Why has New York City become one of the great concentrations of people and economic activity in the world? No complete answer can be given to such a profoundly complex question. However, environmental and spatial factors contribute partial (necessary, although not sufficient) explanations.

Environmental factors here include a superb natural harbor, with very small tidal range and very deep water. (The Hudson River here is a tidal estuary). Manhattan Island has rock foundations capable of supporting the highest buildings in the world. Many port cities are built on tidal or delta mud flats, with serious channel silting and foundation problems.

A key spatial factor is that the Hudson-Mohawk River Valley, linking New York's harbor with the Great Lakes, is the only lowland corridor across the Appalachian Mountains from Canada to Georgia. This has made New York City the principal terminal linking Europe with the North American Midwest.

Once it outstripped rival cities, because of its initial advantages, New York's increasing size made it a growing magnet for the great inflow of European immigrants, whose labor, skills, and economic needs reinforced its position as the dominant North American City. (Source: *The Port Authority of New York and New Jersey.*)

Figure 1.6 Wind blowing soil from Midwest farmland in 1930. (Source: *USDA—Soil Conservation Service.*)

AN EXAMPLE OF ECONOMIC LANDSCAPE EVOLUTION

Changes on the Upper Peninsula of Michigan during the past century provide a dynamic example of economic landscape evolution. The Pre-Columbian Indian population there had recognized as a resource some exceptionally rich native copper deposits and had mined and traded copper over much of eastern North America for centuries. When Europeans later found these deposits, they developed the region into a leading copper producer in the world. Later, in the early 1900s, most of the copper mines closed when the high-grade ores became depleted. The economic landscape of "The Copper Country" on the Keeweenaw Peninsula still contains evidence of the former flourishing copper mining industry: pit-head structures, tailings pond deposits, nearly empty or abandoned mining hamlets, and so on.

A second exploitive boom, which began about a century ago, centered on the high-grade stands of white pine that covered much of the Upper Peninsula. After several decades of rapid cutting for the burgeoning national lum-

14

ber market, the landscape contained vast cutover areas, most of which now have second or third growth forests. The forest resource now is of much lower quality for lumber production, but supports several large pulp mills.

Iron ore provided the impetus for a third economic boom, beginning in the early part of this century. This development concentrated in Marquette County, near the center of the Upper Peninsula. After the World War II industrial boom, the direct-shipping grade iron ores became depleted, making iron ores from other states and countries more competitive.

The Upper Peninsula of Michigan in the early postwar period became one of the nation's most economically depressed regions. The small, residual activities of the copper mining, forest product, and iron mining industries did not provide enough jobs for the people, and migration from the Peninsula steadily lowered the population. Most migrants were young adults, and the median age of the remaining group rose well above the national average. The regional malaise became apparent in the economic landscape, as evidenced by inactive mining centers, depopulated settlements, and abandoned farms.

In this setting, early in the 1950s, a technological breakthrough in the iron-ore industry occurred. A large mining company developed a flotation process that could be used to concentrate low-grade, nonmagnetic iron ore found in the region into high-grade iron pellets for use in the blast furnaces of the lower lake steel mills. (The taconite industry of nearby Northern Minnesota is based on magnetic iron ores, which can be concentrated magnetically.)

The company, after investing large amounts of capital in the new process, was able to tap the large reserves of ore containing less than 30 percent iron that underlie much of the area. The new iron-ore industry differed radically from the old; it was open-pit and required very high inputs of capital equipment, electric energy, and water for the mining and concentration operations. During the past quarter century, a number of very large mines and concentrating mills of this type have been constructed in Marquette County. These operations provided jobs, taxes for local governments, and other income in the form of industrial purchases. Clearly, the region has received important economic benefits from the revitalized iron-ore industry.

However, there was another aspect to the low-grade iron-ore development—a disturbing one with long-range environmental implications. Very large amounts of water must be used in the iron flotation process. The finely milled iron ore was only partially removed from the mill water effluent in the tailings basins. The finest particles remained in permanent suspension, making the effluent water a reddish color. The suspended mineral matter also gave the water an ecologically lethal potential. As a result, the water leaving the tailings basins of the mills and flowing into local streams constituted a serious form of counterproduction that affected sections of the regional hydrology.

Groups concerned about long-range environmental values became alarmed, and public debate over the issue developed into a classic "production versus pollution" controversy. The companies involved made additional large investments in facilities to help alleviate the problem.

This case illustrates a number of points: how a resource base can be expanded through technology; how a production process can result in social costs through environmental degradation; and, finally, how these things are expressed in a dynamic economic landscape.

ECONOMICS AND ECONOMIC GEOGRAPHY AS COMPLEMENTARY FIELDS

In the latter part of the eighteenth century in Europe, a succession of theorists, starting with Adam Smith, began to create the modern discipline of economics. These scholars developed the models of classical economic theory.

In contrast to this, economic geography began primarily as an empirical endeavor, having antecedents in the general field of geography. Geography was given a strong impetus by the expansion of European people to all parts of the world in the sixteenth through the nineteenth centuries. It became a practical enterprise concerned with accumulating and organizing information, and with describing and interpreting the rapidly developing global economic system. The product of this important effort was information for governmental and commercial planning and operations. This took the form of maps, data inventories, environmental monographs, regional descriptions, atlases, and other contributions to world knowledge. A major function of geography has since remained the observation and interpretation of the real world directly through field studies, and indirectly by means of maps and other models of the landscape.

During the past half century both economics and economic geography have expanded well beyond their original cores of interest.[2] Economists increasingly made empirical studies as sources of data became available, such as the United States' national income statistics. The severe world depression of the 1930s turned the attention of theoretical economists to practical problems of national economic policy. World War II and its aftermath induced economists to study non-Western models of economic development. During

[2] Robert B. McNee, "The Changing Relationships of Economics and Economic Geography," *Economic Geography,* Vol. 35, No. 3, July, 1959.

16

World War II and the early postwar period, many geographers with specialized knowledge entered government service where they provided important input for the war effort and various postwar programs. For example, the late John Orchard, Professor of Economic Geography at Columbia University, served as chief advisor to Averell Harriman during and after the war in a succession of foreign-aid and economic reconstruction programs.

In the early 1950s a number of economic geographers in the United States and elsewhere began to expand the use of applied mathematics and computer methods in their teaching and research. A new interest also developed in the earlier works of the German location theorists—von Thünen, Weber, Christaller, and Lösch. The strengthening of the theoretical and analytical aspects of economic geography has been a highly productive development. Twenty years ago location theory was rarely discussed in courses in economic geography outside of graduate seminars. Today, it is rare to find an undergraduate course that does not attempt to introduce its central concepts.

Like economics, economic geography has expanded its intellectual horizons to meet contemporary local, national, and world problems. In expanding their perimeters of interest, both fields have grown together in some

---

ZIMMERMANN ON THE COMPLEMENTARITY OF ECONOMICS AND ECONOMIC GEOGRAPHY

Nearly half a century ago an American economist, Professor Erich W. Zimmermann, wrote perceptively about the relationship between economics and economic geography in terms more relevant today than ever:

That economic life as all social life rests on a physical basis is axiomatic. Realizing this evident relationship of their science to economics, some geographers have vigorously pushed their research into the borderland which separates the two disciplines. Economists, on the other hand, perhaps preoccupied with the tantalizing and fascinating problems of value, price, distribution of income, and with similar phases of price economy in general, have shown less inclination to explore this border region and to study the physical basis on which the structure of price economy rests. The economic geographer, approaching the study of economic life from the angle of underlying physical realities, pushes upward from the physical basis toward the cultural superstructure. The economist, in turn, whose main task is the exploration of a limited section of the cultural superstructure, probes downward toward the physical foundation. Somewhere the two efforts meet, not in competition, but in cooperation.*

* Erich W. Zimmermann, *World Resources and Industries,* Harper & Row, New York. Foreward to the First Edition, 1933.

---

respects. However, although they now complement each other more than ever, the essential characters of the two disciplines remain distinctive.

Modern economic geography as interpreted in this book focuses on two interrelated aspects of Zimmermann's "underlying physical realities"—the *spatial* aspect and the *environmental* aspect. The spatial approach deals with spatial regularities and patterns that would result from economic and behavioral forces, even if the environment were the same everywhere. The environmental (sometimes referred to as the ecological) approach studies the location and character of economic activity as it is influenced by the real-world distribution of environmental factors. It is important at the outset to emphasize that, although they are often discussed separately for instructional clarity, the two influences operate together in shaping the economic landscape. The dual spatial and environmental approaches to economic activity are developed further in Chapter 3. Chapter 2 reviews the grand, space-time process that has been operating for ten thousand years, and from which the present global economy has evolved.

SUMMARY

The *spatial economy* (*spatial economic system*) can be modelled as a space containing a set of consumers and a set of production establishments. The different spatial patterns of *production* and *consumption* require a third economic activity—*exchange*—to match up supply and demand in space. The entire system is ideally kept in equilibrium through the pricing mechanism. The functions of a spatial economy are best revealed in a primitive system, such as Robinson Crusoe's island. The *economic landscape* is the observable pattern of land use in the real world. Observation and interpretation of the economic landscape create a better understanding of the existing spatial economy and of problems related to it. The economic landscape can be interpreted by means of two explanatory approaches: the *spatial* approach and the *environmental* approach. Even in a hypothetically uniform environment, market forces and the efficiencies of scale and agglomeration would give structure to the spatial economy; this is the subject of the spatial explanatory approach. The environmental explanatory approach considers the influence on economic activities of natural resources and other environmental factors. Together, the interrelated spatial and environmental approaches provide an organizing framework for modern economic geography. Economic geography and economics have evolved as separate but complementary disciplines. In its modern form, economic geography can make important contributions to the solution of a series of growing problems at the local, national, and international levels. Economic geography provides a background for such applied fields as regional planning, land-use analysis, resource management, and environmental planning and management.

Questions

1 Describe the economic landscape (1) within a half mile radius of your home or (2) of your present location. What features can be interpreted as representing production, consumption, or exchange functions?

2 What is meant by the contention that a "New America" must be created by the end of this century?

3 How can the concept of *spatial economy* be used to explain the matching up of economic supply and demand in space?

4 In what ways are economics and economic geography complementary fields?

5 Give examples of (1) a local or regional problem, (2) a national problem, and (3) an international problem that fall within the scope of economic geography.

2

EVOLUTION OF THE GLOBAL ECONOMY: THE SPACE-TIME PROCESS

"The unfolding of Man's patterns over geographic space and through time is a fascinating thing to watch and study, and once you have thought about the processes at work in these fundamental dimensions of human existence you can never wholly return to 'pre-diffusion' thinking."

Peter Gould*

A fundamental theoretical question that can be asked about any distribution is whether or not it is a random distribution. If a spatial distribution is nonrandom, then the presumption exists that it results from some kind of nonrandom process operating in space and through time. The present distribution of economic activity throughout the world is clearly nonrandom. This chapter attempts to develop an understanding of the grand process that shaped that distribution.

THE SPATIAL DIFFUSION OF ECONOMIC CHANGE

Ten thousand years ago there were fewer human beings on earth than now reside in metropolitan Chicago. Several million people then lived in small bands that were thinly scattered across parts of six continents. All humanity—the ancestors of everyone now on earth—lived by the same economic activity, hunting and gathering. Since that time a series of radical changes

---

*Spatial Diffusion, Washington, D.C.: Association of American Geographers, Resource Papers for College Geography No. 4, 1969, p. 1.

20

has taken place in the way people produce, consume, and live in general. These changes have multiplied world population a thousand times—to over 4.5 billion—and have created an interconnected global economy. Each change, or *innovation,* originated in one place—or at most a few places—and spread, or *diffused,* outward to other parts of the world.

It is significant that diffusion of the critical innovations did not take place uniformly over space and time. As a result, while some persons today live in modern cities within high technology nations, others still live as their ancestors did thousands of years ago. The extreme degree of spatial variation in economic activity and performance throughout the world gives the study of economic geography a special relevance in today's world.

Let us assume for a moment that the first astronauts to reach the moon were accompanied on their return by an intelligent being from another part of the universe. Let's further assume that the visitor had the ability to discern spatial information on the earth's surface from the returning space vehicle. The observations and questions of this visitor might give us some interesting insights into our global economy. The planetary visitor would observe that *Homo sapiens'* very large numbers and widespread distribution as a single species are unmatched elsewhere in the higher animal world. Another observation would be that human population and economic activity are not distributed over the land in anything resembling a random manner. See Tables 2.1 and 2.2 and Figures 2.1, 2.2, and 2.3.

Now, if our intelligent observer possesses an earthly curiosity, he/she would surely wonder how these striking variations came about, that is, how the spatially diverse global economy evolved. The economic geographer is interested in the same questions, not only to satisfy intellectual curiosity, but also because the grand process that has shaped the present world economy will continue to influence the location of people and economic activity in the future.

HÄGERSTRAND ON THE DIFFUSION OF INNOVATION

The Swedish geographer, Torsten Hägerstrand, a pioneer in the field of spatial diffusion, has written:

Diffusion of Innovation is by definition a function of communication. One cannot adopt an innovation which is not one's own invention unless one has first seen it, heard of it, or read about it. *

* "Aspects of the Spatial Structure of Social Communication and the Diffusion of Information," *Regional Science Association: Papers,* XVI Cracow Congress, 1965, p. 27.

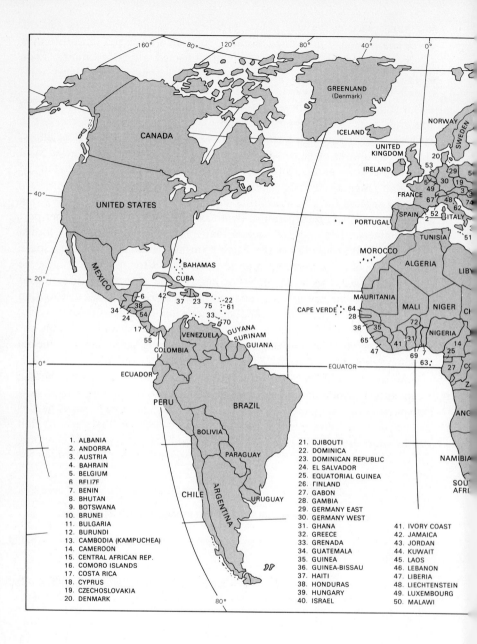

Figure 2.1

EVOLUTION OF THE GLOBAL ECONOMY: THE SPACE-TIME PROCESS

51. MALTA	64. SENEGAL
52. MONACO	65. SIERRA LEONE
53. NETHERLANDS	66. SINGAPORE
54. NICARAGUA	67. SWITZERLAND
55. PANAMA	68. SYRIA
56. POLAND	69. TOGO
57. QATAR	70. TRINIDAD AND TOBAGO
58. RHODESIA (ZIMBABWE)	71. UNITED ARAB EMIRATES
59. ROMANIA	72. UPPER VOLTA
60. RWANDA	73. YEMEN
61. ST. LUCIA	74. YUGOSLAVIA
62. SAN MARINO	75. WEST INDIES ASSOCIATED STATES
63. SÃO TOMÉ & PRINCIPE	

THE SPATIAL DIFFUSION OF ECONOMIC CHANGE

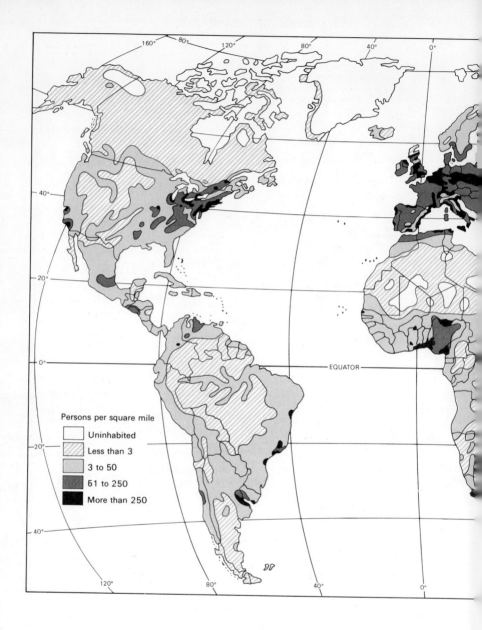

Figure 2.2 At the scale used and with the density classes shown, this map is highly generalized and does not show individual cities.

EVOLUTION OF THE GLOBAL ECONOMY: THE SPACE-TIME PROCESS

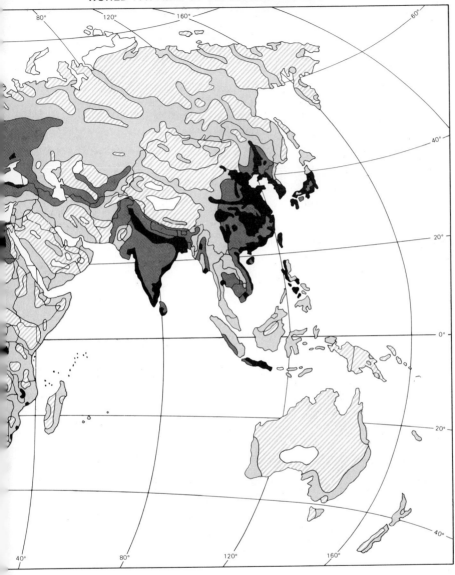

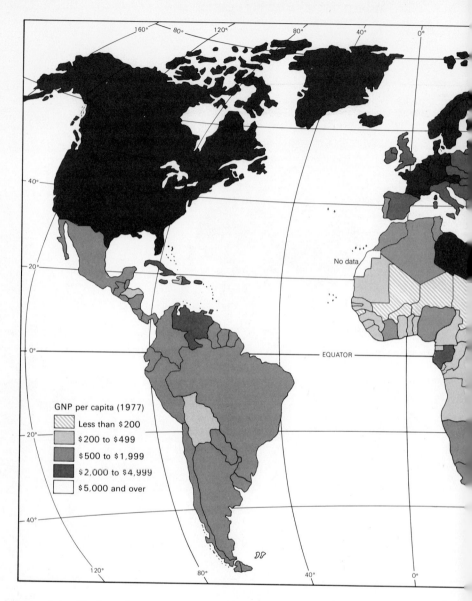

Figure 2.3 *Nations shown are those listed by the World Bank as having populations of one million or more.* (Source: World Bank Atlas, 1979, *World Bank, Washington, D.C., 1979.*)

EVOLUTION OF THE GLOBAL ECONOMY: THE SPACE-TIME PROCESS

GROSS NATIONAL PRODUCT PER CAPITA

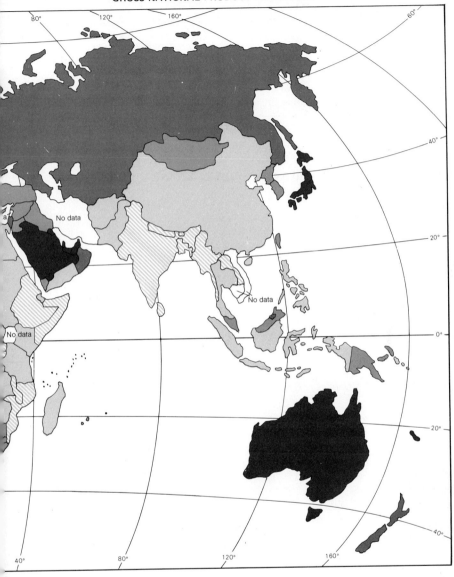

THE SPATIAL DIFFUSION OF ECONOMIC CHANGE

27

Country	Population Number mid-1977 (000)	Population Growth rate (%) 1970-1977	Country	Population Number mid-1977 (000)	Population Growth rate (%) 1970-1977
China, People's Republic of	902,337	1.6	Ethiopia	30,245	2.5
India	631,726	2.1	South Africa	26,952	2.7
USSR	258,932	0.9	Argentina	26,036	1.3
United States	216,729	0.8	Zaire	25,694	2.7
Indonesia	133,505	1.8	Colombia	24,605	2.1
Brazil	116,100	2.9	Canada	23,320	1.2
Japan	113,216	1.2	Yugoslavia	21,738	0.9
Bangladesh	81,219	2.5	Romania	21,648	0.9
Nigeria	78,982	2.6	Morocco	18,310	2.7
Pakistan	74,905	3.1	Algeria	17,152	3.2
Mexico	63,319	3.3	Sudan	16,919	2.6
Germany, Federal Republic of	61,418	0.2	German Democratic Republic	16,857	−0.2
Italy	56,468	0.7	China, Republic of	16,793	2.0
United Kingdom	55,932	0.1	Korea, Democratic People's Republic of	16,651	2.6
France	53,051	0.7	Peru	16,363	2.8
Viet Nam	50,647	3.1			
Philippines	44,473	2.7	Tanzania[a]	16,363	3.0
Thailand	43,326	2.8	Czechoslovakia	15,013	0.7
Turkey	41,949	2.5	Kenya	14,614	3.8
Egypt, Arab Republic of	37,796	2.1	Afghanistan	14,304	2.2
			Sri Lanka	14,097	1.7
Spain	36,298	1.0			
Korea, Republic of	35,953	2.0	Australia	14,074	1.7
Iran	34,782	3.0	Netherlands	13,864	0.9
Poland	34,724	1.0	Venezuela	13,513	3.4
Burma	31,512	2.2	Nepal	13,322	2.2
			Malaysia	12,961	2.7

Table 2.1   (Cont.)

Country	Population Number mid-1977 (000)	Growth rate (%) 1970-1977	Country	Population Number mid-1977 (000)	Growth rate (%) 1970-1977
Uganda	12,049	3.0	Denmark	5,076	0.4
Iraq	11,803	3.4	Guinea	4,989	3.0
Ghana	10,634	3.0	Yemen Arab		
Hungary	10,628	0.4	Republic	4,982	1.9
Chile	10,553	1.7	Dominican		
			Republic	4,980	3.0
Belgium	9,845	0.3	Niger	4,862	2.8
Mozambique	9,691	2.5			
Cuba	9,590	1.6	Haiti	4,749	1.7
Portugal	9,577	0.8	Finland	4,732	0.4
Greece	9,231	0.7	Hong Kong	4,536	2.0
			Rwanda	4,379	2.9
Bulgaria	8,835	0.6	El Salvador	4,256	3.1
Sweden	8,263	0.4			
Madagascar	8,085	2.5	Chad	4,221	2.2
Cameroon	7,882	2.2	Burundi	4,156	1.9
Syrian Arab			Norway	4,034	0.6
Republic	7,835	3.3	Somalia	3,660	2.3
			Israel	3,604	2.8
Saudi Arabia	7,633	3.0			
Austria	7,506	0.2	Honduras	3,322	3.3
Ivory Coast	7,463	6.0	Puerto Rico	3,303	2.8
Ecuador	7,324	3.0	Benin	3,229	2.9
Rhodesia	6,683	3.3	Sierra Leone	3,210	2.5
			Lao People's		
Angola	6,575	2.3	Democratic		
Guatemala	6,436	2.9	Republic	3,200	n.a.
Switzerland	6,327	0.2			
Mali	6,129	2.5	Ireland	3,198	1.2
Tunisia	5,899	2.0	New Zealand	3,148	1.7
			Lebanon	2,939	2.5
Malawi	5,597	3.1	Jordan	2,888	3.3
Upper Volta	5,465	1.6	Uruguay	2,876	0.2
Senegal	5,240	2.6			
Bolivia	5,154	2.7	Papua New		
Zambia	5,128	3.0	Guinea	2,857	2.4

Table 2.1 (Cont.)

Country	Population Number mid- 1977 (000)	Population Growth rate (%) 1970–1977	Country	Population Number mid- 1977 (000)	Population Growth rate (%) 1970–1977
Paraguay	2,810	2.9	Liberia	1,684	3.4
Libya	2,636	4.1	Mongolia	1,530	3.0
Albania	2,545	2.5	Mauritania	1,503	2.7
Nicaragua	2,411	3.3	Congo, People's Republic of		
Togo	2,350	2.6	the	1,423	2.5
Singapore	2,319	1.6	Lesotho	1,250	2.4
Jamaica	2,101	1.7	Bhutan	1,231	2.3
Costa Rica	2,061	2.5	Kuwait	1,137	6.2
Central African Republic	1,867	2.2	Trinidad and Tobago	1,118	1.2
Panama	1,771	3.1			
Yemen, People's Democratic Republic of	1,717	1.9	Kampuchea, Democratic	n.a.	n.a.

[a]Mainland Tanzania.
n.a.—Not available.
Source: 1979 World Bank Atlas, World Bank, Washington, D.C.

The growth and migration of populations and the location of economic activities throughout the world have been influenced by political, military, religious, and other forces. However, these forces have usually been related in some way to underlying economic factors. In this sense, the economic factor is nearly always operating as a locational influence, whether directly or indirectly. We are particularly interested here in the spatial and environmental aspects of the economic factors.

The economic landscape we see today in most parts of the world contains economic functions that originated elsewhere. Most inventions, or innovations, have had a single origin, or at most only a few places of origin. Scholars identify a number of innovations that have resulted in "quantum leaps" in our cultural, technological, and economic development, and which have caused profound changes in our way of life. Three of these have been the

Table 2.2   Gross National Product Per Capita (1977) and Average Annual Growth Rates of Countries with Populations Exceeding One Million

Country	GNP per capita Amount 1977 (US $)	GNP per capita Real Growth rate (%) 1970–1977	Country	GNP per capita Amount 1977 (US $)	GNP per capita Real Growth rate (%) 1970–1977
Kuwait	12,690	—0.9	Spain	3,260	3.6
Switzerland	11,080	0.1	Hungary[b,c]	3,100	5.1
Sweden	9,340	1.2	Ireland	3,060	2.1
Denmark	9,160	2.3	Greece	2.950	4.0
United States	8,750	2.0	Bulgaria[b,c]	2,830	5.7
Germany, Federal Republic of	8,620	2.2	Singapore[d]	2,820	6.6
			Venezuela	2,630	3.2
Norway	8,570	3.9	Hong Kong	2,620	5.8
Canada	8,350	3.4	Trinidad and Tobago	2,620	1.5
Belgium	8,280	3.5	Puerto Rico	2,450	0.1
Netherlands	7,710	2.2	Yugoslavia	2,100	5.1
France	7,500	3.1	Argentina	1,870	1.8
Australia	7,290	1.6	Portugal	1,840	3.1
Saudi Arabia[a]	7,230	13.0	Iraq	1,570	7.1
Libya	6,520	—4.5	Romania[e]	1,530	9.9
Japan	6,510	3.6	Uruguay	1,450	1.3
Austria	6,450	3.8	Brazil	1,410	6.7
Finland	6,190	2.8	South Africa	1,400	1.1
German Democratic Republic[b,c]	5,070	4.9	Costa Rica	1,390	3.2
			Chile	1,250	—1.8
United Kingdom	4,540	1.6	Panama	1,200	—0.1
New Zealand	4,480	0.9	China, Republic of	1,180	5.5
Czechoslovakia[b,c]	4,240	4.3	Mexico	1,160	1.2
Israel	3,760	2.0	Algeria	1,140	2.1
Italy	3,530	2.0	Turkey	1,110	4.5
USSR[b,c]	3,330	4.4	Jamaica	1,060	—2.0
Poland[b,c]	3,290	6.3	Korea, Republic of	980	7.6

Table 2.2   (Cont.)

Country	GNP per capita Amount 1977 (US $)	Real Growth rate (%) 1970–1977	Country	GNP per capita Amount 1977 (US $)	Real Growth rate (%) 1970–1977
Malaysia	970	4.9	Philippines	460	3.7
Jordan[f]	940	6.5	Rhodesia[b]	460	−0.1
Mongolia[b,c]	870	1.6	Zambia	460	−0.2
Nicaragua	870	2.5	Thailand	430	4.1
Syrian Arab			Cameroon	420	1.0
Republic	860	6.1	Honduras	420	0.0
Dominican			China, People's		
Republic	840	4.6	Republic of[b,c]	410	4.5
Tunisia	840	6.5	Liberia	410	1.1
Guatemala	830	3.3	Senegal	380	0.4
Ecuador	820	6.1	Ghana	370	−2.0
Ivory Coast	770	1.1	Yemen, People's		
Colombia	760	3.8	Democratic		
Cuba[b,c]	750	−1.2	Republic of[g]	350	11.2
Paraguay	750	4.3	Egypt, Arab		
Peru	720	1.8	Republic of	340	5.2
Korea,			Sudan[b]	330	2.5
Democratic			Indonesia	320	5.7
People's			Kenya	290	0.9
Republic of[b,c]	680	5.3	Angola[b]	280	−3.4
Albania	660	4.1	Togo	280	5.3
Morocco	610	4.2	Mauritania	270	−0.1
El Salvador	590	2.1	Lesotho[b]	250	9.9
Nigeria	510	4.4	Central African		
Papua New			Republic[b]	240	0.9
Guinea	510	2.5	Haiti	230	2.1
Yemen Arab			Madagascar	230	−2.7
Republic[b]	510	n.a.	Afghanistan	220	2.7
Congo, People's			Benin	210	0.5
Republic of			Tanzania[h]	210	2.1
the	500	0.8			
Bolivia	480	2.9	Zaire	210	−1.4

Table 2.2 (Cont.)

Country	GNP per capita		Country	GNP per capita	
	Amount 1977 (US $)	Real Growth rate (%) 1970–1977		Amount 1977 (US $)	Real Growth rate (%) 1970–1977
Guinea	200	2.5	Somalia[b]	120	−1.1
Pakistan	200	0.8	Ethiopia	110	0.2
Sierra Leone	200	−1.3	Nepal	110	2.4
Niger	190	−1.8	Bhutan[b]	90	−0.3
India	160	1.1	Lao People's Democratic Republic	90	n.a.
Rwanda	160	1.3			
Sri Lanka	160	1.3			
Malawi	150	3.1	Bangladesh	80	−0.2
Burma	140	1.3	Iran	n.a.	n.a.
Mozambique[b]	140	−4.3	Lebanon	n.a.	n.a.
Upper Volta	140	1.6	Kampuchea, Democratic	n.a.	n.a.
Burundi	130	0.6	Uganda	n.a.	n.a.
Chad	130	−1.0			
Mali	120	1.9	Viet Nam	n.a.	n.a.

[a]GNP per capita growth rate relates to 1963–77.
[b]Estimates of GNP per capita and its growth rate are tentative.
[c]For estimation of GNP per capita, see Technical Note, page 22, *1979 World Bank Atlas*.
[d]Excluding the expatriate community, the GNP per capita amounts to US$2,290.
[e]This estimate is not comparable to those for the other centrally planned economies. It has been arrived at, following the *World Bank Atlas* methodology, by adjusting official Romanian national accounts data and converting them to US dollars at the effective exchange rate for foreign trade transactions.
[f]GNP per capita relates to East Bank only. GNP per capita growth rate relates to 1972–77.
[g]GNP per capita growth rate relates to 1973–77.
[h]Mainland Tanzania.
n.a.—Not available.
Source: 1979 World Bank Atlas, World Bank, Washington, D.C.

agricultural revolution, the development of *cities and civilizations,* and the *industrial revolution.*

These three profound revolutions diffused outward from their places of origin in very uneven patterns. Distance from the place of origin was one factor influencing their adoption and development. Another factor was the

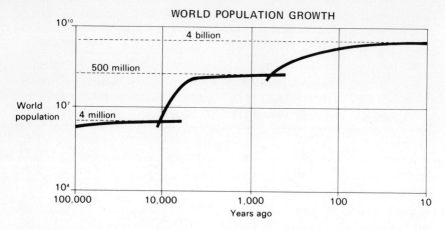

WORLD POPULATION GROWTH

Figure 2.4 This logarithmic growth curve reveals two great advances that have increased world population a thousand times. The first began about 10,000 years ago with the beginning of the Agricultural Revolution, and was sustained by the subsequent emergence of cities and civilizations. The second began about 300 years ago, at the inception of the Scientific-Industrial Revolution in Europe, and its momentum has been maintained up to the present. (Source: Adapted from Edward S. Deevey, Jr., "The Human Population," p. 198. Copyright © September, 1960 by **Scientific American, Inc.** *All rights reserved.)*

environmental character of the places reached by the innovation wave. Thus, places remote from the origin were often not reached, and places with unproductive environments, such as deserts and polar regions, were largely passed over. Both factors operated together as combined influences. Today, remote polar, desert, and mountainous regions still support few people and little economic activity.

The economic revolutions resulted in surges of population growth (Fig. 2.4), and the integration of the world economy from simple, isolated forms to a highly complex, interconnected form. The remainder of this chapter traces the uneven spread of these key innovations and shows how they have shaped the present global economy.

THE SPATIAL ECONOMY OF MAN AS A HUNTER-GATHERER

Over large tracts of land in parts of the world today small groups of people still live as all of our ancestors once did, as hunters and gatherers of food. Until about 10,000 years ago, all humanity lived in roving bands. Population densities were extremely low and human contacts were few. Estimates of the

34   EVOLUTION OF THE GLOBAL ECONOMY: THE SPACE-TIME PROCESS

total population of Mesolithic Britain and Wales (8000–3000 B.C.) are about 3000 to 4000 persons. Under such conditions large groups seldom met together, and the opportunity for the exchange of ideas was extremely limited.

The movements and camping patterns of the bands were influenced by both spatial and environmental considerations. The distance to hunting and gathering sites and their environmental quality as sources of food were interrelated factors. The spatial pattern of fresh water hydrology was (and remains today) especially important. Stream and lake environments were not only ecologically rich sources of food and water, but they also formed pathways along which people, information, and goods could freely move. By the late pre-historical period, waterways had become main routes of transportation and trade in many parts of the forested world.

The relationship between production, storage, and transportation of goods, which is a fundamental one in modern spatial economies, had its beginning in the prehistoric hunting and gathering societies. Gorillas and other large primates gather only the food they need when hungry. Humans came to behave in a fundamentally different manner, which was directly related to the way in which they occupied and utilized their environmental space. Hunting and gathering groups ranged in size from two or three dozen to over a hundred persons. These bands occupied a territory that normally provided at least one square mile per person.

Human mobility and the propensity to travel over a large territory had profound ecological and economic consequences. Ranging over a large area

---

COON REFLECTS ON WHY HUNTING-GATHERING SOCIETIES STILL EXIST IN THE WORLD

An intriguing question arises here: Why did successive waves of economic change affect some hunting and gathering people and not others? Another way of putting it is to ask why hunting-gathering economies still exist in a world where Man has reached the moon? An answer to this by anthropologist Carleton Coon suggests dual explanations based on distance (spatial) and productivity (environmental) factors: "First," writes Professor Coon, "is geographical isolation or sheer distance. Because of their remoteness from the centers where food production began . . . the techniques of husbandry had not yet reached them." Second, "some of the hunters still live in climatic regions beyond the range of profitable agriculture." A third possible reason, Coon notes, is simply that they may not have wanted to trade off the advantages of a life "free from tedious routine".*

* Carleton Coon, *The Hunting Peoples,* Little, Brown and Co., Boston, 1971, p. 3.

brings hunters and gatherers in contact with many varied micro-environments and enables the group to utilize a variety of seasonal food sources. This activity requires an intimate knowledge of the flora and fauna of a region. Although the large territory provides a greater availability and variety of food resources, the hunter must weigh this advantage against the energy and time needed to move about in the area.

The study of Man as a hunter-gatherer can furnish a useful perspective for modern societies. For example, economic and location models, as we see in later chapters, are usually based on the notion of a hypothetical *Economic Man*, who strives to maximize his material income. However, survival within hunting bands is based on a sharing concept, which anthropologists have called "kinship-friendship economics."

THE ORIGIN AND DIFFUSION OF AGRICULTURE AND PERMANENT SETTLEMENTS

About 10,000 years ago, when the last glacial ice sheet still covered parts of North America and Eurasia, a radical change began in the way of life of certain people. They began to grow food, domesticate animals, and live in permanent settlements. This profound change eventually resulted in the domestication of all the important cereal grains, root crops, vegetables, fruits, and livestock that provide today's world food supply. The change was of such moment in our cultural and economic evolution that it is called the *agricultural revolution.*

According to present archaeological findings, agriculture began at about the same time—around 7000 B.C.—in two widely separated places. One was a series of environmentally favorable upland valleys in the Middle East, which are in parts of present-day Iraq, Iran, Turkey, and Syria. The other place of origin was in Middle America, near present-day Mexico city. Thus far, the oldest evidence of plant cultivation and domesticated animals is from sites excavated at Jarmo, in northern Iraq. The people of Jarmo grew barley and two kinds of wheat, and domesticated goats and sheep.

Agriculture and animal husbandry permitted an enormous increase in food supply from a small area, and permanent villages made possible the storage of food surpluses from the surrounding fields. Wherever it occurred, agriculture permitted Man to channel a growing part of his collective energy and time into activities other than food production. The development of relatively dependable food surpluses was followed by a rapid rise in the population of the new agricultural societies. After the introduction of garden plots and domesticated animals in Britain, by the Middle Bronze Age (1400-900 B.C.), the population there increased tenfold. It is estimated that by domesticating food plants Man reduced the space required for supporting each person by a factor of over 200.

For several thousand years agriculture, animal husbandry, and village life diffused outward from the Middle East to other parts of Eurasia and Africa. In the Western Hemisphere by 2000 B.C., permanent agricultural villages had spread outward from the region around present-day Mexico City and were appearing in many places in both North and South America. In some places, the combination of crop agriculture and permanent villages set the stage for spiraling cultural, technological, and economic advances. The hundreds of millions of peasant farmers in Asia today are descendants of Neolithic peoples who adopted agriculture there thousands of years ago.

An offshoot of agriculture, *nomadic herding* (also called *subsistence herding*), had a very different space-time development. In the Old World it became—and still is—a land use found extending over vast areas of semi-arid grassland and arctic tundra, where sedentary agriculture is difficult or impossible. Nomadic herding supports only sparse populations. For reasons not entirely clear, nomadic herding, except for fringe areas in northern Alaska and Canada, did not develop in the New World (Fig. 2.5).

THE ORIGIN AND DIFFUSION OF CIVILIZATION AND URBAN LIFE

THE EMERGENCE OF CIVILIZATION

For several thousand years after the beginning of irrigated agriculture and village life in the Middle East, the farming population grew rapidly and pressure mounted on the local water and soil resources. Some people began to migrate to virgin land on the broad flood plains of the Tigris and Euphrates Rivers. The settlement of the alluvial valley gradually took place. Here, in Mesopotamia—literally, the place between the rivers—in present-day Iraq, civilization is thought to have had its origin in the Old World.

A similar settlement of the delta and flood plain of the Nile River by village-dwelling farmers in Egypt also occurred. By 3000 B.C. the spatial diffusion process resulted in the appearance of a third civilization in the Indus River Valley, in present-day Pakistan. This Harappan culture mysteriously disappeared about 1500 B.C.[1] Around 1500 B.C. a fourth civilization emerged in the Han River Basin, a tributary of the great Yellow River

---

[1] The Harappan civilization was long thought to have been destroyed by conquerers from the north, but a newer theory of destruction by overintensive land use provides an intriguing alternative explanation.

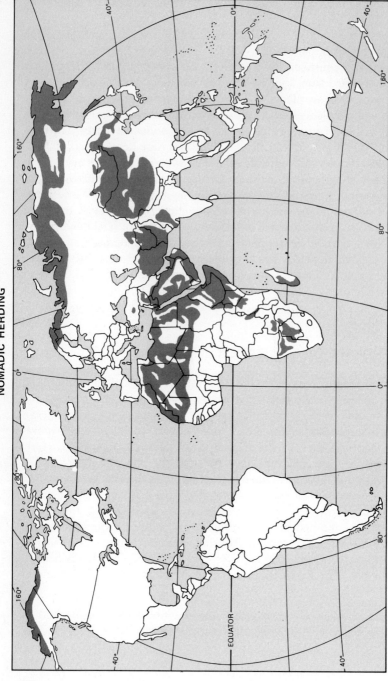

NOMADIC HERDING

Figure 2.5   Regions of the world where nomadic herding is carried on. These are very sparsely populated areas, where little or no other economic activity is found. The herds must continually move about as the scanty forage is consumed. Caribou herds account for the activity in the northern fringes of Eurasia and North America. Note the correspondence between this map and the map in Figure 6.3, which shows regions of aridity and short growing season.

(*Huang Ho*) in China. Unlike the Harappan civilization, the Chinese civilization continued to develop and to diffuse outward to other places in South and East Asia that were environmentally favorable for the production of irrigated rice.

All four early Old World civilizations emerged in riverine corridors, on the rich alluvial flood plains of large rivers (Fig. 2.6). All four riverine environments were located in arid or semi-arid climates, where nonirrigated agriculture was either impossible or very limited. The combination of irrigation water, level topography, alluvial soil, and a sunny climate gave these places exceptional advantages for the production of grain surpluses. The diffusion outward of the agricultural way of life, and then of civilization, took place by a "leap-froging" action to special environments where irrigated grain could be grown. The geographic association of intensive grain production with environmental features, especially water, soil, and level topography, is one that persists down to the present day in Asia.

The riverine settings of the first Old World civilizations were advantageous in a second important way. The great valleys of the Tigris-Euphrates, Nile, Indus, and Yellow River systems provided transportation corridors and crossroads that carried a flow of people and goods, prompted the exchange of information and ideas, and stimulated further economic innova-

LOCATIONS OF THE WORLD'S EARLIEST CIVILIZATIONS AND CITIES

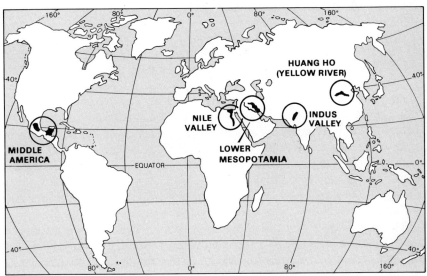

Figure 2.6

tion and diffusion. Both environmental and spatial factors thus help to explain the location and economic character of the earliest civilizations in the Old World.

In the New World another grain, maize (corn), became the support for other civilizations (Fig. 2.6). By 1000 B.C. the inhabitants of Middle America had developed a high culture, which by 800 A.D. resulted in the stunning architectural, astronomical, and mathematical achievements of the Classic Mayan period. Later, in the last centuries before Columbus, the great Aztec and Inca empires flourished. The New World civilizations, unlike those in the Old World, did not develop in riverine environments. They did, however, practice intensive, irrigated farming.

THE DEVELOPMENT AND DIFFUSION OF URBAN LIFE

The city evolved as the spatial concentration and the highest expression of the phenomenon called *civilization*. The processes of urbanization and of civilization cannot really be separated. In fact, the word *civilization* is derived from the Latin *civilitas*, which refers to city dwelling.

The first true cities in the world are believed to have evolved around 3500 B.C. from agricultural settlements established much earlier on the flood plains of the Tigris and Euphrates Rivers in Lower Mesopotamia. These first cities had populations that today we would consider very small. In these places people engaged in a variety of economic activities, and a cross-fertilization of ideas was promoted.

Along with civilization, urban living diffused outward from Mesopotamia and became established as a way of life in the three other riverine corridors mentioned above. There is evidence of early cities in the Nile delta by 3100 B.C. By 2500 B.C. the cities of Mohenjo-Daro and Harappa appeared on the flood plain of the Indus River. By the year 2000 B.C., irrigated wheat and barley were supporting a population in the Mesopotamian city of Ur estimated to be over 30,000. When Abraham, Patriarch of the world's three great monotheistic religions, left Ur, leading his people on their epochal journey around the Fertile Crescent to Egypt, he encountered many long-established urban centers along the way. By 1500 B.C., urban centers of the Shang Dynasty appeared in China. Shortly later, important cities emerged within the flourishing civilizations of Middle America (Fig. 2.6).

The city, from its inception, exhibited certain time-invariant attributes; among these was its role as a trade, religious, political, and military center. Growing urban centers were an efficient spatial response to the demands of a growing regional economy. The city, then as now, was an intensive spatial concentration of economic activity.

By 1000 B.C., civilization and cities were spreading around the Mediterranean Basin and elsewhere. Several centuries later the Greek cities arose and extended the sea-trade network established earlier by the Phoenicians. Meanwhile, diffusion spearheads from the Middle East and China continued to spread to many parts of the rice-growing Asian sub-tropics.

So much has been written about the military and political impact of the Roman Empire that its role in integrating a continental spatial economy has been understated. Roman engineering and administration made possible the extension of its commercial influence from Britain to the Middle East in a single, interconnected economic system. Under Roman rule, population increased and urban life spread throughout what is now Italy, France, Spain, Britain, the Low Countries, Switzerland, and Germany west of the Rhine.

After the collapse of the Roman Empire in the West, urban life declined. During the Dark Ages, Western Europe became fragmented into hundreds of primitive feudal economies. While Western Europe was in cultural and economic decline, the Eastern or Byzantine Empire remained at least partially intact. In the seventh century A.D., the surging wave of Islam moved out of Arabia to spread over North Africa and the Middle East—even to Spain and Southern France—in a sprawling, loosely organized spatial system that is still discernible today as the group of modern Islamic nations. By the thirteenth century, Europe had reached the High Middle Ages, and the robust Italian city-states had become flourishing trade centers. The fabulous journeys of Marco Polo and his family formed a tenuous first link between the European and Far Eastern economic spheres.

By the close of the fifteenth century, those parts of Eurasia and North Africa that could support crop farming formed a vast collection of agricultural economies, connected by trade routes. However, the Old World was then not even aware that another hemisphere existed with its own great civilizations, urban centers, and economic wealth.

EUROPEAN EXPANSION AND THE ESTABLISHMENT OF GLOBAL TRADE NETWORKS

So much happened so fast to change the global economy following Columbus's voyage that it staggers the mind. Much of what followed 1492 was shaped by the Europeans, who surged out of their small continent to occupy or control lands over much of the globe. Within only 30 years after Columbus's voyage, the Spanish presence had become established in most of what is Latin America today, except for Brazil which was claimed by the Portuguese. Thus, in a few short decades, Europeans from two nations gained economic control over vast areas of the New World, and the plundering of two continents began. By 1570, a flood of gold and silver from the mines of Mexico and Peru was pouring into Europe through Spain, causing severe economic repercussions all over that continent.

The economic geography of Latin America today can be traced back to this violent incursion of European guns and culture on the Indian populations of the New World. The regional character of economic production, the distribution of population and cities, the political foundations of the new nations—all these evolved from the conquest.

The initial success of Spain and Portugal in the New World led other maritime nations of Europe to follow their lead. The Dutch, English, and French began a highly competitive struggle that carved up the remainder of North America into colonies and other possessions. The thinly scattered Indians north of the Rio Grande could not long withstand the impact. Great numbers of slaves were brought to the New World from West Africa to supply labor for burgeoning New World enterprises.

In the eighteenth and nineteenth centuries some European nations turned their attention to other environmentally attractive parts of the world. Present-day United States, Canada, Australia, New Zealand, and Soviet Asia were occupied by Europeans, who in time established their own laws and governments. In addition, large parts of Africa and Asia became colonies of European maritime nations.

All this was accompanied by the establishment of ocean trade routes, leading outward from European ports to all parts of the world. Magellan's fleet had no sooner circled the globe for the first time, in 1522, when the Spanish established a regular trading run—The Manila Galleon—to connect the Philippines and Mexico across the Pacific Ocean. English, Spanish, Dutch, French, and later American ships explored and established trade centers on many islands and coasts of the world. From trading centers and military posts thus established, traders, military expeditions, and settlers moved overland to exploit resources and establish trading monopolies.

Thus, while the transportation, agricultural, and industrial technologies of the world were still preindustrial, the sailing ships from a few European nations had spanned the globe with trade routes and diffusion pathways. Naval men-of-war and merchant ships from these maritime powers established far-flung world markets in many commodities, with decision making centers in London, Paris, The Hague, and other European capitals. Through conquest, settlement, colonization, and conversion, Europeans had interconnected many isolated regions throughout the world for the first time into a spatial economic system of global dimensions. As a result, by the time the Industrial Revolution began, much of the world was already partially integrated, and diffusion pathways had been established that would carry the coming waves of industrial innovation.

THE ORIGIN AND DIFFUSION OF THE INDUSTRIAL REVOLUTION

The Industrial Revolution, which had its origin in England about two centuries ago, marked the beginning of a quantum leap in Man's cultural and economic development. One way to begin to comprehend the meaning of the Industrial Revolution is to put ourselves within the mind of a citizen of the Roman Empire, transported in time and space to England or Colonial America 200 years ago. Except for firearms, the scene around him would reveal techniques of agriculture, industry, commerce and transportation very similar to his own. All nonhuman forms of energy would be supplied by animals, windmills, and small waterfalls. The movement of persons and goods would be by horses or other draft animals. Boats and ships would depend on oars or sail. Agriculture and manufacturing would be largely manual operations. In contrast, if the Roman citizen were transported in time only another 200 years ahead, to the present, he would see things that he wouldn't have dreamed possible in the wildest flights of his imagination.

Like the innovations that preceded it, the Industrial Revolution spread outward to places in various parts of the world. This diffusion followed the paths of prior innovations, and in doing so also followed the spread of European people to their new homelands.

Before the Industrial Revolution, the only way energy could be spatially concentrated and applied to perform large-scale work was by mobilizing large groups of men or draft animals. The invention of a practical steam engine in England changed all that. The steam engine enabled Man to convert a great source of potential energy, coal, into mechanical energy through an intermediate conversion to heat energy.

After the establishment of steam-powered machinery, each passing decade saw changes in the economic landscape in parts of England, Wales, and lowland Scotland. Mining centers and industrial towns grew as labor flowed from rural areas to these places. Mines, smoking factories, and grim mill towns became part of the economic landscape. A poignant account of this transformation in Wales and its human effects can be read in Richard Llewellyn's famous novel, *How Green Was My Valley*.

By the early 1800s, the Industrial Revolution had spread across the English Channel and the North Sea to other nations in Europe. Northern France, the Low Countries, Northern Germany, and the southern fringes of Scandinavia were soon being transformed. Somewhat later, the wave of industrial change crossed the Atlantic, and when the Civil War in the United States began in 1861, New England was able to mass produce guns, ammunition, uniforms, and other material for the Union armies. Over the past century, industrialization has also spread to Southern Europe, much of Temperate North America, Japan, parts of Latin America, South Africa, throughout much of the Soviet Union, and to certain sections of India, China, and other Asian nations.

Wherever industrialization took hold it radically changed the spatial economy through the introduction of low-cost transportation. In the early 1800s the steam engine was made so efficient it could be mounted on a boat or railway car where it could carry not only its own supply of fuel, but a payload as well. This opened up the great era of railroad building in North America and Europe (Fig. 2.7).

During the same period, steam-driven ships were improved to the point where they displaced the sailing vessel for river, lake, coastal, and ocean shipping. The new, steam-powered navies enabled a few nations in Europe to strengthen and extend their overseas colonial authority and trading position. Growing world markets for such staples as cotton, wool, and metals came to be centered in European manufacturing cities. Increasing concen-

DIFFUSION OF RAILROAD SERVICE IN EUROPE

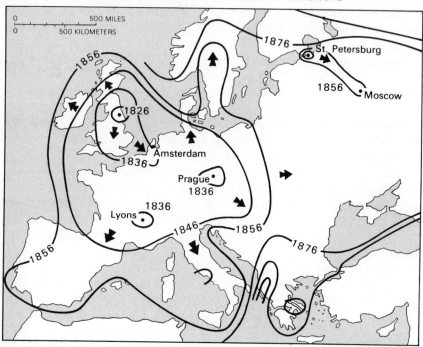

Figure 2.7 (Source: *Peter R. Gould, Spatial Diffusion, Washington, D.C.: Association of American Geographers, Resource Papers for College Geography No. 4, 1969, Figure 57, p. 52. Reprinted by permission.*)

DIFFERENCES IN THE ACCEPTANCE OF INDUSTRIALIZATION

The "opening up" of feudal Japan in the mid-1800s and its subsequent rapid industrialization represents one of the most dramatic examples of innovation acceptance on record. The situation in China was very different. As late as the 1920s, intellectuals and leaders in China were rejecting industrial development as a smoky, vulgar way of life, far inferior to the classical Chinese culture. This attitude changed drastically after industrializing Japan marched on Manchuria in 1931. Chinese leaders were then confronted with the choice of industrializing themselves or being conquered by mechanized outsiders.

trations of industrial capacity in certain European and European-peopled nations enabled them to support large military establishments. Railroads and steamships permitted soldiers, traders, and administrators to penetrate areas in the tropical and subtropical world and control them as sources of raw materials and as markets for manufactured products. The Industrial Revolution thus reinforced the political and economic dominance of European people and their descendants.

The cataclysmic effect of two World Wars in the first half of the twentieth century set the stage for a realignment of political and economic power around the globe. Major developments of the postwar era have been the loss of political influence by European and European-derived countries (*the West*), the creation of a large group of politically independent (*Third World*) nations, and the emergence of Japan as a leading industrial power.

ECONOMIC DEVELOPMENT AND THE DIVERGENCE OF HIGHLY DEVELOPED COUNTRIES (HDC'S) FROM LESS DEVELOPED COUNTRIES (LDC'S)

The world economy has continued to change substantially in recent decades. In any attempt to assess these changes, three major events can be identified. One was the termination of most European-controlled possessions in Asia and Africa following World War II, and the creation in the 1950s and 1960s of scores of new, politically independent nations. A second event was the acceleration of population growth throughout the world following the diffusion of low-cost, disease-control measures from the United States and other industrialized nations to the Third World nations. A third event, related to the first two, was an income divergence of the industrialized world from the Third World. The second and third events are discussed in the remainder of this section.

DIFFUSION OF DEATH-CONTROL TECHNIQUES AND THE WORLD "POPULATION EXPLOSION"

After World War II, international agencies such as the World Health Organization (WHO) were formed to give advice and assistance for the dissemination of death control measures to the less developed world. The results were rapid and dramatic. The spread of disease-prevention techniques was simple, inexpensive, and immediately effective. A few dollars worth of chemicals and medicine applied quickly by technicians greatly reduced the infant mortality rate in communities almost literally overnight. In this way many killer diseases were largely eradicated or brought under control—malaria, smallpox, cholera, plague, and diphtheria are examples. Such effective, low-cost techniques became incorporated into national planning in much of the nonindustrial world.

Wherever infant mortality was lowered, large numbers of babies survived who, within 15 to 20 years, would themselves be of childbearing age. The result of the sharp drop in death rates and the continuing high birth rates was an unprecedented population growth rate—well over 3 percent per year in many countries (see Table 2.1). Among other things, high population growth rates caused a lowering of the median age. A country with a high proportion of children in the population has a relatively low number of economic producers (persons in the 15 to 65 age group) (Fig. 2.8).

In the United States the birth rate dropped during the 1970s until 1977, when it rose slightly to 15.4 births per 1000 population, apparently due to births among women in their mid-twenties to mid-thirties who had postponed having babies at earlier ages.

Problems resulting from the growing world population are compounded because nations are also undergoing urbanization. As people migrate to the larger towns and cities, from the smaller towns and the rural countryside, for better jobs and other economic advantages, the urban agglomerations become the setting for serious economic, social, and political problems.

THE GULF BETWEEN THE HIGHLY DEVELOPED COUNTRIES AND THE LESS DEVELOPED COUNTRIES

Since the end of World War II, a great deal of world attention and concern has focused on improving the economies of Less Developed Countries.[2] De-

---

[2] Over the years many terms have been used to describe these nations: "Undeveloped," "Underdeveloped," "Developing," and so on. In this book the widely accepted designations "Highly Developed Countries" (HDC's) and "Less Developed Countries" (LDC's) are used wherever appropriate.

spite all this effort there remains, after more than three decades, a world that can roughly be divided into "high income" and "low income" nations. About a third of the world's population lives in relatively modern, industrialized, urban economies with high per capita consumption of energy, re-

POPULATION BY AGE AND SEX (1975 AND 2000)

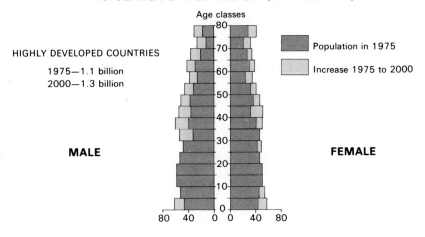

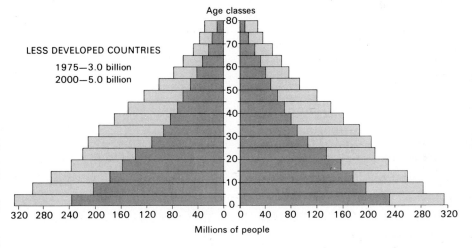

Figure 2.8   Data for 2000 represents U.S. Bureau of Census medium estimates. The higher growth rates in the Less Developed Countries will result in an enormous absolute growth of population. (Source: Adapted from U.S. Bureau of the Census and U.S. Department of State, Agency for International Development.)

sources, goods, and services. The other two-thirds, living in the Less Developed Countries, have a much lower per capita consumption of these things. Professor Paul Samuelson defines a Less Developed Country as, "simply one with real per capita income that is low relative to the present-day per capita incomes of such nations as Canada, the United States, Great Britain, and Western Europe generally."[3]

This dichotomy is, of course, only a convenient generalization. Within both types there may be great inequalities of income and opportunity. There are desperately poor people in Highly Developed Countries, and extremely rich persons in Less Developed Countries. Moreover, many nations can be considered as having an intermediate position between the two groups.

The term *Third World* is another that is used commonly, but it lacks precision since it has both economic and political connotations. Some writers apply the term *Fourth World* to very poor nations designated "least developed" by the United Nations.

The reasons for the persistence of low incomes and low states of economic development among nations are complex. For one thing, many nations are simply too small in terms of population to be able to achieve scale economies of production. Of all the political and economic consequences of World War II, none was more significant than the breakup of colonial possessions controlled by European powers. Many of the newly independent nations, especially in sub-Saharan Africa, were created on the basis of political compromise and therefore were not realistically conceived as viable spatial economies. Some are so small in terms of market demand and human and physical resources as to be greatly handicapped. Even in the larger nations, independence was often accompanied by a policy of economic nationalism that inhibits economic cooperation in larger, more efficient multinational confederations. Compounding the problem of economic viability for many of the newly independent nations is that of internal political instability.

Despite a growing degree of global economic integration, the gulf between the Highly Developed Countries and the Less Developed Countries has continued to deepen through the 1970s.

THE CYBERNETIC FEEDBACK CONCEPT APPLIED TO ECONOMIC DEVELOPMENT

Positive and negative feedback loops can be found universally in natural and artificial systems. The sciences, including the social and management sci-

---

[3] *Economics,* Ninth Edition, McGraw Hill Book Co., New York, 1973, p. 765.

PHILOSOPHICAL ARGUMENTS FOR AND AGAINST ECONOMIC DEVELOPMENT AND MATERIALISM

As stated in Chapter 1, the decade of the 1970s was one of reevaluation, and a feeling now exists that economic modernization is creating, as well as solving, serious problems. The debate over economic growth versus long-range ecological viability will persist for a long time. To put the problem in perspective, here are two contrasting points of view. The first is a quotation from the Irish statesman, Francis Hackett:

*I believe in materialism. I believe in all the proceeds of a healthy materialism,—good cooking, dry houses, dry feet, sewers, drain pipes, hot water, baths, electric lights, automobiles, good roads, bright streets, long vacations away from the village pump, new ideas, fast horses, swift conversation, theatres, operas, orchestras, bands,—I believe in them all for everybody. The man who dies without knowing these things may be as exquisite as a saint, and as rich as a poet; but it is in spite of, not because of, his deprivation.**

On the other hand, the concept of economic growth as a model for national planning is questioned by many. Economic criteria are considered to be too narrow, failing to take into account other factors of human well-being, and focusing too much on values perceived by materialistically oriented Western social scientists. What about the *development* of latent musical talent? Or, for that matter, athletic abilities? Perhaps most important of all, what about the *development* of values or states of mind that can be described as "serenity" or "contentment"? Many people who rank high in such measures rank low in terms of economic criteria.

Dr. Samuel Rosen, an ear specialist from New York, has studied a group of Mabaan tribesmen in Sudan and found that, although living in very poor material circumstances, they are exceptionally healthy and long-lived. Dr. Rosen suggests that their amazingly acute hearing, lack of high blood pressure and heart disease, and other indications of good health are the result of absence of noise, a peaceful life, and the lack of emotional stress. He feels that getting away from the fierce pressures of modern existence might increase one's life span dramatically. This tends to be verified by the experiences of the Mabaan tribesmen who leave their homes. When one of them moves to Khartoum, the nearest city, he too becomes subject to heart attacks, ulcers, and other "civilized" ills.

We can only hope that planning policies will ultimately be worked out that will combine material and nonmaterial objectives, leading toward improvement in the overall quality of life for all humanity.

---

*Quoted in Paul A. Samuelson, *Economics,* Ninth Edition, McGraw-Hill Book Co., New York, 1973, p. 765.

CYBERNETIC FEEDBACK MODELS

(a)

Example of a positive feedback (self-amplifying) system

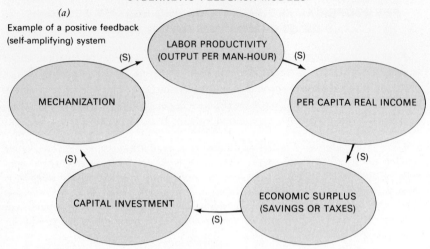

An increase or decrease in any component will induce a change in the same (S) direction in the next component. The result is an upward or downward spiraling effect in the system as a whole.

(b)

Example of a negative feedback (self correcting) system

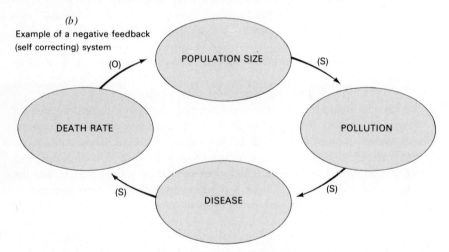

An increase or decrease in any component except the Death Rate will induce a change in the same (S) direction in the next component. However, a change in the Death Rate will cause a change in the opposite (O) direction in Population Size. Thus, an increase or decrease in any component will loop back on itself to induce a corresponding decrease or increase, respectively in that component.

Figure 2.9.

ences, are increasingly using the powerful concepts of cybernetics to model, simulate, and hence better understand otherwise incomprehensible complex systems. (The word *cybernetics* is Greek for "helmsman" or "steersman.") Examples of feedback system behavior, occurring in this book, will help in understanding various kinds of economic phenomena.

Positive feedback provides a powerful model (Fig. 2.9) that helps to understand the complex process of economic development. Swedish social scientist Gunnar Myrdal, over two decades ago, described the plight of Less Developed Countries in terms of "the principle of circular and cumulative causation,"[4] which induces regions or nations to spiral downward because of a series of self-reinforcing disadvantages. For example, undernourished people become less able to produce, and this deepens their poverty and hunger. Greater investment risk raises interest rates on capital in Less Developed Countries, and this impedes investment in capital projects; as a result, productivity is lowered, further reducing incomes and savings. Another downward spiral is created when the lack of job opportunities at home force the highly educated professional people to seek employment in the Highly Developed Countries. As this "brain drain" continues, the Less Developed Country suffers from a lack of professional and management leadership, which further impairs productivity and economic development.

Reviewing the downward spiraling process also provides insights into the opposite, upward spiraling process, which characterizes economic development in a Highly Developed Country. Here, an early advantage often provides the initial "kick," and other advantages continue to reinforce each other in an ascending spiral. In the economic growth process rising incomes increase savings and supply investment capital for labor-saving machinery, which in turn increases labor productivity, and therefore incomes. The upward spiral continues until other factors begin to exert negative responses, such as congestion, pollution, and environmental damage.

SUMMARY

Ten thousand years ago all humanity consisted of a few million people living in small, scattered bands as hunters and gatherers. Today's highly integrated global economy of over 4.5 billion persons has evolved as the result of a space-time diffusion process. A series of critical innovations, including agriculture, permanent settlements, civilization, urban living, and the industrial

---

[4] *Economic Theory and Under-Developed Regions*, Gerald Duckworth and Co., Ltd., London, 1957.

revolution, originated in a few places and spread unevenly throughout the world. The spread (diffusion) of the innovations has been, and continues to be, influenced by spatial and environmental factors. Where adopted, the innovations dramatically increased productivity, wealth, and population. As civilizations expanded and technologies advanced, larger and larger spatial economic systems were created. The outpouring of European people to all parts of the globe following the discovery of the New World led to the establishment of ocean trade routes and global markets. The increases in economic productivity and wealth brought about the Industrial Revolution were adopted for the most part by Europeans or European-derived nations. A by-product of applied science and the Industrial Revolution has been the world "population explosion," resulting from increased food production and the control of disease. Industrialization has created regions of specialized production, interconnected by means of low cost transport and communication networks. Persons in Highly Developed Countries (HDC's) have relatively low cost market access to goods from all over the world. On the other hand, most persons in Less Developed Countries (LDC's) still live in agricultural communities that are largely self-sufficient, but which provide only very low incomes for the fast-growing populations. The HDC's produce about 90 percent of the world's industrial output and account for correspondingly high levels of world resource use and global pollution. Despite a growing degree of world economic integration, the gulf between the Highly Developed Countries and many Less Developed Countries has continued to deepen through the 1970s.

Questions

1 How do combined spatial and environmental factors help explain the location and character of the four earliest civilizations in the Old World?
2 Describe the complex process of economic development in terms of the positive feedback model.
3 Using data and information from the tables and maps in Chapter 2, show how population and economic activity vary in the extreme within the global economic system.
4 Describe the growth in world population over the last ten millenia, and how it will probably continue through the end of this century.
5 Using the spatial diffusion model, trace the adoption of economic changes in what is now your home community over the past 10,000 years. How would your answer differ if you were a resident of Cairo? Rome? Mexico City? Peking? Brasilia?

3

SPATIAL AND ENVIRONMENTAL APPROACHES TO ECONOMIC LOCATION AND LAND USE

". . . two general classes of explanations . . . have appeared in all of our work. One of these involves nearness to customers and minimization of transport costs to market, while the other is based on favorable conditions from the standpoint of production costs and the procurement of materials."

H. H. McCarty and J. B. Lindberg*

The use to which a piece of land is put in a free market economy is very largely governed by its capacity to create economic benefits. The owner of land can be presumed to be interested in gaining the most from the land, whether as a site for a residence, farm, factory, or skyscraper. Questions such as who derives the income or other benefits from a plot of land[1] or what kind of land reforms may be needed to correct inequities are vitally important, but they involve social and political judgments and are not dealt with here.

The economic benefits capable of being produced per unit area govern not only the kind of land use, but also the intensity of a given land use. Land-use intensity can vary greatly for even a single product. For example, wheat is grown under extensive conditions with much marginal land, much machinery, little labor, and low yields (output per acre) in Australia. Wheat is also grown under intensive conditions, with smaller plots of high quality land and greater yields, in Denmark.

An important point here is that profitable locations for intensive wheat

---

* *Preface to Economic Geography,* Prentice-Hall, Englewood Cliffs, N.J., 1966, p. 224.
[1] All references to *land* here mean the natural land, not Man-made structures or other capital improvements.

53

production are not profitable locations for extensive wheat production, and vice versa. This underscores the idea introduced in Chapter 1 that an interrelationship often exists between the location and the character of economic activity.

SPACE AND ENVIRONMENT AS LOCATION FACTORS

In places where a free market in land exists, a bidding process goes on as land is bought and sold (Fig. 3.1). This bidding process establishes the way in which various land uses are allocated within the economic landscape. We know that land prices vary greatly, sometimes over very short distances. These variations reflect competitive bidding pressure from different land uses. Land prices are based on the perceptions, judgment, and decisions of countless home owners and home buyers, farmers, business executives, government officials, and other parties. Since World War II the price of land throughout most of the United States and much of the world has continued to rise.

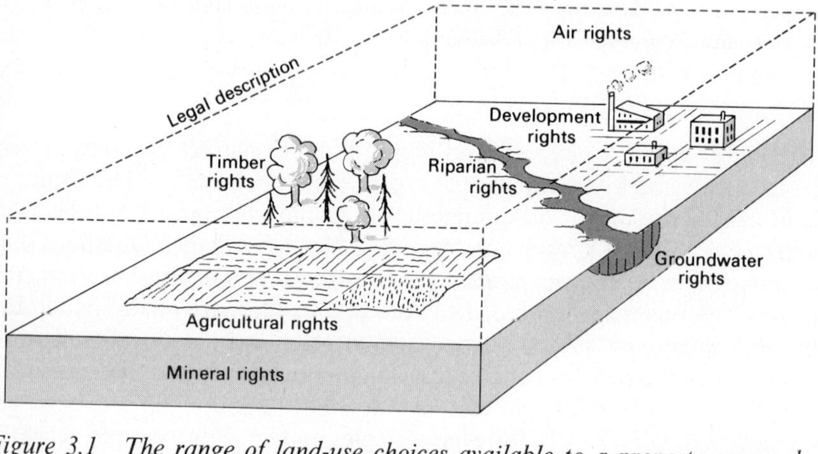

THE GEOGRAPHY OF LEGAL RIGHTS IN LAND

Figure 3.1   The range of land-use choices available to a property owner depends on the nature and extent of the ownership interest that he or she holds. The highest and most complete ownership interest or "title" in land is the "fee simple absolute," making the title holder sovereign "from the center of the earth to the heavens above." The fee simple owner may sell certain rights in the land, such as timber rights or mineral rights, to someone else. (Source: Rutherford H. Platt, Land Use Control: Interface of Law and Geography, Washington, D.C., Association of American Geographers, Resource Papers for College Geography, No. 75-1, 1976, Figure 1, p. 4. Reprinted by permission.)

54   SPATIAL AND ENVIRONMENTAL APPROACHES

Even in Communist countries and others where a free market in land doesn't officially exist,[2] the location of economic activity and the pattern of land use are influenced by the land's perceived potential for economic return. In such countries, however, market signals for the allocation of resources are largely missing, and the State replaces the collective judgment of millions of citizens as decision maker.

The location of economic activity throughout the world has also been influenced by noneconomic forces. Value systems and environmental perceptions held by different people have influenced the location of specific kinds of economic activity. For example, the landscape of Wisconsin or New Zealand cannot be explained without reference to the special place dairy farming holds in the cultural heritage of the North European peoples who settled those regions. Cultural differences from place to place can account for spatial variation in consumption patterns as well as production patterns. The cattle economy in parts of East Africa cannot be understood without knowing the special dietary habits of the Masai people. On a broader geographic scale, some of the worldwide commodity markets, such as those for coffee and tea, are based on the taste preferences of consumers. The per capita consumption of tea is high in the British Isles, while coffee is the favorite beverage in The Netherlands. Nevertheless, the dominant influence in most land-use decisions throughout the world remains an economic one.

Among the economic factors that affect economic location and land use, two classes are of particular importance. These can be referred to as the *spatial* and *environmental* factors. The spatial and environmental approaches to economic location are analogous to the classical geographic concepts of *situation* and *site,* respectively. Acting in a combined fashion, the spatial and

---

ALONSO ON THE DUAL CONCEPT OF LAND

Regional planner William Alonso emphasized the dual economic nature of land when he wrote:

When a purchaser acquires land, he acquires two goods (land and location) in only one transaction, and only one payment is made for the combination. *

* "A Theory of the Urban Land Market," *Papers and Proceedings, Regional Science Association,* Vol. 6, 1960, p. 149.

---

[2] In Yugoslavia and elsewhere in Eastern Europe, some agricultural land can be bought and sold by private parties.

environmental factors can be thought of as making up the "physical basis" of economic life expressed by Erich Zimmermann (Chapter 1).

THE SPATIAL FACTOR: DISTANCE TO MARKETS AND OTHER TRANSPORT COSTS

In the spatial approach to economic location, the principal variable is *distance,* or, more accurately, the costs of overcoming distance. We live in space as well as in time and must therefore overcome distance in all economic activities. Time and energy losses are part of the real costs of moving people, goods, and information. A basic behavioral assumption exists that people normally strive to minimize the costs of overcoming distance. In view of this it seems curious that the field of economics, as it developed in the English speaking world, should have understated the distance factor as it did.

Land-use patterns revealed in the economic landscape result from human decisions related to production, exchange, and consumption. Even if, hypothetically, all the resources in a spatial economy were evenly distributed, the

---

ISARD ON THE SPATIAL ASPECT OF ECONOMIC ACTIVITY

Economic geographers and others interested in spatial economic systems owe a large debt to Professor Walter Isard. In the late 1940s, Isard, a young economist with a Ph.D. from Harvard, began a campaign to establish a greater role for location studies in American academic economics. In 1949, Isard wrote the following in a leading economics journal:

Theoreticians of today are chiefly preoccupied with introducing the time element in full into their analyses. . . . Yet who can deny the spatial aspect of economic development: that all economic processes exist in space, as well as over time? . . . Unfortunately . . . the architects of our finest theoretical structures have intensified the prejudice exhibited by Marshall. They continue to abstract from the element of space, and in so doing they are approaching a position of great imbalance. . . . In this sense the factor of space is repudiated, everything within the economy is in effect compressed to a point, and all spatial resistance disappears.

The approach to absurdity which is inherent in such a treatment . . . can be interpreted as treating an anomalous and ridiculous field: a one-point world, which somehow or other is conceived as divided into n parts, representing n nations, between which trade and trade barriers exist.*

* "The General Theory of Location and Space-Economy," *The Quarterly Journal of Economics,* Vol. LXIII, No. 4, November, 1949, pp. 476-478.

---

movement of consumers and the flow of goods and services would create spatial structure within the economic landscape. Assuming uniformly distributed resources, locational options would exist because of different substitution possibilities. An example would be the substitution of transport costs for production costs as the size of an operation increases. In many operations, unit production costs fall as the volume of output increases—at least up to a point. This is due to *scale economies,* resulting from the use of larger, more efficient plant and equipment, large-volume purchases, and other forms of savings. Increasing the scale of operation, however, may require some firms to bring in raw materials from a larger supply area (for example, a sawmill would need a larger forest supply area). To expand production, other firms might have to expand their marketing area, as in the case of a newspaper, which must reach out for more customers. Either case will involve greater transport costs per unit of output. Such situations set up a series of "trade off" possibilities between production costs and transport costs (Fig. 3.2).

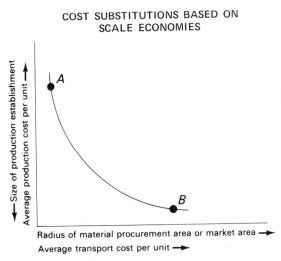

COST SUBSTITUTIONS BASED ON
SCALE ECONOMIES

Figure 3.2   Substitution possibilities between unit production costs and unit transport costs for a hypothetical operation subject to economies of scale where the environment is uniform. Points A and B have the same total unit costs for a given product. Condition A represents high unit production costs (smaller output) and low unit transport costs (smaller market or supply area). In condition B, larger-scale production results in lower unit production costs but higher unit transport costs. Normally, condition A would result in decentralized production, with many small plants, while condition B would result in a relatively few large plants.

THE ENVIRONMENTAL FACTOR: SPATIAL VARIATION IN NATURE

The second explanatory approach to economic location and land use relates to the variation of the natural environment from place to place. This approach helps to clarify the critical link between ecology and economics.

In contrast to the spatial approach, the environmental approach has been mainly an empirical kind of scholarly inquiry. It has not, thus far, been the subject of intensive deductive theoretical development. Environmental factors that vary spatially include climate, geology, hydrology, soil, topography (landforms), and natural vegetation. Environmental factors have a direct influence on *primary* forms of economic production, such as agriculture, mining, forestry, and fishing, in which wealth is extracted directly from the natural environment.

The influence of physical environment on the location and nature of economic production can be seen in the most direct form in mining industries. Some mineral ores are found in only a few places in the world. An example is nickel ore. Economic activity linked to a single physical resource is also clearly apparent in a desert oasis, where the local economic, political, and social system is directly geared to the available water supply.

Chapters 5 and 6 are devoted to a fuller treatment of natural resources and other environmental aspects of economic activity.

COMPLEMENTARITY OF THE TWO APPROACHES

In the case of certain economic activities, locational explanation will be provided mainly by the environmental approach. For example, the huge aluminum refining plant located at Kitimat, on the remote, mountainous coast of British Columbia in Western Canada, owes its location to a single environmental advantage: the very large, low-cost hydroelectric power capacity of the site. On the other hand, most urban land uses are located mainly on the basis of the spatial factor, particularly accessibility to markets and other concentrations of economic activity.

The spatial and environmental factors should be viewed as interacting ones. This is important because it means that economic location is not rigidly deterministic. Land-use decisions depend on human perceptions, values, and judgments. The decision maker, as pointed out above, is usually presented with alternatives (Fig. 3.3). For example, Robinson Crusoe (Chapter 1) might have had the option of digging for shellfish at a nearby, poor supply area, or at a distant, richer source. By exploiting the distant, richer supply, he substitutes transport costs (walking to the distant site and carrying the catch back) for the higher production costs (fewer shellfish dug per hour) at the nearby site. It is obvious that this trade-off would not be possible if shellfish were uniformly distributed in Crusoe's spatial economy.

58

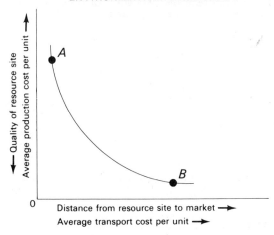

COST SUBSTITUTIONS BASED ON
ENVIRONMENTAL VARIABILITY

Figure 3.3 Substitution possibilities between unit production costs and unit transport costs under conditions of environmental variability. Market for the resource is at "0." A lower-grade resource deposit near the market (A) and a distant, higher grade deposit of the same resource (B) have the same total delivered costs per unit. Other possible cost combinations may lie on or near the curve.

The choice between local supplies of lower-grade resources and distant supplies of higher-grade resources applies in spatial production systems up to the international level. For example, some steel companies in the United States switched in the postwar years to higher-grade, foreign iron ores, as nearer, domestic ores became higher cost through depletion.

ECONOMIC RENT AND LOCATION RENT: FORMALIZING THE ENVIRONMENTAL AND SPATIAL APPROACHES

People bid for land on the basis of its perceived advantages for given types of land use. As William Alonso implied, the purchaser of land receives two things: the intrinsic environmental characteristics of the site, and its location with respect to all other economic activity. The concept of *rent* helps in understanding the nature of these advantages and the dual influences of space and environment in economic activity.

We are faced at the outset with some semantic problems. First, the formal concept of rent discussed here is related to, but is not the same as, the familiar notion of rent (contract rent), which is an agreed on sum paid periodically to the owner of land or other durable property for its use. Further confusion exists because the two kinds of rent discussed here, *location rent* and *economic rent,* are called by different names in the literature. The term *economic rent* is often used to mean both types. Also, *location rent* is sometimes referred to as *land rent, geographic rent,* or *site rent.* We will try to avoid confusion here by consistently referring to *location rent* in connection with the spatial aspect of economic activity, and *economic rent* in connection with the environmental aspect.

In simplest terms, rent expresses the net benefits derived from a unit of land because of advantages resulting from its location (location rent) or its environmental quality (economic rent). Ideally (assuming that demand exists), the land use that yields the highest combined economic and location rent per acre will come to occupy a piece of land, and other land uses will be allocated to other sites where they, in turn, provide the highest combined rent per acre.

The two very different but complementary rent doctrines were conceived in Europe in the early decades of the nineteenth century. The concept of *economic rent* originated with the pioneer economist, David Ricardo, in England; the concept of *location rent* was created by a German landowner-scholar, J. H. von Thünen.[3]

ECONOMIC RENT

David Ricardo's doctrine of economic rent became an important part of classical economic theory. Formulated around 1817, it relates land (environmental) quality, measured by such things as natural soil fertility, to farm income. Farm income per acre is greater where soil is more fertile, since more output can be gained per acre for the same inputs, assuming that other production costs and commodity prices are the same. Looking at it another way, economic rent is the difference between the product obtained by the use of two equal quantities of labor and capital. It is that part of the income of a production process that results from "nature's contribution." The difference in quality between two sites determines the rent on the higher quality land.

An essential feature of Ricardo's version of rent is the assumption of

---

[3]Although it is contended ideologically that land has no value—and therefore no cost or price—under socialism, the existence of differential rent is implicitly acknowledged in the Soviet Union by the administration of levies on the users of land, including differential tax levies, differential procurement prices on quota deliveries payable by the State, and differential turnover taxes on a given product produced in different regions, payable on the basis of natural advantages.

60

spatial variation in land quality. Because of this and the fact that land is fixed in quantity and immovable, progressively lower quality land must be used as population and economic demand rise. Owners of the higher quality land receive the same prices at the market, but their production costs per unit of output are lower, giving them surplus returns. This surplus constitutes economic rent (Fig. 3.4).

The natural cause of rising rents, in Ricardo's view, is explained in terms of diminishing returns for the last unit of production. Consequently, no economic rent would be produced if there were limitless land available of the same quality.

Ricardo emphasized that the price of agricultural land is a consequence of its rent, not vice versa. Also, the rent of an acre of land is not fixed, but is dependent on market price. If it were found, for example, that a commodity such as coffee shortens life, the demand and therefore the market prices would fall (presumably), reducing the rent acquired in the coffee producing regions.

Although he centered his attention on the role of land quality in the creation of rent, Ricardo did recognize the existence of a spatial factor. He wrote, "the most fertile, *and the most favorably situated* land will be first cultivated"; and, again, "thus, by bringing successively land of worse quality *or less favorably situated* into cultivation, rent would rise on the land previously cultivated"[4] (italics mine).

THE CREATIVE MIND OF RICARDO

David Ricardo (1772-1823) was one of the intellectual giants who established the field of economics. Unlike other classical economists, his ideas had universal appeal, finding acceptance by Marxist as well as neo-classical and post-Keynesian schools of economics.

Ricardo never attended a university but instead made a fortune as a stockbroker in London. Retiring from business at an early age, he became interested in the writings of Adam Smith. He turned to scholarship and the result was his famous *Principles of Political Economy and Taxation* (1817). Ricardo also became a member of Parliament, where he sponsored a number of landmark parliamentary acts.

Besides the doctrine of economic rent, Ricardo originated other fundamental concepts, such as the *law of comparative advantage,* discussed later in this chapter, and the *law of diminishing returns,* treated in Chapter 5.

---

[4] David Ricardo, *Economic Essays,* George Bell and Sons, London, 1923, p. 229.

ENVIRONMENT, SPACE, AND ECONOMIC RENT

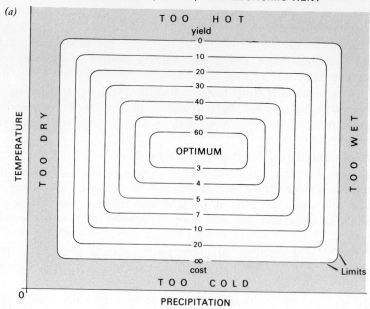

62

SPATIAL AND ENVIRONMENTAL APPROACHES

Figure 3.4 (see facing page) Temperature and precipitation are two environmental variables that have a quasi-systematic spatial distribution. The connection between these variables and economic (Ricardian) rent is shown here for a hypothetical agricultural land use. In (a) variations in yield are shown related to the two factors, together with corresponding unit production costs. In (b) a price of 7 per unit is introduced, which establishes the amount and areal extent of rent produced. A change in the climatic variables or in the price would change the amounts of rent produced and the configuration of the profitable region of production. (Source: *Harold H. McCarty and James B. Lindberg,* A Preface to Economic Geography, *Prentice-Hall, Englewood Cliffs, N.J., 1966, Figures 3.3 and 3.4, pp. 61 and 62.*)

LOCATION RENT

Although Ricardo recognized location as a factor in the creation of rent, it was a German contemporary, J. H. von Thünen, who developed a concept of rent, *location rent,* which made *distance to market* the key variable in explaining the spatial pattern of agricultural land use.

Unlike Ricardian economic rent, location rent is not concerned with spatial variation of land quality. Instead, location rent reflects the advantage of nearness of production to the market. Everything else remaining equal, farms close to the market have a greater location rent per acre than those at greater distances because the unit costs of shipment are lower, and all farmers receive the same price at the market.

Location rent models based on von Thünen's ideas derive a location rent curve that allocates land use in ordered patterns around market centers. Von Thünen's model and the subject of location rent are examined further in Chapter 4.

RENT AND LAND-USE INTENSITY

Land-use intensity varies in the extreme for various kinds of land use. Millions of dollars worth of goods or services can be produced annually by certain kinds of manufacturing or service establishments on less than an acre of land. On the other hand, a ranch needs a square mile (640 acres) or more to support one family in many parts of the semi-arid Western rangeland. The intensity with which a plot of land is used depends on the combination of economic rent and location rent it is capable of generating per acre.

The notion of *marginal land use* is important in both Ricardian (economic) and von Thünen (location) rent doctrines. If, because of a combination of poor quality land and remoteness from markets, the combined rent capacity per acre of a site is barely above zero for its most profitable land use, then the land is considered marginal. If the combined rent generating capacity is below zero for all land uses, then no matter how much labor and capital are applied per acre, no economic activity can be carried on that will cover costs and be competitive with other production sites.

Extensive kinds of land use having low returns per acre are associated with economically marginal areas, and only low population densities can be supported in such places. An example would be sheep grazing areas in many parts of the world. Because of the combined aridity and remoteness from markets in parts of the American West, and in Australia, Southern Argentina (Patagonia), and elsewhere, the only regional land use that is profitable is the grazing of sheep for distant wool markets.

In moving from marginal areas to those with greater rent-producing capacity—that is, places with more productive environments and/or more accessible to markets—more and more kinds of land use become profitable, and the bid price for land rises. As this happens, the land is used more intensively; that is, it pays to use more inputs of labor or capital per acre of land, and more output per acre is realized. A farmer in Iowa can gain more income from sheep raising per acre than a rancher in Wyoming because of Iowa's more productive agricultural climate and the proximity to Chicago and other large markets. However, sheep grazing in Iowa must compete with many other land uses, most of which are more profitable per acre. As a result, we find sheep ranching an important land use in Wyoming (see Fig. 1.4) while corn and other Corn Belt products are dominant in Iowa. This is discussed again when we explain the von Thünen land-use model in Chapter 4.

Extremely wide variations in the intensity of agriculture and other land uses exist between and within nations. In many cases these differences are the result of internal pricing structures. Variations in intensity are influenced by the relative prices of the three principal factors of production—land, labor, and capital. In the United States and Canada, land is relatively abundant and labor relatively scarce, and this leads to *extensive* agricultural practices. Farm sizes of several hundred acres or more are common in Anglo America. However, in China, India, and Japan, where for centuries high population densities have had to subsist on very limited arable land, agriculture is very *intensive* and farm sizes are very small, averaging as low as a few acres per farm family. In the United States and Canada, agricultural land is priced low relative to labor. The opposite is true in Asia. In every case, the farmer strives for the least-cost combination of land, labor, and capital inputs. The price of these factors of production act as signals for input substitutions and for product options. This helps explain why Argentina produces so much cattle (very extensive land use) and why Japan produces so much paddy rice (very intensive land use). Arable land is plentiful in Argentina

SPATIAL AND ENVIRONMENTAL APPROACHES

relative to population (the people-land ratio is low), while the opposite is true in Japan.

So far we have been using illustrations from agriculture, but the principles here apply to other kinds of land use. For example, rich farm land a few miles from an urban center is subject to strong competition from suburban land uses. Since these uses are much more intensive than even very intensive farming, excellent farm land may be purchased for use as a shopping plaza, a drive-in movie, or a tract home development (Fig. 1.3).

While it is true that rich resource deposits—copper ore or petroleum would be examples—can form the bases for "islands" of intensive land use, as a general rule most intensive concentrations of economic activity occur in urban places, where accessibility peaks and where location rents (and, consequently, land values) can reach extraordinarily high levels (Fig. 3.5).

COMPARATIVE ADVANTAGE, REGIONAL SPECIALIZATION, AND TRADE

ABSOLUTE REGIONAL ADVANTAGE

We have seen that location rent and economic rent express two kinds of natural advantages for places. In addition to these fundamental advantages, there can be others resulting from accumulations of human or capital (Man-made) resources, such as skilled labor, industrial buildings, transportation systems, communication networks, educational systems, and so on.

One reason for the great economic performance of the United States is its possession of regions with superb combinations of natural, human, and capital advantages. Grain from the Midwest and coking coal from Appalachia, for example, are produced and transported so efficiently (i.e., at such low unit costs) that, despite being bulky commodities, they can be delivered to markets in many parts of the world and sold at competitive prices.

Regional advantages for production can change over time. These changes can be rapid and dramatic, as when there is a sudden breakthrough in technology, or where a new resource deposit is discovered, such as gold was in California in 1848. Throughout history, regions and nations have gained or lost economic advantages for different kinds of production.

Regional advantages are particularly sensitive to the impact of transport changes. If a new highway built from one city to another passes close to Town A and not to Town B, then Town A will gain lower transport costs to the two cities and will be able to deliver products to markets at costs below those of Town B. (Assuming, of course, that the two towns are otherwise equally efficient producers.) This can also work in a reverse manner. If a limited-access super highway is built that bypasses a town formerly on the old highway, the local gas stations, stores, and other businesses lose their

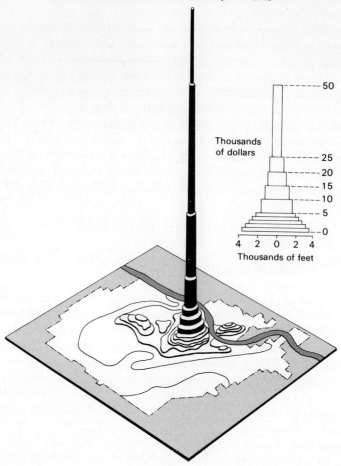

LAND VALUES IN TOPEKA, KANSAS

Figure 3.5   The peaking of land values at the centers of cities is illustrated dramatically in this isometric model of Topeka, Kansas. The graph is based on assessed land values for the period 1954–1959. A similar model for larger cities would reveal a series of subsidiary peaks surrounding the main one. (Source: Duane S. Knos, The Distribution of Land Values in Topeka, Kansas, *The University of Kansas Institute for Social and Environmental Studies, 1962, Figure 2.)*

66   SPATIAL AND ENVIRONMENTAL APPROACHES

previous locational advantage. Dense networks of roads and other integrated transport facilities in industrial regions provide very low-cost access to production materials and labor pools. Such regions are linked by low-cost transport to markets all over the world.

Thus far we have been viewing places in terms of absolute advantages. It is clear that regional specialization and trade on the basis of absolute advantage makes sense. If A can make bows better than arrows, and B can make arrows better than bows, then it clearly pays both to specialize and trade their surplus. In this case both parties end up with more goods (bows and arrows) per hour worked. In a similar manner, regions can devote their natural and human resources to those types of production in which they are most efficient, trading their surpluses for commodities that other regions produce more efficiently. Florida oranges are, in effect, traded for Alaskan crabs. This assumes, of course, that a demand exists for these products and that transport costs between the regions are not prohibitive.

RICARDO'S LAW OF COMPARATIVE ADVANTAGE

David Ricardo threw a whole new light on regional differences as the bases of specialization and trade. In 1817 he formulated his *Law Of Comparative Advantage,* showing that, even if Country A produces, say, both shoes and sugar at lower costs than Country B, specialization and trade in these products could still be advantageous to both. This may appear confusing, and so it will be helpful here to consider an intuitive example:

> Imagine a small community with one medical doctor, who also happens to be the best typist and clerical worker in town. From the purely economic point of view, should he work part time as a physician and part time taking care of the clerical chores in his office? Clearly not. Since his income per hour as a doctor is much greater than as a typist, he can maximize his income by working all of his time as a physician and hiring someone to handle office work, *even though this person may be less productive as an office worker than the physician himself.* Here we can say that the physician has absolute advantage in both areas, but *greatest absolute advantage* as a provider of medical services. Likewise, the clerical worker, since he or she is capable of doing clerical work but not capable of any medical tasks, has the *least absolute disadvantage* as an office worker. These can now be expressed as *comparative advantages*— the physician has a *comparative advantage* in medicine and the clerical worker has a *comparative advantage* in office work.

Ricardo's Law of Comparative Advantage can be illustrated by means of a simplified, two-nation, two commodity model. Table 3.1 shows this model, where production costs are measured in terms of units of labor input. The model relates to countries, but applies more generally to regions of all sizes. It is assumed that surpluses can be produced and a demand exists for the surpluses. Shipping costs are not considered. For Country A, 1 unit of shoes

Table 3.1 A Two-country, Two-commodity Model in which One Country Has Absolute Advantage in Both Commodities, But Where Specialization and Trade Based on Comparative Advantage Benefits Both Countries

Commodity	Production Costs Measured in Units of Labor Required Per Unit of Product	
	Country A	Country B
Shoes	1	3
Sugar	2	4

Two units[a] of labor will produce:	1.0 unit of shoes	.33 units of shoes
Without specialization and trade (assuming one unit of labor for each commodity)	.5 units of sugar	.25 units of sugar
	1.5 units of both	.58 units of both
	2.08 total units produced	
With specialization and trade. Country A has comparative advantage in shoes and Country B in sugar.	2.0 units of shoes	0.0 units of shoes
	0.0 units of sugar	0.5 units of sugar
	2.0 units of both	0.5 units of both
	2.50 total units produced	

[a]Two units are arbitrary. Other numbers of units could be used.

Source: Adapted from Paul A. Samuelson. *Economics,* Ninth Edition, 1973, McGraw-Hill Book Co., Table 34-1, p. 671.

costs 1 unit of labor, and 1 unit of sugar costs 2 units of labor; in Country B, 1 unit of shoes costs 3 units of labor and 1 unit of sugar costs 4 units of labor. The critical thing here is the ratios of these labor costs. If Country A specializes in shoes and Country B in sugar and they trade (even though A can produce *both* cheaper), both countries are better off. This can be seen by comparing the case without specialization and trade and the case with specialization and trade.

In the case with trade, 1 day's work (by one worker) in Country A will now produce the same amount of shoes as before, but a second day's production of shoes (assume 2 units of labor input) can be traded for imported sugar. Thus, for the same 2 day's labor, a worker in Country A can now purchase a larger *combination* of the two commodities. Under these condi-

SPATIAL AND ENVIRONMENTAL APPROACHES

tions, Country B produces less total physical output. Nevertheless, a worker in Country B can buy more of the lower cost imported shoes for a day of his labor, and since he gets the same real wage in sugar, he too can afford more of the combination of shoes and sugar. Thus, *for the same effort, workers in both countries now enjoy a higher real income.*

Ricardo's example considered labor costs, but the principle is much broader, and modern trade theory takes into account national differences in land and capital as well.

In the real world, of course, distance costs are always a factor and create spatial resistance to trade, especially for bulky items. Nevertheless, regional specialization and the exchange of regional surpluses by means of low-cost, mechanized transport have become the hallmarks of modern industrial economies.

Ricardo's Law of Comparative Advantage, together with the doctrines of economic rent and location rent, can be used to interpret the economic landscapes observed throughout the world. Because of its greater rainfall (higher economic rent) and proximity to urban markets (higher location rent), Illinois can grow both corn and wheat better than Kansas, but Illinois specializes in the more intensive (more profit per acre) corn production in which it has comparative advantage (greatest absolute advantage), while Kansas specializes in wheat (on larger farms) in which it has comparative advantage (least absolute disadvantage). In this way, the incomes of both regions are increased through regional specialization and trade.

In looking around the world we find many regions of specialization where it is clear that optimal environmental or spatial conditions for production do not exist. Canada, Argentina, the United States, and Australia have large, semi-arid regions specializing in the export of wheat. Yet, many European nations that have imported wheat over the years have more productive and more accessible wheat environments and can produce much higher yields (Table 3.2). Wheat growing in the former regions provides a greater combi-

Table 3.2   Wheat Yields for Selected Countries in Metric Tons per Hectare, 1948-1952

European Producers		Exporting Nations	
Denmark	3.65	Canada	1.28
Netherlands	3.65	Argentina	1.15
Belgium	3.22	Australia	1.12
United Kingdom	2.72	United States	1.12

Source: Adapted from Michael Chisholm, *Rural Settlement and Land Use: An Essay In Location,* John Wiley and Sons, Inc., 1962, Table 13, p. 105.

nation of economic rent and location rent than any other land use, since aridity and remoteness from markets limits other exports. However, in Denmark or England wheat growing must compete with many other (usually more profitable per acre) forms of land use such as dairy farming, truck farming, and urban or industrial land uses.

To repeat, the Law of Comparative Advantage holds that specialization in types of production for which places have comparative advantage (not necessarily absolute advantage) can result in increased incomes for all trading partners. This is the classical argument for free trade between regions and among nations.

SUMMARY

The location and character of economic activity throughout the world has been, and continues to be, influenced by interacting *spatial* and *environmental* factors. The spatial and environmental explanatory approaches to economic activity have formal counterparts in two complementary rent doctrines: von Thünen's (*location rent*) and Ricardo's (*economic rent*). The spatial approach emphasizes distance costs and applies to all economic phenomena. The environmental approach is based on spatial differentiation of the natural environment. The concept of economic rent establishes a link between human ecology and economics. A specific land use ideally comes to occupy a given plot of land on the basis of the land's ability to generate a combination of location rent and economic rent. The intensity as well as the type of land use varies from place to place, and is also based on rent-producing capacity. Ricardo's Law of Comparative Advantage relates to both spatial and environmental advantages, and provides a fundamental explanation for specialization of production and the resulting trade of surpluses among localities, regions, and nations. Specialization in types of production for which places have comparative advantage (not necessarily absolute advantage) can, through trade, result in increased wealth for all trading partners.

Questions

1 Explain how regular spatial patterns (structure) could develop in a hypothetical spatial economy, even if the natural environment were assumed to be everywhere the same.
2 Give an example of the interaction of spatial and environmental influences on economic activity. Show how such an interaction can be related to substitution between production and transport costs.

3 Describe, with simple examples, the concepts of *economic rent* and *location rent.*
4 Wyoming has no Standard Metropolitan Statistical Area (SMSA) (Figure 13.2) and a small overall population. Explain this in terms of location rent and economic rent, and the principle of regional comparative advantage.
5 In May 1978 the U.S. Government began a new program to protect the domestic steel industry from imports. Discuss the implications of such a policy.

4

LOCATION THEORY: SPATIAL EXPLANATION THROUGH DEDUCTIVE MODELLING

"One way to deal with complex problems is to simplify them. . . . Our earth is almost infinitely complex. . . . The easiest way to simplify this problem so that we begin to see the nature of it is to imagine an unreal earth populated by a hypothetical people."

George F. Carter*

The advances of modern science have come about through the development of theory. The attempt to theorize can be described as a search for order in nature. It is an intellectual device that helps to explain real world phenomena, and to predict the future states of these phenomena. The idea of theory as an explanatory device recurs over and over again in the literature of the philosophy of science.

Deductive theorizing is a reasoning process in which key variables are identified, assumptions are made, and logical conclusions are drawn about the behavior of the variables. This is sometimes referred to as "arm-chair" theorizing, in contrast to *inductive* reasoning in which the emphasis is on finding order through observations of the real world, or through laboratory experimentation.[1]

---

* *Man and The Land: A Cultural Geography* (Third ed.), Holt Rinehart and Winston, New York, 1975, p. 34.
[1] The productive interplay of the deductive and inductive modes in scientific inquiry is well illustrated in the field of physics. Albert Einstein's "arm-chair" deductions established the Theory of Relativity, but actual measurements of the speed of light, later made experimentally by others, provided the empirical verification of Einstein's theory.

Classical location theory provides the deductive foundation for much of the analytical work in modern economic geography. The key variable in location models is *distance,* or more accurately the costs in money, time, and inconvenience of overcoming distance. This makes location theory a *normative* theory, which means that it assumes optimizing behavior on the part of an ideal, completely rational and fully informed population of decision makers. The economic landscape shows things as they actually are (Chapter 1); normative theory, on the other hand, indicates what things *ideally* should be under the stated assumptions.

Location models in many places play an important role in planning. In Sweden, the Soviet Union, a number of East European countries, and elsewhere they have been used for regional planning, transportation systems, school systems, medical services, and many other forms of public facilities.

The use of normative models in planning and research has been questioned by some writers. The concept of *economic man,* based on the assumption of *maximizing* money income, may not always reflect reality. People often exhibit *satisficing* behavior instead. For example, many persons are willing to work at jobs that pay less but give them more time off. Similarly, many small business owners prefer to keep their firm local and small, rather than moving to a large city where the business could be greatly expanded. While satisficing behavior is common, it is difficult to incorporate into economic models.

Criticism is also leveled at normative location models for dealing with economic efficiency, and not with the distribution of wealth—that is, with the size of the pie and not with how it is shared.[2] Nevertheless, the study of classical location theory provides insights into the processes of economic location and land-use evolution that can be gained in no other way.

As the quotation from Wolfgang Stolper in Chapter 1 suggests, a completely general theory of the location of economic activity is very likely an unattainable ideal. This has led to the development of *partial theories,* which

---

THOUGHTS ON PERFECTION BY T. L. SAATY

The need to be satisfied with less than perfection in attempting to apply models to real world problems was philosophically expressed by the pioneer in operations research, Thomas L. Saaty: "Operations research is the art of giving bad answers to problems to which otherwise worse answers are given."*

* *Mathematical Methods of Operations Research,* McGraw-Hill, New York, 1959, p. 3.

---

[2] See, for example, David Harvey, *Social Justice and the City,* Edward Arnold, London, 1973.

attempt to explain different aspects of spatial economic systems. Partial approaches involve the consideration of certain factors, while ignoring others or assuming them to remain constant. (In economics, a common expression for this is the Latin *ceteris paribus*.) This chapter introduces the partial approaches of three pioneer theorists, whose deductive models laid the foundations for modern location theory.

VON THÜNEN AND THE ORIGIN OF LOCATION THEORY

Location theory had its beginning in northern Germany in the 1820s when Johann Heinrich von Thünen published his classic work, *The Isolated State*.[3] Although he wrote over 150 years ago, his methods and ideas still have undiminished relevance today.

Von Thünen was aware that his English contemporary, David Ricardo, had based his notions of economic rent on environmental differences, such as soil quality. Von Thünen, however, emphasized the pervasive role of distance costs. He originated the idea that rent also varies with the distance from market. He showed that rent is generated by the distance factor *even if the environment is assumed to be everywhere the same.* To this kind of rent we apply the term *location rent* (Chapter 3). We will see in later chapters that location rent is an explanatory device for many kinds of economic activities.

Von Thünen is the intellectual ancestor of those who emphasize the spatial approach in explaining economic location.[4] Like Ricardo, von Thünen's background included a balance of analytical rigor and practical experience. His early inclination was toward mathematics, but he came under the influence of a famous agricultural economist and studied for the management of his family estate, *Tellow,* near Rostock.

Von Thünen recognized that there exists a collective reluctance on the part of society—at least where a choice is possible—to expend more effort in the movement of people or goods than is necessary in fulfilling economic demands. At work here is the behavioral principle that Man attempts to use space efficiently by minimizing efforts to overcome distance. This can be geographical distance, or some function of it such as money costs, time, energy, or inconvenience. But whatever form it takes, the factor of distance becomes for von Thünen, and for subsequent location theorists, a universal variable underlying the spatial structure of economic activity.

[3] *Der Isolierte Staat in Beziehung auf Landwirtschaft und Nationalökonomie,* Rostock, 1826. Translated into English by Carla M. Wartenberg as *The Isolated State,* Permagon Press, Oxford, 1966.

[4] See, for example, M. Beckmann and T. Marschak, "An Activity Analysis Approach To Location Theory," Publication P-649, The Rand Corporation, Santa Monica, California, April 5, 1955.

As with most theorists, von Thünen's creative impulse began with an intellectual "problem," that is, a sense of curiosity about something observed in the real world. Von Thünen gazed out over his economic landscape and wondered why plots of land with the same environmental features had very different land uses. He eventually singled out *distance* as the key explanatory variable.(As in the case of so many theoretical advances, a creative break-through seems simple and obvious after it has been achieved.)

Von Thünen reasoned that, since prices for agricultural commodities were fixed by supply and demand levels at the central market town, the kind and intensity of land use surrounding the town depended on the distance of the production sites from the market center. Accordingly, the single variable in his agricultural land-use model became *distance from the farm gate to the market town.*

INITIAL MODEL ASSUMPTIONS

The model assumptions made by von Thünen are clearly expressed in the opening lines of his classic work: "Imagine a very large town at the center of a fertile plain, the soil is capable of cultivation and of the same fertility.[5] Far from the town, the plain turns into an uncultivated wilderness which cuts off all communication between this State and the outside world. There are no other towns on the plain."[6]

Von Thünen was one of the first writers to use the assumption of *economic man.* Under this assumption all persons behave alike in economic matters, have similar demands and consumption habits, have similar abilities and production efficiencies, possess total knowledge, behave rationally, and seek to maximize their incomes.

Von Thünen's hypothetical population exists on a flat, *isotropic plain*— one containing uniformly distributed people, environmental characteristics, and natural resources. Unlike Ricardo's economic rent model, all the land has identical productivity. The single market town purchases all the agricultural production of the surrounding region. Transportation between farms and the town takes place along the shortest routes, unconstrained by natural barriers; transportation costs are a function of straight line distance, but are based on different commodity transport rates, depending on perishability as well as weight. The whole system is closed, so that no influence is exerted from outside.

These initial model assumptions were perhaps not as unrealistic in von Thünen's day as they would seem now. The north German plain in the first

---

[5] Note the direct contrast here with Ricardo's approach (Chapter 3).
[6] *The Isolated State, op. cit.*

decades of the nineteenth century was, indeed, a flat economic landscape with a rather evenly distributed rural population of small farmers. Also, in that pre-railroad era "horse and wagon" transport existed, consisting of a finely textured network of primitive roads, which approximated a uniform transport surface.

THE SINGLE LAND USE MODEL

Under these hypothetical conditions von Thünen employed the single variable, *distance from farm to central market town,* to generate ordered zones of agricultural land use surrounding the market town.

If agriculture were a spatially concentrated activity, such as manufacturing, then all the farm output needed to supply the town could be grown very near the town. In such a case distance costs to market would be negligible. Since all farmers are equally efficient producers and since all receive the same market price in the town for each commodity, the income per acre for a commodity produced adjacent to the market town, because of the negligible transport cost, would be the same for all farmers.

However, since agriculture requires a great deal of space per farm, the provision of agricultural products for a town or city requires production over a large surrounding area. This means that the farms will be located at varying distances from the central market. As a result, farm products must be shipped varying distances to market from different farms, thereby incurring variable transport costs.

The location rent equation for the general case can then be written as:

$$R = o(p - c) - orD \qquad (1)$$

where R = location rent in dollars (any monetary unit) per acre (any areal unit)

o = yield (output per unit area; for example, tons per acre)

p = price at the market center (for example, dollars per ton)
c = production cost per unit of output (for example, dollars per ton)
r = shipping rate, expressed in money units per unit output per unit distance (for example, dollars per ton-mile)
D = distance from farm to market in miles or kilometers

Equation (1) gives the location rent per acre produced by a specific commodity or land use at any distance from the market. It combines terms representing the rent that would be generated by a commodity on an acre at the market, and the reduction of this value by the cost of transporting the commodity to market.[7]

Note that there is only one *variable* on the right side of this equation, the independent variable, D. The other four letter symbols represent *parameters*, whose values vary for different commodities but are everywhere the same for a given commodity or land use.

By assigning different values to the variable, D, and by computing the location rent per acre, R, which would be produced at different distances from the market, Equation (1) generates the location rent graph shown in Figure 4.1. An examination of Equation (1) and Figure 4.1 will illustrate the fundamental relationships in the location rent model. The distance of the

GRAPHICAL INTERPRETATION OF THE LOCATION
RENT EQUATION

GENERAL FORM OF A LINEAR EQUATION

$Y = a - bX$

Y intercept (a) = value of Y at $x = o$

Slope of graph $(b) = \Delta y / \Delta x$

LOCATION RENT EQUATION

$R = o(p-c) - or D$

R intercept $[o(p-c)]$ = value of R at D = o (at the market)

Slope of graph $(-\Delta R / \Delta D) = -or$

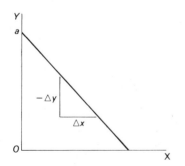

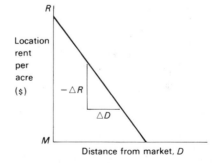

Figure 4.1

[7] For a detailed development of this equation see E. S. Dunn, Jr., *The Location of Agricultural Production,* University of Florida Press, Gainesville, 1954, Chapter Two.

rent graph above the horizontal axis is determined by the first term of the equation, $o(p - c)$. Increase in market price or decrease in production cost raise the graph to a higher position, but the slope remains the same since there is no change in r. This makes that land use more competitive both at the market and at all places distant from the market (Fig.4.2). The opposite changes in one or both parameter values would result in a lower graph position and a correspondingly smaller radius of production.

If, on the other hand, the first term of the equation is unchanged and the parameter r (shipping rate) in the second term is increased, then the graph changes as shown in Figure 4.3. A real-world example of this would be an increased shipping rate that decreases the radius of production. A decrease in r, which would be the case for the introduction of low-cost mechanized transport, would have the opposite effect, extending the profitable radius of production (Fig. 4.3). The effect of changes in yield (o) is more complicated, since this parameter appears in both terms of Equation (1).

THE MULTIPLE LAND USE MODEL

From Equation (1), the location rent per acre, R, at any given distance from the market, D, depends on the values of the four parameters. The values of the parameters, in turn, depend on the different physical and economic characteristics of the products. This can be illustrated by a two crop (two land use) system consisting of tomato production and wheat production.

It is reasonable to suppose that the price per pound at the market will be higher for tomatoes than for wheat (we assume here the sale of wheat as

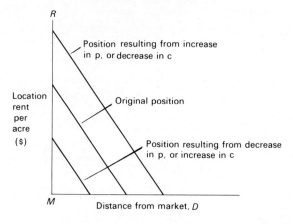

CHANGES IN LOCATION RENT RESULTING
FROM CHANGES IN PARAMETER VALUES FOR
A GIVEN LAND USE

Figure 4.2

78

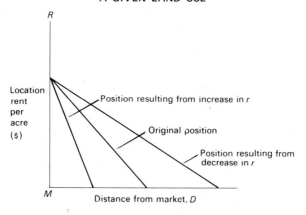

CHANGES IN LOCATION RENT RESULTING
FROM CHANGES IN PARAMETER VALUES FOR
A GIVEN LAND USE

Figure 4.3

grain, not flour, at the market). Since tomatoes are highly perishable, they must be handled carefully and shipped quickly to market, which results in a high transport rate compared to wheat. These and other differences give tomatoes a different set of parameter values from wheat, assigning the two commodities different location rent graphs.

The hypothetical land use pattern generated by the location rent graphs for tomatoes and wheat is shown in Figure 4.4. In the case of tomatoes, return per acre near the market is high. Since r is large for tomatoes, the slope has a correspondingly high *negative* value; this causes the location rent to drop off rapidly until, beyond B tomatoes cannot be raised profitably. Similar reasoning explains the position of the location rent graph for wheat.

Under the assumptions of the model, which include isolation from other regions, the commodity (land use) generating the greatest location rent per acre will occupy that site. Line *LRC* in Figure 4.4 represents the highest levels of location rent for the two-crop system. By dropping a vertical line from point R to point T on the horizontal axis, a critical radius, MT is established. Within the circle established by this radius only tomatoes will be grown, since they will generate the higher return per acre. Beyond this radius and out to C only wheat will be grown, because in that outer zone wheat will produce a greater return per acre. Beyond radius MC transport costs to market are too high and profitable production is impossible; this corresponds to von Thünen's "outer wilderness," where no location rent is produced. The concentric zones of tomato and wheat production, created when radii MT and MC are rotated 360 degrees about the market, correspond to the "rings" in von Thünen's original land-use system (Fig. 4.5).

In any multiple land-use system, such as that in Figure 4.4, we would

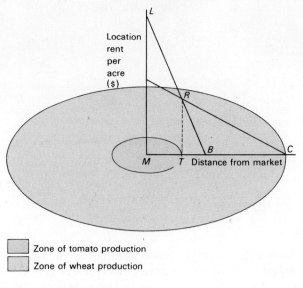

Zone of tomato production
Zone of wheat production

Figure 4.4   The inner portions of both the zones of tomato production and wheat production are farmed more intensively than the outer portions. Location rent per acre is higher (transport costs to market are lower) in the inner portions.

expect the inner portions of each zone to be used more intensively than the outer portions. Higher location rents there, relative to the outer parts of the same zone, enable farmers to increase labor and or capital inputs per acre, and thereby gain greater returns per acre.

Of course, real life farms are usually more complex than this, involving combinations of crops and other rural land use. Nevertheless, the fundamental principles expressed in mathematically explicit terms in this model furnish insights into far more complex land-use patterns in urban as well as in agricultural landscapes.

EQUILIBRIUM FEATURES OF THE MODEL

The land-use model based on von Thünen's original ideas defines a hypothetical landscape in which the rational and completely informed farmers have moved toward a spatial equilibrium of incomes. Through the bidding process land prices will adjust competitively to location rent, and will therefore be highest near the central market, dropping off to zero at the outer,

80   LOCATION THEORY

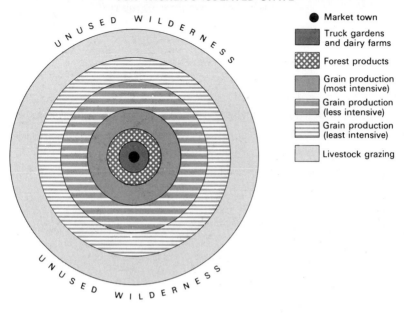

VON THÜNEN'S ISOLATED STATE

● Market town

Truck gardens and dairy farms

Forest products

Grain production (most intensive)

Grain production (less intensive)

Grain production (least intensive)

Livestock grazing

Figure 4.5   Perishable truck crops and milk are produced intensively in the inner ring. In von Thünen's time forests were the source of fuel for cooking and heating as well as for construction lumber, and this zone had to be close to the market. Since von Thünen assumes here a homogeneous environment, land-use intensity and location rent per acre drop off as the only variable—distance from the market—increases. Beyond the grazing zone lies the outer wilderness, where no land use is profitable.

unproductive zone. Ultimately, farmers who locate near the market will have smaller farms of higher priced land. Because of the high location rent of the land there, it pays them to apply greater inputs of labor and capital in order to raise high priced crops that produce high income per acre. Conversely, the farmers who come to occupy the outer margins of the "isolated state" enjoy similar incomes by carrying out extensive farming operations (such as sheep grazing) involving very little input and return per acre, but with larger farms permitted by the low price per acre.

RELAXING INITIAL MODEL ASSUMPTIONS

After establishing the relationship of location rent to land use, von Thünen then modified his model to more nearly approach real world conditions by relaxing some initial assumptions. If the assumption of a uniform environ-

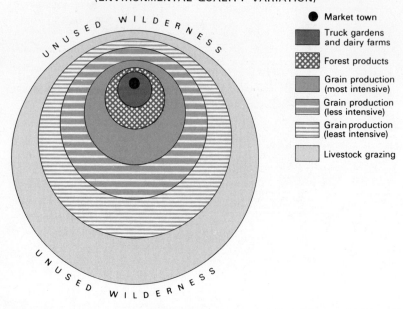

VON THÜNEN'S MODEL WITH VARIABLE PRODUCTION COST
(ENVIRONMENTAL QUALITY VARIATION)

● Market town

Truck gardens
and dairy farms

Forest products

Grain production
(most intensive)

Grain production
(less intensive)

Grain production
(least intensive)

Livestock grazing

Figure 4.6   When von Thünen's assumption of a uniform environment is dropped, the effect on his land use rings would resemble this. Here, the ordered zones are not concentric but are extended southward, assuming higher quality land in that direction.

ment is relaxed and a Ricardian fertility variation is introduced, the alteration of the original concentric zone pattern might appear as in Figure 4.6. A low-cost transportation artery such as a navigable river or a highway through the center of the "isolated state" will extend the inner zones of land use along the new route. In effect, farmers near the route now have lower cost access to the market, and this increases their location rent. If multiple market centers are postulated in addition to low-cost transport routes, the hypothetical land-use pattern then appears as in Figure 4.7.

In the horse and wagon transport system of von Thünen's day, the assumption that shipping costs are linearly proportional to distance did not greatly violate reality. However, where mechanized transport is available, longer trips create savings per ton-mile, and the corresponding location rent graphs would be curved as in Figure 4.8. This would have the effect of extending each land use out farther from the market center.

In all cases of model modification, the ordered pattern of land use around market centers is preserved and remains identifiable, and the intensity of production consistantly drops off with distance from markets.

82

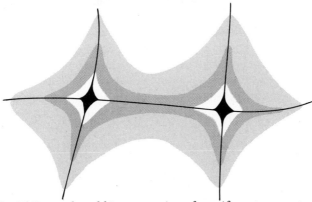

Figure 4.7   Thünen relaxed his assumption of a uniform transport cost surface by passing a navigable river through his hypothetical Isolated State. This reduces transport costs (increases location rent) for farmers near the river. A highway or other improved form of transport would have the same effect. He also considered multiple, competing towns rather than a single market center. The land-use pattern shown here reflects low cost transport routes and two market centers. Note, however, that the ordering of zones surrounding the market centers remains consistent. As the model assumptions are relaxed, the hypothetical land-use patterns resemble more closely real-world economic landscapes.

EXTENSION OF LAND–USE ZONES RESULTING
FROM LONG HAUL ECONOMIES

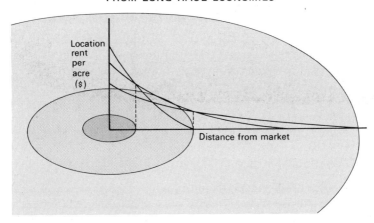

Figure 4.8   Tapering freight rates resulting from long haul economies (Chapter 12) change straight location rent lines to curvilinear form, as shown, and extend all land-use zones outward.

EMPIRICAL VERIFICATION OF THE MODEL

An important question comes up here. Is the Thünen land-use model merely an idealized exercise in logic, or does it actually help understand real world economic locations and land-use patterns? The answer to the second part of the question is unquestionably *yes*. If the mosaic of economic landscapes throughout the world is viewed with the explanatory model in mind, endless examples can be cited of spatial ordering of land use on the basis of location rent. Although the model applies in all countries, it is particularly observable in Less Developed Countries, where unit shipping costs have not been reduced by modern forms of transport and where, consequently, the uniform transport surface assumption of von Thünen has not been greatly distorted.

Spatial economies in Highly Developed Countries also reflect land use ordering based on distance costs. Within the United States or Canada mechanized transport and low shipping rates have had the effect of extending the pattern of economic zonation to continental dimensions (Chapter 7). The Thünen model also has important applications for land uses other than agricultural ones. In later chapters it will be referred to as a principal explanatory device for the location of other kinds of economic activity.

CHISHOLM'S EXAMPLES OF VERIFICATION

In a highly documented study, British geographer Michael Chisholm* cites numerous cases that add verification to the Thünen model. All over the world, the zonation of agricultural production around rural villages reflects the pervasive role of distance costs. Examples are given from Sicily, Sardinia, Italy, Spain, Yugoslavia, Bulgaria, Romania, and other European nations. Chisholm's evidence also includes examples from Nigeria, Ghana, and other African nations, as well as India. Other cases, drawn from various historical periods, illustrate the universality of the Thünen principle. Chisholm's examples also include economic activities other than agriculture. He points out, for example, that the strong zonal patterns of forest despoliation in Queen Elizabeth's England were directly related to distance to the market for the wood products.

* *Rural Settlement and Land Use: An Essay in Location,* John Wiley and Sons, New York, 1967.

ALFRED WEBER'S INDUSTRIAL LOCATION THEORY

Three generations passed in Germany after von Thünen's pioneering contributions before Alfred Weber's major work appeared in 1909,[8] adding an

[8] *Ueber der Standort der Industrien,* Part I, *Reine Theorie des Standorts,* Tubingen, 1909. Translated by C. J. Friedrich as *Alfred Weber's Theory of the Location of Industries,* University of Chicago Press, Chicago, 1929.

important extension to location theory. Weber drew on the work of his predecessor, especially in the adoption of deductive reasoning to interpret aspects of the economic landscape. Weber also followed von Thünen in emphasizing distance costs as the key variable for systematic analysis. Like von Thünen's, Weber's model represented a minimum cost approach.

Weber's view of the world was very different from that of von Thünen, three generations before. North Germany was undergoing rapid industrialization in the first decade of this century, and von Thünen's assumption of ubiquitous (available everywhere) resources clearly did not apply to the iron and steel, chemical, and other heavy manufacturing industries that were rapidly developing. Also, instead of a uniformly distributed rural population, Weber observed growing concentrations of population and urban development close to the coal and iron ore deposits in England, Germany, and other industrializing nations.

MODEL ASSUMPTIONS

Weber sought to develop a *pure theory*—that is, one that would apply within any social or political system. At the same time, his location theory is a *special theory* in the sense that it applies chiefly to heavy manufacturing operations that are transport-oriented. Weber's use of distance and transport costs as his major explanatory variable places him directly in the mainstream of location theory. However, his model differs from both the Thünen model and from the later Central Place models in an important way. His initial assumptions *do not* include a spatially homogeneous natural environment. He assumes instead a highly irregular occurrence of certain resources, such as coal and iron ore, which he calls *localized resources*. These are given a fixed site for each locational analysis. Weber observed that the location of transport-oriented production is related both to distance from the localized resources and distance to the market. He also recognized that plant location is sometimes influenced by two other factors: spatial differences in labor costs, and the efficiencies of firm agglomeration (clustering).

Like von Thünen, Weber considers market centers to be fixed in space, thus establishing the pattern of consumption as a spatial constant. Weber also assumes a fixed, but not necessarily uniform, spatial pattern of labor costs; at any place the supply of labor at constant wages is considered unlimited and immobile. Thus, while the location of production sites is influenced by the location of markets and labor, the location of markets and labor is not, in turn, influenced by the location of production.

Although Weber's mode of transport was mechanized—railroads, contrasting with von Thünen's horse and wagon era—he assumed, as did von Thünen, a uniform transport surface. He did not, however, account for long-haul economies.

THE GEOMETRIC MODEL: SOLVING WITH RESPECT TO TRANSPORT COSTS

Weber's simplified industrial landscape consists of localized resource or fuel deposits and markets, all designated as points in a plane. A simple case would be two raw material deposits (one could be fuel) and one market, forming a *locational triangle* (Fig. 4.9). The problem for Weber is to establish the lowest-cost location for a manufacturing plant producing a single product.

While this seems to be an unrealistic production system, there are manufacturing processes with simple resource and market patterns that resemble this. Plants producing cement or plate glass are examples. Others are mineral processing and certain food processing operations. For such production establishments the costs of assembling bulk raw materials and shipping a

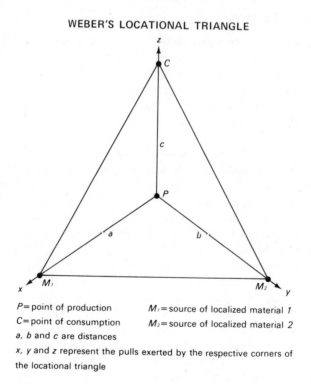

WEBER'S LOCATIONAL TRIANGLE

P = point of production M_1 = source of localized material 1
C = point of consumption M_2 = source of localized material 2
a, b and c are distances
x, y and z represent the pulls exerted by the respective corners of the locational triangle

Figure 4.9 (Source: *Adapted from David M. Smith,* Industrial Location: An Economic Geographical Analysis, *John Wiley and Sons, New York, 1971, Figure 8.1, p. 115*).

LOCATION THEORY

bulky product to market represent a large proportion of total costs, and depend on the location of the plant.

The first stage in Weber's analysis deals only with his major explanatory variable, distance. Production costs and technology are assumed equal everywhere; that is, costs of all production inputs except transport are assumed to be independent of location. Transport costs are a function of both weight and distance moved. The plant ideally will be located at a point where total transport costs are minimized. The point where the costs of the combined movement of materials to the plant and product to the market are minimized constitutes the solution. Finding a spatial solution to this problem is not as obvious as it may seem, even in the case of the simple location triangle.

In Figure 4.9 each corner of the triangle exerts a "pull" on point P measured by the weight to be transported from or (in the case of the market) to that corner. (Transport rates are assumed to be uniform). The manufacture of one unit requires x tons of material M_1 and y tons of material M_2, with the finished product weighing z tons to be transported to the market at C. If P is the point of production and a, b, and c are the unknown distances PM_1, PM_2, and PC respectively, the problem is to find the location of P that minimizes $xa + yb + zc$. The point P can be found geometrically, or by means of a mechanical-graphical analog called Varignon's Frame. For problems more complex than this simple case, mathematical solutions are required for which computer algorithms are available.

Weber recognized that a least transport cost solution depends on the nature and use of the production materials as well as on their location in nature. Resources found nearly everywhere (such as sand, gravel, and water[9]) he termed *ubiquitous materials.* Since these materials could hypothetically be obtained nearby wherever the plant was located, they would involve negligible transport costs and would not, therefore, act as an attracting force. Where only ubiquitous materials are used in a process, the market center becomes the only magnet for the plant.

To repeat for emphasis, Weber termed *localized resources* those, such as mineral ores, that occur irregularly in the environment. Where localized resources are required to produce a product, they, as well as the market, act as magnets for the plant. The "pull" of each localized resource depends on the amount used and the degree to which its weight is incorporated into a unit of the product. Weber makes an important distinction between what he calls *pure* and *gross* materials (although he doesn't allow for varying grades of resources). Pure materials all become part of the weight of the product,

[9] Typical of writers from humid environments, Weber's perception of water as a commonly occurring resource is very different from that held by persons in arid regions.

while gross materials undergo a weight loss in the production process. Examples of pure materials by this classification would be crude petroleum as a raw material for refinery products and tomatoes used in food processing. Examples of gross materials would be iron-ore and saw logs. Fuels and cooling water, of course, would be gross materials since they do not become part of the product. Since gross materials lose weight in the manufacturing process, their locations tend to attract the production site; this is not the case for pure materials.

It is necessary in the least-transport-cost solution for Weber to consider weights and distances moved both for material assembly and shipment of the product to the market. For each manufacturing process these values depend on the amounts of localized resources used to produce one unit of product. Weber expressed this in the form of a *Material Index* (MI), which is the ratio of the weight of the localized resources used to make one unit of product to the weight of the unit product itself.

$$MI = \frac{\text{Weight of localized resources used per unit of product}}{\text{Weight of unit product}}$$

For pure materials, the MI will be 1.0, since the weight of the materials is the same as the weight of the product. For gross materials, the MI is greater than 1.0. For some processing operations, such as the concentration of low-grade mineral ores, the weight of the product is very small compared to the weight of the unprocessed ore. In such cases the Material Index would be very high.

In order to specify the total weight to be moved within his spatial production model, Weber computed what he termed the *Location Weight*. Location weight for a given production process is computed by adding 1.0 (representing the weight of a unit product) to the Material Index (MI). Location weight thus gives the total weight to be moved per unit of product. In processes having high values of location weight, the plant location is drawn toward the gross materials in order to minimize movement before their weight is reduced in processing. On the other hand, a low value for location weight will draw the plant to the market. In a study of the iron and steel industry in Mexico, Kennelly computed a Material Index of 4.0 and a Locational Weight of 5.0. These relatively high values reflected a strong orientation to the raw material sources.[10]

[10]Robert A. Kennelly, "The Location of The Mexican Steel Industry," *Revista Geográfica*, Tomo XV, No. 41, 1954, pp. 109–129; Tomo XVI, No. 42, 1955, pp. 199–213; Tomo XVII, No. 43, 1955, pp. 60–77.

As noted above, if some materials used in a process are ubiquitous resources, this will reinforce the attraction of the market, because such resources will be available at the market as well as anywhere else.

LABOR COST AS A SUBSIDIARY LOCATION FACTOR

In the rapidly developing industrial landscape of Weber's Germany, it became evident to him that spatial differences in the cost of labor could also influence plant location under certain circumstances. Weber therefore relaxed the von Thünen assumption that labor costs were everywhere the same; instead, he considered differential labor costs as one of two possible corrections to the minimum-transport-cost solution.

Weber used a graphical technique to illustrate the labor variable. In Figure 4.10, P is the minimum transport cost production point. Surrounding P are concentric lines, called *isodapanes,* showing how total transport costs (material procurement transport costs plus product delivery transport costs) increase away from point P, as measured in dollars per unit of production. At point L_1 a source of low cost labor is hypothesized (in reality, this could

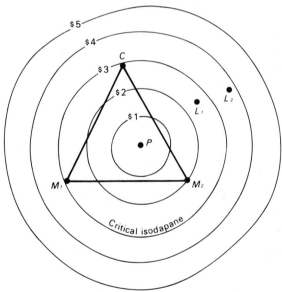

Figure 4.10 (Source: *Adapted from David M. Smith,* Industrial Location: An Economic Geographical Analysis, *John Wiley and Sons, New York, 1971, Fig. 8.2, p. 117*).

reflect lower wages, higher labor efficiency, or both), which would reduce labor costs by $3 per unit of production. Assuming here that labor does not move in response to wage differentials, the question becomes: how is the new labor variable likely to affect the original minimun transport cost solution?

Weber called the isodapane that has the same value as the savings in labor cost the *critical isodapane*. Since L_1 is nearer to P than the critical ($3) isodapane, moving production from P to L_1 would result in less than a $3 increase in unit transport costs, which means that L_1 would be the overall lowest cost production point. On the other hand, if the low cost labor site lies outside of the critical isodapane, as L_2 does, the increased transport cost in operating there would not be offset by the lower labor cost, and P would remain the overall lowest cost production point.

AGGLOMERATION EFFECTS AS A SUBSIDIARY LOCATION FACTOR

Weber was also able to perceive within his developing industrial landscape that certain manufacturing firms benefit from being located near each other. This results from savings due to shared access to specialized labor, services, suppliers, and markets. Agglomeration savings are realized up to the point where congestion and the competition for land drive other costs up and offset them. The agglomeration factor has evolved as a strong influence on the location of a large class of manufacturing industries. Weber, however, did not have the data or methods available to later location analysts, so his approach to this variable was understandably naïve and incomplete.

MODERN ASSESSMENT OF WEBER

Alfred Weber's pioneering work in industrial location theory stimulated many later scholars, some of whom have pointed out deficiencies is his model. One shortcoming was Weber's treatment of transport costs, particularly his disregard for terminal charges and long-haul savings. Weber was also criticized for oversimplification of the spatial aspects of demand. He did not account for the possibility of different resource extraction costs and limitations on the size of resource deposits and he also ignored the relationship between price and resource availability, the possibility of multiple-plant operations, and the implications of scale savings.

Weber recognized limitations in his model. In some cases, they were the price to be paid for the higher explanatory value the model had for a special class of manufacturing activity. The Weberian model represents, as do all models, a compromise between abstract generality and real-world applica-

90

bility. By emphasizing the locational importance of bulky, localized resources, he was able to explain a great deal about the spatial pattern of heavy manufacturing industries, such as iron and steel, heavy chemicals, mineral concentration, petroleum refining, pulp and paper, glass, and cement production. In these industries transport costs make up a large proportion of the total costs, and the processes have simple raw material procurement patterns.[11]

Despite its limitations, Weber's work has inspired a considerable literature in applied industrial location studies. A good example is Isard and Cumberland's study of New England as a possible location for an integrated iron and steel plant. Concerning this research, Isard wrote, "Indeed, it is only by utilizing chiefly the Weberian approach with supplementary economic data that the writer has found it meaningful to analyze the locational structure of the iron and steel industry."[12]

CENTRAL PLACE THEORY: THE CONTRIBUTIONS OF CHRISTALLER

Most of humanity today lives gathered together in communities of various sizes—hamlets, villages, towns, and cities—where economic activities are spatially concentrated. These communities are economic centers from which services and certain goods are made available to surrounding, dispersed markets. Settlement patterns are of great interest to economic geographers, and Central Place Theory is regarded by many as the most important contribution yet made toward a general theory of urban places.

In 1933, slightly more than a century after von Thünen's work appeared and a generation after Weber's contributions, geographer Walter Christaller's classic work[13] was published in Germany, marking the beginning of Central Place Theory. Central Place Theory continues the deductive tradition of the earlier German location theorists. Christaller used many of von Thünen's ideas, and wrote: "Therefore, the economist, as well as the geographer, must return to the fundamental and guiding work of von Thünen, *The Isolated State*, if he wishes to solve economic-geographical problems."[14] Whereas von Thünen was concerned with the agricultural landscape and

---

[11] Weberian analysis is not necessarily confined to manufacturing industry. It can find application wherever transport cost minimization is sought, even in the case of farm layout or industrial plant design.

[12] Walter Isard, *Location and Space Economy,* The MIT Press, 1956, p. 37.

[13] *Die Zentralen Orte in Süddeutschland,* (1933); Translated as: *Central Places in Southern Germany,* by Carlisle W. Baskin, Prentice-Hall, Englewood Cliffs, N. J., 1966.

[14] *Ibid.,* p. 6.

Weber with the manufacturing landscape, Christaller deals with the distribution and functions of urban settlements.

Central Place Theory deals with the spatial distribution of consumer demand, and the locational pattern of service industries and of certain market oriented manufacturing industries. (This is the kind of manufacturing that Alfred Weber's industrial location model does *not* deal with—manufacturing not drawn toward localized resources, but instead toward urban markets.) Central Place Theory can be viewed as a logical and spatial complement to von Thünen's agricultural land-use theory, with the inputs of one system becoming the outputs of the other.

Christaller's Central Place Model helps to explain two interrelated aspects of urban development: (1) the location of settlements as optimal distribution centers for services and certain goods, and (2) the way in which these services and goods are distributed within the spatial system of urban places. Central Place Theory, however, does not apply to the small proportion of towns and cities dominated by heavy manufacturing (Gary, Indiana), federal government (Brasilia, Brazil), mining (Johannesburg, South Africa), or with special environmental conditions (Hot Springs, West Virginia, or Aspen, Colorado).

INTUITIVE INSIGHTS INTO THE CENTRAL PLACE CONCEPT

Studies made in nations all over the world show the central place system expressed universally in the economic landscape. Human behavior and decision making are influenced by models about the world that we carry in our heads. For example, as we approach an unknown community by car we employ a mental model derived from prior observation of many other communities. Even if we have never heard of the place, we can make certain deductions from the size of its population alone. If, before entering the community, we read a sign saying that it contains, say 500 inhabitants, we estimate a high probability of finding a gas station or a small grocery store there.

On the other hand, if we wish to attend a movie, or desire the services of a lawyer, we will not expect to find them there, but must plan to move on to a town, since our mental model of a "town" includes, among other things, movies and law offices. If we need a specialized surgeon or a stockbroker, we will probably have to travel on to the nearest "city," perhaps passing many villages and towns along the way, to get these services. Significantly, our mental model of a city also tells us that we will be able to find there, not only these services, *but also all the other services and goods found in the hamlets, villages, and towns.*

We tend to take our mental models for granted. However, if we carefully

92

observe and map the location of various service and manufacturing establishments, we will find, not a random spatial distribution, but instead a highly structured pattern of central place functions in the economic landscape.

If our experience includes travel in other parts of the world, we will perceive that our mental models of settlements in the United States or Canada may not apply in other countries. One can travel for hundreds of miles in the Soviet Union, Brazil, or India, for example, without seeing an American-style gas station.

WALTER CHRISTALLER'S UNIVERSAL QUESTION

Let us consider for a moment a hypothetical island-nation with an area of 25,000 square miles (about the size of West Virginia) and a population of ten million inhabitants. Given only this information, how is the population likely to be distributed on the island? Conceivably, all the inhabitants could live in one great city located on one part of the island. Again, conceivably, all families could live in evenly spaced rural homesteads covering the entire island. Other logical possibilities falling between these extremes include: ten cities of 1 million each; a hundred cities of 100,000 each; a thousand cities of 10,000 each; and so on. Now, if we consider various size mixes, the number of possible combinations of settlement size and number becomes mathematically astronomical.

Common sense (really our mental models of islands and nations) rejects most of these logical possibilities as improbable. Most persons would have an intuitive "feel" (call it a primitive theory) that—no matter who they are—the inhabitants of the island would probably have evolved spatially over time into one or two large cities, a number of smaller cities, many more towns, and hundreds or even thousands of small villages.[15]

Notice that we haven't yet said anything about *where* all these various-sized places are likely to be located in relation to each other. If we do, students of mathematics will recognize that the possible combinations now become "even more astronomical."

Christaller's importance lies in the fact that he attempted a solution to this seemingly insoluble problem. "Are there laws," he writes, "which determine the number, sizes, and distribution of towns?" Again, Christaller asks, "But why are there, then, large and small towns, and why are they distributed so irregularly?"[16] These questions, which initiated the creation of his theory,

---

[15] A real-world example is Sri Lanka (formerly Ceylon), which has an area of about 25,000 square miles and a size distribution of urban places roughly as described.

[16] Christaller, *Die Zentralen Orte in Süddeutschland, op. cit.,* p. 1.

sound deceptively simple. They are, however, among the most profound queries in the study of human affairs.

Christaller's theory has the mark of elegance because of its universality and its simplicity. From a few initial assumptions and the consideration of only two parameters, he was able to deduce hypothetical landscapes showing the number, relative size, and spacing of central places, ranging in size from hamlets to metropolitan centers.

MODEL ASSUMPTIONS AND PARAMETERS

Although he wrote a century after von Thünen, and in a different part of Germany, Christaller's model assumptions were similar in many respects to those of his intellectual predecessor. Christaller's home in Swabia, a rural South German district in the early 1930s, was still a peasant "horse and wagon" economy. The economic landscape there was still largely unaffected by the industrialization that had had an earlier impact on Weber in North Germany.

Like von Thünen, Christaller assumes that similarly behaving "economic men" are uniformly distributed on a flat, limitless plain, with an even distribution of natural resources. Operating over this space is a primitive transportation system on which the cost of movement is a linear function of the point to point distances travelled.

Christaller envisions an original landscape of farm families. The evolution of small settlements, *central places,* takes place to satisfy their day to day trade requirements. Christaller first postulates a single entrepreneur who desires to produce a surplus of some good or service, say bread, to sell to the neighbors. This will be possible only if the proposed enterprise can "break even"—that is, can do enough business to at least cover all costs. This critical question is determined by the values of two parameters.

The first parameter, *threshold demand,* is simply the smallest population (this translates here into the smallest area, since the potential customers are evenly distributed) which must be served to break even. The threshold demand obviously varies greatly with each type of business enterprise (Table 4.1).

Economic theory states that the quantity of a good purchased is a function of its price. But prices reflect the psychological perceptions of a group. The demand curve in Figure 4.11 can be used to develop the Central Place model. By inverting the axes, the amount of bread demanded can be shown as a function of distance from the bakery. This is shown in Figure 4.12, where the abscissa value reflects the *real price* of a loaf of bread, which increases with distance from the bakery B because of the addition of transport cost to the market price. Note that the transport cost must be paid by the customer whether he or she travels to the shop or the bread is delivered.

94

Table 4.1 *Threshold Values for Selected Central Place Activities in 32 Ohio Towns, 1964*

Activity	Threshold Population
Filling station	492
Food store	498
Restaurant	592
Tavern	806
Drugstore	878
Bank	906
Variety store	976
Shoe store	1074
Undertaker	1183
Dry cleaner	1205
Men's clothing store	1216
Hotel	1318
Women's apparel shop	1450

Source: Adapted from Stanley D. Brunn, "Changes in the Service Structure of Rural Trade Centers" (Communication to the Editor), *Rural Sociology, 33,* 1968, Table 2, p. 204.

THE DEMAND CURVE

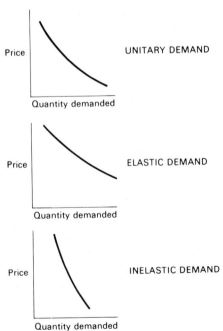

Figure 4.11 A demand curve shows the amounts of a good that would be hypothetically purchased by an individual or a group at different prices. Where demand behavior is unitary, a one percent price decrease will induce a one percent increase in the quantity demanded. In elastic demand (for example, a color TV set or 'other luxury items) a one percent price decrease will cause greater than one percent increase in the quantity demanded, while for inelastic demand (for example, table salt or other staple items) a one percent reduction in price will result in less than a one percent increase in quantity demanded.

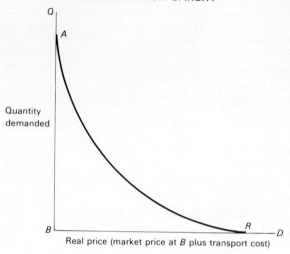

BREAD DEMAND AS A FUNCTION OF DISTANCE FROM BAKERY

Figure 4.12

Although potential customers are spread uniformly over the landscape, the demand for bread drops off as distance from the bakery (real price) increases. Beyond the distance BR the real price is too high to attract any potential buyers. This distance represents the second parameter in Christaller's model, the *market range* of a good or service.

The market range can be defined as the greatest distance (distance costs) that consumers are willing to travel (pay) to purchase a specific good or service at a given market price. Different goods and services obviously have very different market ranges. People are unwilling to travel more than a short distance for small purchases that recur frequently—such as a newspaper or a carton of milk. Expensive items that are purchased rarely, such as a college education or the services of a specialist surgeon, have very large market ranges, extending thousands of miles, and sometimes crossing international borders.

By rotating plane ARB 360 degrees about the vertical axis in Figure 4.12, a volume is generated that represents the total hypothetical demand for bakery bread (Fig. 4.13). If the total demand represented by the volume is *greater* than the threshold demand, the enterprise will theoretically be established. If there is not enough demand within the market range to reach the threshold demand, then commercial bread production is not economically feasible under these conditions and everyone on the plain will continue consuming home-produced bread.

96

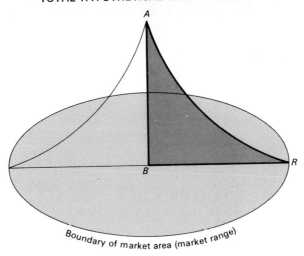

Boundary of market area (market range)

Figure 4.13

A SINGLE FUNCTION CENTRAL PLACE SYSTEM

According to Christaller's Central Place model, if bakery bread[17] production begins at some random point in the demand plain, then a whole spatial system of similar bakeries can be deduced. The location of the first bakery destroys the homogeneity of the plain. A concentration of labor—at first very small—will gather at the point of production, which now becomes a tiny *central place,* distributing bread to customers in a circular trade area (called by Christaller the *complementary area*) as well as to its own inhabitants.[18]

Since one bakery cannot supply customers beyond its market range, new bakeries will theoretically spring up to serve the uncovered demand all over the plain. Under the assumptions of the model, the values for the threshold demand, market range, market price, and transportation rates are the same for all new bread bakeries. The new establishments will locate so as to avoid the market areas of prior establishments. Since the location of each new bakery is constrained by the location of all before it on the plain, a growing

---

[17]Note that, unlike manufacturing in Weber's Industrial Location Model, bread productio uses ubiquitous materials—wheat and other farm products—that are everywhere available in the farming region.

[18]It is still the custom today in France and other countries to buy freshly baked bread each day from a local shop. While it means a daily trip for someone, often a small child, the taste of such bread an hour or two from the oven is something few Americans can enjoy.

CENTRAL PLACE THEORY: THE CONTRIBUTIONS OF CHRISTALLER   **97**

competition arises for the uncovered market areas. As time passes, and as entrepreneurs come and go, new producers will continue "shouldering" each other for space, and the bakeries will pack together under the combined influence of two forces: (1) the entrepreneurs' desire to serve uncovered market areas, and (2) the need for each producer to maintain a market area large enough to meet the threshold demand. If the threshold demand isn't met, the producer is eliminated from the competitive field.

This dynamic process ideally continues until a spatial equilibrium is ultimately reached (Fig. 4.14). In this equilibrium state the opposing forces are balanced. No potential market area is left uncovered, and all bakery market areas have become regular hexagons with equal areas just large enough to satisfy the threshold demand. This is the most efficient way the plane can be "packed." Marketing distances (costs) are minimized, and all customers are supplied with bread at lowest real prices.

MULTIPLE-FUNCTION HIERARCHICAL SYSTEMS

The notion of an economic landscape containing incipient settlements where bread is produced and distributed in surrounding hexagonal market areas may seem somewhat fanciful. However, the hypothetical pattern generated

DEVELOPMENT OF IDEAL HEXAGONAL MARKET AREAS

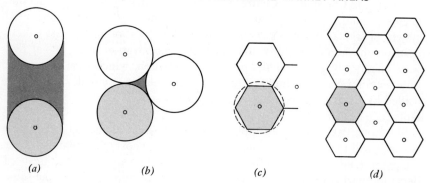

(a)   (b)   (c)   (d)

Figure 4.14 (a) Nontangent market areas for a single good or service. Shaded areas are unserved by any market. (b) Packing of market areas into positions of tangency. (c) Further packing reduces each circular market area to hexagonal form. (d) Resulting ideal landscape consists of equal, regular hexagon market areas, just large enough to contain the threshold demand. (Source: *August Lösch,* The Economics of Location, *Translated by William H. Wóglom, Yale University Press, New Haven, Conn., 1954, Figure 23, p. 110. Originally published by Gustav Fischer, Verlag, 1938.*)

by the single-function Central Place model provides a starting point for a much more complex multiple-function system.

A key concept in understanding the development of a multiple-function system is that of *high order* and *low order* goods and services. Another related concept provided by Christaller is that of *hierarchical structure.* Since threshold demand and market range vary enormously for different central place goods and services, it obviously is impossible for all the central place functions to be carried on in all communities. Goods and services that have large threshold demands require large market areas for a single establishment. These are called *high order functions,* and are located in only the largest central places. Examples would be an opera house or a stock exchange. On the other hand, *low order functions* are those that have low threshold demand and can therefore be supported by a small market area. Low order functions are found in all central places; examples are post offices, gas stations and grocery stores. Between the two extemes, all other central place functions can be ordered approximately by the size of the market area they serve. (Fig. 4.15)

A multiple-function (here a two-function) system can now be generated by superimposing a second (higher order) function on the spatial system of bakeries. Let us assume the second function is shoe repair. Trips for shoe repairs would be less frequent than trips for bread, and the minimum number of potential customers for shoe repair services would be greater. Therefore, both the threshold demand and the market range would be greater for shoe repairs than for bread. We will conveniently assume, following Christaller's model, that a shoe repair shop has a market area three times greater than that for a bread bakery, and that this meets the threshold demand for the shoe repair function.

The first shoe repair establishment will be randomly located in one of the existing, bread-supplying central places and will set the spatial pattern for all others. The ratio of three to one for the two market areas, referred to as the *K = 3 system* by Christaller, generates the two-function hierarchical system shown in Figure 4.16. "Hierarchical" here means that the higher order establishments (shoe repair shops) are superimposed geometrically and functionally on the spatial system of lower order bakeries.

The evenly spaced shoe repair establishments are eventually located in one-third of the bread-producing central places. Central places containing both functions can now be referred to as the *higher order central places;* they have larger populations than the *lower order central places.* Each higher order central place serves the market area for one shoe repair shop (larger hexagon), which contains the equivalent of three lower order market areas.

More and more central place functions can be added to this geometric structure by setting the market area in each case as a multiple of three of the

TYPES OF SERVICE CENTERS IN THE UPPER MIDWEST

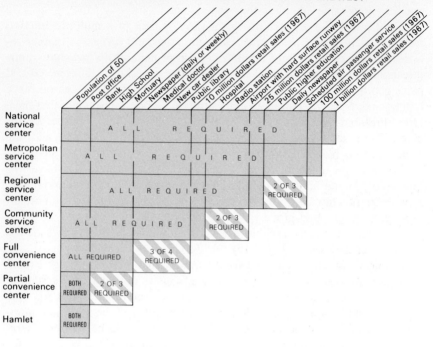

Figure 4.15   The hierarchical structure of central places and their functions ranges from hamlets to a national service center (Minneapolis-St. Paul). (Source: Neil C. Gustafson, "Recent Trends; Future Prospects: A Look at Upper Midwest Population Changes," Upper Midwest Council, Minneapolis, 1973, Chart 8, p. 41.)

lowest order market area. Christaller referred to this as the *marketing principle.*

As in other models, the K = 3 system optimizes one thing (the most efficient marketing of central place goods and services from the smallest number of central places) but leaves others unoptimized. Christaller recognized that a transport network in the K = 3 system, directly linking larger central places by straight line routes, would not pass through many smaller central places. In order to provide an alternative system, Christaller rearranged his original design so that more lower order central places would fall on the routes connecting the larger ones. However, this change makes the higher order market areas larger than those next below them by a factor of *four* instead of three. Christaller called this version of his model the *K = 4 system,* and the optimizing logic on which it is based he termed the *transpor-*

100

A TWO–FUNCTION (K = 3) CENTRAL PLACE SYSTEM

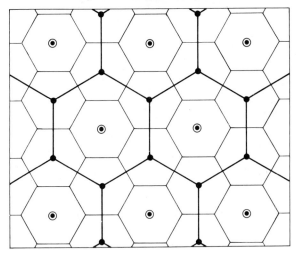

⬡ Boundary of market area for shoe repair establishment

⬡ Boundary of market area for bakery

◉ Central Place containing relatively high order function
(shoe repair establishment) and low order function (bakery)

● Central Place containing low order function (bakery)

Figure 4.16 Hexagonal arrangement based on Christaller's Marketing Principle. (Source: *Based on Walter Christaller,* Central Places in Southern Germany, *Translated from* Die Zentralen Orte In Süddeutschland *by Carlisle W. Baskin, Prentice-Hall, Inc., Englewood Cliffs, N.J., 1966, Figure 2, p. 66.)*

tation principle. The K = 4 system provides the basis for a more efficient transport network (Fig. 4.17).

Both Christaller's market principle and transportation principle are based on minimum cost considerations. However, he realized that political or administrative factors can also influence settlement patterns and urban systems. This led to the conception of his third principle, the *administrative principle.* This version of his model is based on the notion that, from an administrative standpoint, central places and their complementary regions (market areas) should not be partitioned, but ideally should remain intact within political units. A two-function hierarchical system based on the administrative principle would appear as in Figure 4.18. Here, the area of the higher order center contains the areas of seven lower order centers. For this reason, Christaller calls this the *K = 7 system.*

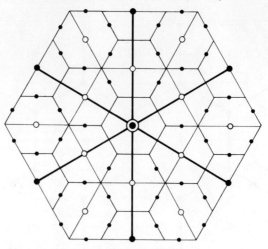

CENTRAL PLACE SYSTEM (K = 4)

● First order Central Place (large city)
● Second order Central Place (small city)
○ Third order Central Place (town)
• Fourth order Central Place (village)
— Straight-line transport routes connecting large cities

Figure 4.17 Christaller's traffic *or* transportation *principle.* (Source: *Same as for Figure 4.16, p. 75.*)

CRITICAL EVALUATION OF CHRISTALLER'S CENTRAL PLACE MODEL

After nearly half a century, interest in Christaller's work continues undiminished and an ongoing extension and revision of his work has produced an international body of literature on Central Place Theory.

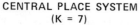

CENTRAL PLACE SYSTEM
(K = 7)

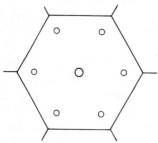

O Higher order Central Place
○ Lower order Central Place

Figure 4.18 Christaller's administrative principle. (Source: *Same as for Figure 4.16, p. 78.*)

A fundamental criticism of Christaller's work has focused on the rigidly mechanistic outcomes of his deductive model. Christaller himself, however, advised his readers to take such outcomes *cum grano salis,* that is, with a grain of salt! While the outcomes generated by the model are deterministic, they are nevertheless logically consistent, based on the stated assumptions. Their importance is that they provide otherwise missing insights into the process of formation of dynamic urban systems. In this connection, Lösch reminds us that, "The question of actual location must be distinguished from that of the rational location. The two need not coincide." [19] Christaller's three hierarchical systems, based on the market principle, the transportation principle, and the administrative principle, represent different approaches to spatial efficiency. Real-world economic landscapes should be interpreted in terms of all three principles.

Some of Christaller's model assumptions have been modified by later writers. For example, changes in transportation and production technology that drastically affect market ranges and threshold demands have been accounted for. Recent economic history illustrates this; small towns throughout the country have been bypassed as new highways enable consumers to drive to larger central places or to regional shopping plazas. The special attraction of larger central places for multiple purchases has also been taken into account by Christaller's successors.

[19] Lösch, *ibid.,* p. 4.

Central Place Theory has been verified by empirical evidence from all over the world. This is particularly evident in regions with comparatively homogeneous natural and cultural environments. Field work in the United States Midwest, for example, has shown a well-developed hierarchy of urban centers and central place functions.[20] It can be universally observed that large cities everywhere have high order functions with national or international market ranges, but also have thousands of lower order establishments predicted by the Central Place Model.

SUMMARY

Space must be overcome in all economic activities. Throughout its long period of development, location theory has focused on distance and relative position as the key variables in explaining spatial economies. Modern developments in location theory are very largely extensions of the classical models of von Thünen, Weber, and Christaller. The work of these pioneers continues to be studied, evaluated, and modified by scholars today on an international level. Von Thünen, Weber, and Christaller all employed the powerful deductive mode of reasoning to interpret the economic landscapes they observed within their particular space-time perspectives. Their models are universal ones that apply worldwide and across the years. The advent of computers and modern mathematical methods has in no way rendered classical location theory obsolete or irrelevant. Von Thünen's ordered zonation of land use is associated with agriculture and other large-space-using activities, but it also finds application in urban land-use analysis and planning. Weber's model relates to industrial landscapes and transport-oriented industries that require evenly distributed "localized" resources, such as coal and iron ore. Christaller's Central Place Model provides a rationale for the settlement patterns and functions of urban places. The location models of von Thünen, Weber, and Christaller, taken together, furnish a substantial measure of explanation for existing economic landscapes and can improve land-use planning.

Questions

1 Describe the different economic landscapes, and the questions they inspired, that led to the location models of J. H. von Thünen, Alfred Weber, and Walter Christaller.

[20] John R. Borchert and Russell B. Adams, *Trade Centers and Tributary Areas of the Upper Midwest,* Minneapolis, Univ. of Minnesota, 1963.

LOCATION THEORY

2 Using the equation for location rent, discuss the changes in parameter values and the corresponding changes in the location rent graph and radius of profitable production that would result from the following conditions:

(a) a decrease in transport rate

(b) an increase in market price

(c) an increase in production cost and an increase in transport rate

3 How would you describe the problem attacked by Christaller in such a way as to suggest the importance of Central Place Theory?

4 Give examples, from economic landscapes you are familiar with, of land-use patterns that can be explained with the help of the models of classical location theory.

5

NATURAL RESOURCES, PRODUCTION, AND WASTE: THE INTERACTION OF ECOLOGY AND ECONOMICS

"Our main inference would be that the common explanation of comparative advantage in terms of only the two factors, capital and labor, is oversimplified, and that theory should place considerable emphasis on the limitational role of natural resources . . ."

Hollis B. Chenery and Paul G. Clark*

In Chapter 4 the location models of von Thünen and Christaller are based on initial assumptions of uniformity of the physical environment. Spatial differentiation of the natural world is considered only if the initial assumptions are relaxed, and then only as a modifying factor. The variations of specific factors in the natural environment and their influence on economic activity will be covered in Chapter 6. This chapter establishes the connection between ecology and economics in the production process. Development of this connection is important in view of the traditional lack of emphasis on natural resources and wastes as influences on regional comparative advantage.

A GENERAL MODEL OF ECONOMIC PRODUCTION

Figure 5.1 shows the economic production process in generalized system terms. System inputs are represented by three variables: the classical economic production factors of *land, labor,* and *capital.* The labor input repre-

* *Interindustry Economics,* John Wiley and Sons, New York, 1959, p. 245.

106

sents a broad set of human contributions, ranging from unskilled to highly skilled types, priced in money wages or the equivalent.

Capital, unlike land and labor, is an input created by the production process itself; the output of producer goods and services become used in further production. Capital can be viewed in familiar physical terms as man-made objects, such as machines, tools, factory buildings, power stations, and so on, which are used to make new goods and services. (A technical description would distinguish between capital, such as a machine with a specified useful life, and other producer goods, such as parts or components, that reenter the production process and are sometimes referred to as "intermediate goods.") According to traditional capital theory, the cost of capital is the interest rate charged. Physical capital is highly concentrated in space.

The *land* input in the model refers to *natural resources.* It is the production factor that has been the most difficult to treat theoretically. We will return to a discussion of natural resources in the next section.

Two other elements of the production model are the parameters *technology* and *management,* which are assumed here as constant. In the real world,

A GENERAL MODEL OF ECONOMIC PRODUCTION

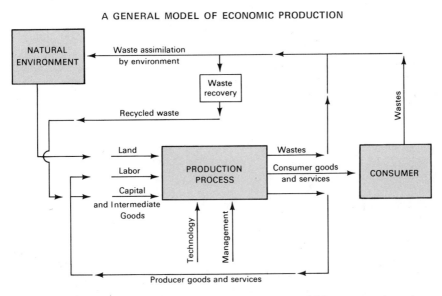

Figure 5.1   This model of the production process could be expented to show other relationships. For example, "environmental quality" is now viewed in economic terms by some as a form of "consumer good."

technology and management can vary greatly and thus affect production in a major way. However, since these influences are very difficult to assess, they are not treated as variable quantities in most discussions of production.

The production process results in two broad classes of outputs, *goods* and *services*. These, in turn, can be classified as *consumer* or *producer* goods and services. Examples of a consumer good and service would be a television set and a haircut; examples of a producer good and service would be a bulldozer and engineering consulting services. Producer goods and services as mentioned above are not sold to the consumer, but are redirected back into the production process. Another system output, often neglected in the past, is *waste*. All production processes produce some form of waste.

This chapter is devoted to a closer look at the interrelated concepts of natural resource, production, and waste, all of which influence the location and character of economic activity, and find expression in a dynamic economic landscape.

NATURAL RESOURCES: THE LAND FACTOR OF PRODUCTION

THE CONCEPT OF LAND

In order to meet their economic needs—including the basic ecological requirements of water, food, clothing, and shelter—people undertake the production of goods and services by extracting *natural resources* from the environment. All three sectors of the natural environment provide raw materials: the solid portion of the earth (*lithosphere*), the water portion of the earth (*hydrosphere*), and the gaseous envelope of the earth (*atmosphere*).

In the language of economics, the term *land* refers to natural resources, and is therefore of central importance to the environmental planner, geologist, engineer, agronomist, forester, water resource manager, wildlife manager, recreation specialist, and others—including many applied geographers—who work directly with natural resources. Instead of assuming a "uniform environment," these people are specifically interested in spatially variable environmental factors.

It was mentioned in Chapter 1 that the next two decades will witness "acute problems" of land-use planning and management, requiring, it is estimated, the physical equivalent of a "Second America" to be built by the end of the century. Despite this, a tendency has existed to neglect or to underplay the role of the land factor (natural resources) in production, or to treat it so abstractly that it is of little value in the solution of practical problems.

NATURAL RESOURCES, PRODUCTION, AND WASTE

Part of the problem stems from the fact that the term "natural resource" is without a universally accepted definition. The student will encounter many—often confusing—versions in the literature. For example, some writers view climate as a fundamental natural resource. On the other hand, the interpretation of economists has generally been quite different. Even mineral ore deposits in the ground are now treated by some economists as capital.[1]

A new term, *common property resource,* has emerged within recent decades, referring to environmental components such as air, water, and ecological systems. Common property resources are conceived to be a class that cannot, or can only imperfectly, be priced and held in private ownership.

The term *land quality* is also not a very precise one. Land with a special combination of environmental advantages for one product may not be at all suitable for another. Tomatoes require a relatively low night temperature for fruit to form; consequently, tomatoes do poorly in the lowland tropics, where sugar cane flourishes.

Another aspect that makes the notion of land a fuzzy one is that labor and/or capital can be applied to improve land productivity. Examples would be smudgepots, fences, wells, and hillside terraces. Recall from Chapter 1 that the economic landscape reflects Man's *modification* of the natural environment. A farm or a city is neither purely natural nor purely man-

---

[1] "Best known for his work in minerals supply and competition in the minerals industry, Herfindahl (Orris C.) advanced the now widely accepted view that ore deposits are better treated as capital than as 'land'." (RFF Announcement, October, 1974, Resources for the Future, Inc., Washington, D.C.)

made, but a combination of both. A national forest wilderness area would certainly seem to be a wholly natural area, and yet programs of fire control and pest management prevent natural controls, such as naturally occurring forest fires, from operating, and thereby change the ecological character of such forests. Even local microclimate and hydrology can be altered to increase production by means of irrigation systems, drainage systems, fog dispensers, and smudge pots, and topography can be modified by means of terracing.

One last reason for confusion over the land concept is its dual nature. An important point here is that capital investment in the form of roads, railroads, canals, and other mechanized transport lowers the cost of movement and can "create" resources by making them economically accessible. This point must be stressed because the notion of natural resource involves *both* environmental and spatial considerations.

CONFLICTING CONCEPTS OF SCARCITY

A conventional classification of natural resources usually begins with a division into *renewable* and *nonrenewable* groups. The *renewable* resources are defined as those capable of reproducing themselves. Examples are forests and fisheries. Generally speaking, renewable resources are associated with the vegetative or animal components of the environment. By contrast, the *nonrenewable* (also called *stock* or *fund*) *resources* are not replaced in relation to human time horizons; examples here are mineral resources. Water is sometimes termed a *flow resource.*

Time plays an important role in the economic analysis of natural resources. It is the key variable in the concept of *conservation* and in the economic opposite of conservation, *depletion.*

Anyone reading the multidisciplinary literature relating to natural resources will discover two broad schools of thought, which can roughly be characterized here as the *pessimistic school* and the *optimistic school.* A large and diverse group of scientists and others view with concern what they consider to be a growing natural resource scarcity resulting from world population increase and economic growth.

A more optimistic (or at least a less pessimistic) view of future resource availability is held by others. This group places strong faith in the economic doctrine of *substitutability*—the ability, within an economic production process, of substituting one resource for another, or of substituting labor and/or capital for natural resources. These persons consider the arguments of the pessimists unsupportable both empirically and theoretically, and emphasize the role of technology in creating "new resources" from common substances in the environment.

110

THE FUNCTIONAL CONCEPT OF RESOURCES

One of the most perceptive treatments in the literature on natural resources remains that by the American economist, Erich Zimmermann. In 1951, Zimmermann wrote, "The word 'resource' *does not refer to a thing or a substance but to a function which a thing or a substance may perform or to an operation in which it may take part,* namely, the function or operation of attaining a given end such as satisfying a want."[2] Zimmermann's functional approach helps to relate human perception of the environment to economic production, and hence to economic landscape evolution.

The functional view of resources stresses the idea that Man's mind is the ultimate resource, and that people perceive their environment through the lens of their culture. Since cultures and technologies have varied greatly from time to time and from place to place, people's perception of the utility of the various elements within their natural environment has also varied greatly. The American Indians living on Michigan's Upper Peninsula mined copper for centuries before the arrival of the Europeans, yet the nearby rich deposits of iron-ore were useless to them. When the Europeans arrived there they developed great iron ore ranges in the region. The same landscape in the Kalahari Desert of Southwest Africa that appears lifeless to a European actually contains all the resources needed to sustain the native inhabitants. In a primitive culture, a tree provides shade, fuel, a stick for defense, and perhaps wild fruit. To the modern forest manager, the same tree can provide a broad range of chemical raw materials as well.

In Chapter 2 we saw that certain productive parts of the earth have been occupied for thousands of years and have high rural population densities, while other large regions are still without dense populations. In addition to culture, an important factor influencing the economic landscape is regional population density. This is sometimes expressed as the *man-land ratio* or the *man-resource ratio.*

A trend in recent decades has been to study scientifically the physical environment with the specific objective of discovering new resources. Around the turn of the century, science and industry for the first time became functionally integrated with the rise of the heavy chemical industries.

The development of the Haber process in Germany in 1914 proved to be a technological threshold. Under demand for explosives during World War I, and with the control of the Chilean nitrate fields in the hands of Great Britain, chemists Fritz Haber and Karl Bosch in Germany invented a process to produce industrial ammonia by a high-pressure catalytic fixation

---

[2] Erich W. Zimmermann, *World Resources and Industries,* Harper and Row, New York, 1951, p. 7.

CLAWSON ON THE INFLUENCE OF CULTURE AND POPULATION DENSITY ON LAND USE

Resource economist Marion Clawson hypothesized how the combined factors of culture and population density might operate to affect the land use of one region:

Suppose that the Indian chiefs of 200 years ago asked you to manage for them the lands, grass, game and other resources of Colorado. Under the technology of that day and with the culture and interests of the indians, the use of these resources will be very different from the use today. Or suppose that the state of Colorado had a population density approaching that of a more densely settled part of the Orient and you were asked to manage these resources so as to support that population. Obviously, the use of the resources would be very different from the use in our example from long ago and almost equally different from the use today. Yet climate, soil, topography, elevation, and many other aspects of resources would be wholly unchanged.*

*In *Resources Development: Frontiers For Research*, Edited by Franklin Pollak, University of Colorado Press, Boulder, 1960, pp. 217-228.

method. This made possible the production of synthetic nitrates, which are the raw material for a wide range of industrial products, including explosives and fertilizer. The process was most significant because it used *air* as a "raw material" to provide the element nitrogen. This revolutionary development freed the producer from dependence on the few commercial deposits of mineral nitrate found scattered around the world, and it brought about a spatial rearrangement of world production, exchange, and consumption of industrial nitrate. Among other things, it caused the decline of the nitrate mining industry in northern Chile.

Through this and other creative advances in applied chemistry (sometimes called "molecular engineering"), plentiful common earth substances have become resources in the functional sense. For example, sea water has become a commercial source of magnesium. Dow Chemical's sea-water plant at Freeport, Texas, is the world's largest producer of magnesium. In 1977, production at this plant reached 100,000 tons, which represented over half of all Western World output. It has been estimated that if magnesium were extracted from the ocean at the current rate of iron and steel demands for the next million years, only one-one hundredth of one percent of the supply would be gone. Air, sea water, coal, petroleum, salt, limestone, and other common earth materials more and more provide chemical elements as building blocks that are synthesized into raw materials to make countless consumer and industrial products (Fig. 5.2).

112   NATURAL RESOURCES, PRODUCTION, AND WASTE

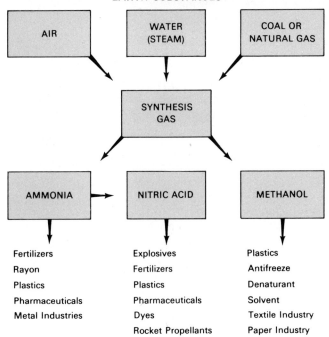

CHEMICAL INDUSTRIES BASED ON COMMON
EARTH SUBSTANCES

Figure 5.2

This trend has forced a reconsideration of the entire doctrine of economic scarcity, and makes Zimmermann's functional concept of resources now seem more valid than ever.

THE PRODUCTION PROCESS: A CLOSER LOOK

Economic production is defined in abstract terms as a process in which an object or a set of objects is made more valuable for satisfying an economic want. The increase in value, also called *utility,* can be brought about in three physical ways:

1. By changing the form of materials. An example would be the construction of a fence from a pile of boards (*form utility*).
2. By changing the location of materials. Moving a ton of coal from minehead to power plant is an example (*place utility*).
3. By changing the time something is used. An example would be storing water behind a dam for the dry season (*time utility*).

Under this abstract definition, transportation and storage are interpreted as forms of production. For our purposes, however, it is more convenient to use the traditional three-part classification of economic activity introduced in Chapter 1—that is, *production, exchange* (including transportation), and *consumption.*

The spatial character of even simple production processes is not always recognized. (Recall the Robinson Crusoe example in Chapter 1.) Between the "raw materials" of the farm, mine, or forest and the ultimate consumer, a series of intermediate production stages usually exists. Thus, marketing a simple box of breakfast cereal involves growing the wheat, milling the flour, baking the flour and other ingredients, and packaging and delivering the product. Transportation and storage can occur between all stages. After the wheat is grown, each succeeding production stage can be performed by different firms in different places.

The term *consumption* refers to use by the ultimate consumer to fulfill his or her demand—eating a loaf of bread, for example. Any intermediate purchases of wheat by the miller or of flour by the baker are not consumption in this sense. The price of the materials purchased at each stage of production reflects the amount of income created up to that point.

As shown in the general production model (Fig. 5.1), the factor inputs are variables that can take on a wide range of values. As a result, a given product can be created by many different combinations of inputs and input levels.[3] For example, dams are built in some parts of the less developed world with very little capital equipment and very much hand labor—areas where labor is plentiful compared to capital (Fig. 5.3). In the highly developed parts of the world large inputs of capital equipment are substituted for labor—areas where labor is scarce compared to capital. As mentioned in Chapter 1, the notion of substitutability of factor inputs in production is important in interpreting the economic landscape. Processes that produce the same output but with different combinations of inputs can have very different locational patterns.

The economic landscape throughout the world has evolved by the substitution of labor and capital for land (natural resources) in the production process. For some nations, the rapid substitution of capital and technology for scarce land resources has been the very basis of their economic survival. Israel is an example of a nation with very limited land, but with a substantial productive base made possible through large substitutions of capital, labor skills, and technology. The history of the Netherlands is unique. Here, 30 percent has actually been added to its land area by reclamation from the sea,

---

[3] The term *production function* is applied to the technical relationship between physical inputs and physical outputs, assuming a given state of technological development.

NATURAL RESOURCES, PRODUCTION, AND WASTE

Figure 5.3   Example of labor intensive production. Men and women are working on the upstream apron of the Chainat Dam 120 miles north of Bangkok, Thailand. (Source: *United Nations.*)

through the massive application of capital and labor, over the centuries.

One of the most dramatic ways in which the substitution of capital and technology changes the economic landscape is by lowering the cost of movement of people, goods, and information through the development of mechanized transport and electronic communications systems. This will be treated more fully in Chapter 12.

THE LAW OF DIMINISHING RETURNS

This brings us to another important principle of economic production, David Ricardo's *Law of Diminishing Returns,* or more precisely, the *Law of Diminishing Marginal Physical Product.* This law (*tendency* is perhaps a better term) states that if one factor of production, say, labor, is increased one unit at a time while the others are held constant, the marginal (the term "marginal" can be translated simply as "additional") product will at first increase, but ultimately will decline.[4] Of course, in the real world the other factors of production are not held constant while one is increased in a con-

---

[4] It has been stated that knowledge is the only production input that is *not* subject to diminishing returns.

trolled manner. Nevertheless, the hypothetical case shows us limiting behavior that is normally too complex to be perceived in real life.

The Law of Diminishing Returns can be illustrated by a simple example of potato production. Let us assume a fixed land input of one acre—roughly the size of a football field—and gradually increase the labor input. (We will ignore the capital input for this simple example.) Assuming that all workers are equal producers, we would find by experiment results similar to those shown in Figure 5.4. One worker alone can produce 100 tons per season. However, two workers can produce 250 tons; this is so because, together, they can do certain tasks that are difficult, impossible, or inefficient for one person to perform (filling sacks or operating a two-person tool, for example).

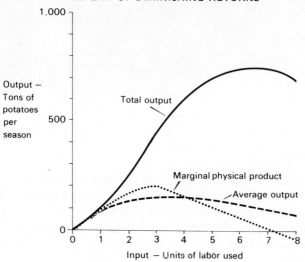

Units of labor used	Marginal (additional) physical product (tons)	Total output (tons)	Average output (tons)
0	0	0	0
1	100	100	100
2	150	250	125
3	200	450	150
4	150	600	150
5	100	700	140
6	50	750	125
7	0	750	107
8	−50	700	88

Figure 5.4   Hypothetical potato production on a fixed area of land, with labor input the only variable.

116   NATURAL RESOURCES, PRODUCTION, AND WASTE

Introduction of a third worker on the acre plot will likewise result in both a greater total output and a greater marginal product. The addition of a fourth worker, however, results in a decrease in the marginal product. At this point the limiting land factor is beginning to exert a constraint. There are no additional jobs that can be done with increasing collective efficiency, and although the total output increases with the addition of the fourth through the sixth worker, the marginal product continues to decline until, with the addition of the seventh worker, it drops to zero. With the addition of the eighth laborer, there are so many workers on the acre plot that they are getting in each other's way and impeding efficiency. At this point on the graph the marginal product becomes negative and the total output actually drops.

By similar reasoning it can be shown that the Law of Diminishing Returns applies to the land or capital factors of production. If, for example, we assume a variable land input with a fixed labor input held at, say, 20 workers (again, ignoring the capital factor), we are likely to find total output and marginal product changing as above. Twenty workers confined to one acre are crowded and inefficient. As land is increased, the efficiencies of the 20 workers increase until the marginal product peaks. Here, spatial efficiency is optimal as each laborer works just the right amount of land to maximize his or her output. However, as more land is added (even assuming uniform land quality), the space to be covered by each worker increases, adding higher and higher transport costs and lowering the productivity of each worker.

The applications of the Law of Diminishing Returns are countless in the study of land use. For example, it furnishes an insight into rural crowding and underemployment in many developing countries. It also illuminates the dilemma faced by nations, such as Brazil, where development of vast, sparsely populated interiors is handicapped by the lack of transport systems and other capital projects. Capital investment for such places is limited, and a danger exists of "diluting" it in space by attempting to develop too much land within a given time frame.

NEGATIVE EXTERNALITIES RESULTING FROM PRODUCTION

In Chapter 1 economic landscapes were shown to reveal not only the physical evidence of production, but also the evidence of environmental damage and other forms of "counter production." In the past Man has not always known the ecological consequences of his economic activity. Examples can be found in all parts of the world and in all periods of history. The removal of forests in Ancient Greece, China, and the Mediterranean lands; the erosion of top soil from the American Great Plains; the destruction of agricul-

ENVIRONMENTAL IMPACT IN ANCIENT GREECE AND ROME

Plato lamented in his *Critias,* "There are mountains in Attica . . . which were clothed, not so very long ago, with fine trees producing timber suitable for roofing the largest buildings . . . there were also many lofty cultivated trees, while the country produced boundless pasture for cattle. . . . The annual supply of rainfall was not lost as it is at present through being allowed to flow over a denuded surface to the sea."

Ecologist G. E. Hutchinson provided an intriguing example from Rome. He reported that an analysis of fossil material from the bed of Lake Monterosi, Italy, revealed that the lake had undergone a radical change around the third century B.C.—from a deep, slightly acidic, soft-water lake to a shallow, somewhat overfertilized, hard-water lake. The change is attributed to the construction of a Roman Road, the *Via Cassia.**

* Reviewed by A. D. Hasler, "Limnologists and Oceanographers Discuss Lakes, Rivers and Aquatic life," *Science,* Volume 138, pp. 698, 700, 703; 9 November 1962. Copyright 1962 by the American Association for the Advancement of Science.

tural land in the Indus River Valley of Pakistan through waterlogging and salinization from excessive irrigation—these and countless other examples of environmental damage (also referred to as *ecological backlash*) have been documented.

In all these cases, the environmental disturbance was a consequence of some form of economic production. A technical term for this is *negative external effect,* or *negative externality.*[5] External effects can be positive as well as negative. A positive externality can be defined as a favorable effect (benefit) on a person, group, or firm that results from the action of a different person, group, or firm. For example, if in pumping water out of a flooded mine, a neighboring mine is also drained, the neighboring mine benefits from a positive external effect. Although we speak in terms of "benefits" and "costs," it is important to note that prices cannot be assigned to externalities.

Our main concern here is with negative externalities, particularly environmental pollution resulting from the generation of wastes.[6] Two things about negative externalities must be stressed. First, they are growing more serious over time as production increases; second, their worst manifestations result from production in the Highly Developed Countries. As the global economy

[5] Other terms for these effects appear in the literature. "External diseconomies" and "negative spillover effects" have been widely used in the past, for example.
[6] An interesting semantic innovation in recent years has been to refer to environmental pollution as a "public bad," the opposite of a "public good."

NATURAL RESOURCES, PRODUCTION, AND WASTE

becomes more and more interconnected, the international impact of environmental deterioration increases. There is evidence, for example, that industrial activity may be causing an increase in the level of carbon dioxide in the atmosphere, with possible long-range effects on the global climate.

WASTES AND WASTE MANAGEMENT

When the economists of the last century were writing about negative externalities resulting from production, one of the favorite examples given was the smoke and foul water that made the industrial towns in Great Britain so unattractive and unhealthy. Environmental pollution created by production wastes has had, in recent decades, a major impact on the location and performance of economic activity. The cost of all pollution control measures in the United States is expected to total nearly $500 billion for the decade ending in 1984 (Table 5.1).

THE CONCEPT OF WASTE

According to the physical laws of conservation, there is neither the creation nor the destruction of matter in any production process—only the rearrangement of matter in space and time under different energy configurations. A corollary to this is that all production processes result in unwanted material or energy by-products, which are defined as *wastes*. Wastes are an inevitable consequence of economic activity (Fig. 5.1), becoming the source of environmental pollution, which occurs in solid, liquid, and gaseous form. Pollution also takes the form of unwanted energy emissions, such as heat, noise, or radiation.

Table 5.1   Pollution Abatement Costs as a Percentage of Gross National Product for Selected Countries, 1971–1975

	Investment	Operating Costs	Total
United States (1971–1980)	0.7	1.5	2.2
West Germany	0.9	0.9	1.8
Italy	0.4	0.2	0.6
Japan	2.2	n.a.[a]	n.a.
Netherlands	n.a.	n.a.	1–1.5
Sweden	0.7	n.a.	n.a.

[a]Not available.

Source: D. W. Pearce, *Environmental Economics,* Longman, 1976, Table 6.9, p. 138.

Natural ecological communities do not have a "pollution problem," since the waste products of organisms are decomposed chemically into substances that provide food for new cycles of metabolism. Some organisms use the wastes of others directly as food. The group called *decomposers,* consisting primarily of fungi and bacteria, consumes organic wastes and keeps them from accumulating. In this way, chemical elements and energy necessary for life are recycled in a constant space-time flow.

For most of his existence on earth, Man also did not disturb the ecology by more than a negligible amount. By the time he had developed agriculture, however, Man was using his environment in such a way as to disturb material and energy cycles. As shown in Chapter 2, the record of Man's role in evolving the global economy has been one of progressive intervention in natural systems in order to produce greater quantities of goods and services for an expanding population.

SPATIAL ASPECTS OF WASTE MANAGEMENT

As long as agrarian economies were dominant, the management of wastes was a simple, local matter. The biological nature of the wastes and their lack of spatial concentration prevented most serious problems. This changed, however, with the growth of industry and large cities.

As Man grew in numbers and concentrated in urban places, his principal strategy for combatting disease and discomfort from waste accumulation was to diffuse it into the environment—usually into bodies of water—where natural processes could convert the organic wastes into inoffensive earth substances. As cities grew very large, however, this strategy became less effective, and death rates in cities were very high.

The viability and growth of cities has always been directly related to the metabolic problem of waste transfer from the city to outlying places of low population density. Streams, lakes, bays, and estuaries were principal depositories of municipal wastes. The flowing water carried away, diluted, and decomposed the waste materials. The great surge of sewer building in the mid-nineteenth century enabled cities in industrializing nations to grow still larger by systematically collecting and moving waste water to rivers and other water bodies.

In a similar way, the constant motion of the atmosphere was relied on to carry smoke, particulate matter, and gases away from cities and towns and to disperse them over wide areas, where the damage they caused would be minimized.

The generation of pollutants and their concentrated discharge into the surrounding environment has increased greatly in recent decades under the

NATURAL RESOURCES, PRODUCTION, AND WASTE

compounding influences of population growth, economic growth, and urbanization. Pollution from the industrialized nations bordering the North Atlantic creates negative externalities of international dimensions. An example of this is the growing pollution of the North Sea. The postwar expansion of chemical industries in France, Switzerland, West Germany, and the Netherlands resulted in a great increase in waste discharge into the Rhine River. In 1963 an international commission was established to deal with the matter. Resulting tighter controls on the dumping of chemical wastes into the Rhine, however, led to an increase in dumping into the North Sea.

The waste assimilating capacity of the ocean fringes, bays, lakes, estuaries, rivers, and other water bodies is reaching upper limits in parts of the world. In economic terms this is causing cities, industrial plants and other polluters to modify their operations in such a way as to reduce their free dumping of wastes into the environment.

In addition to industrial and municipal effluents, the waters of ocean stretches are being polluted by discharges from ships at dock, at anchor, or underway at sea. Oil well operations and accidental tanker discharges are always a threat, and attempts by governments to control routine tanker discharges in coastal waters are often unenforceable. A number of intrepid sailors who have navigated small sailing craft on long ocean voyages in recent years have brought back disturbing reports of encountering garbage and other waste matter in mid-ocean.

Just as the earth's waters are finite and have waste assimilating limitations, so is the lower atmosphere subject to pollution overload. Gaseous and particulate wastes concentrate near the emission sources. Thus, where discharges are massive, such as in cities and industrial regions, the lower atmospheric space for miles around can be adversely affected and the population threatened (Fig. 5.5). Sometimes the effects of regional air pollution from a

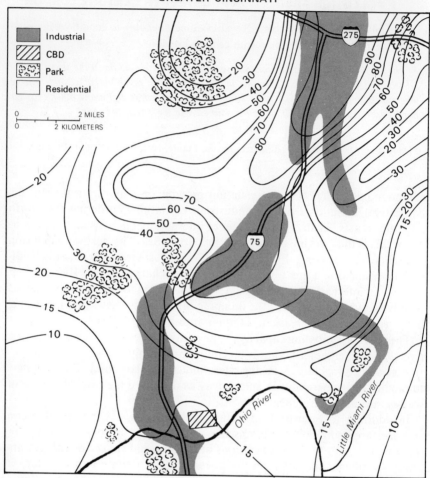

Figure 5.5 *Contours show the values of particulate matter (dust) concentra-tion (μ/m^3) at an elevation of 3000 feet above Greater Cincinnati, as measured on May 27, 1970. Note that the maximum levels of pollution occured over the industrial sections of the city.* (Source: *Adapted from Wilfred Bach and Thomas Hagedorn, "Atmospheric Pollution: Its Spatial Distribution Over An Urban Area,"* Proceedings of the Association of American Geographers, *3, 1971, p. 21.*)

concentrated source are clearly apparent in the economic landscape. Fumes from mineral smelters in some parts of the world have destroyed vegetation and poisoned the environment over a wide area surrounding the smelter (Fig. 5.6).

The city or industrial region is also a concentrated source of solid waste. The management strategy for solid wastes has followed the pattern for liquid and gaseous wastes—get them away from population centers as quickly as possible. However, solid wastes must be collected, stored, and moved by costly land transport (Fig. 5.7).

Compounding the global pollution problem is the fact that the technologically advanced nations are continually developing production processes that create more and more "exotic" industrial wastes. Each year thousands of new chemical substances are developed for use by the chemical and other industries. These compounds find their way into waste effluents. No one knows for certain the long-range health effects many of these new wastes will have on humanity. Strontium is an example of a problem element. Strontium's commercial growth began in the mid 1800s, resulting from the development of a process for beet sugar refining. It was used in an increasingly large group of products: enamels, glass, welding fluxes, liquid heat-

Figure 5.6   Prior to 1919 smelter fumes killed all vegetation in this area. The fumes were controlled in 1919, but this photograph, taken in 1928, shows the persisting environmental damage. Sacramento River drainage basin, California. (Source: USDA—Forest Service.)

WASTES AND WASTE MANAGEMENT

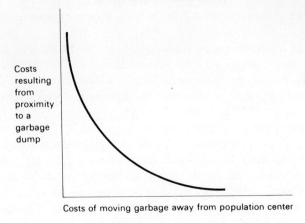

COST TRADE–OFFS IN SOLID
WASTE MANAGEMENT

Costs
resulting
from
proximity
to a
garbage
dump

Costs of moving garbage away from population center

Figure 5.7   Proximity to a garbage dump creates social costs—smell, flies, rats, and possible disease—that can be eliminated by substitution of money costs to move the wastes away. Possible combinations of the two kinds of costs might occur at points on the graph whose locus is suggested by the curve. The substitution of a landfill or incinerating operation can neutralize some, but not all, of the offensive characteristics of the waste.

treating baths, signal flares, and many others. As a result, strontium is now found concentrated in a number of places in the environment.

It bears repeating here that a significant aspect of the global waste-management problem is the imbalance between waste generation in the highly developed and the less developed worlds. Both in terms of national totals and per capita averages, the generation of a disproportionately high output of waste is characteristic of urban-industrial regions of the globe.

SHEAFFER'S APPROACH TO WASTE MANAGEMENT

A creative professional in the environmental management field is Dr. John R. Sheaffer, a geographer and planning executive based in Chicago. Sheaffer's approach to waste management is based on three fundamental principles:

1. *The environment is a single system with air, land, and water interacting and affecting, and being affected by, human occupancy.*
2. *The environmental system for planning purposes is closed. Sheaffer writes, "Examine briefly a modern refuse incinerator which seeks to destroy material—a basic violation of this principle. The gases emitted from the stack are*

NATURAL RESOURCES, PRODUCTION, AND WASTE

pollutants—mercury vapor, chlorinated hydrocarbons, acids of nitrogen. The wet scrubbers to reduce particulate matter emissions may make a water pollution problem and the ash residue has the potential to leach into the ground water and attract flies and rats. Today our urban life systems are planned and designed as open-ended systems that must discharge either to the air or water in order to function. Consequently, they violate this second principle in our conceptual framework."

3. *Pollutants are potential resources out of place. Pollutants in an urban environment are simply dislocated resources that should be relocated, reclaimed, reprocessed, or recycled so that they can become resources. Sheaffer gives the following example: "Accelerated cultural eutrophication of a lake is caused primarily by the nitrates, phosphates, and potassium. These nutrients are to a large extent dissolved in wastewater and conventional secondary treatment processes are ineffective in their removal. When these nutrients are discharged to a water body, they stimulate plant growth such as algae and water weeds. However, if those same nutrients were applied to the land, they would be called fertilizer. They would be resources; however, because they are dislocated in the environmental system they are called pollutants."**

* John R. Sheaffer, "Contributions of Geography to Urban Waste Management," Paper delivered at Annual Meeting of The Association of American Geographers, Boston, Mass., April 20, 1971.

REGIONAL SOIL EROSION: AN EXAMPLE OF THE INTERACTION OF ECOLOGY AND ECONOMICS

Soil erosion is a natural earth process in which soil particles are moved progressively down slope toward the ocean by gravity and running water, and are replaced by fresh mineral particles from the underlying bed rock. The rate of this natural process is, by human standards, exceedingly slow, and is determined by rock type, slope, elevation, and other factors. When people disturb this process by plowing fields, cutting timber, excavating for a highway, or building a dam, they introduce a new system variable. Large-scale earth movement by humans causes sediment to be displaced down-slope rapidly in large volumes, creating a serious negative externality. Table 5.2 gives estimates for earth excavation of different types in the United States. The yearly volume is far greater than generally suspected.

Not only is top soil removed and gullies produced (Figure 5.8) in this process, but the deposition of the soil where it is not wanted by wind and water also creates serious problems. For example, each year in the United

Table 5.2   Estimated Amounts of Earth Moved on Construction Projects in the United States, 1979

Type of Project	Volume Moved in Millions of Cubic Yards
Highway construction	475
Dams, canals, levees	160
Residential construction	500
Industrial and commercial construction	500
Airports and railroads	40
Agricultural development	1000
Dredging	750
Surface (open pit) mining	7547

Source: Caterpillar Tractor Co., Peoria, Illinois, Private Communication, November 16, 1979.

Figure 5.8   Massive gullying formed by water erosion in Coffee County, Alabama. (Source: *USDA—Soil Conservation Service.*)

NATURAL RESOURCES, PRODUCTION, AND WASTE

States it costs the public over a hundred million dollars to dredge sediment from harbors and waterways alone. In addition, another hundred million dollars in reservoir capacity is lost each year from deposition of stream-borne sediment. This does not take into account less tangible losses from sedimentation damage, such as impaired recreational facilities.

The "dust bowl" disaster of the 1930s was a tragic chapter in American history. The ecological disruption and economic losses caused by attempts to bring parts of the Great Plains under the plow are well documented. The rapid occupation of this ecologically "fragile" region took place by farmers who lacked arid land experience, and who, consequently, did not appreciate the protective role played by the grass cover in their new environment.

It is a climatic feature of semi-arid regions that droughts of several years duration occur from time to time. Under the twin stimuli of a series of relatively wet years and high wheat prices, large areas of the Great Plains were exposed by the plow in the 1920s. Then came plummeting grain prices and drought during the early 1930s. In a desperate effort to cut their losses by planting more, the farmers used their land more intensively, but this only increased the wind erosion of the dried-out soil. By the time the long drought was over, the rich top soil of vast stretches of the Great Plains had been stripped away and deposited elsewhere as unwanted silt. The economic losses that resulted from the dust bowl disaster, to say nothing of other forms of human suffering, were staggering.

The lesson of the American Dust Bowl, learned the hard way, resulted in the adoption of land use policies and practices more compatible with the long-range potential of regions subject to erosion (Fig. 5.9). The hard lesson, however, had to be learned all over by the Soviet Union during its Virgin Lands Program of the 1950s.

Despite the more enlightened farming practices in the United States since the 1930s, man-induced erosion still represents a serious problem in many places. In Iowa, for example, unprotected, sloping cropland is stripped of an average of 13 tons of soil per acre annually. This roughly amounts to two bushels of soil lost for each bushel of corn harvested. And that is an average figure; in bad years, such as 1974, soil losses per acre reach 40 to 50 tons per year.[7]

The problem of soil erosion is worse in many Less Developed Countries where heavy population growth has forced agricultural production up steeper slopes. Fields planted on such slopes are highly vulnerable to erosion when cropped. A compounding problem—another legacy of rising world

---

[7] Resources for the Future, Inc., *Annual Report 1977,* Washington, D.C., p. 38.

Figure 5.9   The owner of this gullied land in Buncombe Co., N.C. (A), planted the area with pine and locust seedlings in the late 1930s. The same tract nearly 20 years later is shown in (B) *(Source: Tennessee Valley Authority.)*

128   NATURAL RESOURCES, PRODUCTION, AND WASTE

petroleum prices—has been the trend in many Less Developed Countries to strip trees and brush from the land in a desperate search for cooking and other fuel needs, leaving the topsoil more exposed to wind and water erosion, even in areas not under cultivation.

SUMMARY

A general model of economic production shows the relationship between *natural resources* (the *land* factor of production), *production,* and *wastes.* Natural resources affect the comparative advantage of regions and nations. Opinion varies with respect to the future availability of resources, particularly the nonrenewable group. Zimmermann's *Functional Concept of Resources* is more valid today than ever before as depletion and prices continue to increase and as applied science creates new sources of raw materials from common earth substances. Production adds *utility* to objects, increasing value by using variable combinations of land, labor, and capital. Different input combinations can result in different optimal production locations. Many production stages, often in different places, are usually required before a final product reaches the consumer. All production inputs except human intelligence are subject to the *Law of Diminishing Returns.* Economic production results in *negative externalities,* which are unwanted and often unanticipated. A large class of negative externalities results from the generation of pollution in the form of solid, liquid, and gaseous wastes. As production increases and becomes spatially concentrated, the management of wastes becomes a growing factor in the location and character of economic activity. Most environmental pollution occurs in urban areas and industrial regions, sometimes creating problems of global proportions. Accelerated soil erosion is caused by poor agricultural methods and other forms of production, and provides an example of the interaction between ecological and economic processes.

Questions

1 How do differences in culture and population density affect land-use management? Give examples.
2 With a simple example, such as commercial bread baking, shoe repair, or the growth of Christmas trees, analyze the production process by use of the general production model.
3 What is meant by the *Functional Concept of Resources?* Give examples. Why is the concept of such importance to the United States' and world economies in the 1980s?

4 Explain the general idea underlying Ricardo's *Law of Diminishing Returns* with a simple example and a graphical illustration.
5 What is meant by the term *negative externality?* Give examples of the evidence of negative externalities from economic landscapes you are familiar with.
6 Develop a case study to illustrate how improved waste management has affected economic activity in your community.

6

ENVIRONMENTAL FACTORS INFLUENCING ECONOMIC ACTIVITY

"One important explanation of high American wages, therefore, lies in the sphere of economic geography. Compared with the size of our working population, we have been generously supplied with land, coal, iron, oil, and water power. The per capita supplies of these vital sinews of modern industrial production are less in Europe and still less in many other regions."

Paul A. Samuelson*

By now, a major theme of this book should be fixed in the reader's mind: space and environment act together to influence economic activity. In this chapter we concentrate on the way in which spatial variation of environmental factors—Ricardo's land quality—influences the location and character of economic activity, and along with it human settlement. However, throughout this and succeeding chapters it is necessary to keep in mind the role played by distance in all forms of economic activity.

The physical environment affects the comparative advantage of a place, region, or country for different kinds of economic production. Climate and geology can be considered as two "master variables." Climate and geology also affect economic activity indirectly through their influence on landforms, soils, vegetation, and hydrology.

The combined effect of the environmental variables accounts in considerable measure for the location of agriculture, grazing, forestry, fishing, mining, and other forms of *primary production,* which are based directly on the

---

* *Economics,* 9th Edition, McGraw-Hill Book Co., New York, 1973, p. 572.

natural environment. The location of primary production, particularly agriculture, in turn explains a great deal about the location of all other forms of economic activity and human settlement.

We look at environmental factors individually here; however, comprehension of the economic landscape requires that a region be considered in its totality.

SPATIAL VARIATIONS IN CLIMATE AND BIOLOGICAL PRODUCTION

Climate can be considered as weather generalized over space and time. Weather is determined by the interaction of a set of factors, including latitude, elevation, relief, wind systems, and the spatial arrangement of land and water masses. Surprisingly similar climatic conditions exist in widely separated parts of the earth. For example, the Town of Nazareth in Northern Israel has a climate very similar to that of Mill Creek, California.

The occupation of the earth by humanity has always been influenced by the distribution of climatic types. Some scientists suggest that *Homo sapiens* evolved to their present form as a response to the climatic challenge of the *Pleistocene* (continental glaciation) period of the recent geologic past. We do know that Man's invention of clothing and shelter, and his use of fire, enabled him to extend his hunting and gathering activities to a wide range of climatic types around the world.

After the Agricultural Revolution, man's occupation of the cold-winter regions of the world was made possible by the selective development of grain crops requiring short, intense growing seasons.

Nature, of course, does not recognize "good" or "bad" climates. These terms indicate our perception of a climate's suitability for agricultural production and other human activities. The viability and growth rate of each plant species are functions of environmental factors, which vary greatly from place to place. Choice tomatoes can be grown under an artificial climate at the South Pole, but they will be very high cost tomatoes indeed.

JEN-HU CHANG'S COMPARISON OF TROPICAL AND TEMPERATE REGIONS FOR AGRICULTURE

"It is a common misconception that tropical regions have a very high agricultural potential and that the low productivity there is largely the result of technological incompetence. . . . In addition to the disadvantage of high nighttime temperatures, which accelerate respiration, tropical regions, especially the wet tropics, usually have lower radiation than temperate zones during their normal growing season. In July, the average daily radiation is 440 langleys at Madras, India (13% N), as against 680 langleys at Fresno, California (36% N), and 450 langleys at Fairbanks, Alaska (64% N).. . . Although the productivity of annual crops is usually higher in temperate regions, the tropics have the advantage of year-round crop production. Tropical lands are best suited for crops with a long vegetative. Able to intercept light to a maximum extent. The average annual yields for such crops as sugar cane, cocoa, and oil palm are indeed impressive, and they rank among the highest."*

*Jen-hu Chang, *Climate and Agriculture: An Ecological Survey,* Aldine Publishing Company, Chicago, 1968, pp. 59-60

Climate affects economic location through its role in the biochemistry of all plant and animal life. Looking at the grand scheme of the biosphere, we see that the key process is *photosynthesis,* which links the inorganic and the organic worlds. The radiant energy from the sun enters the biological cycle through the photosynthetic production of organic matter by chlorophyll-bearing organisms. Green plants on the land, algae in fresh water, and phytoplankton in sea water utilize the sun's energy to convert carbon dioxide and water into carbohydrates, with oxygen released as a waste product. The accumulation of plant and animal material produced by photosynthesis is called *biomass,* and its spatial distribution reflects the distribution of the climatic factors that control photosynthesis.

Among all the requirements for biological production, the two most critical are solar energy and water. The space-time distribution of these essentials is very irregular. Much solar energy falls on deserts where water is the scarce and limiting factor; on the other hand, there is much surplus water in some environments, where energy receipt is very limited. Where either solar energy or water are limiting factors for plant photosynthesis and animal metabolism, there results, in terms of modern physical geography, a *low work environment.* In such environments chemical reactions, biological functions, and decay are all retarded; examples include polar regions and deserts (see Figs. 6.1, 6.2 and 6.3).

Figure 6.1 Building on highway south of Fairbanks, Alaska. Heated portion of building has subsided into thawed permafrost. Front porch was unheated. (Source: *U.S. Geological Survey.*)

A separate volume could be filled with examples of climate as a location factor at the regional and local levels. Because of water's high specific heat, it stores heat energy from the sun very effectively during the summer and releases it slowly to the air during the winter. This "hot-water-bottle effect" accounts for the mild climate of Western Europe. The warm North Atlantic Drift (continuation of the Gulf Stream) carries an enormous quantity of heat from the tropical latitudes to the North Atlantic, where Westerly winds carry the warm, humid air over Western Europe, creating a very productive climate for agriculture.

The same principle works in reverse to create conditions that make New York an important wine producing state. The water in large lakes, such as Erie, Seneca, and Cayuga, remains cold in the spring and chills the air above. This cooler air moves eastward over the land and retards the development of the grapes until early summer, when the danger of a killing frost is past.

The role of climate on Man as a direct physiological factor has often been

Figure 6.2 A much-attended "tree" at the Chuquicamata copper mine in northern Chile. This is on the eastern fringes of the Atacama Desert, perhaps the driest region in the world. No other vegetation of any kind is visible. The presence of great copper reserves in this remote, hostile environment brought capital and labor in to form one of the largest open pit mining operations in the world. A tailings pile from the mine appears in the background.

overstated. What does appear verified is that lower economic efficiency in many tropical countries results from debilitating diseases and poor nutrition rather than any direct influence of the climate on human performance.

A significant contrast in latitude exists between the United States and the Soviet Union (Fig. 6.4), giving the two countries very different climatic patterns and agricultural productivities.

SPATIAL VARIATIONS IN GEOLOGY AND LANDFORMS

DIRECT INFLUENCES OF GEOLOGY

The spatial variation of geologic forms can have an important influence on the occurrence and type of economic activity. The geographic location, size, shape, and coastline configuration of land masses are all the results of tec-

ENVIRONMENTAL CONSTRAINTS ON HUMAN HABITATION AND ECONOMIC ACTIVITY

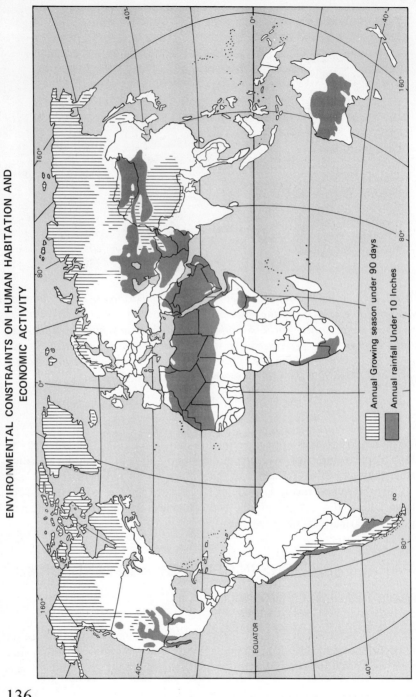

Annual Growing season under 90 days

Annual rainfall Under 10 Inches

Figure 6.3   (see facing page) Compare this map with the map of world population density (Fig. 2.2). Regions with short growing seasons or little rainfall usually support few people and little economic activity. An exception is the Nile River Valley in Egypt, which receives water from humid regions a thousand miles upstream. Other environmental constraints are hilly or mountainous land and lack of fertile soils.

CONTRAST IN LATITUDE BETWEEN THE UNITED STATES AND
THE SOVIET UNION

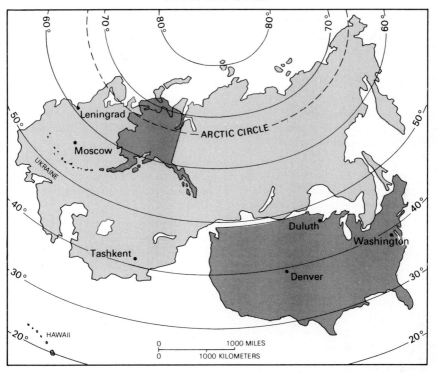

Figure 6.4   A map of the United States superimposed on that of the Soviet Union reveals the latitudinal, and therefore the climatic, disadvantages of the USSR. The Ukraine, in the southern part of European Russia, is the most productive agricultural region in the USSR, yet it lies at the latitude of Duluth, Minnesota. Leningrad's latitude matches that of southern Alaska. Much of the Soviet Union south of the 49th parallel, which is the border between the U.S. and Canada, is semi-arid or desert. (Source: Adapted from U.S. Army Corps of Engineers.)

FIELD'S COMPARISON OF ENVIRONMENTAL QUALITY AND LAND PRODUCTIVITY IN U.S.S.R. AND NORTH AMERICA

Canadian geographer N. C. Field made a comparative analysis of the agricultural land base of the Soviet Union and North America (United States and Canada) on the basis of two climatic measures. He explains the higher productivity of the United States in terms of temperature and moisture advantages (see Table 6.1). The following is quoted from his study:

From a cropland base 25 per cent larger than that of the United States, the USSR has been obtaining an agricultural output only about 70–75 per cent as great. Thus, on a per acre basis, the productivity of Soviet cropland has averaged not more than 60 per cent that of the United States. Relative to the combined cropland resources of Canada and the United States, Soviet cropland might be rated as about two-thirds as productive per acre.

Climate is without question the major factor contributing to broad regional gradients in the productivity of the arable land resource within both the USSR and North America. Spatial variations both in the yield of individual crops and in the overall crop composition, or type of farming, are closely related to differences in thermal and moisture conditions.

The arable land base of North America as a whole, and that of the United States in particular, is thus much more favorably endowed from the standpoint of environmental quality than that of the Soviet Union. Canada's land resource, on the other hand, is of even lower average quality than that of the USSR.

Given equal technology and capital inputs the Soviet Union can never hope to achieve, in the author's view, an average level of productivity from its cropland resource approaching that of the United States or the North American region as a whole. *

* N. C. Field, "Environmental Quality and Land Productivity: A Comparison Of The Agricultural Land Base of the USSR and North America," *Canadian Geographer,* Vol. 12, 1968, pp. 2, 5, 9, 11, 12.

---

tonic forces. Although it is impossible to quantify such factors, their influence can be profound. The fact that Norway, with a population of Greater Detroit, has one of the largest merchant fleets in the world is associated, of course, with its maritime location and tradition. The shape of a nation or a region can also have an important effect on its spatial economy. Other things being equal, a nation with a compact shape has an economic advantage over a nation, such as Chile, which has an extremely elongated shape.[1] An un-

[1] Kevin R. Cox, *Man, Location, and Behavior: An Introduction to Human Geography,* John Wiley and Sons, Inc., New York, 1972, p. 125.

Table 6.1   Cropland in the United States and USSR Classified by Thermal and Moisture Zones (Percentage Distributions)

Moisture Index[a]	United States Degree Months				USSR Degree Months			
	100–199	200–299	300 and over	Total	100–199	200–299	300 and over	Total
90–100	8	30	19	57	26	0.1	0.3	26
80–89	2	5	2	9	14	1	—	15
65–79	5	7	3	15	18	6	—	24
0–64	4	7	8	19	22	9	4	35
TOTAL	19	49	32	100	80	16	4	100

[a]Moisture Index, as a percentage, is given by (annual evapotranspiration/potential evapotranspiration) × 100.

Source: Adapted from N. C. Field, "Environmental Quality and Land Productivity: A Comparison of the Agricultural Land Base of the USSR and North America," *Canadian Geographer,* Vol. 12, 1968, Table V, p. 10.

usual example of an entire regional economy adversely affected by the absence of surface water, due to an extremely advanced karstic geological condition, was the subject of research completed in 1973.[2]

Another influence of geology has been called the "geological lottery." This refers to how mineral deposits useful to Man were concentrated in highly irregular spatial patterns millions of years ago. The fixed nature of these deposits continues to have an important influence on Man and his economic activities throughout the world. The "geological lottery" will be the basis for a discussion of mining location and mineral production in Chapter 9.

SLOPE AND PRODUCTION COSTS

Through the ages people have attempted to increase their production of food and other products on uneven topography by leveling the surface of the land. They do this because, with few exceptions, the cost of economic activity is rendered higher when it must be performed on an uneven surface. It is a physical principle that if a person or a bale of hay or a gallon of water or a vehicle of any kind must be elevated in going from one place to another, the process requires more energy. Moving loads up a grade or simply walking uphill is not compensated in energy terms by going down the other side.

[2]Donald O. Doehring and Joseph H. Butler, "Hydrogeologic Constraints on Yucatan's Development," *Science,* November 15, 1974, Vol. 186, pp. 591-95. Copyright 1974 by the American Association for the Advancement of Science.

Elevation above sea level is not necessarily the critical factor here; there are rather level plateau surfaces at higher elevations throughout the world. (It is true, however, that these regions are often isolated by surrounding, higher mountain ranges, as in the case of the *Altiplano* of Peru and Bolivia.) Instead, production and transportation costs are related to the degree of terrain roughness, since uneven togography requires a constant up and down displacement. Most of the world's cropped farmland is found in plains, valleys, or in other relatively level areas (Figs. 6.5 and 6.6). Economically speaking, regions with rough terrain require higher costs for most economic

SPATIAL RELATIONSHIP BETWEEN FLAT LAND AND CASH
GRAIN FARMING IN THE MIDWEST

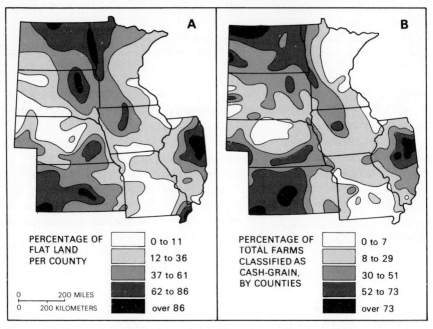

Figure 6.5   In a study published in 1963, J. J. Hidore tested the hypothesis that a spatial association exists between the distribution of flat land (sloping 3° or less) and the distribution of cash-grain farms in several Midwestern states. Hidore's analysis for county units showed that nearly half the total variation in cash-grain farming was accounted for statistically by variation in the variable "flat land." The general congruence of the two spatial variables is shown cartographically in Maps A and B. (Source: J. J. Hidore, "The Relationship Between Cash-Grain Farming and Land Forms," Economic Geography, Vol. 39, 1963. Figures 1 and 4. Reprinted with permission of the author and editor.)

Figure 6.6   Many of the world's great grain producing regions are character-ized by flat or gently rolling land on which highly mechanized cultivation can take place. This is a view of the Canadian prairie in southern Saskatchewan where 15,000,000 acres are under wheat cultivation. (Source: United Nations and Canadian Government Travel Bureau.)

activities because they need greater inputs for a given output. This helps explain why hilly regions are very often low income regions.

In the case of transportation, the disadvantage of hilly terrain can be directly expressed in terms of money costs by means of civil engineering analysis. Not only are construction costs affected, but so are maintenance and operation costs. Road maintenance in a hilly or mountainous region must contend with rock slides and other forms of mass earth flow. In terms of operating costs, the energy required to lift a railroad car or automobile up a grade increases as a power of the grade. Very often a roundabout route is designed to maintain the design grade, but this requires a much longer route, and hence increases other costs.

Some exceptions do exist to the generalization that rough topography is economically disadvantageous. Certain economic benefits are directly asso-ciated with hilly and mountainous regions, such as scenic, recreational, and wilderness values. Upland forest areas in humid regions are also very good water storage areas, and have an advantage for hydroelectric development.

Certain mountainous or hilly regions, such as the Urals in the USSR, the Black Hills in South Dakota, and the Canadian Shield, are crystalline rock masses containing great mineral wealth.

Variations in elevation and in sun and wind exposure in humid tropical uplands result in a complex pattern of climate and land use. The terrain affects the spatial economy of such regions in a profound way. On the one hand, there tends to be isolation of communities; on the other, the different environmental conditions at different elevations stimulate a "vertical trade" up and down the mountains in different commodities.

SOILS AND VEGETATION AS LOCATION FACTORS

Soil is a highly complex substance made up of mineral particles, organic material, air, and water. Most soils are full of microscopic plant and animal life. Soils are highly dynamic and can change rapidly; even hourly changes in bacteria populations may occur. In this sense they are especially sensitive to Man's impact. The processes that form soils are based on the two primary environmental variables: climate and geology. Soils are also influenced by the other, derivative variables: landforms and vegetation.

The speed of soil formation varies greatly. Thousands of years are required to produce an inch of soil on hard rocks, such as granite or basalt. On softer rocks, such as shale, and in unconsolidated material, such as glacial moraines, sand, and river deposits, soils can develop within a few decades or even a few years. In most cases, soils are covered by a plant cover.

Unlike climate, soil is an environmental variable that can be managed by people. The application of labor (hoeing, plowing, terracing) and capital (tools, tractors, equipment) can bring about marked changes in a soil. Today the soils of Western Europe are far more productive than they were in the Middle Ages.

Oddly, the influence of soils on settlement patterns in the United States has been understated in economic history. The Mayflower Pilgrims stepped off Plymouth Rock onto soils that were comparatively unproductive (Gloucester and Merrimac soils) and had to depend on sea food and Indian corn from the interior to survive the first few years of the colony. In 1635 Thomas Hooker took his followers inland to the Connecticut Valley, where they established a string of settlements between what is now Hartford, Connecticut, and Springfield, Massachusetts. Each settlement was established on rich, alluvial soils found in the valley. So highly valued were these soils that they became the object of town and lot survey divisions carried out to tenths of an inch.

The huge land grant of William Penn, farther to the south, was on a zone of very productive, gray-brown podzolic soils. In 1709 two men purchased for 500 pounds 10,000 acres in what is now Lancaster County. Even then the fertility of the soil was perceived so high that this price was double what Penn had established for other land. This transaction has been referred to as one of the best land bargains ever made in Colonial times. These are the famous Hagerstown soils, which helped Pennsylvania to become the granary of the colonies.

When population growth in post-revolutionary America created pressure to move into new areas, many settlers moved south along the extensions of fertile limestone soils in the Cumberland and Shenandoah Valleys. Many families, such as the Boones and Lincolns, passed through the Cumberland Gap and followed the fertile soils westward. This route became the famed Wilderness Road that the settlers in their covered wagons followed to the rich blue grass basins of Kentucky and Tennessee.

The spatial distribution of natural vegetation in the world today varies considerably from that when Man first developed agriculture 10,000 years ago. Labor and capital inputs to the land, particularly in the form of plows, axes, and grazing stock, have radically changed the original distribution of vegetation in the middle latitudes.

In the humid middle latitudes, as technology advanced and the land could be cleared, forest regions were transformed into agricultural regions. Cultural perceptions of the environment were important in this process. The settlers from Northern Europe in America felt at home in the forests, while those from the Mediterranean lands preferred the open grasslands. Prairie grasslands were a hindrance to agricultural settlement, however, until a steel plow was developed that could turn over the thick sod. As the high prairie grass was removed, the world famous "Cornbelt" began to develop, centered around what is now Eastern Iowa.

In the humid tropical regions of the world, the rapid, year-round growth of vegetation exerts a constraint on many economic activities. Only where enough capital is available for heavy, specialized equipment for the control of vegetation are large-scale economic activities feasible. An even greater handicap to intensive agricultural production and economic development in the humid tropics is the presence there of low-yielding lateritic soils (Fig. 6.7). We will see in Chapter 7 how this constraint affects agricultural land use over large tracts of tropical forest around the globe.

WATER AND ITS RELATION TO ECONOMIC ACTIVITY

Water, like soil, is an environmental variable over which Man exercises considerable control. Water resource management is one of the most important aspects of land-use planning and environmental management. The highly irregular distribution and quality of fresh water in space and time are factors that affect the location and character of economic activity. Both the spatial and the environmental explanatory themes in economic geography are needed to understand this influence.

Water is necessary for physical, chemical, and biological processes and is the medium of life functions. Protoplasm is, on the average, three-quarters water; plants use about 450 tons of water in the production of one ton of dry organic matter. When water is a limiting factor, ecological processes slow down or stop altogether.

Man, himself, is largely an aqueous system. Humans sweat over most of their body surface in controlling their temperature and must have two or three quarts of water daily in some form as a replacement. In addition, all the biotic resources that make up our food supply depend on the presence of large quantities of water in the liquid state.

The lack of water in the form of droughts and the excess of water in the form of floods have always been problems for Mankind. They are recurring themes in the Bible and other ancient literatures.

SPACE-TIME VARIATIONS IN WATER OCCURENCE

Water is considered a *flow resource,* which means that it is renewable in terms of human use. However, the irregular space-time occurrence of fresh water creates a special class of planning and management problems.

The two major sources of fresh water are surface and sub-surface supplies. The *surface water* includes lakes, ponds, streams, estuaries, wetlands, and artificial impoundments. The sub-surface supplies, or *groundwater,* are found in underground *aquifers,* which are water-bearing rocks, gravels, or sands. It is highly significant for modern water management that the surface and sub-surface water sources are interconnected hydrologically.

The rates of replenishment of the surface and sub-surface supplies are related to precipitation. Annual precipitation (rainfall, or the rainfall equivalent of snow, hail, or sleet) varies from nearly zero in some deserts, such as the Atacama in Chile, to over 400 inches in places in the foothills of the Himalaya Mountains in India. Where average precipitation is low and temperatures are moderate to high, surface water supplies are scanty or absent entirely,[3] and regional groundwater supplies lie deep and have very low

Figure 6.7   (see facing page) A misconception long existed concerning tropical soils, because of the lush vegetative growth associated with them. In recent decades it has been shown that most soils underlying the tropical and subtropical forests and grasslands are laterites, which are poor for the cultivation of most food crops. Lateritic soils, rich in minerals but poor in organic matter, create an obstacle to increased food production in many Less Developed Countries.

[3] An exception here is the "exotic stream," such as the Nile, which rises in a humid climate and is large enough to be sustained through a desert region.

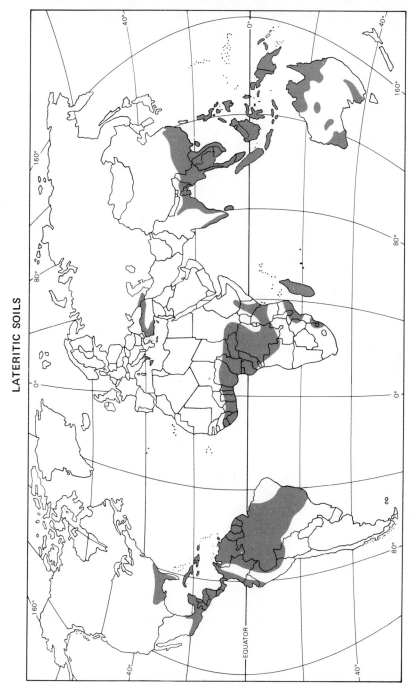

LATERITIC SOILS

145

recharge rates. In humid regions, on the other hand, surface water supplies normally abound, the *water table* (the upper surface of the saturated groundwater zone) lies near the surface, and the rate of replenishment of the groundwater is high (Fig. 6.8).

The hydrologic function of streams as nature's "spillways" gives them a pulsing behavior that has always posed a fundamental management problem (Fig. 6.9). The high degree of variability of streamflow is not generally appreciated. Measured flows on the Missouri River at Kansas City have ranged from a maximum of 573,000 cubic feet per second to a minimum of only 1500 cubic feet per second (Fig. 6.10).

In the case of droughts, a compounded problem confronts humanity. Normally, the more arid a region is, the greater the deviation of its annual precipitaion about a long-range mean value. Places such as Cairo, Egypt,

AREAS OF NATURAL WATER SURPLUS AND NATURAL WATER
DEFICIENCY

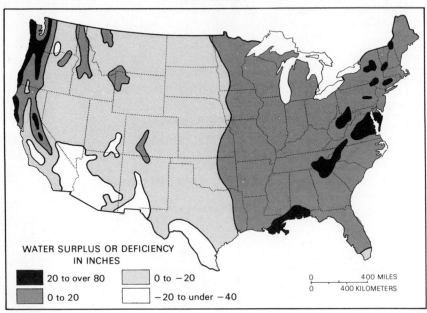

WATER SURPLUS OR DEFICIENCY
IN INCHES

■ 20 to over 80   ▢ 0 to −20
▨ 0 to 20   □ −20 to under −40

0   400 MILES
0   400 KILOMETERS

Figure 6.8   Values in inches were computed by subtracting values of potential evapotranspiration from average precipitation. The map shows a general natural water surplus in the eastern half of the country and a general natural water deficiency in most of the western half. The deficiency shown in southern Florida is the result of very high evapotranspiration—not low precipitation. (Source: U.S. Water Resources Council.)

may go rainless for long periods of time, and then suffer a damaging deluge. This makes water mangement in arid or semi-arid regions a critical decision process.

THE PRODUCTION OF BENEFITS AND COSTS THROUGH WATER REGULATION

As prehistoric Man developed culturally and diffused to occupy the globe, his needs for fresh water were by no means matched in space and time by natural supplies. Evidence exists that people were constructing small dams by 7000 B.C. in early attempts at irrigated agriculture. This same activity, the altering of the space-time occurrence of water, is referred to today as *engineering regulation,* or merely *regulation.*

The benefits from a modern dam project can be multiple, and may include water for municipal supplies, industry, or irrigation; hydroelectric power; flood control; low-flow augmentation for pollution control; improved navigation; and recreation (Fig. 6.11). In many Highly Developed Countries a large proportion of the total stream runoff has been brought under some degree of regulation. The Missouri and Tennessee in the United States are rivers that now consist largely of a series of regulated impoundments.

Large-scale investments in water management facilities are essential for any developing region or nation. Yet, internal capital for such projects is

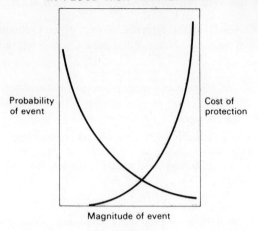

PROBABILITY AND CHOICE
IN FLOOD RISK MANAGEMENT

Probability
of event

Cost of
protection

Magnitude of event

Figure 6.9   The planner's dilemma. Many natural hazards, such as floods, follow a probability model shown by the curve on the left. The question becomes: how does one buy the best protection with limited funds or resources? As the size of the flood increases, the cost of protection rises rapidly. But, the protection costs must be paid every year, while a devastating, low-probability flood may occur this year or not for 100 years. Natural hazard risk management is a most difficult decision problem facing many communities. (Source: Adapted from Elliott W. Montroll and Wade W. Badger, "Introduction to Quantitative Aspects of Social Phenomena, *Gordon and Breach Science Publishers, New York, p. 137.)*

often difficult to generate, since investments in public utilities create long-range, instead of short-range, economic benefits.

A principal concern today is the ecological consequence of water engineering regulation.[4] The question becomes: to what degree are long-range, sometimes irreversible losses (negative externalities) caused by dams or other water engineering projects? Detrimental environmental effects may not be anticipated during the planning and design stages of the project. The vast Indus River irrigation system in Pakistan is an example of a large, water-engineering project in which unforeseen environmental deterioration has

[4]Joseph H. Butler, "Geomorphology and Decision-Making in Water Resource Engineering," Chapter 5 in Donald R. Coates (Ed.), *Environmental Geomorphology,* Publications in Geomorphology, State University of New York, Binghamton, N.Y., 1971.

Figure 6.10   Aerial view of the greatest flood in the history of Kansas City, Missouri, that occurred in July 1951. The long, white arc swinging across the bottom of the picture is the Central Industrial District flood wall. (Source: U.S. Army Corp of Engineers.)

occurred. During the 1930s, under British sponsorship, one of the largest irrigation systems in the world was planned and constructed in the Indus River Valley. It later became apparent that the large amounts of water diverted from the natural river channel to irrigate fields over vast areas were causing two related problems: a rising water table and the accumulation of surface salts. Today, large areas of Pakistan are agriculturally unproductive because of this unanticipated environmental change.

In urban-industrial nations, the locational link between natural water occurrence and economic activity may appear less obvious than in primitive economies. As a nation develops economically and accumulates capital, it can build larger dams, sink deeper wells, construct longer canals, and so on.

Figure 6.11   Boulder (Hoover) Dam on the Colorado River between Nevada and Arizona. Completed in the early 1930s, this multiple-purpose river project became a model for river basin development projects in many parts of the world.

The result is an increased ability to store and move large volumes of water at very low unit costs. In this way the highly developed region can, at least within certain limits, overcome local water deficits by importing from other regions. An example is the movement of water from the Feather River in humid Northern California to the semi-arid Metropolitan Los Angeles Water District, a distance of over 500 miles.

Nevertheless, the influence of water availability on the location of economic activity does exist in highly developed countries. Australia is an example of a Highly Developed Country in which population and economic

150   ENVIRONMENTAL FACTORS INFLUENCING ECONOMIC ACTIVITY

activity are spatially correlated with surface and groundwater supplies. In the United States, most parts of the arid and semi-arid West support few people and only limited economic activity. (The notable exception to this is Metropolitan Los Angeles, but this region, as noted above, imports water from humid regions many hundreds of miles distant.)

WATER AND URBAN DEVELOPMENT

Since people need water daily to sustain life, every community has an absolute minimum water requirement. The ecological concept of water as a limiting factor also applies to the economic function of settlements. Note that this environmental consideration contrasts with, but supplements, Christaller's Central Place explanation for urban distributions in Chapter 4.

COON ON WATER AND VILLAGE LIFE IN THE MIDDLE EAST

Anthropologist Carleton Coon, in a study of contemporary life in the Middle East, stressed the critical role of water as an influence on village size and location.

The location of the village, then, depends on water. . . . There must be sufficient permanent water for drinking, watering the animals, cooking, an occasional bath, and if possible operating a grist mill. . . .

Water will also determine the minimum size of a village. The supply must be more than enough for a single biological family . . . because such a family cannot perform all the tasks needed in the peasant economy at the proper times. . . . A dozen households is about as small as a village can be and still function and perpetuate itself.*

* Carleton Coon, *Caravan: The Story of the Middle East,* New York, H. Holt and Co., 1958, pp. 174, 175.

Towns and cities require the removal of waste water as well as the provision of reliable water supplies. The ability of people to live crowded together in dense urban populations depends now, as it always has, on the control of waterborne diseases.

The water supply and sewerage systems developed by ancient Rome are timeless models of urban water management. The ecological interaction between public health and city size can be traced for centuries in the history of the Roman capital. By 312 B.C., the city had outgrown its local water supply and the Tiber River had become badly polluted. From then until 305 A.D. a total of fourteen aqueduct systems were built to serve the capital, having an aggregate length of 359 miles. By 305 A.D. the water supply system also included 247 reservoirs and furnished the city of Rome with 50 million gallons per day. This supply served over 900 public baths and more than 1200 public fountains.

Waste water disposal in Rome was another prodigious undertaking. The size and complexity of the Roman sewerage system was comparable to that of the water system. At its peak the population of the city of Rome probably exceeded a million persons. Large water supply and sewerage systems were also built by the Romans in Paris, Lyons, Metz, Seville, Segovia, and other cities within the Empire.

The military and political collapse of the Roman world in the West was accompanied by the disintegration of administrative structures supporting the urban water systems throughout the Empire. As a consequence, aqueducts, distribution networks, and other system structures deteriorated and fell into disuse. Lack of potable (drinkable) municipal water supplies and unchecked water pollution contributed to the de-urbanization of the former Empire, a process that set the stage for a thousand years of feudalism in Western Europe. During the Dark and Middle Ages, waterborne pathogenic organisms caused wave after wave of deaths from typhoid fever, dysentery, and cholera.

By the time the New World was opened up to European settlement, the beginnings of modern hydrology and water management began to appear in Europe. In the late fifteenth and early sixteenth centuries, municipal water works were introduced in some of the growing urban centers of England and Germany. Lead pipes were first used in the London water system around the time of Shakespeare. Mechanical pumping was begun in Hanover in 1627, and shortly after that in London. Advances in water engineering and management diffused to America and to other parts of the world, permitting large increases in city size. In the United States, the first municipal water works was built in Boston in 1652, using wooden conduits.

By the early 1800s, under the growing impetus of the Industrial Revolution, large numbers of people in Europe and North America began migrating to the new industrial towns and cities looking for employment. To meet the new public health demands, a simple strategy was adopted—the removal of wastes by dilution in water, and the gravity flow of the sewage to the nearest body of water. Under this method, the harmful effects (negative externalities) were spatially dispersed. The natural waste assimilation capacity of the receiving water bodies was taken for granted as a "free good."

By 1900 England became the first "urbanized" nation, and the Twentieth Century ushered in an era of accelerated city growth. Agglomerations of people grew that never would have been possible without the dual life-support systems of filtered municipal water supplies and waste water removal by sewerage systems.

As cities grew, the surface and subsurface water resources within them became inadequate, and, as in the case of Rome, they began to reach out far beyond their borders to secure additional supplies. By 1842, for example, New York City (then Manhattan Island only) was unable to extract enough water from local wells and ponds, and constructed the Croton water system, which tapped supplies 40 miles north of the city. Subsequent growth, together with the annexation of Brooklyn and other adjoining boroughs, required a further reaching out for new water supplies, first to the Catskill region in 1915, and then, after World War II, to the Delaware River Basin, 125 miles away. New York City (not the entire metropolitan area, but the city alone) now requires watersheds totalling 1969 square miles to supply the water needs of its residents, who are concentrated on fewer than 300 square miles.

ENVIRONMENTAL FACTORS INFLUENCING THE LOCATION
OF COTTON PRODUCTION IN SOUTHEASTERN U.S.

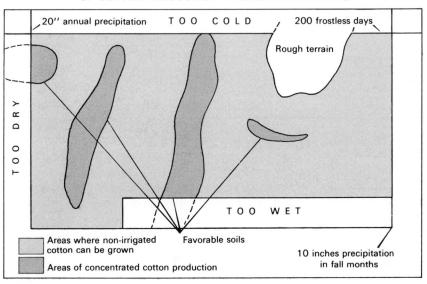

Figure 6.12   The spatial pattern of cotton production has been influenced by: (1) The length of the growing season, (2) the annual and fall season precipitation, (3) the location of particular soils, and (4) the location of rough terrain. The location of environmental influences and limiting boundaries are shown here schematically, along with areas of potential and actual cotton production. (Source: Harold H. McCarty and James B. Lindberg, A Preface to Economic Geography, Prentice Hall, Englewood Cliffs, N.J., 1966 Figure 11-2, p. 220.)

The interurban competition for water supplies in humid regions, while by no means as critical as that in arid regions, does nevertheless exist. A competition, for example, exists between New York City and Philadelphia over the use of the Delaware River water.

Looking into the future and projecting current use patterns within the United States indicates a growing supply problem. For example, the projected water requirement for metropolitan Miami will be an estimated 1.4 billion gallons a day by 1995. By then, under present plans, it will require a watershed area of 2800 square miles to supply Dade County, which contains Miami. This represents an area as large as the Everglades from Lake Okeechobee to Cape Sable.

It is clear from projecting urban water demands into the future that new approaches are going to be necessary. One approach is the use of higher-cost, alternative sources of water, including desalinized sea water and treated waste water. Experience in Santee, California, suggests that political and psychological resistance to recycled waste water is not an insurmountable obstacle.

Thus far we have concentrated on individual environmental factors. In reality, two or more of these factors often combine to influence economic location and activity within a region. Figure 6.12 shows schematically how environmental factors have combined to influence the location of nonirrigated cotton production in the Southeastern United States.

SUMMARY

Spatially variable environmental factors can have direct or indirect influences on economic activity. *Photosynthesis* is essential for biological production and, ultimately, for economic production. The spatial patterns of solar energy and fresh water are fundamental influences on human settlement and economic location. The uneven distribution of mineral resources gives some regions of the world great advantages for mineral based industries and energy production. The effects of slope as a constraint on most forms of economic activity can be observed throughout the world. Intensive economic production and high population densities are generally found in places having level or near-level terrain. Soil type and natural vegetation can be important factors affecting land use. The availability and quality of surface and groundwater supplies continues to be a primary influence on the location and character of economic activity. In Highly Developed Countries capital investment is often used to relieve local environmental deficiencies or to enhance economic production. Nevertheless, the major urban-industrial regions of the world have been developed in areas enjoying favorable combinations of climate, land forms, and other environmental factors.

Questions

1 Compare the world distribution of population with the distribution of arid climates and solar energy deficits.

2 Examine a large-scale topographic map (such as a U.S. Geological Survey grid) of your home community—or some other familiar area—and relate land use to topography.

3 What are some environmental characteristics of the humid tropical regions of the world that may prove to be economic advantages or disadvantages over the coming two decades?

4 Contrast the environmental quality of the United States and USSR for agricultural production.

5 Give examples of the influence of soil types on the historical settlement patterns in America.

6 Describe the geographic pattern of natural water surplus and deficit in the United States, and relate it to the patterns of population density and economic activity. How does the Los Angeles region of California overcome its natural water deficit?

7

AGRICULTURAL SYSTEMS AND WORLD FOOD PRODUCTION

*"A farm with good soil usually commands a better price than one of the same size with poor soil, but only if their locations are equal. The rockiest pasture ten miles from Boston is more valuable than the finest black loam in Central Illinois."**

The provision of food is humanity's most important economic activity. Approximately half the world labor force consists of farmers and farm workers. Nutritional deficiency is perhaps the most widespread cause of human suffering in the world today. Among other things, where malnutrition exists, human resources are diminished for productive effort. Clearly, attempts to alleviate the world food problem deserve the highest priorities. Since agriculture forms the economic base for commercial, industrial, and urban development, a better knowledge of world agriculture provides a foundation for understanding the global economy.

THE DIFFUSION OF WORLD AGRICULTURE

The land under permanent cultivation is only a fraction of the total inhabited area of the globe (Fig. 7.1). The world average cultivated area per capita is now about one acre. However, arable land is distributed very unevenly among the nations (Table 7.1).

The present pattern of agricultural land use around the globe is the outcome of a ten thousand year space-time process of *spatial diffusion* (Chapter

---

*Jean Gottmann, *Megalopolis: The Urbanized Northeastern Seaboard of the United States,* The M.I.T. Press, Cambridge, Mass., 1961, p. 263. © 1961 by The Twentieth Century Fund, Inc.

156

Table 7.1   *Arable Land Per Capita[a] in Selected Countries, 1977*

Country	Acres of Arable Land Per Capita
Australia	8.10
Canada	4.62
Argentina	3.31
USSR	2.22
United States	2.15
Chile	1.36
Denmark	1.31
Mexico	1.09
Tanzania	0.94
Nigeria	0.89
France	0.86
Brazil	0.79
India	0.64
Zaire	0.59
Italy	0.54
Saudi Arabia	0.37
China	0.37
Israel	0.30
United Kingdom	0.30
Egypt	0.20
Netherlands	0.15
Japan	0.10

[a]This table does not reflect variations in the quality of arable land.

Source: Adapted from Food and Agricultural Organization of the United Nations, *Production Yearbook 1977.*

2). Of all the thousands of potentially edible plants in Man's environment, relatively few have been cultivated as a source of food. The earliest civilizations were based on a few key grains: wheat, oats, rye and barley in the Middle East, Europe, and North Africa; rice, wheat and millet in South and East Asia; and corn (maize) in Pre-Columbian America. The cereal grains are highly nutritious, are less bulky and less perishable than other foods, and are easy to store and ship. So successful were these grains that they remain to this day among the great food staples of the world (Table 7.2).

Paradoxically, the diffusion of crops throughout the world did not result in the successful adoption of many middle latitude staples in the humid tropics. For example, in the tropics high soil temperatures have been shown

APPROXIMATE LOCATIONS OF PERMANENTLY CULTIVATED LAND

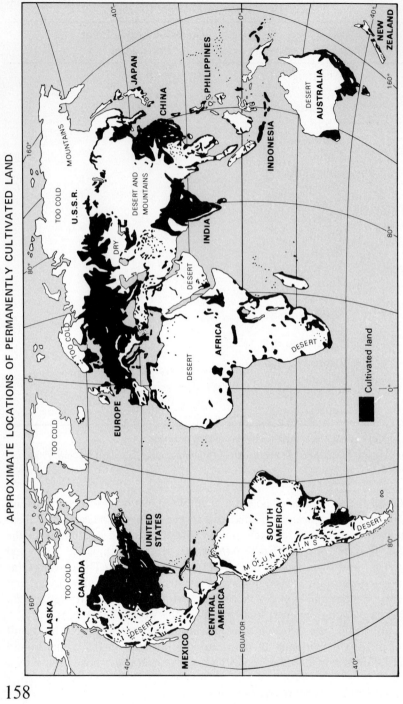

158

Figure 7.1   (see facing page) Four great concentrations are conspicuous in the northern hemisphere—all in humid regions with ample growing seasons. These are also the regions of great population densities (see Fig. 2.2). (Source: U.S. Department of Agriculture, Office of Foreign Agricultural Relations.)

Table 7.2   Major Producing Nations of the Principal Grains

	WHEAT	
	Production (Thousand Metric Tons)	
Place	**1961–1965 Average**	**1976**
World	254,427	418,383
USSR	64,207	96,900
United States	33,040	58,307
China	22,230	43,001
India	11,191	28,846
Canada	15,364	23,587
Turkey	8,585	16,578
France	12,495	16,150
Australia	8,222	11,713
Argentina	7,541	11,200
RICE		
World	255,324	350,260
China	88,138	129,054
India	52,733	64,363
Indonesia	12,396	23,300
Bangladesh	15,048	17,627
Thailand	11,267	15,800
Japan	16,444	15,292
Vietnam	9,629	10,800
Brazil	6,123	9,560
Burma	7,786	9,307
Korea, Republic of	4,809	7,243
Philippines	3,957	6,455
United States	3,084	5,246
MAIZE (Corn)		
World	216,291	334,276
United States	95,561	159,173

Table 7.2 (continued)

	MAIZE (Corn)	
	Production (Thousand Metric Tons)	
Place	**1961–1965 Average**	**1976**
China	22,636	33,114
Brazil	10,112	17,845
Romania	5,853	11,583
USSR	13,122	10,138
Yugoslavia	5,618	9,106
Mexico	7,369	8,308
South Africa	5,248	7,312
India	4,593	6,257

Source: Adapted from *United Nations Statistical Yearbook 1977.*

to cause deterioration of the tubers in potatoes. Tubers will not grow at all in soil temperatures above 84 degrees F (29 degrees C). Research has shown that the high temperatures below ground in the tropics destroy the roots of certain plants. Some researchers believe that properly designed irrigation would allow tropical countries to grow such middle-latitude vegetables as peas, broccoli, lettuce, and cabbage. Another problem with tropical climates for many middle latitude crops is the lack of cool night temperatures. This explains, for example, why tomato production is low in the humid tropics. The night temperatures there remain above the optimal fruit-setting range.

Until Columbus' voyage, the plants cultivated for food in the New World differed totally from those in the Old World. However, the linking of the two hemispheres and the subsequent contact of peoples and cultures stimulated the diffusion of crops. Transported species often did better in their new environments, and this led to great increases in the ability of certain regions to support populations. The potato is a good example. When it was carried from its place of origin in South America to northern Europe, it became a very successful food staple that permitted rapid population increases. The population rise in Ireland was drastically reversed, however, when the potato-blight organism ruined crops overnight in the 1840s and created a catastrophic succession of famines.

Except for the turkey, North America received all its livestock and poultry species from the Old World. Corn (maize), found only in the New World before Columbus, is now grown in many places around the globe. Grain sorghum, which came to America from Africa on slave ships, has become a top-ranking feed grain in the United States.

The process of crop and animal diffusion and the resulting productive increases have been more dynamic than ever in recent years. The soybean, for example, introduced commercially into the United States from China, is now a leading farm export from the United States.

In addition to the principal grains—wheat, rice, and corn (maize)—other food crops that have chief world importance today are: three root crops—potato, sweet potato, and cassava; two sugars—beet and cane; four legumes—peas, beans, peanuts, and soybeans; and, two tree or tree-like crops—coconuts and bananas. These few plant species provide the bulk of food today. With the exception of the coconut and banana, the plants listed above are annuals, which are planted, grow, produce food, and die in one season. Unlike trees, annual plants are short-rooted and therefore cannot tap soil nutrients that lie more than a short distance below the surface.

GENERAL CHARACTERISTICS OF AGRICULTURE

Crops, agricultural techniques, farm size, yields (output per acre), productivity (output per man hour), and farm incomes all vary from place to place throughout the world. To some degree this is the result of political and social forces. For example, the *Latifundia* system of large estates has impeded the upgrading of peasant agriculture in much of Latin America since the conquest.

Great differences also exist in diets from place to place in the world. In industrialized nations many people overeat to the point of shortening their lives. On the other hand, the diets of most people in Less Developed Countries are based largely on grains, often with a critical shortage of protein. Diets in the Highly Developed Countries, which contain many animal products, require much more agricultural land per person. About 70 percent of the food ingested by grazing animals is used by them for energy simply in moving about. Only part of the remainder is available as food for human consumption. Animal grazing is therefore an inefficient use of scarce arable land, and is rarely found in the crowded parts of Asia.

Unlike manufacturing, commerce, and mining, which are concentrated in space, farming has a very large spatial requirement. Since a great deal of land is required per unit of output, agriculture is a poor competitor for sites that are also attractive for more concentrated forms of economic activity. Agriculture's high land requirement also means that distance costs have a critical bearing on agricultural land-use at all scales, from individual farm layout to world regionalization of production. This forms the basis for von Thünen's land use model (Chapter 4). All over the world, kitchen gardens, which require much hand labor and frequent visits, are invariably located as close as possible to the farm dwellings to minimize the amount of human energy and time expended in tending and harvesting them.

Space requirements in agriculture are affected by input factor prices and substitution. A bushel of rice can be grown by using much land and capital and with very little labor; or, it can be grown with little land and capital, but with much labor. This is a very important consideration in economic geography, because different combinations of factor inputs can have different optimal locations.

A characteristic of agriculture in most parts of the world is the existence of relatively small producing units. The majority of peasant farmers and farm workers in the world live, not on individual farmsteads as in the United States and certain other countries, but in rural villages from which they travel daily to surrounding fields. The bulk of India's population, for example, lives in *half a million* farm villages—a fact of profound implications for that nation's spatial economy.

In many Less Developed Countries the fragmentation of farm plots leads to many difficulties, including reduced farm income. This can be explained in terms of spatial efficiency. If one of a farmer's plots is a long distance from the main dwelling, it will yield relatively low return, because so much of the farmer's time and effort must be spent in travelling to and from the plot with tools, equipment, and so on. If this plot is nearer *another* farmer's dwelling, however, it could generate a higher return for the second farmer. This is why the consolidation of fragmented holdings into more efficient units should be an important part of rural land policy in the Less Developed Countries.

As noted in Chapter 2, people living in Highly Developed Countries and in the more modernized parts of the Less Developed World are tied together by trade that links regions of specialization. These regions have comparative advantage for the commodities in which they specialize, such as wheat, beef, wool, dairy products, coffee, tea, or cotton. Trade provides low cost access to worldwide food supplies for the people in the HDC's. On the other hand, in LDC's people living in small, isolated farm villages are not part of the world exchange economy. Here, virtually all the food consumed is locally produced by labor-intensive methods.

It needs to be emphasized that the location and character of agriculture are influenced by the interaction of spatial and environmental factors. An example at the international level would be the case of European agricultural land use. Western Europe has long displayed a strongly developed zonation around an intensively farmed inner core centered on the Low Countries. This part of Europe enjoys both a highly productive agricultural environment and low cost accessibility to great urban and export markets, with both advantages tending to reinforce each other (Fig. 7.2).

There are many ways of classifying world agriculture. For our purposes, a simple, economically oriented classification is used, consisting of three highly contrasted agriculture systems that together represent the great bulk of world farming activity (Fig. 7.3). The first system is called *shifting cultivation*, which is prevalent over much of the world's thinly populated tropical forests. The second is *intensive subsistence farming* found throughout South and East Asia, where half the world's population presses heavily on very limited agricultural land. The third system is *capital intensive agriculture* in the industrialized nations.

SHIFTING CULTIVATION IN THE TROPICAL FORESTS

Large regions in the humid tropics of the world still support shifting subsistence cultivators (Fig 7.4). These primitive farmers represent a way of life that has, in many ways, remained unchanged for thousands of years.

Variants of shifting cultivation were once the prevalent forms of agriculture over much of Europe and other forested regions of the world. In the Middle Ages it was practiced in Britain, where it was called "swiddening," a derivative of an Old Norse word meaning to "singe," and it persisted in remote parts of Sweden until well into this century. Shifting cultivation is called by different names in different places around the world. *Slash and burn* is a widespread term; in Latin America, the common expression is *milpa*.

Shifting cultivation requires very large areas of land. Labor inputs are only sporadically intensive. The capital input is extremely limited; the hoe

INTENSITY OF AGRICULTURAL PRODUCTION IN EUROPE

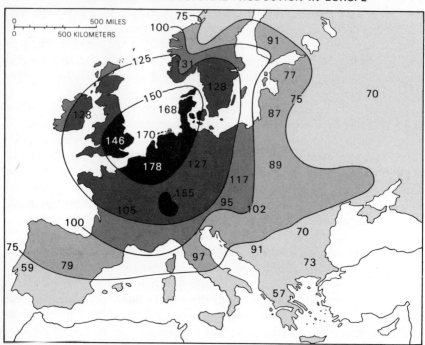

Figure 7.2   The index of 100 is the average European yield per acre of eight main crops: wheat, rye, barley, oats, corn, potatoes, sugar beets, and hay. The region of highest intensity has a productive climate, level topography, and good soils (Ricardian environmental advantages), and contains London, Amsterdam, Paris, Hamburg, Rotterdam, Copenhagen, and other great urban markets (Thünen market accessibility). In the outer fringes of Europe—southern Spain, southern Italy, northwestern British Isles, northern Scandinavia and the Balkans—both environmental and spatial factors are less favorable, the combination of economic rent and location rent per agricultural acre is correspondingly lower, and rural population densities are less. (Source: Adapted from S. van Valkenburg and C. C. Held, Europe, 1952, John Wiley and Sons, New York, Map A, p. 102.)

and digging stick are used commonly as the principal tools. Studies in the field by anthropologists, geographers, and others in recent years have dispelled much of the ignorance surrounding shifting agriculture. No longer is the stereotype valid that holds it to be a very simple, inefficient, and wasteful

MODELS OF THREE CONTRASTING AGRICULTURAL SYSTEMS

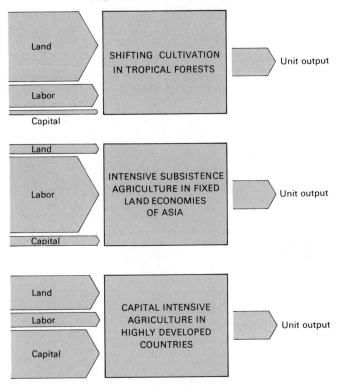

Figure 7.3 "Land" and "Labor" represent the natural environment and direct human inputs, respectively. "Capital" includes tools, equipment, machines, and the like. The width of the input bars should not be interpreted numerically; these bars indicate typical proportions of factor inputs used in each system. In the capital intensive model, considerable variations of input levels would exist in different countries. The characteristic feature, however, is the large-scale replacement of hand labor by mechanized equipment, whether in "land rich" HDC's, such as New Zealand, Canada, or the United States, or in HDC's with very limited land resources, such as The Netherlands. In regions where the capital intensive system is found, the productivity and incomes of the farmers are much higher than in the two other systems.

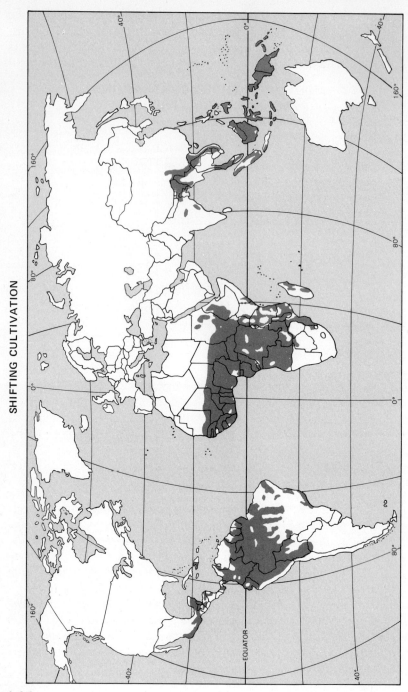

Figure 7.4 (see facing page) The shaded portion of the map includes some areas where nonshifting forms of primitive subsistence agriculture exist. Around the fringes of the regions shown, the two types are sometimes interspersed.

PELZER'S DEFINITION OF SHIFTING CULTIVATION

Shifting cultivation has been defined by geographer K. J. Pelzer as, "an economy of which the main characteristics are rotation of fields rather than crops; clearing by means of fire; absence of draught animals and of manuring; use of human labor only; employment of the dibble stick or hoe; short periods of soil occupancy alternating with long fallow periods."*

*Pioneer Settlement in the Asiatic Tropics, American Geographical Society, New York, 1945, p. 17.

---

system. Instead, this age-old form of subsistence farming, even when practiced by illiterate peoples, is a sophisticated production system requiring an intimate knowledge of soil, climate, and other environmental factors (Fig. 1.1).

In shifting cultivation Man replaces part of the natural bio-mass with other species of plants that supply food and other useful material such as gourds, poles for house and fence construction, matting, thatch, fuel, and possibly even cotton for garments. All this is done without the benefit of machines or inanimate forms of energy, except fire. The principal mechanism for maintaining soil fertility and yields—shifting production from one forest clearing to another every few years—is based on the very low storage capacity of lateritic soils for water and nutrients (Fig. 6.7). While the trees have roots that can tap nutrients deep in the tropical soils, the small, annual plants making up most food crops have roots that are short and therefore rapidly deplete the upper few inches of soil, particularly of phosphorus, after two or three years of cultivation. (Where alluvial, volcanic, or other special soils are present, this is not a problem.)

Many variants of the system have evolved over the centuries in different parts of the world, but the shifting mechanism remains the fundamental response to fertility decline in all. In every case a selected portion of the forest, after a careful weighing of many factors, is partially cleared by slashing the bush and small trees, and by girding the larger ones (cutting an incision around the tree that severs the life-sustaining cambium layer just beneath the bark, and ultimately kills the tree). At the end of the driest part of the year, the slash is burned. Burning this material forms a loose and friable soil, enriched with ashes containing the vital minerals, in which the cultivator can plant with a simple digging stick. The beneficial effects of the burn—fertilizing the land and destroying the weeds—decrease over time. (In some cases where the slash is too moist to burn, as in the Chocó region of Colombia, it is removed by hand or allowed to remain and rot.) After a few years of continual cultivation and declining yields, the garden patch is abandoned and the forest takes over and restores the natural fertility after about two decades or so. Meanwhile, the farmer has cleared other patches for cultivation.

The diet of shifting cultivators, particularly if supplemented by poultry and swine as scavengers, can be not only very nutritious, but greatly varied as well. Because it is organic farming, this system supplies trace elements vital to health that are often missing in processed foods.[1]

The size of settlements in a shifting cultivation economy is normally small. The communities are hamlets or dispersed settlements of fifty to a few hundred inhabitants each. Not only are the gardens changed every few years, but the houses or the whole community may be moved as well from time to time, depending on circumstances. This means that the distance factor is

---

COLIN CLARK ON THE KEY ROLE OF TRANSPORT

In view of their low incomes and sporadic labor input, one may wonder why shifting cultivators and other subsistence farmers in the tropics do not produce more for commercial sale. Agricultural economist Colin Clark provides this explanation, drawn from experience in Africa:

... *most of the cultivators in Africa are still only occupied for a fraction of what we would regard as a normal working year—two to four hours a day, on the average. Then why do they not produce more? The reason is that there are limits to the amount a subsistence cultivator wishes to, indeed is able to eat, and that if he has any more output he would have great difficulty in selling it, if he has to carry all his produce a long distance to market on his head. The first and most urgent step required to improve the position of the subsistence cultivator is the provision of transport. It is not until roads and vehicles are available, and also an adequate supply of industrial products at reasonable prices to exchange for his produce, that the farmer is willing to produce anything substantially above his own family's subsistence requirements.**

* Colin Clark, *Population Growth and Land Use,* St. Martin's Press, Inc., MacMillan & Co., Ltd., 1967, p. 139.

---

[1] The decline in soil fertility and crop yields over time affects only the quantity of food produced, not its nutritional quality.

AGRICULTURAL SYSTEMS AND WORLD FOOD PRODUCTION

always an important one in the community decision process. The natural tendency is to clear and farm the forest near the dwellings. Transport costs to and from the nearby gardens are thus minimized. As the nearby garden plots becomes exhausted, cultivation must be carried on farther away, where the transport costs to and from the plots are greater. This is another example of the familiar trade-off between production costs and transport costs.

Soil exhaustion and erosion are common land-use problems around permanent towns and cities throughout the humid tropics. Studies by the East African Royal Commission have shown that cultivation near coastal villages resulted in serious damage to the forest, while land remained uncleared farther inland because of the higher transport costs.

Throughout the realm of shifting cultivation certain forces are tending to modify or eliminate the system. These are forces both internal and external to the system. The external forces include the impact of the jet age culture, and mainly affect the younger members of the community. Outside institutional influences can also be very strong. The national policies of some countries call for strenuous efforts to "modernize" the remaining subsistence cultivators.

Perhaps the most important influence of change is an internal one, although it too is derived from the outside in the form of more effective disease control. This is the pervasive force of population growth, which creates a system disequilibrium. Deterioration of the agricultural base, we have seen, results from a too-rapid rotation of the more accessible forest land under pressure to produce more food. The overall regional system is not likely to collapse suddenly. Changes will come about first in areas that are more accessible to outside economic activity, such as coastal zones, river valleys, islands, and other places on the fringes of the world exchange economy.

LABOR-INTENSIVE AGRICULTURE IN THE FIXED-LAND ECONOMIES OF ASIA

It is a fact of profound world significance that over half of all humanity lives in South and East Asia. The land use that makes this possible is a form of largely subsistence agriculture (Fig. 7.5). This type of farming is extremely labor-intensive, and the economies of South and East Asia are, for the most part, severely land-limited or *fixed land* in character.[2]

---

[2] Some authors include the Valleys of the Tigris-Euphrates and the Nile, in present-day Iraq and Egypt, in a classification of labor-intensive, subsistence agriculture. There are also grounds for including some agricultural economies surrounding the Mediterranean and elsewhere in this category. However, here we concentrate attention on the huge farming population in South and East Asia.

INTENSIVE SUBSISTENCE CULTIVATION

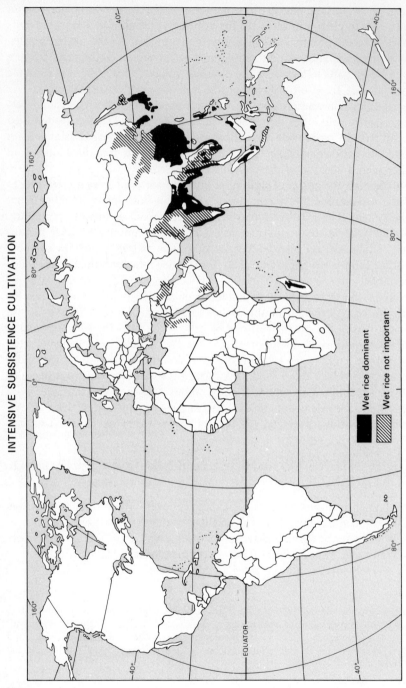

Wet rice dominant

Wet rice not important

170

Figure 7.5 (see facing page) This map is necessarily generalized and includes farming of a partly commercial nature as well as truly subsistence farming. In all cases, however, the distinguishing characteristic is extremely large amounts of hand labor required per unit of output.

LONG-INHABITED, DENSELY POPULATED AGRICULTURAL LANDSCAPES

The lands of South and East Asia have been inhabited by agriculturalists for thousands of years. As food-producing techniques became more efficient over the centuries, population densities increased. In turn, as population expanded, it forced the intensification of production on the limited arable land already under cultivation. The resulting agricultural system requires prodigious inputs of human labor to substitute for the paucity of both cultivable land and capital.

Most of the people in this part of the world are peasant farmers who dwell in over a million rural farm villages (Fig 7.6). Agricultural technology, methods of storage, marketing methods and modes of travel have changed suprisingly little over the centuries.

The chief occupation of these farmers is simply growing enough food and other agricultural products for survival. The bulk of the food grown consists of cereal grains and vegetables for home consumption. Only a very small proportion of total agricultural output moves out of the region or leaves the country as exports.

The dense rural populations of these countries are concentrated on the limited level or terraced areas that have adequate water for irrigation. Rural population densities in the productive areas run very high, sometimes exceeding 2,000 per square mile. This gives very low ratios of arable land to agricultural worker in this part of the world (see Table 7.1).

Because of the very large inputs of labor required by agriculture, productivity and per capita incomes remain low (see Table 2.2). With a preponderance of persons making their living in low-income agriculture the national economies, except for Japan and a few others, have the characteristics of Less Developed Countries. The low level of economic surpluses results in low rates of capital formation. Lack of capital investment in mechanized transport means high cost movement of commodities, and this inhibits regional trade based on specialization.

The literature contains countless references to the influence of the physical environment on agriculture in Asia. As expected, the climate becomes more productive (growing season lengthens and temperatures rise) in a southerly direction. As a result, where water is present, the economic rent and the price of the land increase toward the south. A farming family in the southern

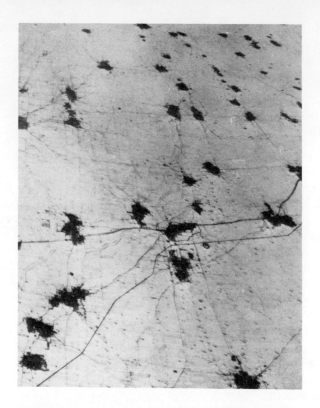

Figure 7.6   This remarkable oblique air photo was taken over the North China Plain in 1943. A light snow has fallen, which has melted in places, showing the spatial pattern of agricultural villages, connecting roads and trails, and even, in the foreground, the outlines of the individual fields. (Source: U.S. Air Force Photo.)

part of Japan can subsist on about one hectare (2.47 acres) of lowland soil. Farm sizes are much larger on the northern island of Hokkaido.

Large stretches of level or gently rolling agricultural land, such as those in the North American Midwest, the Argentine Pampa, or Russia's Ukraine, are missing in South and East Asia. Over 80 percent of the islands of Japan are too steeply sloped for cultivation. Where conditions permit, it has been the practice to actually "create" level land by building and maintaining earth terraces by hand (Fig. 7.7). Combining the climatic, topographic, and soil factors, an extraordinary correlation is found between river flood plains and deltas, on the one hand, and agricultural production on the other. (A

Figure 7.7   The famed Banawe rice terraces in the mountainous Ifugao Province of the Philippines. The terraces, buttressed by reddish clay walls, are among the most extensive in the world. First developed 2000 years ago, they are still in use, although their intricate irrigation system needs constant maintenance. Even if capital were available for large, mechanized farm equipment, it could not be used on such terraces. (Source: United Nations.)

notable exception would be the high population density and intensive agricultural production on the rich soils of volcanic origin on the Island of Java in Indonesia.)

THE SPECIAL ROLE OF LOWLAND (PADDY) RICE

The spatial patterns of agricultural production and population density throughout South and East Asia are directly related to the critical role played by *lowland* or *paddy rice*. It is difficult for anyone who comes from a supermarket economy to realize what rice means in this part of the world. From the standpoint of food production per unit of land farmed, nothing compares to irrigated rice. Careful measurements have shown rice production in Japan to have a photosynthetic efficiency approaching an absolute maximum.

Ideal soils for rice are alluvium, two to three feet deep, with a clay subsoil to keep the water from draining down too fast. However, the roots of lowland rice are able to obtain sufficient nutrients from even poor soils. On soils of low quality, if weeds can be suppressed and the fields flooded with a few inches of water during the growing stage (both requiring great hand labor), one or even two crops of rice can be grown year after year with no artificial fertilizer.

Most varieties of paddy rice are transplanted from seed beds to save space. Transplanting of the three week old rice plants requires so much stoop labor that it is rarely practiced outside Asia (Fig. 7.8). Where the temperature, hydrology, or topography are unsuitable for paddy rice, other grains are grown on the productive land: wheat, barley, sorghums, and dry (upland) rice. Near the village dwellings are found the garden vegetables; beans, peas, corn, peanuts, yams, sugar cane, and melons are typical crops.

Figure 7.8   Farm worker in central Java, Indonesia, transplanting rice plants, one by one, into an irrigated field. This is the ultimate in labor-intensive agriculture, contrasting with mechanized rice production in California and other places with capital-intensive agriculture. (Source: *United Nations.*)

In many places, hogs, chickens, or ponded fish, such as carp, are kept as scavengers and sources of animal protein.

A comparison of rice farming in the Far East and the United States makes an interesting and instructive case study. Rice farms in the United States are the most highly mechanized and capital intensive in the world, requiring less than two man hours of labor per acre for all growing and harvesting operations. By contrast, in Asia a labor requirement of more than 400 man days (9600 man hours) per acre is not uncommon.

NUTTONSON'S PRE-REVOLUTIONARY ANALYSIS OF CHINESE AGRICULTURE

Since China contains approximately a fourth of the world's population, and since over 60 percent of its people are engaged directly in farming, an analysis of its agriculture is meaningful in world terms. In 1947, two years before the Communist revolution swept through China, M. Y. Nuttonson published an analysis of Chinese agriculture.[3] This section is excerpted from that study.

[3] M. Y. Nuttonson, "Ecological Crop Geography of China . . .," International Agroclimatological Series, Study No. 7, American Institute of Crop Ecology, Washington, D.C., 1947.

Topographically, the greater part of China's land area is not suitable for cultivation. Climatically, wide stretches of the country are subject to conditions unfavorable to crop production. On the whole, less than one-fifth of the total area of China is under cultivation. The cultivated land is estimated to represent less than one-half of the crop acreage of the United States, yet China feeds a population more than three times as large.

Two-thirds of the entire population of China is engaged in agriculture and the average farm unit consists of less than five acres of land. The small farm is frequently expected to provide not only food but also clothing for the entire household. Since production of cereals and vegetables for direct human consumption is more economical than growing of feed for livestock, the latter is of relatively minor importance in the agricultural economy of China. Multiple cropping consists of planting in the same field alternate rows of different crops which is done at various intervals during the year. The painstaking system, a result of land scarcity, allows various crops in different stages of development on the same parcel of land so that while one matures the other is only half developed or just being planted. To fertilize the soil, the rich silt from the numerous river channels and waterways is removed and then carefully spread over the fields.

The major crop areas of China and its only extensive level land are the plains of North China, and the basins and delta of the Yangtze river. The other important crop areas are the terraced hillsides, the river valleys, and the plateaus. Nearly all the cultivated soils are alluvial. About half of all the cultivated land is under irrigation and irrigated land is largely planted in rice. Water from the river canals is often brought to the field by farm labor using buckets or operating an endless chain. In general, as much cultivated land is devoted to rice as rainfall and irrigation facilities make possible.

The Tsingling Mountains form an approximate dividing line between regions of the most important crops of China, i.e., between the rice in the South and wheat in the North. South of the Divide abundant precipitation and warm climate often permit crop production during the entire year and two rice crops per year from the same field are not unusual. In many areas of South China even three crops per year from the same land are possible; these are usually two rice crops and one winter crop. On the other hand, in the northernmost agricultural areas of China only a single, summer crop is harvested.

The field practice in the rice growing regions is to sow rice in seedbeds and set out the seedlings in the field. In view of the laborious procedure and time required to establish such field conditions, the Chinese peasant is reluctant to rotate the rice crop with crops that may disturb these conditions.

Frequently, in order to utilize his small acreage to the fullest extent, the Chinese farmer plants his summer crop between rows of wheat. Thus, in Central China cotton seed is broadcast in the wheat field three to four weeks ahead of the wheat harvest.

In addition to the two major food crops and the main fiber crop, a great number of

176   AGRICULTURAL SYSTEMS AND WORLD FOOD PRODUCTION

other cultures are of importance in the various parts of China. The small holdings of the Chinese farmer are devoted to a variety of plant crops depending on the ecological and economical factors of a particular region.

CHINA'S AGRICULTURE TODAY

Despite massive agricultural development programs, and after three decades of radical political and institutional change, the basic elements of crop geography in China remain in many ways similar to those Nuttonson reported in 1947. Rice and wheat are still dominant in South and North China. Production of these staples and other crops, including cotton, is highly concentrated in arable lowlands, where alluvial soil and water are available. The rugged topography over much of the nation still creates a highly fragmented mosaic of productive regions separated by mountains, resulting in very high-cost transport, and consequent lack of economic integration at the national level.

The basic problem of feeding the huge and growing Chinese population remains an acute one, aggravated each year by the addition of about ten million new people. Three decades after the revolution, over 60 percent of the labor force still remains working in labor-intensive, and therefore low-productivity, agriculture. In 1979, shipments of grain from the United States to China reached significant levels.

THE DIFFICULTY OF CAPITAL SUBSTITUTION IN FIXED-LAND ECONOMIES

In terms of productivity, agriculture in Asia and in other areas of labor-intensive production is grossly inefficient.[4] In such countries as India or China, where a large proportion of the work force is engaged in low productivity agriculture, incomes—and therefore surpluses for capital investment—are very small. Even where income surplus is generated, its use to provide capital as a substitute for labor is often constrained by plot size and environmental limitations.[5] Very often the topography is simply not suitable for tractors or other mechanized equipment. Hand-created terraces and irrigation systems would be obliterated by heavy machines.

[4] The word "efficiency" can be used in different ways when comparing agricultural systems. The general statement for efficiency is O/I, output divided by input; however, the variables I and O can stand for different things. Bushels of rice produced per acre (yield) is one measure of efficiency, while bushels of rice produced per man hour (productivity) is a very different measure. In considering per capita incomes and human welfare, the productivity of agricultural labor is a critical measure.

[5] See J. M. Blaut, "The Economic Geography of a One Acre Farm on Singapore Island," *Malayan Journal of Tropical Geography*, Vol. I, 1953, pp. 37-48.

In a few areas in Asia where incomes and capital formation permit, such as in Japan, this problem is partly overcome by a compromise with nature in which hand-operated mechanical cultivators and other small machines are used. However, in order to make such capital equipment effective, the farmers must become adequate mechanics, and must also be able to purchase fuel and spare parts. These are by no means easy to accomplish in Asian rural communities, especially since the sharp rise in petroleum prices.

This means that in the fixed-land economies of Asia, especially under present levels of population growth, it is extremely difficult for farmers to break out of a vicious circle and to make the substitution of capital and other variable inputs for human labor, a substitution that accounts for the high productivity and high farm incomes of the industrialized world. The effects of population growth on this situation are potentially ominous (see Fig. 2.8).

CAPITAL-INTENSIVE AGRICULTURE IN HIGHLY DEVELOPED COUNTRIES

THE NATURE OF CAPITAL-INTENSIVE AGRICULTURE

The third system of agricultural production (Fig. 7.3) represents a type found in the industrialized nations and in the more developed parts of certain other nations. The dominant economic feature of this type is its capital-intensive (and therefore energy-intensive) nature (Fig. 7.9). This does not mean that all farms in these regions are highly capital-intensive; there are many marginal, subsistence farms in Switzerland, Canada, and the United States. It does mean, however, that the capital-intensive farms dominate the agricultural economies in these countries and produce by far the greatest share of agricultural products that enter interregional or international trade.

Of the three models of agriculture discussed in this chapter, this one is by far the most dynamic in terms of changes in the economic landscape. Modifications can occur rapidly, particularly around the urban fringes (Fig. 1.3). The rapid development of capital intensive agriculture over the past century and its influence on regional specialization and world trade are closely related to the process of industrialization. A direct association can be made between industrial development, capital investment in agriculture, high farm productivity, and high per-capita farm incomes.

Although it is difficult to measure directly in economic terms, technological change goes hand in hand with capital investment in agriculture. The application of science to agriculture has taken many forms. An example is improved plant and animal strains. The rapidity with which these have in-

Figure 7.9   A chisel planter operated by one man in Ida County, Iowa, typical of the highly mechanized agriculture in the American Midwest. With this machine, it is not even necessary to plow prior to planting. (Source: USDA—Soil Conservation Service.)

creased productivity and yields in the industrialized world has been described as phenomenal (Fig. 7.10).

The rapid improvement of technology has had marked effects on the location as well as the character of agricultural production.[6]

New strains of drought resistant grain sorghum, sometimes called "dryland corn," rose in the late 1950s from near obscurity in the United States to the fourth largest grain crop in only a few years. More recently, an improved version of the once ignored soybean became in the 1970s a leading cash crop in the United States, and its most valuable farm export in some years. The soybean has more protein per pound than red meat and grows exceptionally fast in the United States Midwest. In recent years it has created export demand as a source of animal feed and human food. It is now found in this

[6] See, for example, H.G. Roepke, "Changes in Corn Production on the Northern Margin of the Corn Belt," *Agricultural History* 33, 1959, 126-32.

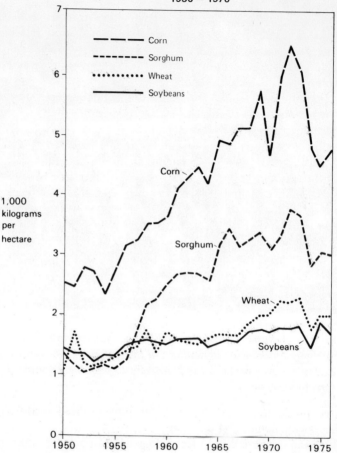

YIELD TRENDS FOR MAJOR U.S. CROPS,
1950 – 1976

1,000
kilograms
per
hectare

Corn
Sorghum
Wheat
Soybeans

Corn

Sorghum

Wheat

Soybeans

Figure 7.10   Sharp increases in agricultural yields were achieved by American farmers following World War II. The gains were due to better plant strains and to large increases in fertilizers, pesticides, irrigation systems, and improved equipment. Fluctuations in supply were mainly the result of weather or blight. (Source: Harrison Brown, The Human Future Revisited, W. W. Norton and Co., New York, 1978, Fig. 6.1, p. 126. Based on data from U.S. Dept. of Agriculture, Economic Research Service.)

country in supermarkets as a low-cost "extender" of hamburger and other higher cost foods.

Capital investment and associated technological improvements have also radically changed farm mechanization, transportation, irrigation, pest and disease control, and chemical fertilization. In contrast, improved productivities and yields have been the exception instead of the rule in labor-intensive agricultures of the Third World.

Capital intensive agriculture can be roughly divided into two sub-groups, one in nations with relatively low ratios of arable land per agricultural worker, and a second group in nations with relatively high ratios. The first group includes most European nations and Japan, which have small land areas and limited arable land supporting high population densities. These nations supply a large part of their own food and other agricultural needs by a moderately capital-intensive agriculture, but this is supplemented with purchases from abroad paid for by selling industrial exports.

The second group, which includes the United States, Canada, Australia, New Zealand, and Argentina, has very large per-capita arable land resources[7] and the comparative advantage to export large surpluses of grain, animal products or other agricultural commodities. Significantly, most of the surpluses exported by these nations are sold to European nations, or Japan, which have the foreign exchange to purchase food imports. Thus, one of the chief characteristics of capital-intensive agriculture throughout the world is that it is the main source of agricultural exports, most of which are sold to other industrialized nations.

The richer the nation, in terms of per capita income, the smaller the proportion of income spent on food, the greater the nonessential foods in the diet, and the greater the amount of land required to feed one person. The high per capita intake of meat, dairy products, and other nongrain foods in the Danish, American, or Canadian diet requires much more land per person to produce than the corn and bean diet found over much of Latin America, or the rice and vegetable diet of the Asian peasant. Compared with Asian farms, those of the industrialized nations are extremely large. In parts of the United States, the traditional 160 acre farm (one quarter of a square mile section) is no longer considered adequate to support a commercial operation.

Another feature of capital-intensive farming is the small proportion of the national labor force required to work in the agricultural sector (Fig. 7.11). A small fraction of the population in these countries can feed the nonfarming

[7] For example, up through the 1970s, over 5000 acres of potentially ideal wet rice land remained unused in the Kaitana region of New Zealand's North Island.

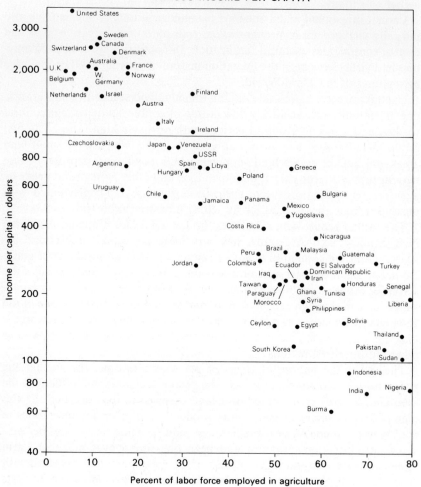

PERCENT OF LABOR FORCE IN AGRICULTURE VERSUS INCOME PER CAPITA

Figure 7.11 This graph shows the inverse correlation between per capita incomes and the percent of the labor force employed in agriculture for a large number of countries. The low incomes in the Less Developed Countries reflect the prevalence there of low productivity agriculture. (Source: World Bank, Washington, D.C., "Agriculture: Sector Working Paper," June, 1972, p. 12.)

182   AGRICULTURAL SYSTEMS AND WORLD FOOD PRODUCTION

population and often produce surpluses. In countries that have developed a capital-intensive agriculture, the trend has been for surplus rural labor to migrate to towns and cities, where the expansion of manufacturing (secondary) and service (tertiary) industries absorb them, thus keeping rural wages and incomes from becoming depressed. This adjustment is not, unfortunately, taking place in most Less Developed Countries, where population growth is maintaining high densities, underemployment, and depressed wages in the rural farm villages, which cannot be relieved in the already crowded cities.

SUBSTITUTION OF CAPITAL AND OTHER VARIABLE INPUTS FOR LIMITED LAND RESOURCES

In Highly Developed Countries with limited arable land, emphasis has been placed on the substitution of capital or other inputs for the relatively scarce land factor. While "land rich" nations such as Canada and the United States were able to develop unused land as populations grew, this was not possible for most European nations, and especially for Japan. As a result, these nations increased yields on existing cropland by the heavy application of chemical fertilizers. Countries such as Germany, the Netherlands, and Japan thus became, decades ago, heavy users of commercial fertilizers. In nations that can afford substantial expenditures for fertilizer, and have productive climates, up to 300 pounds of plant nutrients are applied per acre per year. In areas of adequate rainfall the application of chemical fertilizer can double, triple, or even quadruple the yields of intensively farmed soils. Later, as competition increased for land in the United States, it too turned more to the use of chemical fertilizers as a substitute for new land. Heavy fertilization in the United States began with World War II.

Modern irrigation systems, another form of input substitution, have been built on a massive scale in many nations. By changing the space-time flow of water through the use of dams and other engineering structures (Chapter 6), the capacity of the regions for agricultural production has been greatly improved. Capital investments in irrigation have altered the economic landscape radically in many arid parts of the world.

An extreme degree of capital substitution for land has been reached with the commercial development of chemical farming, sometimes called *hydroponics*. Here, soil is actually replaced by manufactured gravel pits containing carefully controlled plant food solutions. In this environment, all the production inputs can be controlled, and a conventional farm's output can be produced on a fraction of the area. By this method, for example, 200 to 300 tons of tomatoes can be produced from plants that would produce only a few tons by conventional farming methods.

An example of a system approaching the ultimate in "landless" farming is one that has been operating for over a decade in Austria and West Germany. Here, tower greenhouses over 100 feet in height produce flowers or high value vegetables on conveyer belts under assembly-line conditions.

THE TREND TOWARD INDUSTRIALIZED AGRICULTURE

What we really see in the Highly Developed Countries is a process of industrialization of large segments of the agricultural economy, involving heavy substitution of machines and energy for human and animal labor. In the first few decades of this century, the development of the internal combustion engine and mechanized farm machinery resulted in a quantum leap in agricultural productivity. Mechanization not only increased the farmer's output many times, but also released, in the United States alone, 70 million acres of land that had been necessary for feeding horses.

Mechanized agriculture, in ecological terms, is a highly energy-deficit operation. If we take into account the calories of energy consumed by farm machinery, the energy used to build and deliver that machinery, the energy to mine the original raw materials, and the energy to transport the crops and to fertilize and protect them by pesticides, we would find that the total exceeds by many times the calories of energy in food produced. It is thus a characteristic of capital intensive agriculture that it uses a very large amount of inanimate energy to produce one unit of food energy.[8]

In some industrialized nations, very high levels of productivity have been reached by employing automated techniques. The United States offers many examples of this. Some dairy farmers now have machine operated milking parlors where up to 60 cows can be milked each hour by one worker. On automated poultry farms, one laborer can care for 75,000 broilers. A principal strategy of Midwest American farmers operating capital-intensive enterprises is the daily and seasonal allocation of family labor inputs so that little, if any, hired labor will be required.

Computer assisted recordkeeping and production programming are being used increasingly to improve productivity. The farmer managing such operations must be a competent business manager, with a knowledge of machinery maintenance, plant and animal husbandry, and marketing.

---

[8] Significant exceptions to the extravagant use of energy in modern agriculture exist in the United States. The Amish people and certain other groups have religiously based restrictions on the use of mechanized equipment. Their large, productive farms in Pennsylvania and parts of the Midwest are truly models of energy conservation.

Other phases of farming are coming more and more to resemble highly organized industrial operations. Farmers in some parts of the United States can hire crop harvesting and other specialized machine operations. Custom combine harvesting has been available throughout the wheat growing areas for decades. Custom harvesting is also now available for corn, grain sorghum, barley, cotton, rice, and many other crops. Even alfalfa hay, grown in the San Joaquin Valley of California, is custom-baled by specialized operators. In some places in California dealers rent out farm tractors and trucks by the month, similar to the rent-a-car operations. Entire corn-growing operations in the central Corn Belt can be subcontracted as a package. Much of the rice in California, as shown above, is grown by specialized custom service that includes planting, fertilization, and pest control performed by airplanes.

One of the most far reaching impacts of industrialization on world agriculture results from the sharp reduction in transport costs. Low cost, mechanized forms of transport have led to the widespread creation of regions of improved and specialized production. For example, the construction of railroads in France permitted the transport of bulky lime at low cost to areas with poor soils, thereby increasing agricultural yields in those areas.

Today, commodities can be moved to distant domestic or foreign markets because of low bulk transport rates. Not only do shipments of agricultural staples, such as wheat, move around the world, but so also do perishable goods and other agricultural products. Pineapples and papayas are flown from Hawaii to New York; ripe strawberries and freshly cut flowers are flown from Florida to Chicago; and vine-ripened melons and fresh lettuce reach Boston by air from California.

THE SPECIAL ROLE OF U.S. AGRICULTURE IN THE WORLD ECONOMY

Nowhere in the world has the trend toward capital-intensive, science-based farming resulted in higher levels of productivity than in sections of the United States and Canada.

It must be repeated here that by no means can all farms in the United States be characterized as highly capital-intensive, or even profitable enterprises. There is a strong regional character to the distribution of farm incomes in the United States. In Appalachia, the Ozarks, upper New England, and the northern Great Lakes region for, example, environmental disadvantages and isolation contribute to low farm incomes. We are focusing here on the large, highly capitalized, scientifically managed farms that supply the great bulk of our national and export markets (Fig. 7.12).

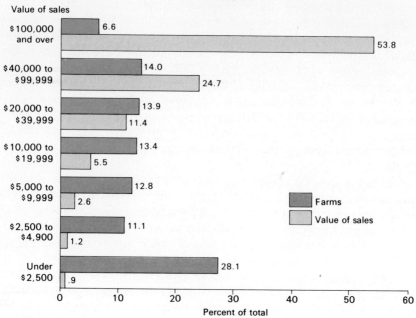

NUMBER OF FARMS AND VALUE OF AGRICULTURAL
PRODUCTS IN UNITED STATES SOLD BY
SIZE OF SALES, 1974

Figure 7.12 (Source: *U.S. Dept of Commerce, Bureau of the Census,* 1974 Census of Agriculture, *Volume IV, Part I,* Graphic Summary, *Chart 3., p. xxviii.*)

REGIONAL SPECIALIZATION

Much of the American Midwest and certain other sections of the country have superlative combinations of environmental factors for various kinds of agricultural production. A major reason for the success of American agriculture has been the specialization of various agricultural land uses in those regions where they enjoy comparative advantage. In rent terms, various agricultural products are grown where they can generate the largest combination of location rent and economic rent (Chapter 3).

This was illustrated cartographically in a study of the United States by John F. Kolars and John D. Nystuen.[9] Figure 7.13A shows the hypothetical agricultural land-use zones based on location rent generated per acre, as-

[9] *Physical Geography: Environment and Man,* McGraw-Hill Book Co., New York, 1975, p. 239.

AGRICULTURAL SYSTEMS AND WORLD FOOD PRODUCTION

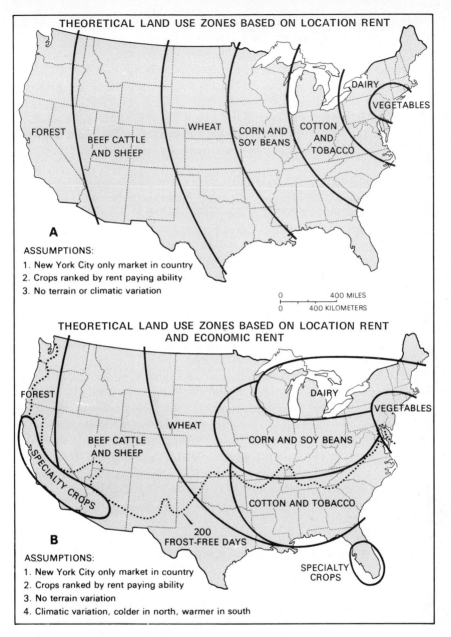

THEORETICAL LAND USE ZONES BASED ON LOCATION RENT

DAIRY

VEGETABLES

FOREST

BEEF CATTLE
AND SHEEP

WHEAT

CORN AND
SOY BEANS

COTTON
AND
TOBACCO

A

ASSUMPTIONS:
1. New York City only market in country
2. Crops ranked by rent paying ability
3. No terrain or climatic variation

0   400 MILES
0   400 KILOMETERS

THEORETICAL LAND USE ZONES BASED ON LOCATION RENT
AND ECONOMIC RENT

FOREST

DAIRY

VEGETABLES

SPECIALTY CROPS

WHEAT

BEEF CATTLE
AND SHEEP

CORN AND SOY BEANS

COTTON AND TOBACCO

200
FROST-FREE DAYS

B

ASSUMPTIONS:
1. New York City only market in country
2. Crops ranked by rent paying ability
3. No terrain variation
4. Climatic variation, colder in north, warmer in south

SPECIALTY
CROPS

Figure 7.13 (Source: *Adapted from John F. Kolars and John D. Nystuen,*
Physical Geography: Environment and Man. *Copyright 1975, McGraw-Hill
Book Co., p. 239, Fig. 10–14. Used with permission.*)

suming a von Thünen model in which New York City is the market for national production, and also assuming uniform environment. Next, Kolars and Nystuen relaxed the environmental assumption and postulated a temperature variation based on latitude—cold to warm in a north-south direction. In the resulting map (Fig. 7.13B), the land-use zones have readjusted in response to temperature differentials. Pasture for dairy herds can grow in shorter, cool growing seasons (similar to northwest Europe). Corn and soybeans require 150 frost-free days and hot summers. Cotton cannot be grown north of the 200 frost-free day line, and specialty crops require regions with mild winters.

This second map, based on both location rent (spatial) and economic rent (Ricardian environmental quality) considerations, can be seen to approximate the actual agricultural land-use pattern in the 48 United States. Compare the hypothetical land use map in Figure 7.13B with the actual distributions in Figures 7.14 through 7.21.

If the terrain and soil factors were considered as well, the hypothetical map would resemble reality even more closely.

THE U.S. AS GRAIN SUPPLIER OF THE WORLD

The natural advantages of the American Midwest for agriculture have been enhanced by capital and other inputs in that region. Investments in machinery, fertilizer, equipment, improved seed and animal varieties, and pesticides have greatly improved productivity and total output. In addition, large investments in transport facilities facilitate the movement of bulk agricultural commodities from the farms to national and international markets via truck and rail connections to Great Lakes and other United States ports. As a result, by the mid 1970s, in the words of a Resources for the Future, Inc., report,[10] "The American Midwest had become the grain and soybean supplier of the world." More recently, large exports of agricultural commodities have helped offset the debilitating drain of foreign exchange to pay for price-inflated oil imports.

As it has many times over the past years, the U.S. Department of Agriculture in the spring of 1979 announced a series of sales of United States grain to the Soviet Union. Private American exporters, under these sales, are sup-

[10] *Resources,* Washington, D.C., Winter, 1976.

Figure 7.14 (see facing page) (Source: Courtesy of Oxford University Press.)

AGRICULTURAL SYSTEMS AND WORLD FOOD PRODUCTION

MAJOR LAND RESOURCE REGIONS AND BUILT-UP AREAS

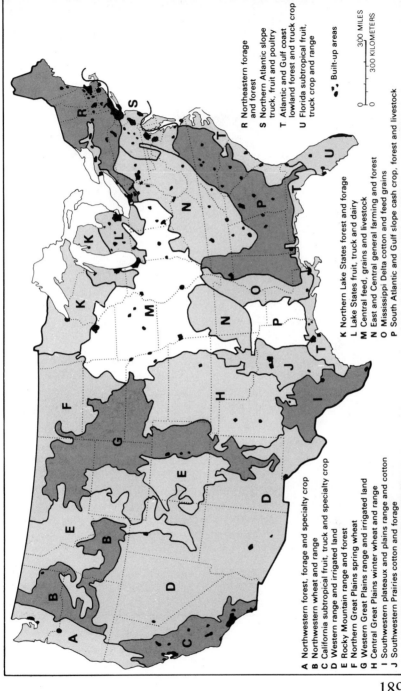

A Northwestern forest, forage and specialty crop
B Northwestern wheat and range
C California subtropical fruit, truck and specialty crop
D Western range and irrigated land
E Rocky Mountain range and forest
F Northern Great Plains spring wheat
G Western Great Plains range and irrigated land
H Central Great Plains winter wheat and range
I Southwestern plateaux and plains range and cotton
J Southwestern Prairies cotton and forage

K Northern Lake States forest and forage
L Lake States fruit, truck and dairy
M Central feed, grains and livestock
N East and Central general farming and forest
O Mississippi Delta cotton and feed grains
P South Atlantic and Gulf slope cash crop, forest and livestock

R Northeastern forage and forest
S Northern Atlantic slope truck, fruit and poultry
T Atlantic and Gulf coast lowland forest and truck crop
U Florida subtropical fruit, truck crop and range

•••• Built-up areas

0   300 MILES
0   300 KILOMETERS

189

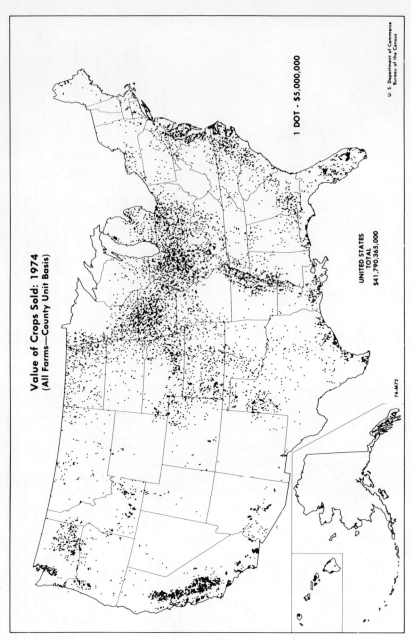

190

Figure 7.15 (Source: U.S. Department of Commerce—Bureau of the Census.)

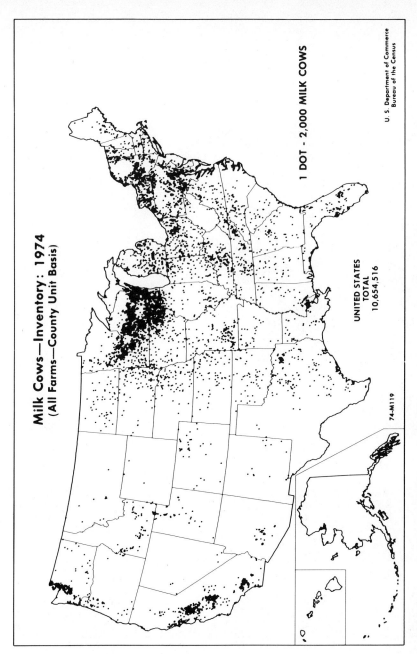

Figure 7.16 (Source: U.S. Department of Commerce—Bureau of the Census.)

191

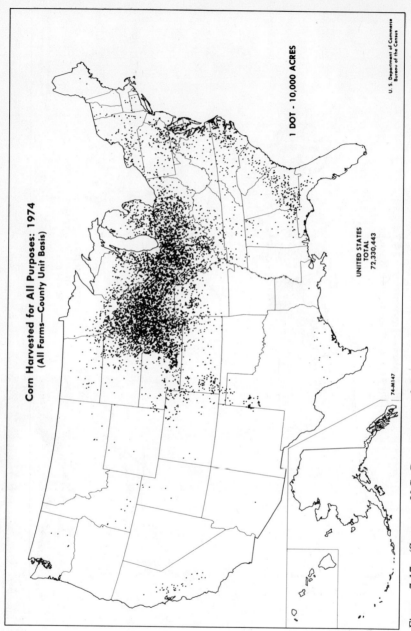

Figure 7.17 (Source: U.S. Department of Commerce—Bureau of the Census.)

192

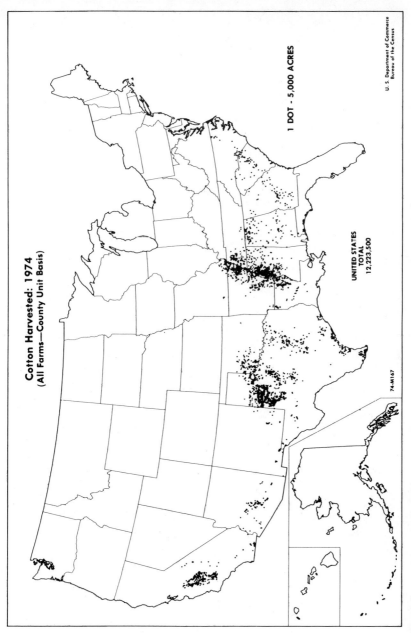

Figure 7.18   (Source: U.S. Department of Commerce—Bureau of the Census.)

193

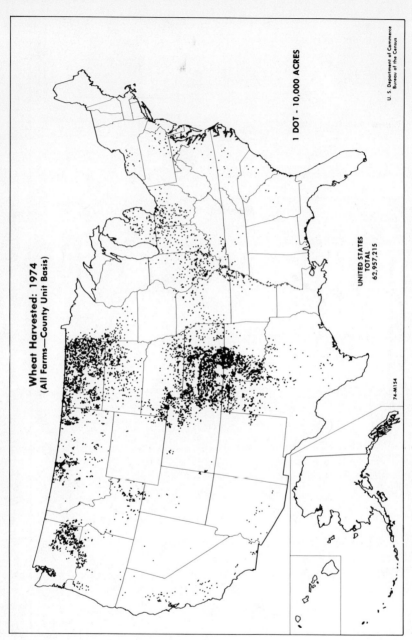

Wheat Harvested: 1974
(All Farms—County Unit Basis)

1 DOT - 10,000 ACRES

UNITED STATES
TOTAL
62,957,215

74-M154

U. S. Department of Commerce
Bureau of the Census

Figure 7.19 (Source: *U.S. Department of Commerce—Bureau of the Census.*)

194

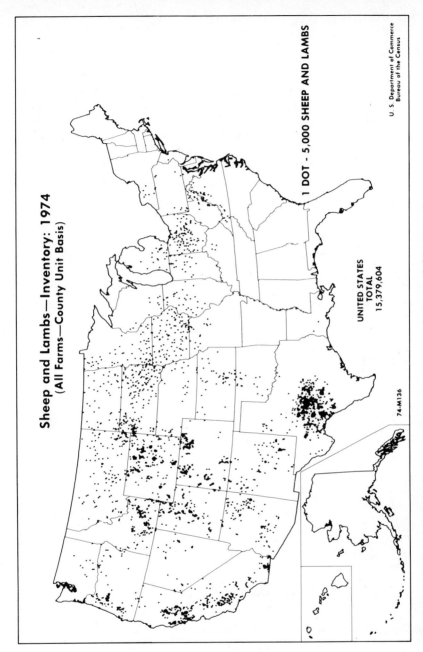

Figure 7.20 (Source: *U.S. Department of Commerce—Bureau of the Census.*)

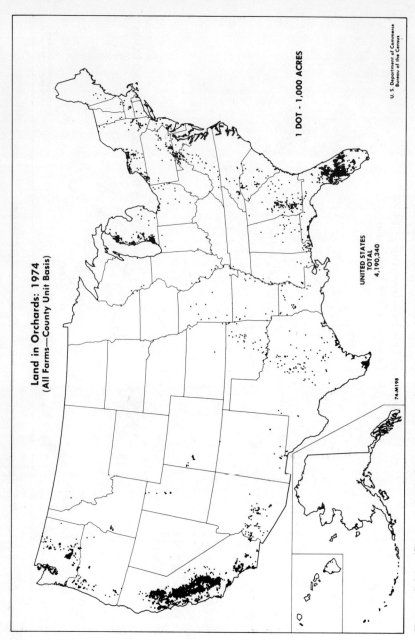

Land in Orchards: 1974
(All Farms—County Unit Basis)

1 DOT - 1,000 ACRES

UNITED STATES
TOTAL
4,190,340

74-M198

U. S. Department of Commerce
Bureau of the Census

Figure 7.21 (Source: *U.S. Department of Commerce—Bureau of the Census.*)

196

plying 250,000 tons of corn and 160,000 tons of wheat during the market periods of 1979 and 1980.

The Soviet Union has been plagued with serious problems in its agricultural sector since its inception. Part of the problem is environmental in nature (Chapter 6); however, another part results from institutional weaknesses.

Despite receiving favorable treatment from the State, the ideologically favored *state farms* (*sovkhozes*) lack efficiency and are unpopular with the workers. The dominant socialized unit is the *collective farm* (*kolkhoz*), which is a forced cooperative under the management of a chairman elected by the Communist Party.

State managed agriculture in the Soviet Union is said to suffer from a severe misallocation of resources. On the collective farms, labor has a higher marginal product per unit produced than capital, while the state farms are overcapitalized, resulting in the wasteful use of machines. The nature of agricultural planning, which is bureaucratic and clumsy, and the lack of free

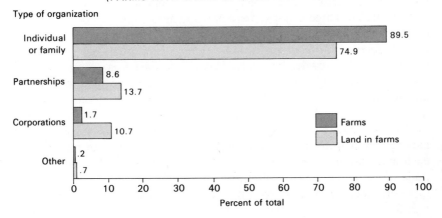

NUMBER OF FARMS AND LAND IN FARMS BY TYPE
OF ORGANIZATION, UNITED STATES, 1974
(FARMS WITH SALES OF $2500 AND OVER)

Figure 7.22 In 1974, there were 1,695,047 farms recorded with sales of $2,500 and over; total land area of these farms was over 905 million acres. Despite the consolidation of farm holdings into bigger units and the growth of corporate farming, agriculture in the United States is still dominated by the family farm. (Source: *U.S. Dept. of Commerce, Bureau of the Census,* 1974 Census of Agriculture, *Volume iv, Part I,* Graphic Summary, *Chart 6, p. xxx.*)

market pricing result in planning inflexibility. Workers on collective farms in recent years have been given the privilege of tilling a small plot (about two acres) for themselves. Today, a substantial share of vegetables, eggs, and poultry consumed in the USSR are grown on these private plots and sold for profit at local markets.

Despite the trend toward larger farms, farm consolidation, and the industrialization of agriculture, farming in the United States remains primarily a family operation (Fig. 7.22). In the middle 1970s, small farms were being eliminated at a slower rate than a decade earlier. Significantly, perhaps, Pennsylvania reported 2000 more farms under cultivation in 1976 than in 1974. The interest in home vegetable gardens, organic gardening and nutrition, and the growing revolt against highly advertised junk food appear to be more than passing fads.

SUMMARY

Farming is humanity's most universal occupation, and forms a foundation for other economic activities. Since the agricultural revolution 10,000 years ago, the population of the earth has increased a thousand times. Agriculture diffused to certain parts of the earth, from origins in the Middle East and Central America, and was adapted where environmental and spatial factors were favorable. Three major systems of world agriculture can be contrasted: (1) *shifting cultivation,* an age-old system found over vast areas of the world's tropical forests; (2) *labor-intensive agriculture,* supporting over half of all humanity on the crowded lowlands of South and East Asia, where low labor productivity results in low incomes and little surplus for capital investment; and (3) *capital-intensive agriculture,* associated with industrial nations, which has radically transformed the production, distribution, and consumption of food throughout the world. Very high labor productivities, surpluses, and incomes result from investment of capital and technology in regions with environmental and spatial advantages for specialized production, and the trade of surpluses. Industrialization of agriculture in the environmentally superior American Middle West has given this region comparative advantage for the production and export of grain and other agricultural products to food deficit nations all over the world.

Questions

1 Describe the global distribution of permanently cropped land. Why is it confined to only a fraction of the populated regions of the world?
2 Compare irrigated rice farming in East Asia with that in California.

3 What are some problems related to increased food production in the humid tropics?

4 Show how the location of specialized agricultural regions in the United States can be interpreted in terms of the location rent and economic rent models.

5 Discuss the essential features of the three contrasting world agricultural systems: shifting cultivation, labor-intensive agriculture of Asia, and capital-intensive agriculture of the Highly Developed Countries.

6 Give your interpretation of the statement, "Agriculture is the Achilles heel of the Soviet Union."

7 Suppose you were a summer intern for your congressman and were asked to draft a one page summary analysis of Chinese agriculture for presentation at a briefing session for the congressman in one hour. Write your draft.

8

RENEWABLE FOREST AND OCEAN RESOURCES AND RELATED PRODUCTION

"Applying the economic Principle of Comparative Advantage, the comparative disadvantage of the cold climates for forestry is much greater than their comparative disadvantage for agriculture. In the long run therefore we may expect to see the world's supply of forest products increasingly derived from the tropics and temperate zones . . ."

Colin Clark*

"The present harvest of the oceans is roughly 55 million tons a year, half of which is consumed directly and half converted into fish meal. A well-managed world fishery could yield more than 200 million tons."

S. J. Holt†

FORESTS AND OCEANS AS SPATIALLY VARIABLE RESOURCES

Compared with agriculture, forest-based and ocean-based production is relatively minor on a global basis, accounting for only a small percentage of the world's working force and value of product. Nevertheless, in certain countries—Iceland and Finland, for example—fishing or forestry are dominant economic activities. Fishing and forestry are also regionally important in many nations of the world.

---

* *Population Growth and Land Use,* St. Martin's Press, Inc., MacMillan & Co., Ltd., 1967, p. 150.
† "The Food Resources of the Ocean," *Scientific American,* September, 1969, p. 178.

Along with mining, forestry and fishing[1] are classified as *primary* or *extractive industries,* which means that they involve materials extracted directly from the natural environment. An obvious spatial aspect of extractive production is that it is confined to locations where the resource occurs naturally or where it can be cultivated. Since trees and marine life (and minerals, in the case of mining) are found in highly irregular spatial patterns of quantity and quality, these patterns are a fundamental factor in the location of the industries on which they are based. Thus, the spatial resource pattern provides a *necessary* (but not a *sufficient*) explanation for the location of the extractive process. Many other factors enter into the decision to establish an extractive enterprise, but its location will necessarily be mapped into the spatial pattern of the resource.

The output of extractive industries can be in the form of *consumer goods,* such as firewood or fish for direct home consumption. However, extraction is usually the first in a series of production processes in which the original natural resource becomes transformed into a *producer good* (such as wood pulp or animal feed), ultimately to be incorporated into a consumer good (newspaper or hamburger). The extractive industries thus provide the "raw materials" for *secondary production*—that is, for manufacturing and construction industries.

From the standpoint of resource management, a sharp division exists within the extractive industries. Mining deals with mineral deposits, which are *non-renewable.* Mineral resources are therefore subject to inevitable depletion. For that reason, mining will be treated separately in the next chapter, and this chapter will deal with the renewable forest and ocean resources.

The living resources of the forests and the seas are constantly being renewed by natural processes. The rate of renewal depends on the physical environment and the size of the propagating stock. The propagating stock is obviously diminished by harvesting (extraction). For these "self-regulating" resources there ideally exists an optimum rate of extraction that will provide maximum harvest indefinitely. This is called the *maximum sustained yield,* and provides a planning guide for long-range resource management.

There are, of course, conspicuous differences between forestry and fishing operations. Nevertheless, both forestry and fishing are spatial production systems to which the organizing concepts of location rent and economic rent apply. In both cases the resource base varies in quality from place to place in the Ricardian sense, and in both systems distance costs to market are an important locational factor, as in von Thünen's land-use model.

---

[1] The term fishing here will include shellfish, whales, and other forms of marine life unless otherwise specified.

FOREST RESOURCES AND FOREST-BASED PRODUCTION

The forests of the world have been a basis for economic activity since Man's earliest appearance, providing materials for food, shelter, tools, weapons, fuel, and other human needs. Forest-based production today varies greatly between the Highly Developed and Less Developed Countries. In the LDC's firewood is still an important product, while in the HDC's the major products made from *roundwood*[2] are lumber and materials based on wood pulp, such as paper and paperboard. Most international trade in wood products consists of lumber and pulp-based products exported to HDC's.

Forestry and forest based industries are extravagent space-using activities. A large proportion of operating costs is related to the physical effort of collecting logs from a large resource supply area, and transporting bulky products to distant urban markets. For this reason, Weber's Industrial Location Model (Chapter 4) helps in understanding forest industry locations (Fig. 8.1).

The number of persons supported and the income generated is very low per acre, and for this reason forestry is unable to compete with more intensive forms of land use. In rent terms, forestry generates a low combination of location rent and economic rent per acre. In order for forest-based production to be profitable, it must satisfy several conditions. There must be no other land use with higher rent potential competing for the space. Also, the enterprise must be located where its products can be shipped to a market without prohibitive costs. Many forests are located in the tropics or in other places where they are now inaccessible to mechanized transport. Even within the conterminous 48 United States, roughly half the forest area is classified as economically inaccessible (Fig. 8.2).

Large variations exist in the distances that various forest products can be profitably shipped. Pulpwood logs, which have a low value per unit weight, cannot be transported long distances; pulp mills are therefore located as close as possible to the forest supply area. On the other hand, the high-priced specialty woods, such as teakwood, can be shipped long distances.

A profitable forest-based enterprise must be located where the environment is suitable for sufficiently high rates of tree growth of the desired species. This cannot always be established in absolute terms. Production costs based on site quality and transport costs to market can often be substituted for each other. That is, a lower quality forest close to a market may be

---

[2] *Roundwood* is the general term applied to the rough logs after the branches have been removed. In a later stage, wood pulp or lumber are made from the roundwood.

RENEWABLE FOREST AND OCEAN RESOURCES

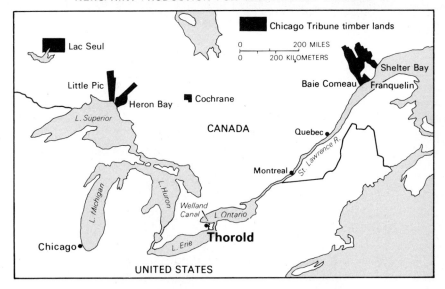

Figure 8.1   An interesting plant location case study is that of the Chicago Tribune's *Canadian subsidiary, the Ontario Pulp and Paper Company. Until 1911, newsprint had been produced in two separate processes and locations: (1) pulp making, near the sources of wood in the Canadian forests, and (2) newsprint manufacture, near the United States urban markets. Following the imposition of a Canadian export duty on unprocessed wood pulp, the expanding* Chicago Tribune *decided to construct a single, integrated pulp and paper mill in Ontario, and to buy specially designed lake vessels to ship the finished newsprint to Chicago. Considering all factors, the company located the plant at Thorold, at the end of the Lake Erie water level on the Welland Canal. The plan was to bring wood from the company's vast holdings along the lower St. Lawrence shore to Thorold for processing into newsprint. Both raw material assembly and product delivery would then be by low-cost water shipment. Other advantages of the Thorold site were: low-cost Niagra hydroelectric power, abundant processing water, low-cost rail access to Appalachian coal, and local paper-making skills. Despite changing economic conditions on both sides of the border over the years, Thorold has remained a low-cost plant site for the* Chicago Tribune's *newsprint production.* (Source: *Edgar C. Conkling and Maurice Yeates,* Man's Economic Environment, *McGraw-Hill Book Co., New York, 1976, Fig. 5-2, p. 120.*)

DISTRIBUTION OF FOREST LAND

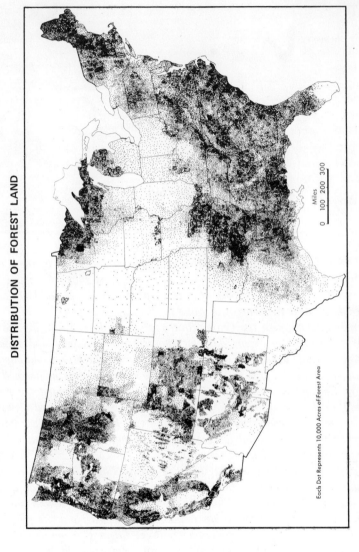

Each Dot Represents 10,000 Acres of Forest Area

Miles
0   100 200 300

Figure 8.2 (Source: USDA—Forest Service.)

just as profitable as a higher-quality forest in a remote region. This is the same principle that applied to agricultural production in Chapter 7.

SPATIAL VARIATION OF FOREST QUALITY

Since the quality of the forest is an important factor in the location of forest product industries, it is advisable to look more closely at the way in which forest quality varies from place to place. The two principal attributes determining forest quality in an economic sense are: (1) the types of trees that grow or can be grown in a place, and (2) the rate of tree growth.

Whether we consider natural forests or artificially planted (cultivated) forests, tree types and growth rates are influenced by environmental factors. The forest tree is a living organism, having a period of rapid early growth, a period of maturity, eventual decay, and final death. Depending on species and environment, the life span may be a few decades or hundreds of years. The forest tree is part of an ecological complex, growing in a stand with other trees, usually with an understory of other woody and herbaceous vegetation. As long as a tree is living it is protected against microorganisms, and the wood is held in "storage" until needed. But, eventually the tree dies and the economic value it represented is lost.

Tree distribution is related to climate, altitude, slope, and soil. Forests need a relatively high annual precipitation, although not necessarily uniformly distributed throughout the year. Thus, forests are found in a wide range of latitudes, from wet equatorial to cold subarctic climates (Fig. 8.3).

There are two major classes of trees, *conifers* (*soft woods*) and *broadleaved* (*hard woods*). Softwood refers to pine, fir, and other needle-bearing trees that grow their seeds in cones. Some "softwoods" are actually harder than some species called "hardwoods."

Hardwoods have broad leaves and usually shed them seasonally. In many parts of the world both types co-exist; in other regions, one or the other may dominate. In general, conifers are found in temperate climates, limited in the north, not by low winter temperatures but by low summer temperatures. The July 50 degree isotherm is roughly considered the northern boundary of forests in the northern hemisphere.

Extensive areas of North America and Eurasia are covered with coniferous, or mixed coniferous-hardwood forests. Large areas of coniferous forest are found in mountainous parts of both the western and eastern parts of North America. The lack of large land masses in the middle and higher latitudes of the Southern Hemisphere limits coniferous forests there to small areas, mostly in Argentina, Chile, Australia, and New Zealand. Toward the equator, conifers are displaced by hardwoods, and are missing in the wet tropics, except at higher elevations.

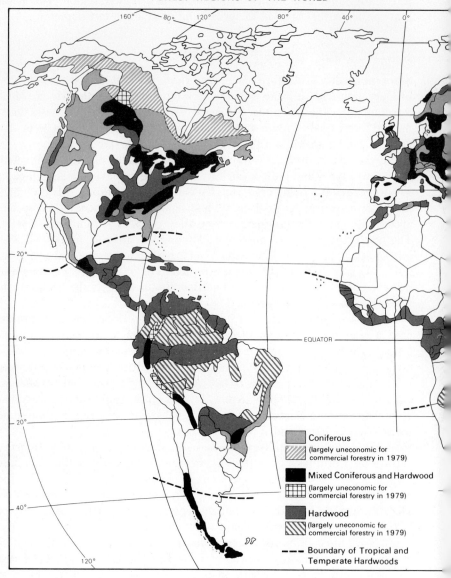

Figure 8.3   This map shows the distribution of forest types based on environmental factors; these are not necessarily regions still heavily forested. Vast areas of forest land in the northern latitudes and in the tropics remain un-

RENEWABLE FOREST AND OCEAN RESOURCES

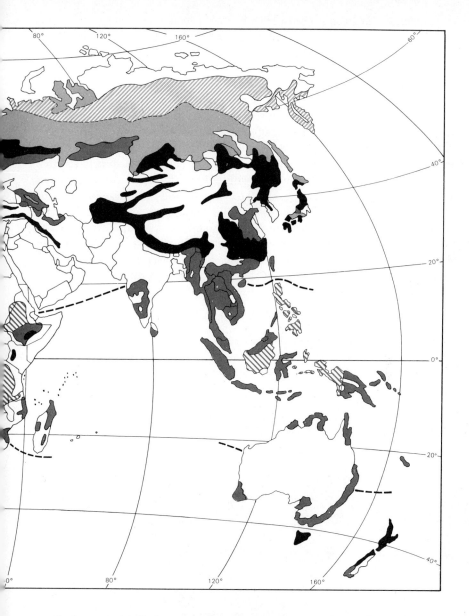

touched commercially because of remoteness from markets. The northern for-
ests also have an environmental disadvantage for production—slow growth
rates. (Source: *Daniel Loetterle.*)

Temperate hardwoods (broadleaved) trees predominate where the mean annual temperatures are between 40 and 65 degrees F and the rainfall exceeds 20 inches per year. Some hardwoods, such as birch, extend northwards almost as far as the conifers. Tropical hardwoods are limited to latitudes that are frostfree and receive more than 20 inches of rain per year.

A wide range of wood types and rates of growth are found within the accessible forest regions. Different tree species have wood with various physical properties, and hence have different market demands. In addition, the same tree species will grow at very different rates under different kinds of moisture and temperature conditions. It is not generally appreciated how fast trees can grow in moist climates with mild winters. For example, a pine tree can grow to pulp size in about 10 to 12 years and to log size in about 20 years in Southeastern United States, while the same growth increments would take three times as long in New England. In Alaska, Northern Canada, or Siberia, it may take 100 years for a tree to attain a diameter of only 8 inches. In southern Brazil, on the other hand, where the climate is very favorable, loblolly pine trees grow at exceptionally fast rates (Fig. 8.4).

THE DEMAND FOR WOOD AND WORLD PRODUCTION PATTERNS

Wood is not a single, homogeneous raw material; instead, it should be viewed as a family of similar materials with variable properties and economic uses. Different species of wood have different cellular structures, re-

Figure 8.4 Cross section of a loblolly pine tree grown in southern Brazil. In 11 years this tree grew to a diameter of 16 inches. (Source: Westvaco Corporation.)

RENEWABLE FOREST AND OCEAN RESOURCES

sulting in different degrees of hardness, durability, workability, and resistance to water. Softwoods have greater strength for weight, have more uniform fibers, and have taller trunks and fewer limbs. This makes them easier to harvest and mill, and they are preferred for construction.

The high consumption of roundwood, primarily in the form of lumber and pulp products, is an economic feature of modern, industrial societies. Certain industrialized nations are the major consumers of forest products. The Soviet Union and the United States are world leaders in production (Table 8.1). Europe as a region is also a major world producer. Considerable trade exists within Europe, mainly from Scandinavia and the Alpine nations to those nations without large forest resources. Other important flows of forest products are to Europe from the Soviet Union, United States, and Canada, to Japan from southeast Asia, and to the United States from Canada (Table 8.2).

The United States consumes about 30 percent of all industrial wood cut in the world. Housing takes about a third of this amount, another third is used to make paper, paperboard, and other pulp mill-derived products, and the final third goes into nonresidential construction, shipping containers, furniture, railroad ties, telephone poles, and so on. In 1972, the United States consumed 14 billion cubic feet of wood, or enough to build a wooden road 12 feet wide and one foot thick to the moon. The U.S. Forest Service estimates that by the end of the century, domestic demand will rise 57 percent

Table 8.1   Roundwood Output in Major Producing Nations

Place	Production (Million Cubic Meters)		
	Coniferous	Broadleaf	Total
World	1098	1400	2498
USSR	322	62	384
United States	258.7	82.7	341.4
China	89.8	105.4	195.2
Brazil	24.0	140.0	164.0
Indonesia	0.4	129.4	129.8
India	5.2	122.3	127.5
Canada	104.7	10.6	115.3
Nigeria		68.9	68.9
Sweden	45.6	6.8	52.4

Source: Adapted from United Nations Statistical Yearbook, 1977.

Table 8.2   United States Production, Imports, Exports, and Consumption of Roundwood

	Billions of Cubic Feet			
	1952	**1970**	**2000[a]**	**2000[b]**
Domestic production	10.8	11.7	21.3	15.7
Imports	1.4	2.4	3.1	5.0
Exports	0.2	1.4	2.4	2.5
Total United States consumption	11.9	12.7	22.0	18.2

[a] Estimated with 1970 relative prices for wood products.
[b] Estimated with rising relative prices for wood products.
Source: *Environmental Quality*, Council on Environmental Quality, Washington, D.C., 1976, p. 312.

for lumber, 119 percent for wood pulp, and 107 percent for veneer and plywood.

HIGH-YIELD FORESTRY AND CAPITAL-INTENSIVE PRODUCTION

The modern concept of high yield forestry views the forest as a complex living system that must be studied scientifically before it can be wisely managed. Modern foresters deal with trees in their total setting, and their control

---

CLARK'S SOLUTION TO THE OVER-CONSUMPTION OF PAPER

Economist Colin Clark, commenting on the habit of using so much paper in the United States, suggests that a policy of greater conservation could be implemented in the form of a tax:

The amount of wood pulp used in the United States clearly seems wasteful, whether we look at the bulk of the Sunday newspapers, or the unnecessary amount of wrappings. Those who are concerned about the conservation of future supplies of wood for pulping would do well to recommend the imposition of substantial tax on current use of fresh wood for pulping. This would have several beneficial consequences; it would encourage the collection of waste paper for repulping; it would hasten the search for other materials (e.g., dry fibre from sugar cane) suitable for pulping; it would conserve forests; and finally, it might reduce the amount of litter left in the streets and public places.*

* Population Growth and Land Use, St. Martin's Press, Inc., MacMillan & Co., Ltd., 1967, p. 150.

---

of the forest must extend through all stages of development. Scientific management techniques, following the sustained yield principle, are aimed at achieving maximum long-range economic benefits while still maintaining the renewable character of the forest resource base.

By carefully designed thinnings and cuttings, the forester can influence the species, sizes, and qualities of the trees grown. Under these conditions, considerable volumes of timber can be harvested that would otherwise be lost to normal mortality in a "natural" forest. Under undisturbed conditions the forest is biologically in equilibrium, with natural death and decay balancing growth increments over the long run. Some managed forests in the United States South now produce as much as three cords per acre per year, whereas in their natural state they would produce about a third of a cord per acre per year. Impressive advances in tree culture and genetic improvement have resulted from cooperative government and industry programs in a number of countries. Seed orchards have been established and superior tree seedlings by the tens of millions have been planted in the United States.

Technological change in harvesting as well as in growing forests has been rapid, and in some cases dramatic. The use of highly specialized equipment has brought about substantial increases in output from existing forest resources. Larger scale, more efficient means of transporting logs now permit handling materials of sizes and qualities previously considered uneconomic, and have made it possible to salvage scattered dead trees. Power driven equipment and large, special purpose machines are being used with great effectiveness (Fig. 8.5). Mechanization also reduces the costs of moving wood to concentrated points for collection and processing. Now, many formerly unacceptable grades of trees are usable, resulting in an enlargement of the resource base represented by the existing forests.

As the costs of transportation have declined over the past few decades, networks of roads, connecting with railroads and waterways, have extended the accessibility of forests. In both North America and Eurasia, lower cost transportation has pushed roundwood production into formerly inaccessible regions. The establishment of new ports and railway lines in the Soviet Arctic, especially east of the Ural Mountains on the Angara, Yenisei, and Lena Rivers, is part of the Soviet policy of expanding its forest resource base.

A trend in recent years has been the establishment of large multiple-product operations. In the United States, Canada, Japan, and certain European countries, these are corporate undertakings. In the Soviet Union and other centrally managed economies, they are state operations. In either case, large amounts of capital are required. Such establishments permit a high degree of production integration, and considerable economies of scale. The large, multiple-product plants can use a high proportion of trees within a

Figure 8.5 In a matter of seconds this chipper consumes an entire tree and loads the chips into a waiting truck. (Source: *Masonite Corporation.*)

given area, which might not provide enough trees of one species for single-product plants to harvest.

FOREST GROWTH AND NEGATIVE EXTERNALITIES IN THE UNITED STATES

It is a misconception that the United States will suffer a serious timber shortage in years to come. Actually, American forests hold the promise of being a growing economic asset in the future. From about the same acreage of commercial forest land, net growth of wood (growth less mortality) was reported 11.2 percent higher in 1977 than in 1970, and exceeded harvests by 53 percent.[3]

The increase in the wood supply during the 1970s has been a continuation of a long-term increase in timber growth. Annual net growth has risen by 56 percent since the Forest Service first began making detailed inventories in 1952.

The reason for the increased national wood supply is that, as the old growth stands were harvested, the areas were opened up to rapid growth of younger stands of timber.

---

[3] *Resources,* Resources for the Future, Inc., Washington, D.C., January–March, 1979, p. 20.

RENEWABLE FOREST AND OCEAN RESOURCES

COMPUTER SIMULATION OF FOREST GROWTH

One of the newer tools for scientific forest management is a technique for computer simulation of forest growth, developed jointly by Yale University School of Forestry and IBM Corporation. Dr. Daniel Botkin of Yale and Doctors James F. Frank and James R. Wallis of IBM created a mathematical model of forest dynamics that permits simulated manipulation of tree stands and environmental factors in order to study the way trees grow and interact with the environment. The system equations take into account soil quality, climate, topography, and competition from other species. The model can simulate the growth of a two and a half acre forest stand at the rate of one year per second, enabling the research investigator at a computer terminal to carry out theoretical studies that would require centuries in an actual forest.

While United States forests are growing year by year, the biological capacity appears to be far from reached. However, forest production, like other forms of production, is subject to negative externalities. As tree removal has become more mechanized, particularly in the practice of clear (block) cutting (Fig. 8.6), problems have developed often far from the production site itself. Soil erosion and the consequent downstream problems of siltation and flooding are examples. Forest removal can cause air pollution over wide areas, resulting from atmospheric dust. Water pollution results from forest-based production, particularly from pulp and paper production, and this becomes a negative plant location factor. Such operations, more and more, are being located away from large metropolitan markets, where extra transport costs must be absorbed.

It is a mistaken notion that centrally managed governments avoid the "pollution versus production" controversy. Lake Baikal in the Soviet Union is one example. (In the Soviet Union, all forests are government property.) Lake Baikal, located in Soviet Asia near the Mongolian border, is the oldest and largest freshwater lake in the world, and has a unique biology of interest to scientists in many nations. However, in 1967, despite strenuous objections from many Soviet scientists and a number of world scientific organizations, a mammoth wood pulp mill at the south end of the lake was put into operation. This episode illustrated the fact that disagreements between environmentalists, on the one hand, and engineers and production managers, on the other, can transcend political systems.

As population grows, the wilderness value of forests becomes more important as a long-range source of public benefits. Wilderness values include the role of natural forests as laboratories for ecological study as well as places for recreation. The loss or impairment of wilderness environments has be-

Figure 8.6   Clear cutting (block cutting) in old-growth Douglas fir-western hemlock forests in the South Fork of the Skokomish drainage basin, Olympic National Forest, Washington. (Source: *USDA—Forest Service.*)

come a highly charged national issue in the United States, one that will have a growing influence on forest utilization in the future. A policy problem arises here over the fact that wilderness, wildlife, recreation, and other public uses of the forest are often incompatible with wood production (Fig. 8.7).

THE UTILIZATION OF TROPICAL FORESTS

At the present time economic utilization of the tropical forests of the world is minor. One set of obstacles is environmental. Many different varieties of trees exist per acre in tropical forests, in contrast to the denser stands in higher latitudes. Rapid growth of underbrush impedes many production operations, and flooding and poor drainage may be problems in low areas. Prop roots in marshy areas also hamper tree harvesting. Another problem relates to transportation. Tropical forests contain few urban-industrial areas and are therefore remote from industrial markets for forest products.

214   RENEWABLE FOREST AND OCEAN RESOURCES

DEGREE OF COMPATABILITY AMONG VARIOUS FOREST USES

Primary use	Maintain attractive environment	Provide recreation opportunity	Wilderness	Wildlife	Natural watershed	General Conservation	Wood production and harvest
Maintain attractive environment		Moderately compatible; may limit intensity of use	Not inimical to wilderness but does not insure	Compatible to most wildlife, less so to a few	Fully compatible	Fully compatible	Limited compatibility; often affects amount of harvest
Provide recreation opportunity	Moderately compatible unless use intensity excessive		Incompatible; would destroy wilderness character	Incompatible for some kinds; others can tolerate	Moderately compatible; depends on intensity of recreation use	Moderately compatible; incompatible if use too heavy	Limited compatibility depends on harvest timing and intensity; roads provide access
Wilderness	Fully compatible	Completely incompatible, can't tolerate heavy use		Highly compatible to much wildlife less so to others	Fully compatible	Fully compatible	Completely incompatible, precludes all harvest
Wildlife	Generally compatible	Limited compatibility; use intensity must be limited	Mostly compatible though some wildlife require vegetative manipulation		Generally fully compatible	Generally fully compatible	Generally limits volume of conditions of harvest
Natural watershed	Fully compatible	Moderate compatibility; may require limitation on intensity	Not inimical to wilderness but does not insure	Generally compatible		Fully compatible	Moderate compatibility; restricts harvest methods but does not prevent timber harvest
General conservation	Fully compatible	Moderately compatible; if use not excessive	Not inimical to wilderness but does not insure	Generally compatible	Fully compatible		Compatible but requires modification in methods of timber harvest
Wood production and harvest	Compatible if harvest methods strictly controlled	Moderately compatible	Completely incompatible; would destroy wilderness	Compatible if harvest methods fully controlled	Compatible if harvest methods fully controlled	Compatible if harvest methods fully controlled	

Figure 8.7 This chart indicates the degree of compatibility between each primary use in the first column, and other uses shown along the same line in the following seven columns. (Source: Resources for the Future, Inc., Washington, D.C., 1974.)

As a consequence of these disadvantages, the practice in many places has been to harvest selectively from scattered, special-purpose, high value trees: mahogany from Mexico, Honduras, and Haiti; Spanish cedar from the West Indies and Brazil; teak from Burma, Thailand, and the Philippines; balsa from Ecuador, and so on.

In coastal areas and other more accessible parts of the tropical forest realm, a growing development of technologically advanced, capital-intensive, wood-based production has taken place for several decades. Large plywood and other wood product plants have been established, for example, along coasts and rivers in parts of Central Africa. An example of the Thünen principle can be seen operating here. The more accessible areas tend to be overexploited. In 1964 The African Economic Commission reported, "Many of the coastal zones that have been commercially exploited are gradually being exhausted and logging is proceeding into belts further inland, which will result in higher transport costs."

Institutional obstacles to future development also exist. Most of the countries with tropical forest resources are LDC's with low rates of capital formation. Modern transport facilities and supporting infrastructure, such as land surveys and maps, are scarce or lacking altogether in these countries. What little capital is available would be spatially diluted, unless concentrated in the more accessible areas. In some cases, political instability also acts as an inhibiting factor.

Despite these problems, some authorities believe that the tropical forests have an enormous, long-run potential for forest-based production. According to this view, forestry, not agriculture, holds the greater promise for attaining the full hydrocarbon production potential of the humid tropics. If this turns out to be the case, future growth is first likely to be concentrated along coastal fringes, or sites accessible to river corridors. An example is the large, new wood pulp mill located on a tributary (Jari) of the Amazon River, near its mouth, in the rainforest of Brazil, financed and managed by the American industrialist, Daniel K. Ludwig.

MARINE BIO-RESOURCES AND PRODUCTION

The waters of the oceans, as well as the soil on the land, establish the critical link between the inorganic and organic worlds—the source of life on earth. The ocean basins, two-thirds of the earth's surface, act as a processing plant to convert solar energy to living protein. The fisheries of the world today, however, provide only a minor fraction of the total animal protein used for

RENEWABLE FOREST AND OCEAN RESOURCES

human consumption. About half of the world fish catch is used for purposes other than for human food. For example, menhaden caught off the east coast of the United States and anchovies caught off Peru in great quantities are converted into animal feed (fishmeal), fish oil, and other industrial products.

On the consumption side, the growth of population and industrialization throughout the world is creating new demands for the resources of the ocean. As a total resource base, the oceans also include water, petroleum, minerals on the bottom, and the elements dissolved in sea water. This section deals only with the renewable bio-resources.

MAXIMUM SUSTAINED YIELD

Fishing can be viewed as the counterpart of hunting on the land, except that the ocean environment is three-dimensional. In both cases there is an ecological interconnection between the hunting rate (the intensity of fishing), the average catch, and the total population of organisms. The long-term equilibrium of a fishery is based on its ability to compensate for deaths resulting from fishing activity. These relationships are shown in Figure 8.8.

In nature without people there are checks and balances that maintain a long-range ecological equilibrium. When Man enters the scene as a predator, his fishing activity can be adapted to long-term production if he understands the dynamics of reproduction. A population of fish is normally largest when it is not being exploited. When fishing starts, the natural equilibrium is upset. At first the changes are small, but as fishing intensity increases on the original stock, the stock is reduced until a *sustained yield* is reached. At this level of fishing intensity the stock neither decreases or increases. Maximum yields occur at intermediate levels of fishing intensity, usually between one-third and two-thirds of the virgin stock. In this intermediate range, the average size of the individual fish will be smaller and their age younger than in the original population. The *maximum sustained yield* is the largest average catch that can be taken indefinitely without causing the fish stock to rise or fall. Fishing intensities above or below this optimum point theoretically create conditions of *overfishing* or *underfishing*.

The theoretical management problem is to determine the fishing intensities that will give maximum sustained yields for specific fish populations, and then to provide the scientific basis for the control of the amount of fishing. This ideal is, however, rarely attainable, because the renewal of stock in nature depends not only on the size of the unharvested population, but also on variations in numerous environmental factors, which are not fully understood.

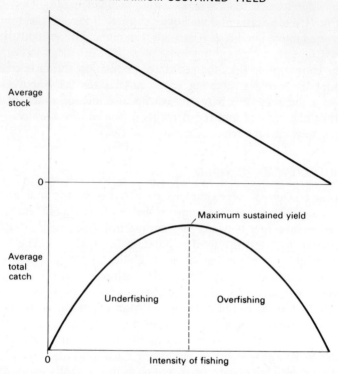

Figure 8.8   See text for discussion. (Source: *Milner B. Schaefer and Roger Revelle, "Marine Resources," in Martin R. Huberty and Warren L. Flock (Eds.), Natural Resources, McGraw-Hill Book Co., New York, 1959, Fig 4.5, p. 101.*)

LOCATIONAL PATTERNS OF FISHING

The model in Figure 8.8 provides insights into the rational management of fisheries. However, it is necessarily simplified and does not treat the ocean as an "unconfined" three dimensional resource space, varying in quality from place to place. Commercial fishing under present hunting methods requires the presence of large schools of fish, containing no more than a few species. These are found in only a relatively few places in the oceans. All the marine species have their own environmental requirements and spatial distributions. The bulk of the fishing harvest throughout the world consists of a relatively few species. For profitable commercial operations, the fish population must

218   RENEWABLE FOREST AND OCEAN RESOURCES

not only be large enough to withstand regular exploitation, but must also be within economic distance of urban markets. Virtually all nations bordering the sea have some fishing activity. However, the bulk of the total world catch is taken by about a dozen and a half nations (Table 8.3).

The spatial variation in fish populations is directly related to ocean fertility. The tiny plants of the ocean (phytoplankton), on which the entire life chain depends, can only survive near the surface, where sunlight penetrates and where photosynthesis can take place. The microscopic plant life near the ocean's surface supports all the larger varieties of marine life. Like the land surface, the ocean surface has wide extremes of fertility. Fish stocks of commercial size and homogeniety are concentrated in coastal waters, shallow banks, and certain other places where the fertility is exceptionally high.

The soluble minerals that serve as plant nutrients in the surface waters

Table 8.3   Countries with Major Catches of Marine Organisms,[a] 1976

	Catch (Thousand Metric Tons)	Percent
World total	73,467	100.0
Japan	10,620	14.5
USSR	10,134	13.8
China	6,880[b]	9.4
Peru	4,343	5.9
Norway	3,435	4.7
United States	3,004	4.1
Republic of Korea	2,407	3.3
India	2,400	3.3
Denmark	1,912	2.6
Thailand	1,640	2.2
Spain	1,483	2.0
Indonesia	1,448	2.0
Philippines	1,430	1.9
Chile	1,264	1.7
Canada	1,136	1.5
United Kingdom	1,063	1.4
Iceland	986	1.3

[a]Excluding whales.
[b]1973 data.

Source: Adapted from "Fishery Commodity Situation and Outlook," Food and Agricultural Organization of the United Nations, April, 1978, Table 1, p. 3.

must continually be replenished. They are depleted by photosynthesis and the slow sinking of plant and animal remains into the deeper waters (Fig. 8.9). The fertility is restored where nutrient-rich, deeper waters are continually forced up to the surface. By this process, the ocean is said to "plow itself." The regions where the process is most vigorous have been called, to use another metaphor, the "green pastures" of the sea. The upwelling of the deeper water is accomplished in three ways: (1) in some places the wind forces surface water away from the coast, and nutrient-rich water surges up from the depths to replace it; (2) in some regions surface waters are cooled to nearly freezing in the winter, increase in density and sink, forcing up richer water from the depths; (3) in some areas the water is mixed by wave or current action in shallow depths, causing the surface fertility to be constantly replenished. It is estimated that the natural upwelling caused by these mechanisms can increase the actual fish catch of an area by a factor of many thousands.

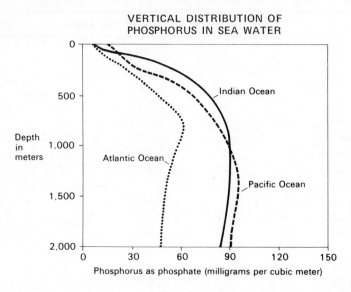

Figure 8.9 Average surface waters of the oceans contain very small amounts of the essential life element, phosphorus. Maximum concentrations occur at depths of about 1000 meters or more. The same general pattern is found for concentrations of nitrogen. In regions of the sea where upwelling of the lower water occurs, these critical nutrients are brought to the surface where they form the foundation, through photosynthesis, of a food chain that supports a flourishing fish population. (Source: Gifford B. Pinchot, "Marine Farming," p. 20. © Dec. 1970 by Scientific American, Inc. All rights reserved.)

220

The fisheries of the world are based on one or more of the three ways of re-fertilizing surface waters. The sardines, anchovies, and mackeral off California, the sardines off South Africa, and the tuna off the West Coast of North and South America live in regions of upwelling, where the deep water is brought to the surface by wind action. The cod, herring, and haddock of Newfoundland, Labrador, Iceland, and Greenland all live in regions of winter cooling and overturning. The sardines off Maine and the flatfish in the shallow Grand Banks thrive where the Gulf Stream and the Labrador Current clash in turbulent mixing. All three processes are important around Antarctica, where whales thrive.

The spatial pattern of ocean fertility provides an environmental explanation for the location of world fisheries. An interrelated, spatial explanation supplements the first. Fishing locations among the regions of high fertility are influenced by distance costs to port. Since commercial fishing follows the hunting model, higher costs of overcoming distance in searching for the fish and in travelling to port with the catch must be compensated for by lower production costs resulting from high concentrations of fish. Fishing location also depends on the price at the market port. The price for tuna is high enough in the United States to enable modern, radar-equipped fishing boats from San Diego, California, to make trips of several months duration to the rich waters off western South America.

The most intensively exploited fishing grounds are those where a high density of desirable fish types are available within range of home port markets—that is, where the combination of economic rent and location rent is high. Very high fishing intensities are found where fertile waters lie off heavily populated coasts, as in East Asia or Northwest Europe (Fig. 8.10).

Spatial patterns of consumption are influenced by cultural perceptions and psychological attitudes, which affect taste preferences. Caviar, the eggs (roe) of sturgeon, is a delicacy for some people and is repugnant to others. One reason for the limited development of the fishing industry in the Indian Ocean, despite the lack of protein in the diet of the dense populations living around it, is a distaste for fish and other marine products. Strong fish taboos are deeply ingrained in some cultures. In parts of South Asia, fish is excluded from the diet on religious grounds.

NEW TECHNOLOGIES AND CAPITAL-INTENSIVE PRODUCTION

A general trend exists within the fishing industry throughout much of the world, whether privately owned or state operated, to become more highly organized, more technologically advanced, and more capital intensive. This trend results from a growing demand for ocean products for human con-

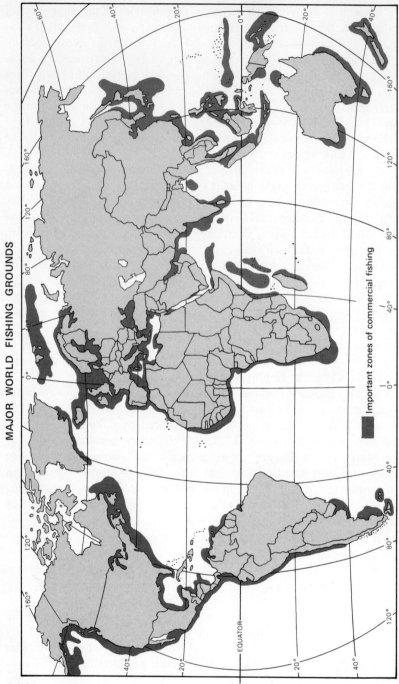

Important zones of commercial fishing

Figure 8.10 (see facing page) Heaviest concentrations of fishing occur in regions where (1) shallow banks or upwelling currents create conditions of high fertility ideal for large fish stocks, and (2) ports serving urban markets are within economic range. Major fisheries are, consequently, located off the heavily populated coasts of nations in East Asia, in the seas surrounding Europe, and off Eastern United States and Maritime Canada.

sumption and other needs, increasing scientific knowledge about the ocean, and capital availability within the developed world.

The general principle underlying these improvements is a simple one: to increase the efficiency of the process by which diffuse fish stocks are found and captured, that is, "strained" out of the enormous volumes of water in which they are found. As Man becomes more efficient in this process, he is better able to exploit the less-intensively fished, fertile zones of the oceans. The direction of capital investment has been toward new technologies and new equipment designed to make production process spatially more efficient. Large, specialized vessels, designed for long cruises and having processing capacity for the perishable fish are able to stay at sea for extended periods, penetrating the distant fisheries in search of fish concentrations.

Japan and the Soviet Union have fleets of large factory ships equipped for long voyages and containing modern freezing and processing equipment. Some ships regularly carry oceanographers, marine biologists, and research

---

STEVENSON'S RESEARCH ON SATELLITE ASSISTED FISHING

Some types of fish are confined to specific water conditions that are discernible by high altitude remote sensing. The flight of Gemini in 1966 and subsequent space flights revealed such information. The combination of computers and satellite photography may be a future key to more efficient fishing operations. Dr. Robert E. Stevenson of California's Scripps Institute of Oceanography is an authority on satellite assistance for fishing. He said, "If we would cut down the hunting time (from 90 percent) to say, 60 percent, we'd be giving a great boost to the industry production."[*]
In November 1973, Stevenson discovered in Skylark photos ocean whirlpools he thinks could help locate new fishing grounds. The whirlpools appear in the photos as swirling eddies of cold water in the warm current flowing off Mexico's Yucatan peninsula.[†]

[*] *New York Times*, November 7, 1967.
[†] *New York Times*, December 7, 1973.

MARINE BIO-RESOURCES AND PRODUCTION

equipment. Some Russian ships are equipped with underwater TV cameras and giant searchlights to learn more about the ocean's bottom deposits and the behavior of fish. This is part of an ambitious program to expand the Soviet fisheries, including the establishment of schools for the training of technicians, biologists, and other marine specialists. Floating factory-type operations are used by other maritime powers, such as Norway, Great Britain, Portugal, and Iceland. These countries employ subsidies to advance their national fishing interests.

Technological change and capital investment are also working on the demand side to expand the markets for fishery products. An example is the processing of fish into fish meal (animal food) and fish flour (human food). These are similar production processes involving the grinding up of the entire fish in bulk lots, followed by cooking, drying, and packaging. Technological improvements and capital investment in overland transport and marketing facilities are extending markets farther into the port hinterlands. However, the lack of cold storage facilities is still an acute problem in many of the Less Developed Countries.

INTERNATIONAL COMPETITION FOR OCEAN RESOURCES: THE GROWING STRUGGLE

In the minds of many persons the most difficult problems in future use of the oceans are not scientific, but of a political nature. There exists a dire need for management policies at the international level that will keep the competition for the ocean's resources from becoming a source of intolerable world tension.

"Freedom of the Seas" has been the International doctrine since 1604, when the three mile limit—the seventeenth century range of cannon shot—was established. The Soviet Union claimed a 12-mile territorial zone in 1927. In 1945, President Truman declared the continental shelf's resources under U.S. control. In 1952, Chile, Peru, and Ecuador extended their fisheries limits to 200 miles. In the intervening years, many more nations have extended their territorial waters to 200 miles (in 1977 alone, the United States, Mexico, Canada, the United Kingdom, India, Norway, and Sri Lanka all joined the list), giving rise to growing conflicts over the world's major fisheries.

In 1974, United Nations Secretary General Kurt Waldheim declared: "It is urgent that we take the first essential steps toward international agreement as quickly as possible. . . . Time is not on our side and delay would be perilous." Despite this note of urgency, no workable international treaty now appears forthcoming.

MARINE FARMING: SPATIAL EFFICIENCY OF PRODUCTION

No matter how sophisticated the searching procedures become, ocean fishing will continue to be spatially inefficient as long as it is essentially a hunting enterprise. Some sort of cultivation, involving direct management of the marine organisms, may ultimately prove the most effective way of tapping the ocean's potential for biotic resources. Some authorities think that certain areas could be developed into highly productive "marine farms." Various management strategies are conceivable, but all are based on the same principle: to minimize or eliminate the distance costs of finding, harvesting, and transporting fishery products to market.

A spatially efficient production system requires the breeding and cultivation of fish or other marine organisms in a confined and controlled environment. One technique is the production in enclosed or partly enclosed bodies of water. In such places the addition of relatively small quantities of chemical nutrients would greatly increase the yield of fish.

The cultivation of marine organisms, both animal and plant, has been carried on in coastal waters for centuries.[4] Ideal marine environments for cultivation of marine organisms are bays, estuaries, tidal lagoons, and so on, which are protected from storms and where a mixing of fresh and ocean waters at shallow depths provide optimum growth conditions.

[4] Pond breeding of fresh water fish, such as carp, has been practiced in the United States and other nations for a very long time. Pond-bred fish are a source of animal protein in many Asian countries.

Numerous examples of marine farming throughout the world suggest the possibilities for a much higher level of world development. Suspension cultures of oysters, cultivated in Japan's Inland Sea, yield thousands of pounds of meat per acre per year. It is estimated that the coastal waters off the Eastern United States could furnish very high yields of shellfish if cultivated on the Japanese model. A particularly attractive feature of coastal marine cultivation is its immunity from competition by foreign powers. Conversely, a growing problem in these areas is pollution of the coastal waters from urban and industrial sources.

SUMMARY

Forestry and fishing are *extractive* (*primary*) industries based on renewable living resources, for which there hypothetically exist *maximum sustained yields*. For both forest-based and marine-based industries the resource varies in quality from place to place in the Ricardian sense, and distance costs must be absorbed as in the Thünen model. Modern forest-based production concentrates on the output of lumber and pulp-based products, such as paper and paperboard, while firewood is still an important forest product in the Less Developed Countries. The Highly Developed Countries, which are the chief consumers, are also the major producers of wood products. The concept of high-yield forestry views the forest as a complex living system that must be scientifically managed. In the HDC'c, new technology and organizational efficiencies have created large-scale, multiple-product operations requiring very large capital investments. Negative externalities in the form of air and water pollution are now important forest industry location factors. Wood production conflicts with other forest land uses in the United States and elsewhere. The forests of the United States have been growing faster than they have been cut for the past several decades. As a renewable and exportable resource, they represent one of America's great natural assets for the future. The forests in the accessible parts of the humid tropics appear to have a substantial potential for further development.

The world fishing industry is still a hunting enterprise, and remains, therefore, spatially inefficient. The fertility of the ocean for marine harvest varies extremely from place to place. Depletion follows the Thünen model, with fertile areas close to ports overfished, and other fertile areas in remote parts of the world underfished. It appears inevitable that conflicts will grow over the control and extraction of ocean resources. Ocean resources can theoretically be managed efficiently through a controlling body that eliminates wasteful duplication of fishing effort. Marine organism cultivation in coastal waters can provide greatly increased, high protein food supplies, if the coastal waters are not polluted by municipal and industrial wastes.

Questions

1 Discuss the benefits and problems associated with expanded economic use of American forests.
2 Describe the characteristic features of high yield forestry.
3 Discuss the negative externalities that result from forestry and forest product industries.
4 What accounts for the very great fertility variations from place to place in the oceans?
5 What is meant by the contention: "Ocean fishing is a spatially inefficient enterprise"?
6 Explain the world pattern of ocean fishing in terms of interacting environmental and spatial influences.

9

MINING
AND
THE
NONFUEL
MINERALS

"The geographic distribution of rich ores has always been responsible for traffic, transportation, and trade, for the intermingling of civilizations, for wars, and for much of human progress."

Richard M. Foose*

A technological revolution occurred when prehistoric humans learned to strike one piece of flint with another in such a way as to flake off chips, and thus fashion crude axes and other tools. These "capital goods" could then be used to fell trees, kill and butcher large animals, make clothes, carve objects of art, and, regrettably, wage war.

Man became a metallurgist sometime between 5,000 and 4,000 B.C., when he first perceived that fire could be used to free valuable metals from their mineral compunds. The first metal so released, probably by accident, was copper, obtained from such compounds as azurite. Metallic copper can be released at a relatively low temperature, like that produced in a camp fire.

After lengthy experimentation, tin was added to the copper to produce the harder alloy, bronze. Tin-bearing compounds are very scarce, however. Cassiterite, the mineral most likely to have been the source of tin in the Bronze Age, is not found at all in the eastern Mediterranean area, where bronze was commonly used. This means that Bronze Age Man must have carried on prospecting and trading in metals over wide regions of the world. These explorations, in turn, were made possible by the increasing use of bronze

*"New Mineral Frontiers," Department of Earth Sciences, Stanford Research Institute.

tools, weapons, and armor. The Phoenicians, from the eastern end of the Mediterranean, obtained tin from the Celts of Cornwall in Southwestern England. The mines of Cornwall have been operating on and off ever since. The invasion of Britain by Julius Caesar is thought to have been undertaken, at least in part, by Rome's growing demand for copper, tin, and lead.

Iron came into use around 1200 B.C. Iron ores are much more common than those of most other metals. However, iron metallurgy is more difficult than copper smelting because much higher temperatures are needed to free the iron from its ore. Iron is by far the major metal used in the modern world, accounting for 90 percent of the total. Indeed, it is not incorrect to say that the world is still in the *Iron Age*.

There are many ways to classify the complex mineral world. It will be useful here to consider three broad groups of minerals: the metallic minerals, the nonmetallic minerals (Table 9.1) and the mineral fuels. The discussion in this chapter will center on the metallic and nonmetallic minerals. Chapter 10 will cover mineral fuels within a general discussion of energy resources.

CHARACTERISTICS OF MINERALS AND MINING

Mining, as in the case of other extractive industries (Chapter 8), does not rank high as an employer of labor or as a direct generator of income within the world economy, compared with agriculture, manufacturing, or service industries. This comparison, however, should not serve to underestimate the incalculably important role played by minerals and mining operations in all modern societies.[1]

The market prices of minerals reflect Man's perception of them as useful in meeting his needs. This, in turn, depends on their different physical and chemical properties. Common building stone, such as granite or limestone, has great resistance to compression (pushing) forces, but very little resistance to tension (pulling) forces. Building stone is therefore ideal for massive structures, such as pyramids, where large compressive loads must be supported, but is virtually useless as a structural beam or slab subject to loading, and therefore to tension forces along its lower face. (A rock slab or beam supported at its ends can collapse under its own weight.) On the other hand, some metals can withstand many thousands of pounds of tension per square inch of cross section. This, plus the ability to withstand shock and vibration and to hold an edge, make steel, which is made from iron, universally impor-

---

[1] Von Thünen (Chapter 4) made a significant concession in his agricultural location model. He violated his own assumption of a uniform environment by considering "indispensable" mineral deposits to be located near his central market town.

tant as a structural material. Steel-reinforced concrete has combined properties designed to withstand both compression and tension forces.

A critically important property of copper and aluminum is electrical conductivity. All industrial societies depend for their existence on this special property.

Table 9.1   Common Groupings of Metals and Nonmetallic Minerals

Metals	Nonmetals
Iron	Building
Iron ore	Limestone
Iron alloy	Sand and Gravel
Manganese	Cement materials
Chromite	Chemical
Nickel	Sulfur
Molybdenum	Salt
Cobalt	Fertilizer
Vanadium	Phosphate rock
Base	Potash
Copper	Nitrates
Lead	Ceramic
Zinc	Clay
Tin	Feldspar
Light	Refractory and flux
Aluminum	Clay
Magnesium	Magnesia
Titanium	Abrasive
Precious	Sandstone
Gold	Industrial diamonds
Silver	Insulant
Platinum	Asbestos
Rare	Mica
Uranium	Pigment and filler
Radium	Clay
Beryllium	Diatomite
	Barite
	Precious and gem
	Gem diamonds
	Amethyst

Source: James F. McDivitt and Gerald Manners, Minerals and Men, The Johns Hopkins University Press, Baltimore, MD., 1974, Figure 1, p. 15.

The nonrenewable character of minerals is a vital planning consideration. Minerals used as fuels are completely consumed in use. A certain amount of recycling of metallic minerals within the economy does exist. These factors hold true for socialist economies as well as for free-market economies. The Supreme Soviet of the USSR, in July 1975 approved a new mineral code that mandates the planned, comprehensive use of mineral resources. The new code, like federal mineral policy in the U.S., is designed to increase the effectiveness of the use of mineral resources and to improve conservation.

Some mineral products, such as gems, are consumed directly by the public. However, most nonfuel mineral products are *producer goods* used in manufacturing, construction, and agriculture. For most minerals (particularly metallic minerals), a series of production processes, each having its own environmental impact, is carried out between the point of origin in the ground and the ultimate market (Fig. 9.1).

CHANGING WORLD PATTERNS OF SUPPLY AND DEMAND

The great increase in mineral use in the modern world (Table 9.2) results from the compounding of three factors: (1) the increasing per capita use in industrialized nations, (2) the spread of industrialization, and (3) the increase in world population.

Geopolitical factors have always had a strong influence on the location of mining enterprises and on the spatial patterns of the mineral industries,

Table 9.2   Total Past Consumption of Selected Resources in the United States for the Period 1776-1974, and Estimates of Future Needs During the Lifetimes of Persons Living in 1974

Resource	Total Consumption Through 1974	Estimated Future Needs During Lifetimes of Persons Living in 1974
Iron ore (tons)	6 Billion	6 Billion
Aluminum (tons)	290 Million	698 Million
Copper (tons)	72 Million	86 Million
Sand and gravel (tons)	30 Billion	42 Billion
Energy (equivalent barrels of oil)	400 Billion	585 Billion
Water (gallons)	4.7 Quadrillion	5.9 Quadrillion

Source: U.S. Geological Survey, 1974.

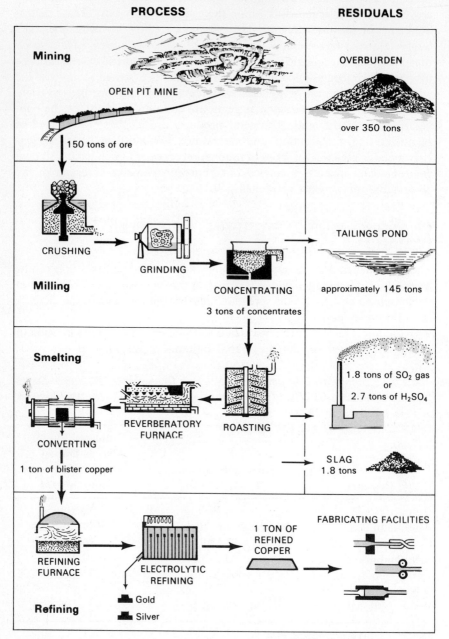

PRODUCTION STAGES AND ENVIRONMENTAL IMPACTS IN THE COPPER INDUSTRY

PROCESS

RESIDUALS

Mining

OPEN PIT MINE

OVERBURDEN

over 350 tons

150 tons of ore

CRUSHING

GRINDING

Milling

CONCENTRATING

TAILINGS POND

approximately 145 tons

3 tons of concentrates

Smelting

REVERBERATORY FURNACE

ROASTING

1.8 tons of SO$_2$ gas
or
2.7 tons of H$_2$SO$_4$

CONVERTING

1 ton of blister copper

SLAG
1.8 tons

Refining

REFINING FURNACE

ELECTROLYTIC REFINING

Gold
Silver

1 TON OF REFINED COPPER

FABRICATING FACILITIES

Figure 9.1 (Source: *James F. McDivitt and Gerald Manners,* Minerals and Men, *The Johns Hopkins University Press, Baltimore, Md., 1974, Fig. 7., p. 71.*)

particularly the metallic mineral group. National boundaries were established in many cases before the mineral wealth of nations was known. This has led to recurring international tensions, sometimes resulting in armed conflict. Tin and other relatively rare metals have been a cause of wars from ancient times to Japan's thrust into Southeast Asia in World War II. Minerals have also been used as weapons in economic warfare; an example would be Russia's stoppage of exports of manganese to the United States in 1948.

Since World War II, the gargantuan demands for minerals by many industrial nations have outstripped their national supplies. High consumption has forced even the mineral-rich, developed nations to rely more and more on imports from Less Developed Countries. Until the 1920s the United States was virtually self-sufficient in minerals. By 1950, however, it was importing over half the aluminum (bauxite), manganese, nickel, and tin it consumed. By 1976, the United States was importing, by value, about 15 percent of its total nonfuel mineral supply, and was dependent on foreign sources for more than half its supply of twenty minerals, many critical to its industrial output (Table 9.3).

Today, nonfuel mineral production is heavily concentrated in a few big

Table 9.3 *United States Imports of Selected Critical Minerals, 1977*

Mineral	Percent Imported	Major Foreign Sources
Columbium	100	Brazil, Thailand, Nigeria, Malaysia
Mica (sheet)	100	India, Brazil, Malagasy Republic
Manganese	98	Brazil, Gabon, South Africa
Cobalt	97	Zaire, Belgium, Norway, Finland
Tantalum	97	Thailand, Canada, Australia, Brazil
Platinum	92	South Africa, USSR, United Kingdom
Bauxite and alumina	91	Jamaica, Australia, Surinam, Guinea
Chromium	89	South Africa, USSR, Turkey
Tin	86	Malaysia, Thailand, Bolivia, Indonesia
Asbestos	85	Canada, South Africa

Source: U.S. Bureau of Mines.

countries having a large share of the world's "geological lottery" (Chapter 6). These include the United States, Canada, Soviet Union, South Africa, and Australia. A large share of nonfuel mineral exports today go to the Highly Developed Countries from Bolivia, Brazil, Chile, Mexico, Peru, and Venezuela in Latin America, from several African nations, and from Malaysia.

SPATIAL AND ENVIRONMENTAL ASPECTS OF MINING ACTIVITY

As with other forms of extractive production, the location and character of mining enterprises are influenced by interacting spatial and environmental factors. A *mineral reserve* (the term *ore* is used for the reserves of some minerals) must, by definition, be potentially profitable.

The economic benefits that can be derived from a mineral reserve are related to its accessibility, including nearness to large industrial markets, and its quality (size, shape, depth, and grade of ore). As in other forms of production, substitution possibilities exist between transport costs and production costs (see Fig. 3.3). A lower-grade copper deposit in Arizona may be a reserve; a higher-grade deposit in Alaska may not be.

An important point here is that the same mineral deposit can change over time from a reserve to a nonreserve, or vice versa, depending on changes in production costs, transport costs, and market prices. A reduction in costs and/or an increase in price will increase the number of known deposits that can profitably be worked as reserves. Conversely, increased costs and/or reduced price will act to decrease the number of reserves. Mining and milling costs also depend on the value of by-products, available technology, the level of taxes and royalties, management recovery policies, and other factors.

Some minerals, such as sand and gravel, have a very widespread occurrence (Fig. 9.2); others, such as the metal nickel, are rare, existing commer-

---

THE DEFINITION OF MINERAL RESERVES

In 1974, the U.S. Department of Interior's Bureau of Mines and Geological Survey jointly adopted new definitions to describe economic minerals more accurately. The classification system is based on two criteria: the extent of geologic knowledge about the resource and the economic feasibility of its recovery. *Mineral resources* are defined as concentrations of naturally occurring solids, liquids, or gases, discovered or only surmised, that are or might become economic sources of mineral raw materials. *Mineral reserves* (ores) are the portion of mineral resources that have actually been identified, and can be legally and economically extracted.

MINING AND THE NONFUEL MINERALS

cially in only a few places in the world (Fig. 9.3). Metals usually occur in chemical combination with other elements from which they must be separated, while nonmetals are often used in the form in which they are mined. Because of this, and since deposits of metals are much scarcer than those of nonmetals, the prices of metals are high relative to those of bulky nonmetals. This has an important influence on marketability. Metals, after concentration, can bear the cost of shipment to distant markets, while the low unit prices for sand, gravel, clay or limestone inhibit their distant shipment. This means that the bulky nonmetals are confined to local or regional trade, while metals become international commodities. (An exception, of course, would be diamonds and other gem stones, which are a special class of nonmetallic minerals.)

Since the output of most mines is in the form of producer goods for industry and not consumer goods, demand is sensitive to the level of industrial activity as well as to price. Aggregate demand for minerals, therefore, tends to be *price inelastic;* that is, an increase or decrease in price does not result in a proportionate decrease or increase in demand (see Fig. 4.11).

An important factor in the mineral industry is that of monopoly control, which varies greatly in its influence on price. Some markets, such as those for diamonds, are highly monopolistic, while those for such metals as lead and zinc are competitive. Another reason why the demand may not always closely follow price signals in the market is that some metallic minerals are produced as a by-product of the extraction of another mineral. For example, most silver produced in the United States is a by-product of copper, lead-zinc, and gold mining. Also, when mineral prices are unstable for any reason, there is a tendency for mining operators to "gut" their ore bodies by rapidly mining out the highly profitable ore.

In analyzing the spatial pattern of mineral production, the location of industrial markets can be assumed as fixed. That is, mines are located with reference to markets, but mineral users generally do not seek locations near the mines.

Many mines have been developed in regions lacking comparative advantage for other kinds of economic activity. These are often regions of desert, rough topography, bad soils, permafrost, or various combinations. Most metallic mineral deposits are found in mountainous or hilly areas. The geological environment that favors metallic concentration is therefore seldom well suited to other types of land use, except possibly for recreation.

Mining settlements in remote regions must depend heavily on the mining activity alone as an economic base. Mining enterprises in such places often support the entire infrastructure of town, roads, schools, and so on. Because of the nonrenewable character of minerals, mining production is limited over time. If no other economic activity can be substituted, the inevitable

PATTERN OF SAND AND GRAVEL PRODUCTION IN GREAT BRITAIN

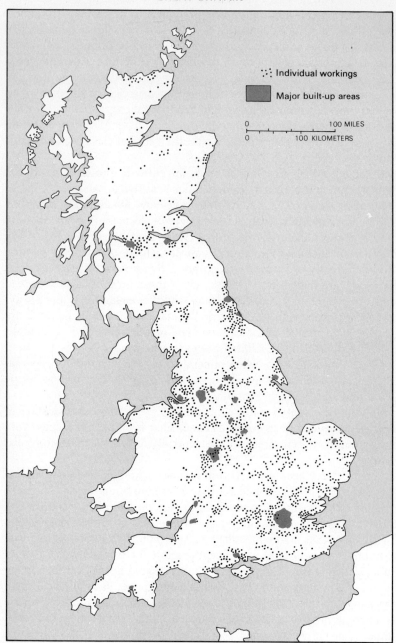

Individual workings

Major built-up areas

0   100 MILES
0   100 KILOMETERS

Figure 9.2   (see facing page) The occurrence and mining of different minerals can have very different spatial patterns. In industrial nations, sand and gravel rank at or near the top in tonnages used, exceeding even petroleum and coal. About 90 percent of all sand and gravel mined is used in construction and road-building. Because of their widespread geological occurrence and low price, sand and gravel are mined in many sites close to their markets. For example, operations of this type are found by the hundreds in Great Britain. (Source: Kenneth Warren, Mineral Resources, John Wiley and Sons, New York, 1973, p. 229.)

decline of the region will follow the mineral depletion. Mining enterprises come and go, and mobility is a strong tradition among miners of all historical periods.

As time passes, negative externalities are becoming a more important location factor. Environmental pollution, ecological disruption, and other undesirable effects of mining and mineral processing are examples. Under-

PATTERN OF WORLD NICKEL PRODUCTION

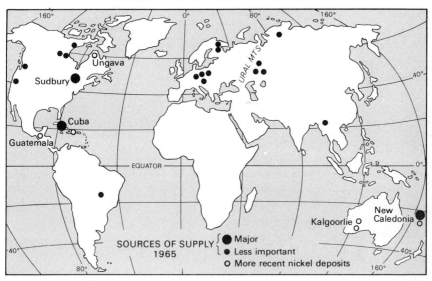

Figure 9.3   In sharp contrast to the distribution of sand and gravel workings (see Fig. 9.2), the mining of the metallic mineral, nickel, occurs in only a few places in the world. Because they are indispensable to modern industrial nations for steel-making and other uses, many of the less common metals, such as nickel, have major geopolitical significance. (Source: Kenneth Warren, Mineral Resources, John Wiley and Sons, New York, 1973, p. 146.)

ground as well as surface mines can create serious environmental problems. Although not always at the mining site itself, mineral smelting operations have been recognized as a special source of environmental degradation for over a century. The fumes and other gaseous emissions from mineral smelters in many parts of the world have destroyed vegetation and poisoned the landscape. Airborne wastes from mineral operations are transported by atmospheric movements over large areas. Copper smelters in the Swansea area of Great Britain created regional devastation for a hundred years. In the United States early in this century, areas in California and other states were desolated by smelter fumes (see Fig. 5.6).

MINERAL DEPLETION AND LOCATIONAL EFFECTS
STRATEGIES AGAINST DEPLETION

In Chapter 5 we noted that forecasts of future resource availability range from very pessimistic to somewhat optimistic. There is common agreement that the world will not literally "run out" of minerals, but that their costs may rise to prohibitive levels as they become more difficult to find, extract, and process. Shortages of nonmetallic minerals are less likely to be critical in the future; they can, in many cases, be met through substitution. Fertilizers make up a large class of nonmetallic mineral resources. Nitrogen fertilizers can be produced from air (Chapter 5). Phosphate is plentiful in the United States, although in short supply in highly populated countries, such as China, India, Japan, and Indonesia. Potash, the third important mineral fertilizer, can be gotten from lake or ocean brines or salt beds in many places throughout the world. More pessimistic views concerning depletion are held about the metallic minerals.

Various strategies have been evolved by nations and firms to counter the effects of the depletion of high grade metallic ores. These strategies include the following and all affect the location of mineral production: substitution of other minerals or other materials; increase in scrap metal recovery; improved technology in the mining and concentration of low grade ores; and increased exploration for undiscovered deposits.

The question of substitution is complex. Perhaps the only thing that can be said now is that some substitutions will be possible as we move into the future, but that general substitution is not anticipated. No known economic substitutes exist for sheet mica in certain electronic applications. Diamonds that serve as abrasives and mercury used in some pharmaceuticals are other examples. Copper and aluminum are the only low cost electrical conductors.

The generation of scrap is an important conservation measure for metals. As the price of new metal rises, a greater rate of scrap recovery is possible. Scrap metal is a major component in the production of steel, lead, zinc, and

238

copper. Minerals used in paint, ceramics, and many other products cannot be recovered as scrap. Minerals used as fuels are of course not recoverable.

Increased technology applied to the mineral industries has usually been accompanied by greater use of new capital equipment and energy. Real costs per pound of metal rise as grade (metallic content) falls off, and more capital and energy must be expended to win a given amount of metal from larger tonnages of low-grade ore. The inevitable increases in energy prices are bound to raise the price of metals in the future.

WORLD EXPLORATION AND THE DEVELOPMENT OF NEW DEPOSITS

The spatial patterns of mineral production are strongly influenced by exploration strategies and operations. As the "cream" of the high-grade mineral ores becomes mined in regions accessible to industrial markets, vigorous programs of exploration and development are undertaken in more remote regions. New exploration methods have greatly increased the efficiency of the mineral search in the unexplored regions of the world. Over the past three decades some unexpectedly large mineral discoveries have been made. Airborne electro-magnetometers found large nickel deposits in Manitoba, Canada. Resistivity surveys helped to find lead-zinc deposits in New Brunswick, Canada. Iron and barite deposits were discovered in Australia, and huge iron ore deposits were found in remote parts of Venezuela and Canada.

Exploration by airborne instruments make an otherwise exceedingly costly operation relatively low cost. With such methods vast areas can be explored in a very short time, and search costs per square mile are low compared to conventional ground methods. Advanced ground exploration methods have also been used successfully. In the United States, seismic surveys resulted in the discovery of sulfur bearing domes in the Gulf Coast region so massive that they altered the world pattern of supply.

Mineral explorations are financially risky operations. They are very often concentrated on areas near existing production or near established markets, where the probability of recovering exploration expenses is reasonably good.

As the geologists and engineers disperse all over the world in a competitive search for new ore bodies, political factors become important considerations in the location of new mining ventures, especially within the Third World. Wherever possible, mineral-importing nations prefer not to rely on supplies from distant, politically unstable nations. Such supplies are vulnerable to sudden stoppage. Industrial nations regard politically stable governments as preferred sources of their critical imports. Industrial nations that are vulnerable to the sudden denial of critical minerals, such as chrome or tungsten for special steels, maintain emergency stockpiles and often seek to protect their home mining industries even when they are relatively inefficient and high cost.

If a mine is closed down for several years, equipment rusts, flooding may occur, and the workers often depart. To keep its home mines operating, governments will sometimes place *quotas* on the importation of certain minerals. *Tariffs* are also used to protect domestic mining by restricting importation through the imposition of taxes. *Subsidies* are sometimes used to aid the domestic industry. All these measures protect higher-cost home production against lower-cost, vulnerable imports. The central question becomes: to what degree should higher-cost domestic production be supported as a guaranteed supply in the event of war or other emergency? The proper balance between home production and lower-cost imports is an important policy consideration for all nations.

THE TREND TOWARD LARGE-SCALE MINING OF LOW-GRADE DEPOSITS

Although many small mines exist throughout the world, the average size of new mining enterprises is steadily growing larger. The trend to bigness provides scale economies at all levels of operation, since mining overhead costs do not rise in proportion to mine output. A new metal-mining operation requires an investment of risk capital of several hundred million dollars (Fig. 9.4). New mining ventures require a total engineering and management sys-

AMAX'S 500 MILLION DOLLAR HENDERSON MINE

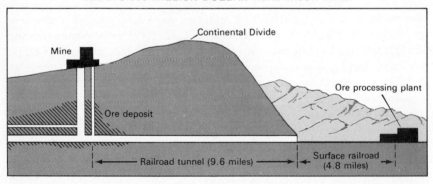

Figure 9.4   The world's largest producer of molybdenum spent an extra 100 million dollars developing this new project 40 miles west of Denver to make it environmentally acceptable. A railroad tunnel nine miles long was blasted beneath the Continental Divide in order to place the ore processing plant where environmental impact could be minimized. The plant began production in 1976, and will have an ultimate design capacity of 50 million pounds per year.

240

tems approach, very different from the primitive "seat of the pants" mining operations of half a century ago.

The large-scale, mechanized mining operations, if successful, result in low labor costs per unit of output, although wages may be high (Table 9.4). However, the large energy requirements of these operations make them sensitive to rising energy prices.

Because of the high requirements for capital and scientific management, large new metal mining enterprises are limited to a relatively few state-managed operations, or to multinational firms. In Latin America and Africa a trend exists toward nationalization of foreign-owned mining operations, either by full ownership by the country, or by partial nationalization in which the country assumes a percentage, often 51 percent, of the ownership.

Capital-intensive mining sometimes takes the form of international joint ventures. In Australia some enterprises are owned by a mining company, Australian investors, and foreign metal customers, such as the Japanese. The complexity of operations of this magnitude can be illustrated by the Bougainville development in Papua, New Guinea. The Bougainville porphyry copper deposit, discovered in 1964 by an Australian firm, is now one of the world's largest copper mines. Gold is also produced as a by-product. The operating company is Bougainville Copper Pty., which in turn, is owned 20 percent by the Territory of Papua and New Guinea and 80 percent by Bougainville Mining Ltd. The last company is owned two-thirds by Conzinc Riotinto of Australia and one-third by New Broken Hill Consolidated. The sale of shares to the public and to certain public and quasi-public organizations further complicates the ownership structure. Construction of the mine and facilities was started in 1969 and completed in 1972 at a cost of a half billion dollars.

The trend for industrial nations to import increasing quantities of metals from foreign sources is not necessarily irreversible. New deposits overseas will continue to supply a large part of the market within the United States. However, in the long run depletion will also occur in the foreign supply areas, and the comparative advantage for the mining of many key minerals is likely to shift back to the United States.

Table 9.4   Labor Efficiencies of Large-Scale Bauxite Mining

Size of Operation (Tons per Year)	Per Capita Output (Tons per Year)
60,000	128
400,000	635
1,000,000	1219

Source: Kenneth Warren, *Mineral Resources,* John Wiley & Sons, 1973, Table 10, p. 90.

The shift back to leaner, domestic ores is likely to follow rising world metal prices (Fig. 9.5). Domestic production will continue to gain scale economies by surface mining with very large, special purpose machinery, in order to recover the lower-grade deposits. This has already been the case in the copper mining industry (Table 9.5). Copper ores of considerably less than one percent grade from Arizona and Utah have been able to compete in United States markets with three percent ores from Chile and Zambia.

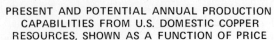

PRESENT AND POTENTIAL ANNUAL PRODUCTION
CAPABILITIES FROM U.S. DOMESTIC COPPER
RESOURCES, SHOWN AS A FUNCTION OF PRICE

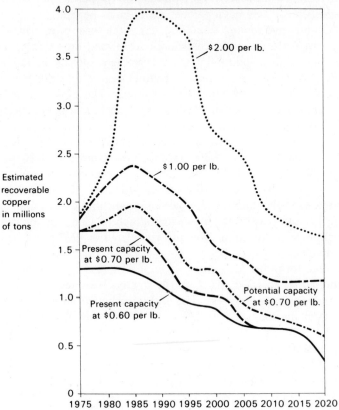

Figure 9.5   As the market price of a metal rises in relation to the cost of extraction, it becomes economically feasible to recover larger amounts of it from lower grade ores. (Source: Environmental Quality, *Council on Environmental Quality, Washington, D.C., 1976, p. 327. Based on data from the U.S. Bureau of Mines.*)

MINING AND THE NONFUEL MINERALS

Table 9.5   Average Grades of Copper Ore Mined in the United States

Year	Average Grade of Ore Mined (Percent Copper)
1900	4.00
1910	1.88
1920	1.63
1930	1.43
1940	1.20
1950	0.89
1955	0.83
1960	0.73
1965	0.70
1970	0.60
1973	0.53

Source: *Environmental Quality,* Council on Environmental Quality, Washington, D.C., 1976, p. 328.

The entire future course of events regarding large-scale mining of low-grade ores may hinge on a factor not anticipated before 1974—the rapid rise in world energy prices.

Speculation exists concerning long-range prospects for metal extraction from entirely new sources. Sea-bed mining appears on the verge of becoming

---

McKELVEY ON FUTURE ENERGY COSTS AND METAL AVAILABILITY

Dr. V. E. McKelvey, former Director of the U.S. Geological Survey, made the following remarks in an address on April 25, 1977:

The end of cheap energy profoundly changes some assumptions we have held about our continued ability to supply our needs for minerals. The notion that we could go on using brute force to mine and concentrate ever greater quantities of ever lower grades of ores now has to reckon with the rising cost of brute force. Moreover, our efforts to get around the geochemical scarcity of metals like copper, tin, and lead by substituting more abundant metals such as aluminum, magnesium, and titanium must deal with the fact that the latter require three to six times as much energy to produce.

THE TREND TOWARD LARGE-SCALE MINING OF LOW-GRADE DEPOSITS   **243**

a global commercial enterprise. One intriguing idea, which is beginning to get legitimate scientific and engineering attention, is "space mining." A number of serious research papers have appeared in recent years discussing asteroids as commercial sources of minerals.

Perhaps the only thing that can now safely be said about such possibilities as sea-bed mining and space mining is that they are likely to pose a greater international political challenge than a scientific one.

SUMMARY

Human use of minerals has gone hand in hand with cultural and economic development for over 6000 years. Modern industrial nations have enormous demands for both metals and nonmetallic minerals. The world's leading nonfuel mineral producers are the United States, the Soviet Union, and a few other Highly Developed Countries. However, the United States and other industrial nations must import certain critical minerals required by their economies. Mineral reserves are very unevenly distributed in space. Some minerals, such as sand and gravel, are commonly found. Others, such as nickel, are found commercially in only a few places on earth. Although the location of mining and milling operations is influenced by political factors, it is still highly responsive to spatial and environmental factors. Depletion of high-grade metal reserves in HDC's is causing accelerated exploration and mining developments in many parts of the world. Multinational firms able to amass capital and conduct international operations are organized to exploit lower-grade ores efficiently through large-scale operations. In the future, the high-grade foreign ores are also likely to become depleted, and the comparative advantage of some forms of mining will shift back to the United States, but at higher price levels. Higher future energy prices will contribute to rises in mineral prices. Sea-bed mining holds future promise, if the difficult problem of international conflict can be overcome, and space mining is being given serious engineering study.

Questions

1 What is meant by the term *mineral reserve,* and how does it differ from mineral deposit?
2 Discuss the causes and some consequences of the accelerated world use of metals over the past few decades.
3 Outline the strategies against nonfuel mineral depletion open to the United States.

         MINING AND THE NONFUEL MINERALS

4 Examine a world atlas showing the distribution of various mineral resources. Which mineral producing regions of the world are likely to become the foci of increased geopolitical tension during the 1980s? Explain your selections.

5 Describe the world trend toward large scale mining of low-grade mineral reserves.

10

CHANGING
PATTERNS
OF
ENERGY
PRODUCTION
AND
CONSUMPTION

"We are an interdependent world and if we ever needed a lesson in that we got it in the oil crisis."

Robert S. McNamara*

The use of inanimate energy is essential to human life in all parts of the globe. However, the kinds and amounts of energy used vary in the extreme from one place to another. In many regions of the world today, men, women, or children gather firewood or animal dung to warm their homes and cook their food. At the same time, individuals in industrialized countries daily consume very large amounts of energy.

The total energy supply of a place, region, or nation consists of a number of different forms of energy having different characteristics. Within the category of commercial energy there are several major types that are only partially subject to economic substitution. We can heat our homes with petroleum, natural gas, coal, firewood, or electricity; we can run our trains on coal, diesel fuel, or electricity; cars, trucks, and planes run on petroleum products—but not coal. It is possible to convert some forms of energy into other forms commercially. Thus, coal can be used to produce liquified gas if the price is competitive. The most important conversion is that of heat energy from the burning of fossil fuels—coal, petroleum, or natural gas—into mechanical energy by the expansion of steam in a steam turbine, and the conversion of the resulting mechanical energy into electrical energy by a

---

*The World Bank, Washington, D.C., March 30, 1974.

246

directly coupled generator. The resulting electric energy is in a form that has myriad uses in a spatial economy—from running a railroad system to energizing miniature electronic components in a computer.

LOW-COST ENERGY AND THE SPATIAL ECONOMY

The Industrial Revolution was based on a revolution in energy use, which started with the invention of a practical steam engine. Now, energy[1] could be harnessed wherever coal supplies could be mined or otherwise obtained. The steam engine radically changed the locational pattern of the fast-growing manufacturing industries, since it made them independent of water power sites. By the middle of the nineteenth century the steam locomotive, made efficient enough to carry its own fuel supply, was rapidly altering the space economy in the industrializing parts of the world.

During the latter part of the nineteenth century the generation and transmission of electric energy became commercially feasible over considerable distances, and this liberated production from direct connection, through shafts and belts, to a steam engine. During the first decades of the twentieth century, hydroelectric energy was developed on a large scale. The first electrochemical and electrometallurgical manufacturing plants were clustered at the sites of low-cost hydroelectric power, such as Niagara Falls, lying between New York State and Ontario, Canada.

The internal combustion engine, developed commercially around the turn of the century, provided a power source not tied to a fixed electrical distribution system. Today, the internal combustion engine is indispensable to industrialized regions and nations everywhere.

In the twentieth century, the use of machines and transport equipment driven by low-cost energy became the hallmark of industrial societies throughout the world. Where it has been acquired, low cost energy has multiplied Man's productive output, and thereby his income, by a very large factor. Each gallon of gasoline used in a small engine, for example, can do the work of a gang of laborers for many hours, or can run a motorcycle for 75 miles. The relationship between per capita energy use and per capita Gross National Product is strikingly shown in Figure 10.1.

---

[1] The words "energy" and "power" are often used synonomously as in *electric energy* and *electric power*. However, technically speaking, they do have different meanings. *Power* is the capacity to do work, while *energy* is a measure of the work done. An automobile with an engine rated at 100 horsepower has that power whether running at full speed or standing in the garage. If the car is driven for three hours, it will expend 300 horsepower-hours (HPH) of energy. These mechanical units of power and energy can be translated into equivalent electrical units. One horsepower is equivalent to 746 watts (.746 kilowatt) of electrical power. The kilowatt-hour is the standard measure of electric energy use in the home.

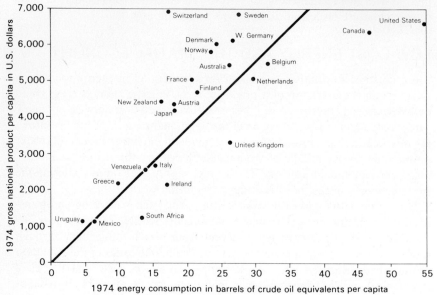

ENERGY CONSUMPTION PER CAPITA AND GROSS
NATIONAL PRODUCT PER CAPITA FOR SELECTED COUNTRIES

Figure 10.1   Extremely high per capita energy consumptions in the United States and Canada are reflections of high incomes, relatively low energy prices historically, and the need to move people, goods, and information over great distances within spatial economies of continental proportions. (Source: The National Energy Plan, Executive Office of the President, Washington, D.C., *April 29, 1977, p. 3.*)

The availability and cheapness of energy not only transformed the spatial economies of the industrializing parts of the world, but also had an integrating effect on the global economy as a whole. Low cost energy applied to a succession of new inventions made possible the efficient, and therefore the low cost, movement of people, bulk commodities, and information. This stimulated regional specialization of production and the exchange of commodities in a worldwide trade network.

The past several decades have also seen great increases in electrical transmission efficiencies. Within urban and industrial regions, electric energy from interconnected central power stations—these can be fossil fuel (coal, petroleum, or natural gas), hydroelectric, or nuclear powered—reach domestic, commercial, industrial, and perhaps even farm consumers through extensive networks of transmission and distribution lines. As time passes, more and more "super" power grids are being developed to interconnect productive regions. In some cases, the grids have been constructed across international boundaries. The United States-Canadian and the various European interconnections are examples; less commonly known electric power linkages also now exist across Kenya-Uganda, Tunisia-Algeria, and Argentina-Paraguay, and a regional network interconnects Ghana, Togo, and Dahomey. Others in Africa and Latin America are in the planning stage.

THE GLOBAL ENERGY CRISIS: CULMINATION OF A FIFTY YEAR TREND TOWARD DEPENDENCE ON MIDDLE EAST OIL

THE IMPORTANCE OF PETROLEUM

Oil seeping to the surface of the ground in certain regions of the United States was considered a nuisance in the middle of the last century. By the end of the century, however, oil had become a major industry. The rapid rise of automobile and truck transport in the first decades of this century stimulated an explosive growth in all aspects of the petroleum industry, particularly in the United States. It has been said that World War II was "run on petroleum." During that war, 60 percent of United States ocean freight tonnage was made up of petroleum and its products.

Unlike coal, petroleum is a twentieth century phenomenon. Unlike coal too, many of the great oil reserves of the world are located in regions of hostile environment, where other forms of economic activity are limited (*e.g.,* Saudi Arabia, Kuwait, Iran, Libya, Iraq etc.) (Table 10.1). While coal was a key factor influencing economic location in Europe and North America in the nineteenth century, the great industrial regions, for the most part, were already established when the demand for petroleum products began to accelerate.

The geographical disparity between industrial markets and the reserves of oil have set the world stage for geopolitical rivalries that seem to grow more acute with time. Their own great reserves did not keep the United States and the USSR from a confrontation over Middle East oil. The United States was ready to back up its stand with the force of arms against the threatened Soviet occupation of Iran, shortly after World War II.

An economic phenomenon of profound significance during the past half century has been the shift in the industrial world away from coal and toward low cost imported petroleum as a primary energy source. The low production costs in the Persian Gulf region are the result of high economic rent, related to environmental advantage. Extremely favorable geological structures and scientifically managed regional extraction methods result in average well production *several hundred times* as great as the average American well.

Table 10.1   Petroleum Output in Major Producing Nations, 1976

Place	Crude Petroleum Production (Thousand Metric Tons)	Percent of World Production
World	2,863,518	100.0
USSR	519,677	18.1
Saudi Arabia[a]	425,804	14.9
United States	401,211	14.0
Iran[a]	295,084	10.3
Venezuela[a]	120,153	4.2
Iraq[a]	112,284	3.9
Kuwait[a]	108,046	3.8
Nigeria[a]	103,479	3.6
United Arab Emirates[a]	95,265	3.3
Libya[a]	93,452	3.3
China	85,000[b]	3.0
Indonesia[a]	74,195[b]	2.6
Canada	62,152	2.2
Algeria[a]	50,423	1.8

[a] OPEC Nations.
[b] Estimated.

Source: Adapted from *United Nations Statistical Yearbook, 1977.*

Also making this shift possible was the development of a great world tanker fleet. Even the United States, with its large reserve, could not keep up with growing domestic demand for oil. In 1920, coal furnished over three-quarters of American energy needs, while oil and natural gas combined furnished less than 20 percent. By 1972, the situation was almost completely reversed (Fig. 10.2). Thus, by 1972, a major feature of the international oil trade was the dependence it created on the Arab oil-producing countries by the large consuming countries of Western Europe, Japan, and, to a lesser extent, the United States (Fig. 10.3). The outbreak of Middle East hostilities and the drastic increases in prices marked the end of a fifty year trend. The year 1973 can be viewed as the last of a long period of ascending world energy use, under the impetus of low energy prices. Looking ahead into the future, there appears to be no likelihood of a return to the low price levels enjoyed before that threshold.[2]

---

[2] The term energy "crisis" is particularly appropriate here if we interpret the word in its original meaning as a "turning point."

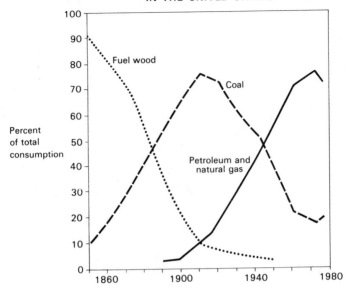

SHIFTS IN FUEL USE PATTERNS
IN THE UNITED STATES

Figure 10.2   (Source: The National Energy Plan, *April 29, 1977, p. 6.*)

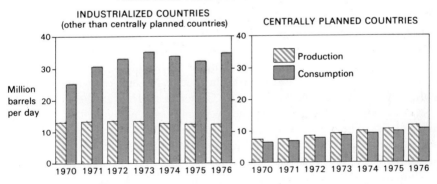

PETROLEUM PRODUCTION AND CONSUMPTION

Figure 10.3   This chart demonstrates in unmistakable terms the energy dilemma of the industrialized Western Democracies and Japan. Compared to the USSR and other centrally planned countries, their consumption of oil continued to far exceed their production, even after the supply crisis and price rises of 1974. (Source: Adapted from World Bank, *"World Economic and Social Indicators", Report No. 700/79/02, April, 1979, Chart No. 8, p. 30.)*

THE GLOBAL ENERGY CRISIS

The nations of the world have since come to feel the impact of higher cost energy in all sectors of their economies. One serious consequence, mentioned earlier, has been that LDC's have found it difficult to pay for petroleum-based fertilizers needed to produce an important share of their food. In a sense the low income people of the Third World feel the problem more acutely than any others, since rising prices restrict their already marginal use of oil for essential cooking, heating and lighting needs.

THE IMPACT ON THE UNITED STATES

With less than six percent of the world's population, the United States accounts for over 30 percent of the global energy consumption. Overwhelmingly, this energy has been supplied by mineral fuels—96 percent in 1976. Every day each person in the United States uses an average of four gallons of oil, 300 cubic feet of natural gas, 15 pounds of coal, and smaller amounts of other forms of energy. This is substantially more than the average of other industrial countries and eight times as much as the world average.

The United States and Canada use more energy per unit of Gross National Product than any other nation (Fig. 10.1). Part of the reason for the prodigious use of energy in the United States and Canada is spatial. These countries are very large and thinly populated compared to most other Highly Developed Countries. The United States spends fully 25 percent of its total national energy budget (over half of its petroleum budget) on transportation. This compares with 10 to 15 percent for the countries of Western Europe and Japan.

Beyond this, however, there has been a tradition of extravagant energy use based on low prices in the United States and Canada. The use of large, high fuel-consuming cars in these countries was encouraged by gasoline prices considerably lower than those in the rest of the world. Lavish use of low-cost energy also characterized other sectors of the American economy. In New York City the World Trade Center, completed in the early 1970s, was designed with an electric energy requirement equivalent to that of a small city. The high use by energy-intensive industry groups in the United States, compared with those in West Germany, is shown in Figure 10.4. The United States was a net exporter of oil in 1948, but by 1972 it was importing 29 percent of its requirement.

Following the oil embargo of 1973-1974, prices of OPEC (Organization of Petroleum Exporting Countries) oil were raised by more than 400 percent precipitating the world recession of 1974-1975 (Fig. 10.5) Despite this, United States oil imports rose from 29 percent to 42 percent of demand between 1972 and 1976, creating a serious balance of payments problem for the United States, and the value of the dollar dropped to record lows on the world currency exchange.

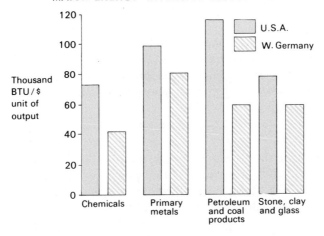

U.S. INDUSTRY ENERGY EFFICIENCY
COMPARED TO WEST GERMANY, FOR
MAJOR ENERGY–INTENSIVE INDUSTRIES

Figure 10.4 (Source: The National Energy Plan, *April 29, 1977, p. 44.*)

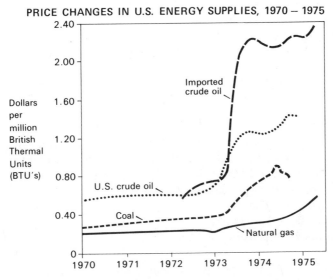

PRICE CHANGES IN U.S. ENERGY SUPPLIES, 1970 – 1975

Figure 10.5   While the increase in the price of imported crude oil was sudden and dramatic in 1973, it also triggered substantial increases in the other major energy fuels for the United States. The repercussions of these and subsequent price increases have been felt in every facet of the economy. (Source: Environmental Quality, *Council on Environmental Quality, 1976, Washington, D.C., p. 105.*)

THE GLOBAL ENERGY CRISIS

ENERGY: THE ACHILLES' HEEL OF THE UNITED STATES?

Late in 1975 the Library of Congress released a report after a lengthy study of the world energy situation. The report stated, "Energy may well become the 'Achilles' Heel' of U.S. foreign policy the same way as agricultural shortages are for the Soviet Union." The study concluded that the United States' reliance on Arab oil would grow rather than diminish. In contrast, it predicted that Great Britain and Norway would become energy-independent by the early 1980s with oil from their North Sea fields.

Oil imports to the United States rose to 8.7 million barrels in 1977, and dropped to 8.1 million barrels in 1978, due to the new contribution from Alaska. The 1978 import figure, however, was fully one-third higher than that in 1973, and represented half of total United States demand.

ADELMAN'S COMMENTS ON FUTURE PETROLEUM AVAILABILITY

An economist's interpretation of future oil availability has been offered by M. A. Adelman of M.I.T. The following is excerpted from a transcript of a discussion between Professor Adelman and William F. Buckley on the television program *Firing Line*, telecast on the Public Broadcasting System on September 23, 1973:

Mr. Adelman: "Apparently our vision expands as fast as our use. So I don't find it convincing to make estimates of what the ultimate findable amounts are because in fact nobody knows, and if it's true that nobody knows, then we need something, some theory or policy to let us live with ignorance, and in fact we have one. . . . ." [Mr. Adelman refers here to the price mechanism] "So, in a very important sense, oil is unlimited in the sense that we'll never get to the end of it. . . . If substitutes don't materialize, then it will become a very scarce and expensive commodity."

Mr. Buckley: "Like perfume."

Mr. Adelman: "Like perfume, and we'll have to treat it and dole it out by the drop."

Mr. Buckley: "And simply readjust our culture."

Mr. Adelman: "Exactly—like it or not."

Mr. Buckley: "Or discover something else."

Mr. Adelman: "Or discover something else."

Mr. Buckley: "Is that in prospect?"

Mr. Adelman: "It's in prospect if you spend enough money to do so."

The sudden drop in crude oil production in Iran following the revolution there, and other events since have rendered the world energy situation more politically volatile than ever. About the only prediction that seemed reasonable in early 1980 was that the United States, along with other nations, will continue its reliance on huge OPEC oil imports through the 1980s in an attempt to buy the time necessary to switch to alternative energy sources. Among other things, the level of future petroleum imports will depend on how much new oil and gas are found domestically, and how costly it will be to produce and market it.

During the coming decade the possibility exists of importing crude oil from what appear to be very large, undrilled formations in Latin America, Africa, and elsewhere (Fig. 10.6).

How to bring about greater self-reliance in energy supply for the United States, without suffering drastic economic dislocations, is an exceedingly difficult problem. Whatever form long-range national energy planning takes, it will have to be based on knowledge of the various alternative energy sources reviewed below.

ENERGY ALTERNATIVES FOR THE UNITED STATES

In any discussion of future energy alternatives, it is imperative to stress the need for greater conservation. The U.S. Energy Research and Development Administration (ERDA), in its revised energy development plan submitted to Congress in 1976, put the highest priority on conservation measures. *The National Energy Plan*, released in the spring of 1977 by the Executive Office of the President, also spoke of the critical need for conservation, and the President reiterated this in his Energy Statement of July 15, 1979.

PROSPECTS AND PROBLEMS OF EXPANDED COAL USE

One policy option for the United States is the expanded use of its enormous coal reserves. Coal is one of its great natural resources in terms of both quantity and quality (Fig. 10.7). The nation is a world leader in production (Table 10.2). A significant part of the reserves are high-grade, thick bedded, near the surface, and located in strata that are unfolded and unfaulted (Fig. 10.8). This provides the opportunities for very high levels of mechanization with special purpose coal mining equipment in both underground and surface mining (Fig. 10.9).

Coal wages in the United States are the highest in the world; however, underground mining in central Appalachia, as well as surface mining there and elsewhere in the United States, is by far the most highly mechanized in the world. As a result, labor productivity in United States coal mines is

WORLDWIDE CONCENTRATION OF OIL DRILLING

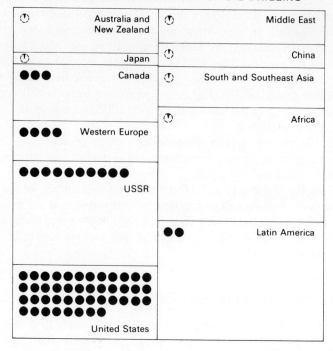

Figure 10.6   Oil drilling throughout the world through 1976, compared to the size of areas favorable for petroleum occurrence. The number of dots are proportional to the number of wells drilled. Note the small number of wells in the Middle East, where the world's greatest production occurs. Extraction techniques used there result in relatively few, widely spaced wells, each producing large amounts in a geologically coordinated unit operation. The significance of Latin America and Africa as possible future sources of petroleum is suggested in this chart. (Source: Dr. Bernardo F. Grossling, Research Geophysicist, U.S. Geological Survey, News Release, Department of the Interior, February 26, 1976.)

much higher than anywhere else (Table 10.3). This, together with low-cost rail and barge transport from the mines to Eastern markets and ports, gives the United States coal industry a very competitive position.

The United States is thus a low-cost producer of high quality coals (including coking coals that have special physical properties necessary for blast furnace operations). Despite the inland location of the mines, United States coal can be exported competitively to many parts of the globe. Immediately after World War II, massive coal exports to Western Europe permitted the

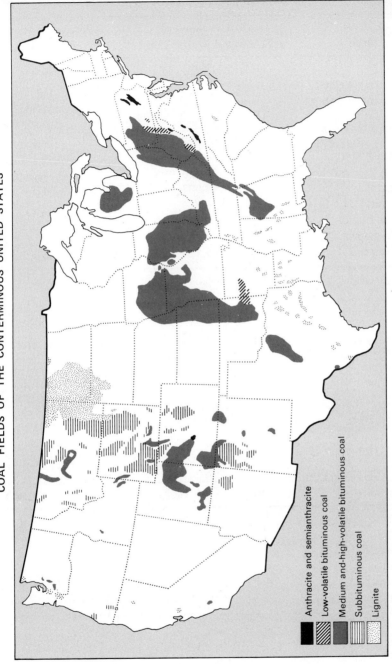

Anthracite and semianthracite
Low-volatile bituminous coal
Medium and-high-volatile bituminous coal
Subbituminous coal
Lignite

Figure 10.7 (Source: *U.S. Geological Survey*.)

Table 10.2   Coal Output in Major Producing Nations

Place	Coal Production[a] (Thousand Metric Tons)	Percent of World Production
World	2,419,993	100.0
United States	585,684	24.2
USSR	494,377	20.4
China	480,000[b]	19.8
Poland	179,303	7.4
United Kingdom	123,822	5.1
India	100,870	4.2
Germany, Federal Republic of	95,902	4.0
South Africa	75,730	3.1
Australia	67,820[b]	2.8

[a] Does not include brown coal and lignite production.
[b] Estimated.

Source: Adapted from United Nations Statistical Yearbook, 1977.

prostrate countries there to survive several critical winters. At one time or another since, coal shipped from special port facilities, such as those at Newport News, Virginia, has been sold in European markets, and even as far away as Chile and Japan.

Compared with petroleum and natural gas, coal reserves within the United States could serve as an energy and raw material source for genera-

Table 10.3   Output per Man Day at United States and European Underground Coal Mines (Net Tons)

	1947	1957	1967	1976
United States[a]	5.49	8.91	15.07	9.10
United Kingdom	1.61	1.76	3.15	2.44
Belgium	0.95	1.27	2.46	1.75
France	1.05	1.85	2.32	1.88
West Germany	1.32	1.75	3.60	3.84

[a] Does not include anthracite mines.

Source: Adapted from National Coal Association, Washington, D.C., Data from Department of Energy and Foreign Official Publications.

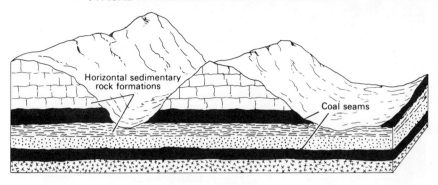

Figure 10.8   Cross section showing a bituminous coal deposit in the dissected plateau region of West Virginia. These are thick, high-grade coal beds lying in unfolded and unfaulted seams at or near the surface. These conditions permit very low-cost, mechanized mining. Most Midwest and Western coal is surface mined, also in highly mechanized operations. Most bituminous coal in Europe is produced underground, in relatively deep shaft mines, where seams are thin and often folded and faulted. Under these conditions, mechanization is limited, and much pick and shovel labor is required to recover the coal. Production of coal in Europe is often supported by State subsidies.

tions, depending on future prices and depletion rates. One estimate shows 1990 domestic coal production to be 1.2 billion tons annually, nearly twice the 1975 production of 670 million tons.

The largest domestic user of coal will continue to be the electric utilities, which will account for perhaps half of domestic coal demand in 1990. By 1990 about 20 percent of projected coal output is expected to be used for the production of synthetic oil and gas. Future production levels will be influenced, as usual, by prices, but will also be affected by mining legislation and the pace of technological advances, such as the development of flue gas desulfurization.

Until recent years "western coal" in the United States remained in a low state of development because it is lower grade and because it is located far from the large urban and industrial markets in the Midwest and East. Now, however, because of its low sulfur content and new pollution regulations, and because it can be strip mined, most future growth in domestic supply is expected to take place in the western coal region. As energy prices rise, the lower grades and the long distance to market become less disadvantageous.

Strip (surface) mining (Fig. 10.10) has certain economic advantages over undergrounding mining. Strip mining, where it is environmentally feasible,

(a)

(b)

Figure 10.9 (see facing page) Continuous mining machines (a) use whirling cutting teeth to rip coal from underground seams. Coal is conveyed backward to shuttle cars (b). Extremely favorable environmental conditions permit a level of mechanization in Appalachian underground mines found nowhere else in the world. (Source: *Joy Manufacturing Co.*)

has a much lower ratio of fixed to variable costs. A strip mine is therefore a much more flexible operation than an underground mine, since the operator can adjust the level of production more closely to market conditions. Strip mining also requires much less labor input per ton, and the rate of coal recovery is higher than in underground mining, where only about half of the coal is recovered. Another advantage of strip mining is that it is safer and healthier for the miners, who do not have to spend a good part of their lives deep underground.

Figure 10.10 Bucket-wheel excavator used in surface coal mining. Note the size of the automobile in the foreground. (Source: *U.S. Geological Survey.*)

ENERGY ALTERNATIVES FOR THE UNITED STATES

The proposed expansion of surface coal mining, however, will create environmental problems and the need for land restoration. Strip mining leaves the land scarred if not reclaimed (Fig. 10.11), and reclamation becomes a cost of production. A 1972 report by the U.S. Council on Environmental Quality stated that 4 million acres of land had been gouged by surface mining, and that about half that area had been reclaimed in some way. New legislation and regulations require greater reclamation efforts. Certain other forms of environmental impact cannot be corrected.

Environmental problems (negative externalities) also result from the burning of coal by the purchaser. In steam electric stations only about 40 percent of the potential energy is converted into electrical energy; 10 percent is exhausted into the stack and 50 percent of the energy is transferred to the cooling water and discharged into the environment (Fig. 10.12). (The need to dissipate heat has long been a key location factor for steam electric power stations; see Fig. 10.13). The burning of coal also releases gases containing

Figure 10.11   Geologic studies suggest that underground mining of coal may cause more environmental damage over long periods of time than surface mining followed by proper reclamation. The subsidence pits shown here resulted from collapse of the surface into voids left by underground mining at the Monarch mine near Sheridan, Wyoming. The mine was abandoned in 1914. (Source: U.S. Geological Survey.)

Figure 10.12   The twin chimneys of the Homer City Electric Generating Station near Johnstown, Pennsylvania, are two of the tallest structures in the world, rising 1216 feet—nearly a quarter of a mile. The capacity of the station is 650,000 kilowatts. The two cooling towers are 367 feet high. Each tower cools 225,000 gallons of water from 120° to 90° F every minute. (Source: New York State Electric and Gas Corporation and Pennsylvania Electric Company.)

known and suspected toxic elements, such as sulfur, arsenic, mercury, beryllium, fluorine, cadmium, selenium, and zinc. These elements may also enter the soil or groundwater during disposal of ash from coal burning plants. The U.S. Geological Survey, Bureau of Mines, and other federal agencies have given the environmental problems of coal utilization top research priority.

OIL SHALE AND OTHER UNCONVENTIONAL HYDROCARBONS

The escalation in energy prices since 1973 has stimulated interest in several unconventional hydrocarbon energy sources. In Canada, the Athabascan tar sands of Northern Alberta have been producing small quantities of oil for decades. (55,000 barrels a day in 1977). Other oil-bearing formations that

ENERGY ALTERNATIVES FOR THE UNITED STATES   263

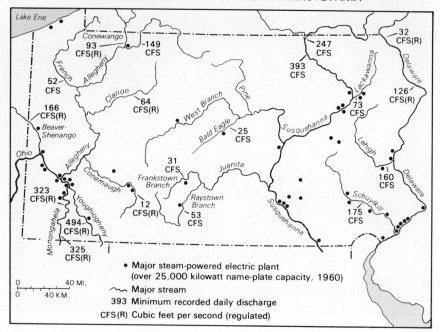

Figure 10.13   The degree to which steam powered electric plants are associated spatially with sources of cooling water is shown by this map. Only a few of the major steam electric generating plants in Pennsylvania in 1960 were not located directly on a river site. Minimum recorded discharge figures at selected gaging stations are shown. The need for cooling water is growing with time, both for nuclear-fueled and fossil-fueled plants. (Source: *George F. Deasy and Phyllis R. Griess,* "Factors Influencing Distribution of Steam-Electric Generating Plants," The Professional Geographer, *Vol. XII, Number 3, May, 1960, Fig. 3, p. 3.*)

are being studied are the oil shales and tar sands of the Western United States, the black shales of the Eastern United States, tight sandstones of the Rocky Mountain Region, and the geopressured zones underlying the Gulf of Mexico and its adjacent coastal plain. All these sources are potentially vast, but much more research must be done on the very difficult problems of economic recovery.

Commercial and environmental feasibility may be close in the case of some of the Western oil shales. Enormous quantities of oil are trapped in the pore spaces of this rock. Some of the high grade oil shales yield over 140 gallons of oil per ton; most shales of potential commercial interest yield from 25 to 65 gallons per ton. Shale containing about 80 billion barrels of oil from the higher grade Western deposits is considered potentially workable with present methods of extraction. The increase in domestic energy prices has shifted much of the oil shale reserves—about 11 million acres in Colorado, Utah, and Wyoming—to a higher, "recoverable" category (Fig. 10.14). However, the full scale production of oil from shale will still require the solution of a number of problems. Very large-scale, capital-intensive surface operations are required to mine the shale and to free the oil from the rock. Daily disposal of huge amounts of waste material is one potentially difficult problem; another is the need to acquire large quantities of process water in the semi-arid climate.

PRINCIPAL OIL–SHALE DEPOSITS OF THE
UNITED STATES

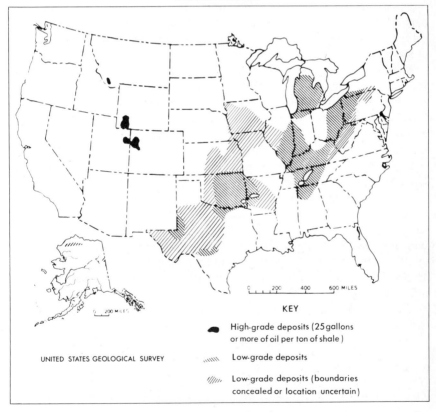

KEY

High-grade deposits (25 gallons
or more of oil per ton of shale)

Low-grade deposits

Low-grade deposits (boundaries
concealed or location uncertain)

UNITED STATES GEOLOGICAL SURVEY

Figure 10.14   (Source: *U.S. Geological Survey.*)

NUCLEAR POWER

In the early 1960s, nuclear reactors used as heat sources for central station electric generation in the United States advanced from the experimental to the commercial stage. By the beginning of 1979, there were 72 nuclear electric power plants licensed to operate in the United States, and 133 more plants in various stages of construction or planning (Fig. 10.15).

Since the crisis at the Three Mile Island Plant on the Susquehanna River below Harrisburg, Pennsylvania, in March 1979, the entire question of future nuclear power development in the United States has become uncertain. Up through 1978, proponents of nuclear energy anticipated that half of this nation's central station electricity would be generated by nuclear plants by 2000 A.D. However, after the incident at Three Mile Island, no one in or out of government could predict the future course of nuclear power with any degree of assurance.

The necessity for very large nuclear power plants for cost effectiveness is part of the problem (Fig. 10.16). The siting of nuclear electric stations is sharply constrained by a series of negative externalities, such as the disposal of wastes.

Another major problem, brought to international attention at Three Mile Island, is the removal of heat from the reactor. In the middle 1970s a decision was made not to erect a nuclear power plant on the shore of Lake Cayuga, near Cornell University in central New York State. The decision was made because the increase in water temperature caused by discharges into the lake would adversely affect its limnology.

Even before the spring of 1979, the location of nuclear power plants in the United States was very strongly influenced by public fears of nuclear catastrophes and other possible hazards to human health and the environment. Construction of proposed plants had been delayed time and time again. The strict regulation of nuclear plant siting diminished greatly the potential locations for new plants, especially in high market potential areas. Despite this, in 1979 within the United States, 10 million people lived within 20 miles of an operating nuclear reactor and about 100 million people lived within 50 miles of one (Fig. 10.17).

Critics of nuclear power point out another problem. Uranium 235 is the fuel used in nuclear powered plants in the United States and nearly all others throughout the world. Uranium 235 is a comparatively rare element,

Figure 10.15   (see facing page) Because of space limitations, symbols may not show precise locations of nuclear generating units. (Source: Adapted from U.S. Department of Energy.)

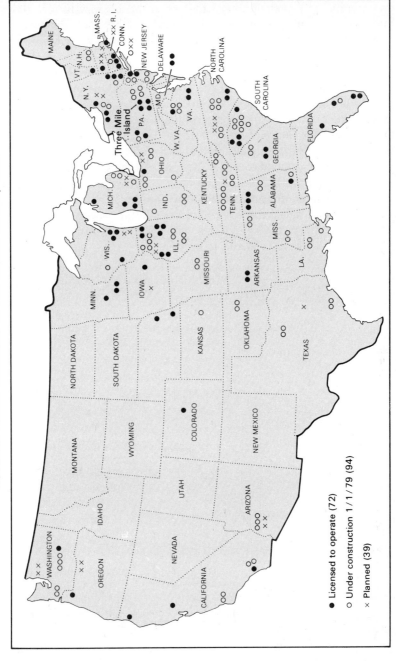

NUCLEAR POWER REACTORS IN THE UNITED STATES, 1979

- Licensed to operate (72)
- Under construction 1/1/79 (94)
- Planned (39)

267

and there is only enough known to exist in this country to fuel about 500 plants for 30 years. Plutonium could be substituted. It can be produced by bombarding Uranium 238, the more common isotope of uranium, with neutrons. A different type of nuclear reactor, called a *breeder reactor,* has been developed here and in Europe to make plutonium at the same time that it generates power. A problem of the greatest magnitude exists here because the plutonium produced could be used to make nuclear weapons. A very small quantity (about 20 pounds) is all that is needed to make a crude bomb. Quite clearly, the future of the nuclear power industry throughout the world is bound up with the critical question of nuclear arms proliferation.

It is therefore difficult to assess the future of nuclear power development elsewhere in the world. During the 1970s, a number of countries, including the Soviet Union, France, Brazil, and—ironically, it would seem—Iran, adopted a "full speed ahead" policy on nuclear power development. To what degree, if any, these programs will be revised in the light of the Three Mile Island experience remains to be seen.

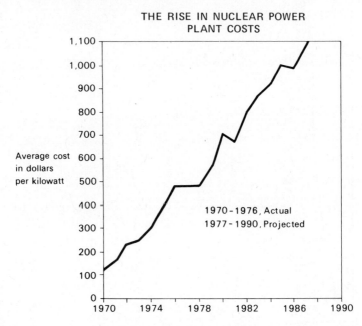

Figure 10.16 The cost of plants going into production was over $500 per kilowatt in 1979, four times the $130 per kilowatt cost for plants completed in 1970. (Source: Henry R. Linden, et al., "Perspectives on U.S. and World Energy Problems," Report published by Gas Research Institute and Institute of Gas Technology, Chicago, Feb., 1979, Chart No. 79.)

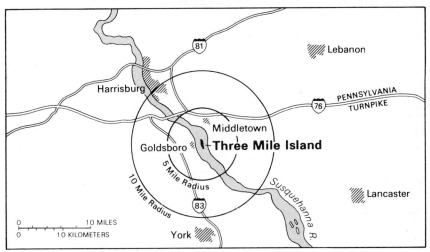

Figure 10.17   The plant is located on an island in the Susquehanna River, which flows southeast into the Chesapeake Bay. The towns of Goldsboro and Middletown lie within a few miles of the plant site; within 10 miles are located a long section of the Pennsylvania Turnpike and the southern edge of the City of Harrisburg, capital of Pennsylvania. Within 25 miles of the plant lie three other cities and a productive agricultural region. (Source: *Adapted by permission from* TIME, *The Weekly Newsmagazine; Copyright Time Inc., 1979.*)

HYDROELECTRIC ENERGY AND PUMPED STORAGE PLANTS

The future role of hydroelectric energy is constantly being reevaluated as energy prices rise, because it does not create the pollution problems that fuel-burning steam electric stations do, and because it does not require the consumption of fossil fuels. Only a small proportion of all electric energy generated in the United States is hydroelectric. In some regions of the United States and some nations, however, the proportion of hydroelectric power is high.

The spatial distribution of hydroelectric plants is related to the costs of producing the energy and of transmitting it to a market. Production costs are a function of two environmental factors: topography and hydrology. Hydroelectric power is based on the principle that water under pressure, a "head," will drive a water wheel or turbine, transforming hydraulic energy into mechanical energy. The turbine is direct-coupled to a generator, which

ENERGY ALTERNATIVES FOR THE UNITED STATES   269

in turn converts the mechanical energy to electrical energy for transmission and distribution.

A region with heavy rainfall and with a hilly topography has an environmental advantage for hydroelectric production in Ricardian terms. However, a site with superior natural features may be of little economic value if it is remote from a market. The familiar production cost–transport cost trade-off applies here as in other forms of economic activity.

In the past, large hydroelectric sites have acted as magnets for industries that require high inputs of low-cost electric energy per unit of product. In some cases, such as at Niagara Falls, the stream discharge is large and the drop in elevation is precipitous, providing a tremendous source of electric energy in the power plant below the falls. In other cases, Man intervenes to provide an artificial head by damming a stream and creating a reservoir.

In the United States and, following its lead, in many other nations, hydroelectric power has been combined with other benefits in very large scale, multiple-purpose river projects (see Fig. 6.11). The best large hydroelectric sites in the United States have already been developed. As a result, hydro's share of electric energy generation in the United States is expected to decline from 15 percent in 1975 to about 8 percent in 1990.

In recent years, however, rising energy prices have increased interest in the development of *pumped storage plants.* These specially designed plants operate within large systems, generating energy for the system at peak hours to help meet peak demands. Then, at low-demand hours, such as at night or on weekends, electric energy from the regional grid is used to run the plant turbines (which are reversible) as pumps to reverse the flow and pump the water from the pool below the plant up to the higher one above the plant, for use in electric generation during the next peak period. An advantage of the pumped storage plant is that it requires only a small impoundment of water, which is used over and over again. Of course, this is not a case of getting something for nothing. The laws of conservation of energy still apply, and there is an overall loss of energy in the system. However, from the economic standpoint, the operation pays off by providing high-value, peak-hour energy to the system and consuming low-value, off-peak-hour energy from the system.

GEOTHERMAL ELECTRIC POWER

The molten core of the earth represents an unlimited source of heat energy. However, under present technology this heat can be tapped in only a few places, where it penetrates upward close to the surface, heating water in the rocks and producing steam under pressure. The steam in such places can be tapped to run a steam turbine, which in turn drives a generator, which produces electricity.

The world's largest geothermal electric power plant is located about 100 miles north of San Francisco, at the site of a very large earth heat source. The plant, which has a capacity of 600,000 kilowatts of power, is part of a federally sponsored research program, which expects to double the plant capacity by 1982. This is part of a project that aims at deriving enough electric energy from Northern California sites to meet the needs of a city the size of San Francisco. Elsewhere in the United States, exploratory drilling has found only very limited sources of underground steam suitable for electric power generation. Among the other nations, Italy, Iceland, Japan, and several others have geothermal power plants operating on a commercial basis.

SOLAR ENERGY

Solar energy has always enjoyed a universal appeal, because it is perpetual and pollution free. By the end of the 1970s, solar energy was being used on a small scale in many places, primarily for space and water heating. The amount of solar energy reaching the earth's surface is exceedingly large, but its concentration and storage on a large scale pose difficult problems. Solar installations require high capital investment for the amount of useful energy produced.

In the summer of 1979, the President announced a solar energy program, setting a goal of meeting 20 percent of the nation's energy needs from all forms of solar energy by the year 2000. However, this includes hydroelectric power, wind power, and other derivative forms not normally classified as solar energy.

One longer range possibility under investigation is the use of satellite solar stations to intercept energy from the sun and transmit it to earth. The dictum bears repeating here that the greatest resource of all is Man's mind.

SUMMARY

The modern world has developed and been sustained by progressively lower cost energy supplies. Global consumption of fossil fuels doubled five times over the last hundred years, as productivity and per capita incomes rose rapidly in the industrializing parts of the world. The year 1973 marked a turning point in the world energy situation, after 50 years of growing dependence by the United States, Western Europe, and Japan on low-priced Middle East oil. A fourfold increase in oil prices brought the era of cheap fossil fuels to an end. Since then energy prices have risen faster than the rate of inflation, creating serious consequences for the Less Developed as well as the Highly Developed Countries. Higher energy prices and increasing political uncertainties have stimulated the quest for alternative sources of energy that will reduce dependence on oil from the OPEC nations. Nevertheless, the United States will continue to be a large net importer of oil through the 1980s. World supplies of petroleum and natural gas are approaching economic limits, and production is expected to peak before the end of the century and then decline. Large reserves of coal represent a major resource asset for the United States, where production and exports are based on thick, high grade seams that permit highly mechanized, low-cost mining. Decisions on energy alternatives for the United States will depend on the public's perception of nuclear energy and on the need to preserve environmental quality, as well as on prices and reliability of supply. The longer run shift away from oil toward other energy sources will require an increased emphasis on conservation. Higher energy prices have stimulated research and development on solar based and other renewable forms of energy. Future changes in the production and consumption of energy will have an impact on the spatial economies of the United States and other nations.

Questions

1 Review the background of the world energy crisis of the 1970s.
2 Analyze the potentials and problems of coal as a future energy source for the United States.
3 Explain the statement "Energy may well become the Achilles' heel of United States foreign policy."
4 Analyze the potentials and problems of oil shale as a future energy source for the United States.
5 Explain the principle of a pumped storage hydroelectric plant.
6 Speculate about the impact on your lifestyle if the prices of all forms of energy were suddenly doubled.
7 What would be some spatial implications for the United States economy of a long-term commitment to (a) coal, (b) nuclear power?

11

INDUSTRIAL REGIONS AND THE LOCATION OF MANUFACTURING

"Industrial locations are usually not distributed at random, but group themselves in economic landscapes . . ."

"There is no scientific and unequivocal solution for the location of the individual firm, but only a practical one: the test of trial and error."

August Lösch*

The diffusion of the Industrial Revolution from Great Britain to various places throughout the world during the past two centuries has been described as the single most important cultural transformation in the history of humanity. The changes brought about in the way people live as a result of the Industrial Revolution have been dramatic almost beyond description. Even that visionary genius, Benjamin Franklin, could not have envisioned what any of us can see today all around us. The evolution of technologically based societies has provided unprecedented material wealth, health, and longer life to large segments of the world population. Where industrialization has taken hold, the use of machines, run by inanimate forms of energy, has increased Man's ability to produce goods and services by a hundred fold or more. This, plus the development of specialization—individual, product, firm, and regional—has increased productivity and therefore incomes by orders of magnitude.

*The Economics of Location, trans. W. H. Woglom, Yale University Press, New Haven, 1954, pp. 255 and 29. (Originally published by Gustav Fischer, Verlag, 1938).

CHARACTERISTICS OF MANUFACTURING INDUSTRY

THE NATURE OF MANUFACTURING

Manufacturing is a type of production involving the addition of *form utility* to an object or a set of objects. The U. S. Bureau of the Census defines manufacturing as a process that meets the following criteria:

The operation must be carried on in factory buildings and not in the field.
The process must involve an occupational division of labor, with individual workers performing separate, successive operations in the same production process.
Power-driven machinery must be used.
The industry must turn out a uniform product, not work made to a customer's order.

The term "manufacturing", specified in this way, does not apply to the large volume of products made throughout the world by hand labor in cottage or household industries. Nor does the term apply to the very important construction industry.

Manufacturing can be classified into two broad categories: the processing of raw materials, and the assembly of previously manufactured components. These are called *processing* and *fabricating* industries (Table 11.1). The pro-

Table 11.1   Breakdown of Manufacturing Industries into Standard Industrial Classification (SIC) Groups

SIC Code	Manufacturing Industry	Number of Establishments	Number of Employees (Thousands)	Value Added by Manufacture (Million Dollars)
	Processing Industries			
20	Food Products	28,184	1,569	$ 35,617
24	Lumber and Wood Products	33,948	691	10,309
26	Paper and Allied Products	6,038	633	13,064
28	Chemicals and Allied Products	11,425	836	32,414
29	Petroleum and Coal Products	2,016	139	5,793

274

Table 11.1   (continued)

SIC Code	Manufacturing Industry	Number of Establishments	Number of Employees (Thousands)	Value Added by Manufacture (Million Dollars)
32	Stone, Clay, and Glass	16,015	623	12,586
33	Primary Metal Industries	6,792	1,143	23,258
	Fabricating Industries			
21	Tobacco Products	272	66	2,637
22	Textile Mill Products	7,203	953	11,718
23	Apparel and Related Products	24,438	1,368	13,487
25	Furniture and Fixtures	9,232	462	6,089
27	Printing and Publishing	42,102	1,056	20,197
30	Rubber and Plastic Products	9,237	618	11,653
31	Leather Products	3,201	273	2,917
34	Fabricated Metal Products	29,525	1,493	26,946
35	Machinery, except Electrical	40,792	1,828	37,563
36	Electrical Machinery	12,274	1,662	30,584
37	Transportation Equipment	8,802	1,719	39,799
38	Instruments and Related Products	5,987	454	10,584
39	Miscellaneous Manufacturing	15,188	446	6,777

Source: Adapted from *Census of Manufactures, 1972,* U.S. Department of Commerce, Bureau of the Census, 1975.

CHARACTERISTICS OF MANUFACTURING INDUSTRY   275

cessing industries involving bulky, localized raw materials are those for which the Industrial Location Theory of Alfred Weber provides an explanatory model (Chapter 4). Referring to the general production model in Figure 5.1, the output of manufacturing production can be either *producer goods* or *consumer goods*. The manufactured producer goods are used further in the production process.

A distinguishing feature of manufacturing in the industrialized countries is high productivity, leading to high per capita incomes. This results from mechanization and the prodigious use of fossil fuels and other forms of energy. The flexibility of most manufacturing operations permits a wide substitution of production inputs. A clay bowl, a wheelbarrow, or even a motor vehicle can be produced under either labor intensive or capital intensive conditions. In Highly Developed Countries the price of capital (interest) is low relative to the price of labor (wages), and production tends to be capital intensive. In LDC's, the opposite condition generally prevails. General Motors produced the subcompact Chevrolet Vega on a completely automated assembly line with capital investment of hundreds of millions of dollars. However, General Motors has also designed and sold components for a "Basic Transportation Vehicle" that can be manufactured under labor intensive conditions in LDC's with a capital investment of under $100,000.

There are many other possibilities for input substitution in manufacturing, depending on the technology of the industry and the prices of the three principal factors of production: land (natural resources), labor, and capital. For example, automobile engine blocks can be made from either cast iron or aluminum; skis and tennis rackets can be made from either aluminum or wood. Since the prices of the factors of production vary from place to place, they influence the decisions by firms about both the type and location of manufacturing operations. Great variations exist in the growth rates of different manufacturing industries. This is a consideration in any analysis of a dynamic economic landscape.

Manufacturing is a spatially concentrated form of economic production. Unlike agriculture, grazing, hunting, recreation, or forestry, manufacturing has relatively small space requirements per unit of product. In his industrial location model, Alfred Weber assumed point locations for manufacturing plants (Chapter 4). Even in densely populated industrial regions, factory areas and workers' homes occupy only a fraction of the economic landscape. During World War II, the Ford Motor Company's River Rouge Plant worked three shifts, totaling 85,000 workers, producing military tanks in a plant complex less than two square miles.

It can be seen from Figures 11.1 and 11.2 that manufacturing production is spatially concentrated much more than population. Two great international industrial regions exist—one in Eastern North America and the other

PRINCIPAL AREAS OF MANUFACTURING

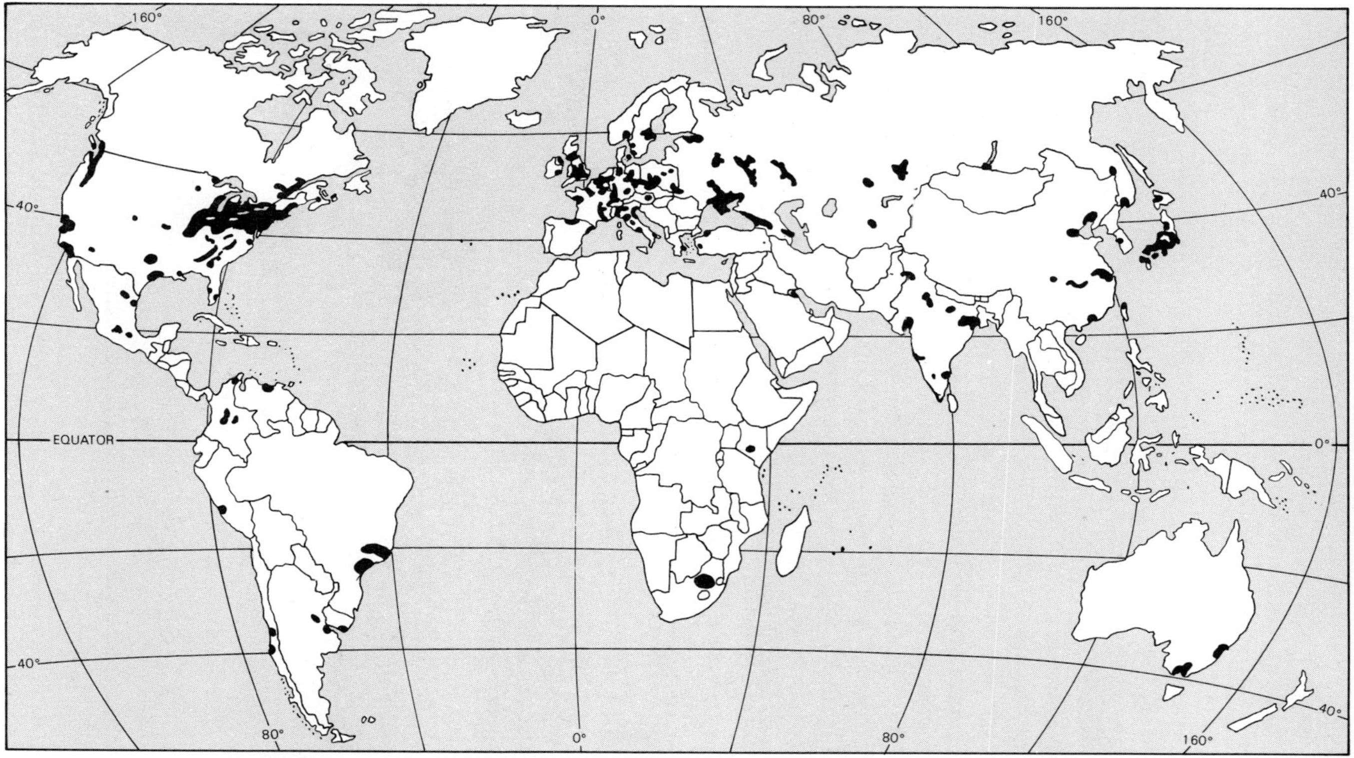

Figure 11.1 (Source: *Daniel Loetterle*).

277

in Europe. In addition, conspicuous national concentrations of manufacturing occur in The Soviet Union, Japan, India, and several other countries. Manufacturing location is highly correlated with urban agglomerations. The city as a location of manufacturing activity is an important topic that we discuss in Chapter 13.

To understand the spatial character of manufacturing we must realize that it is, itself, the source of supply for most manufacturing operations. The producer goods manufactured in one factory—such as parts, components, and subassemblies—become inputs to other fabricating plants. The result is a series of linked production stages that end up as goods and services for the ultimate consumers. This is an underlying reason for the clustering of most manufacturing firms in spatial agglomerations. Within such concentrations an individual firm gains many advantages.

Economic geographers and others interested in manufacturing generally agree that *value added by manufacture* is the most appropriate measure for most purposes. According to the Bureau of the Census, "value added by manufacture" is an approximation of the increase in value of materials as they move through the manufacturing process. Value added is determined by substracting the cost of materials used in the manufacturing process from

MANUFACTURING CONCENTRATIONS IN THE UNITED STATES AND CANADA

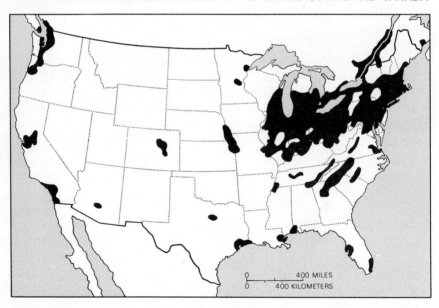

Figure 11.2   Due to different measurement criteria, this map is not totally compatible with figure 11.1. (Source: Daniel Loetterle).

the value of the finished products. Thus, value added includes the following: payrolls and payroll supplements, contract rent, interest on capital, taxes, depreciation, purchased business services such as insurance, legal, marketing, advertising, research, accounting, as well as profit. Value added by manufacture has an important advantage over *value of product,* because it avoids double or multiple counting. Consider this simple case: if we wish to measure the amount of manufacturing resulting from the production of one bakery, it would be misleading to count the value of bread sold, because part of that value was contributed by the miller of the wheat before it was shipped to the baker as flour. The same reasoning can be applied to the milling process. The value of the product of the miller (flour) includes the value of the wheat purchased from the farmer. In order to measure manufacturing activity without multiple counting, only the value actually added at each production site should be counted.

VARIATION IN THE SIZE OF FIRMS AND PLANTS

A wide variation exists in the size of manufacturing firms and establishments (plants). Moreover, one firm can consist of many establishments, referred to as *branch plants,* scattered throughout the nation, or, for that matter, many nations. The differences in size are not random, but are related to technological, economic, and spatial requirements.

A substantial share of world manufacturing is being performed by very large business firms (Table 11.2). General Motors represents a larger economic enterprise than most nations. Of the 50 largest economic entities in the world in the early 1970s, 37 were nations and 13 were multinational corporations. What is especially significant here is that the growth rates of many multinational corporations exceed those for the largest nations. The typical multinational manufacturing firm obtains production inputs from

Table 11.2   Percent Share of Assets Held and Value Added by Manufacture for 100 Largest United States Manufacturing Firms

	1950	1976
Percent share of assets held	39.7	45.5
	1972	
Percent share of total Value Added by Manufacture	33.0	

Source: U.S. Department of Commerce, Bureau of the Census, *Statistical Abstract of The United States—1977,* Tables 923 and 924, p. 565.

In industries such as oil it is no longer possible to be a major producer without operating as a multi-national corporation and competitive forces are likely to make multi-national operations essential in a wider range of industries. . . .

Companies with the best information on foreign plant location are those corporations who make foreign plant location facilities frequently enough to have developed a routine to handle such decisions. . . .

The foreign plant is likely to be established by an industry leader (e.g. Singer, N.C.R., Ford, IBM) anxious to protect business in a large export market threatened by tariffs.*

*Anthony Blackbourn, "The Spatial Behavior of American Firms in Western Europe," F.E. Ian Hamilton, Editor, *Spatial Perspectives on Industrial Organization and Decision-making*, John Wiley and Sons, New York, 1974, pp. 245, 246.

many nations and sells a wide range of products to customers in many nations.

Nevertheless, a surprising share of manufacturing, even in the industrialized nations, is still accounted for by small firms and establishments. This is so because economies of scale are less important in these lines of manufacturing. Small manufacturing firms have an advantage in serving specialized markets, such as those requiring frequent adjustments of style or design. Small firms are predominant in such lines as precision instruments, specialized machinery, and fashion clothing.

CONTRASTING INDUSTRY PATTERNS: BEVERAGES AND INTEGRATED STEEL MILLS

The maps showing World and American manufacturing (Figs. 11.1 and 11.2) are regional composites of many different industries. Specialized books on manufacturing geography and certain atlases show the locations of individual manufacturing industries. Here, we will briefly examine two contrasting industry patterns. Beer brewing and integrated iron and steel production are two extreme types, with respect to spatial distribution and other characteristics. Most other manufacturing industries would fall somewhere between them.

The numerous, highly dispersed breweries located throughout the United States and elsewhere can be understood in terms of several factors. A broad-based consumer demand exists in many nations. In some countries, unsafe drinking water has traditionally encouraged the use of substitutes, such as beer and wine, in which pathogenic organisms cannot survive.

On the production side, the ingredients for making beer—water, grain, yeast and hops—are ubiquitous (available in many places), the capital requirements do not have to be high, the technology is simple, and labor skills are minimal. Since the product is bulky, containing mostly water, it cannot be shipped very far without low cost, mechanized transport.

For these reasons, beer production historically has been found in towns and cities throughout many countries of the world, and it is generally one of the first process industries to appear in LDC's, at least where alcoholic beverages are not prohibited. Actually, much of the beer produced for local or home consumption in many countries is not bottled or canned and labeled, and therefore does not appear in national production statistics. For this reason, maps attempting to show the distribution of beer production are often misleading.

In recent decades in the United States and other HDC's, there has been a trend in the brewing industry toward consolidation and concentration of production in larger breweries. However, as in soft drink bottling and canning, the economies of large-scale plants must be weighed against unit transport costs, which become greater as the market area increases (see Fig. 3.2).

In contrast to beer or soft drink production, basic iron and steel production is concentrated to a very high degree (Table 11.3) (Fig. 11.3). The locational significance of integrated iron and steel mills[1] within an economy is very great. Each mill serves as a source of supply for hundreds of steel fabricating plants. Thus, a spatially interdependent system of supply and demand linkages is anchored back to the few, very large integrated iron and steel mills.

The basis for steel's universal use lies in its flexible set of properties and its low cost, which make it desirable for thousands upon thousands of products, ranging from hairpins to locomotives, from watch springs to suspension bridges. The amount of steel consumption per capita within an economy is a measure of the state of development of that economy.

When iron and steel production became a large-scale enterprise, using coking coal, the early industry in Europe, and later in the United States, developed near the coal mines. As the costs of bulk transport dropped after the advent of the railroads, the steel industry became less tied to coal and iron ore deposits, and more oriented toward the growing urban markets. When the shift to overseas iron ore began in the United States following World War II, a sizable proportion of new steel capacity was established at eastern ports, which are also close to large urban-industrial markets.

---

[1] An integrated mill takes in the basic raw materials—iron ore, coking coal, limestone, and water—produces pig iron, then steel, then rolling-mill products, in one large integrated operation (Fig. 11.4).

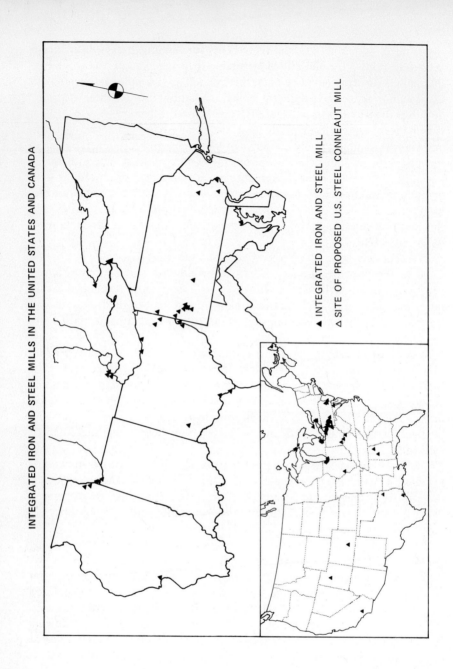

INTEGRATED IRON AND STEEL MILLS IN THE UNITED STATES AND CANADA

▲ INTEGRATED IRON AND STEEL MILL

△ SITE OF PROPOSED U.S. STEEL CONNEAUT MILL

282

Figure 11.3 (see facing page) Although smaller, nonintegrated steel plants, based on local supplies of steel scrap or delivered pig iron, are scattered throughout the country, the bulk of tonnage steel produced in the United States and Canada comes from the integrated mills shown. The U.S. Steel Corporation's proposed new Conneaut Mill, expected to be the largest in the world, will be located on the southern shore of Lake Erie, on the Pennsylvania-Ohio border. This will reinforce the dominance of the Pittsburgh-Great Lakes steel-producing region. (Source: Daniel Loetterle).

Basic iron and steel production, as it has evolved in most industrial regions, is based on the blast furnace-steel furnace-rolling mill sequence shown in Figure 11.4. (In certain places, such as in Sweden where coking coal is absent and hydroelectric power is abundant, electric arc furnace operation makes relatively small tonnages of high-grade steels, which are in demand throughout the world for special uses.) The integrated steel mill must be extremely large to be efficient, that is, to produce at low unit costs. This requires great energy and raw material inputs and a market large enough to absorb the continuous flow of many products and by-products. A preliminary operation that produces coke from coal (coke is used to charge the blast

Table 11.3   Major Steel Producing Nations

	Steel Production in 1976 (Thousand Metric Tons)	Percentage of World Total
World	675,000	100.0
USSR	144,805	21.5
United States	116,121	17.2
Japan	107,399	15.9
Germany, Federal Republic of	42,415	6.3
China	27,000[a]	4.0
Italy	23,446	3.5
France	23,221	3.4
United Kingdom	22,274	3.3
Poland	15,231	2.2
Czechoslovakia	14,693	2.2
Remainder of world	138,395	20.5

[a] Estimated.

Source: Adapted from *United Nations Statistical Yearbook, 1977.*

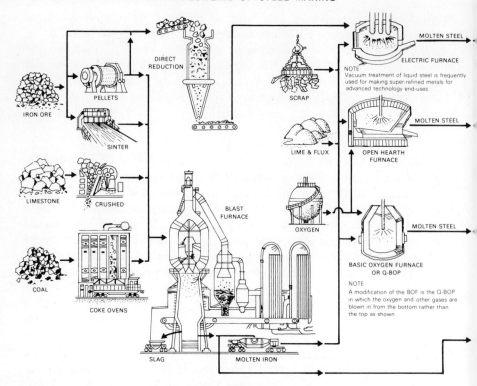

*Figure 11.4   Steel is iron combined with small amounts of carbon (usually less than one percent), and forms a large family of metals produced in hundreds of grades. Small amounts of alloying materials are used to make steels with special properties. The three steel-making processes shown—open hearth, basic oxygen, and electric furnace—normally account for more than 100 million tons each year in the United States. In the 1970s, the basic oxygen process gained leadership over the traditional open hearth method. (*Source: American Iron and Steel Institute, Washington, D.C.*)*

furnace) is a chemical process with many by-products, which require a large industrial market to be sold competitively. The processes of pig iron production and steel making are physically linked within an integrated mill to eliminate reheating and remelting the great masses of iron. Industrial regions generate large amounts of steel scrap, which is also used as an input to the steel furnaces.

The nature of the massive blast and steel furnace operations requires that they function on a continuous basis. Once an integrated mill is shut down, it

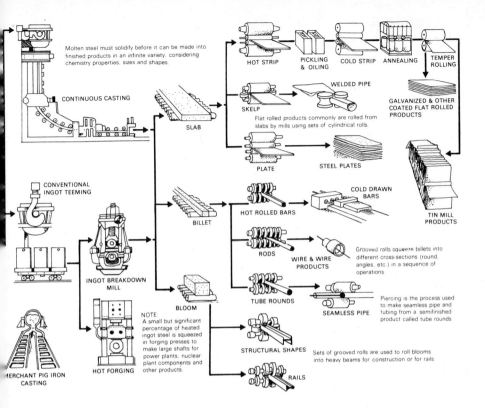

Molten steel must solidify before it can be made into finished products in an infinite variety, considering chemistry properties, sizes and shapes.

CONTINUOUS CASTING

SLAB

CONVENTIONAL INGOT TEEMING

BILLET

INGOT BREAKDOWN MILL

BLOOM

NOTE: A small but significant percentage of heated ingot steel is squeezed in forging presses to make large shafts for power plants, nuclear plant components and other products.

MERCHANT PIG IRON CASTING

HOT FORGING

HOT STRIP   PICKLING & OILING   COLD STRIP   ANNEALING   TEMPER ROLLING

WELDED PIPE

SKELP

Flat rolled products commonly are rolled from slabs by mills using sets of cylindrical rolls.

PLATE   STEEL PLATES

GALVANIZED & OTHER COATED FLAT ROLLED PRODUCTS

HOT ROLLED BARS   COLD DRAWN BARS

TIN MILL PRODUCTS

RODS   WIRE & WIRE PRODUCTS

Grooved rolls squeeze billets into different cross-sections (round, angles, etc.) in a sequence of operations.

TUBE ROUNDS   SEAMLESS PIPE

Piercing is the process used to make seamless pipe and tubing from a semifinished product called tube rounds.

STRUCTURAL SHAPES

Sets of grooved rolls are used to roll blooms into heavy beams for construction or for rails.

RAILS

takes weeks to restart. The operation is thus a very inflexible one with no opportunity for fine tuning the level of supply to changes in demand. The overhead charges for a modern steel mill are so great that a firm (or a country if the industry is nationalized) may be forced to keep producing and selling, even when prices drop below a profitable level, in an attempt to cut losses. This can lead to the "dumping" of steel by one country in another country, sometimes at prices below cost.

For all these reasons, in order to be efficient and competitive in the world market, an integrated iron and steel operation must be extremely large, involving investments of hundreds of million of dollars. Since the per capita consumption of steel in Less Developed Countries remains low, few places outside the major industrial nations have the large and diversified industrial markets required to absorb the output of such massive operations.

It is no wonder that so few integrated iron and steel mills are found throughout the Less Developed World, despite national policies of economic protection. Even in the United States, large regions are without a fully integrated mill (New England, for example). There are only about a half dozen integrated mills west of the Mississippi, despite the fact that the United States accounts for a large share of the world's supply of steel.[2]

The establishment of a new integrated iron and steel mill is not a common occurrence, even in the United States. For this reason, the location of the proposed new Conneaut Mill of the U.S. Steel Corporation will be highly significant. The Conneaut facility as proposed will be the largest steel mill in the world, and will be located on the south shore of Lake Erie, on the Ohio-Pennsylvania border (Fig. 11.3). Total investment for the huge complex would be an estimated 3.5 billion dollars. U.S. Steel must get permits from over 30 government agencies before proceeding with construction, and this may take several years. Of interest here is the selection of the lower Great Lake Region for the new mill, which runs counter to the postwar move to eastern seaboard ports, and reinforces the position of the Pittsburgh-Great Lakes region as a world steel producer. This location signals a decreasing future emphasis on imported iron ores (Chapter 9).

FORMATION AND DYNAMICS OF INDUSTRIAL REGIONS

A POSITIVE FEEDBACK INTERPRETATION

In Chapter 2 it was suggested that the cybernetic positive feedback model lends insight into the complex process of economic development (see Fig. 2.9). The same model can be used to analyze industrial regions, which are themselves dynamic cores of the development process. When applied to industrial regions, the positive feedback model describes the interactions of mutually reinforcing variables that stimulate industrial growth. Once an initial perturbation, or "kick", starts the process—this could be a matter of chance or historical accident—the latent advantages begin to operate and reinforce each other in an upward spiral.

The first great industrial region, in Europe, gots its initial impulse from the development of the steam engine and subsequent technological breakthroughs. The rich coal and iron ore deposits provided advantages for rapid industrial growth in the nineteenth century. This took place within an agriculturally superior region, with maritime access to trade with other productive regions of the world.

As time passed and new wealth was created, the dense agricultural population increased further, urban centers grew, and incomes rose dramatically, creating a growing market for consumer goods. The growing European mar-

---

[2]A certain amount of steel is produced in nonintegrated plants in regional centers such as Boston, Denver, Seattle, Atlanta, and Phoenix. These plants use steel scrap or purchased pig iron, and serve local and regional markets.

ket, in turn, stimulated the growth of new industries. Higher productivity, resulting from the increased use of energy and machinery, created more wealth, which financed more research and capital investment, resulting in still greater production. As this happened, the size of some firms grew very large, and economies of scale became an additional advantage.

There are, however, limiting conditions to this process. The upward spiral of mutually reinforcing advantages continues until congestion, environmental pollution, or other problems grow critical enough to offset the advantages. When this happens, industrial growth stops, reverses, or adjusts in some way to the limiting condition so that growth can continue.

INTERINDUSTRY LINKAGES

During the growth of an industrial region, the various production establishments (plants) do not emerge in random locations. Instead, interindustry spatial groupings tend to appear, whose firms and plants are interconnected by linkages of supply and demand. One common grouping consists of plants producing basic steel, steel fabricated products, machinery, and transportation equipment. The great concentration of these industries along the Lower Great Lakes in the United States and Canada forms part of the *American Manufacturing Belt* (see Fig. 11.2 and 11.5).

Although the United States Manufacturing Belt, extending from Minneapolis-St. Paul and Kansas City in the west to Boston and Washington in the east, still occupies a dominant position in the national economy, it has lost importance relative to other growing industrial regions of the country. For example, a vigorous growth of interlinked industries has taken place over the past few decades along the western Gulf Coast in Texas and Louisiana. Here, oil refineries located on low-cost tidewater shipping sites produce a

MARKET POTENTIAL IN THE UNITED STATES

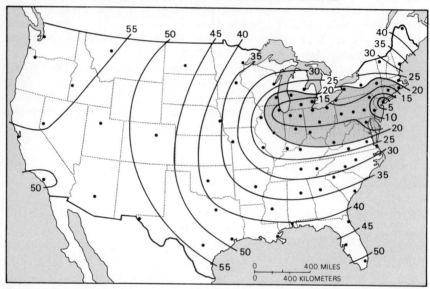

Figure 11.5 Market potential based on retail sales. The shaded area repre-sents the U.S. Manufacturing Belt. *(The inclusion of Canada would alter the pattern somewhat.) Geographer Chauncy Harris in 1954 calculated that half of all the retail sales in the United States were made within the U.S. Manufactur-ing Belt. The market potential is an index of the intensity of possible contact with markets. The dots on the map show places for which calculations were made. The market potential* (P) *is defined as the summation of markets acces-sible to a point* (M) *divided by their distances from that point* (d)

$$P = \Sigma \left(\frac{M}{d} \right)$$

The isolines were drawn to show the generalized surface of potential, with isoline values being the percent of market potential below New York City, calculated on the basis of retail sales and land transport. (Source: *Chauncy D. Harris, "The Market As A Factor in the Localization of Industry in the United States,"* Annals of the Association of American Geographers, *44 (1954), Fig. 4, p. 320.)*

288   INDUSTRIAL REGIONS AND THE LOCATION OF MANUFACTURING

variety of refinery products. In addition, they produce surplus refinery gas that they sell to nearby synthetic rubber plants and other gas-consuming industries. Both the oil refineries and synthetic rubber plants are supplied with sulfuric acid from nearby chemical plants that use local supplies of sulfur. Many other firms of all sizes, specializing in other chemical products or by-products, also find it advantageous to locate in this region to match up their supply and marketing requirements with those of other regional firms. Other important concentrations of manufacturing in the United States are shown in Figure 11.2.

INDUSTRIAL LOCATION: THEORETICAL LIMITATIONS

The Industrial Location Theory developed by Alfred Weber (Chapter 4) and later theorists provides a model for the location of manufacturing facilities in certain industries. However, because of some formidable difficulties a general theory of industrial location does not appear on the horizon. Martin Beckmann and Thomas Marschak have suggested the nature of the challenge:

A complete long-run analysis would . . . explain what caused plant concentrations, and how labor sources and markets developed—would explain, in short, the distribution of human and man-made resources given the distribution of natural (but non-

human) resources. But the powers of theory are limited. There are many incompletely understood relationships even in the short run . . .[3]

Industrial location theory based on the simple assumptions of single plant, single product operations is limited in its application to more complex, real-world situations, particularly those of multinational firms. Plant location decisions, as with other business decisions, are made on the basis of incomplete information. Each manufacturing operation has a special set of technological and economic requirements that influence its scale of operation and its location. For example, the sizes, spatial distribution, and ownership pattern of lumber saw mills are very different from those of pulp and paper mills. Each firm is faced with a constantly changing set of locational influences, including changes in technology, markets, resource availability, and government regulations. These changes are accompanied by shifting factor prices and substitution possibilities.

Another problem in attempting to formalize the location decision process at the plant level is the lack of a single business objective that can be assumed for all firms. Business decisions are theoretically assumed to be based on a profit-maximizing goal. However, for the owners or partners of a small firm, the goals may include certain nonmonetary as well as monetary benefits, such as operating in a familiar community, or having more time off away from business.

Despite its limitations for practical application at the plant level, the literature on industrial location theory provides many instructive analytical guides (Fig. 11.6). Two general lines of approach have been used in analyzing industrial location under the profit-maximizing assumption: (1) the least-cost approach, in which the total of the interacting production and transport costs is ideally minimized, and (2) the market area approach, in which revenues are ideally maximized. The two approaches have, for the most part, been treated separately in the literature. Recall from Chapter 4 that classical location theory involved least-cost solutions, ignoring spatial differences in price. Some writers in recent years have ignored spatial variation in costs in order to concentrate on market area analysis and revenue maximization. Logically, the two approaches are complementary, and the ideal plant location would be the one where the difference between revenues and costs is greatest for the firm.

FACTORS IN PLANT LOCATION PRACTICE

Billions of dollars are invested in new manufacturing plants each year in the United States. The plant location decision process varies greatly from industry to industry and from firm to firm. Smaller firms generally use informal

[3] Martin Beckmann and Thomas Marschak, "An Activity Analysis Approach to Location Theory", Publication P-649, The Rand Corporation, Santa Monica, Calif., April 5, 1955, p. 3.

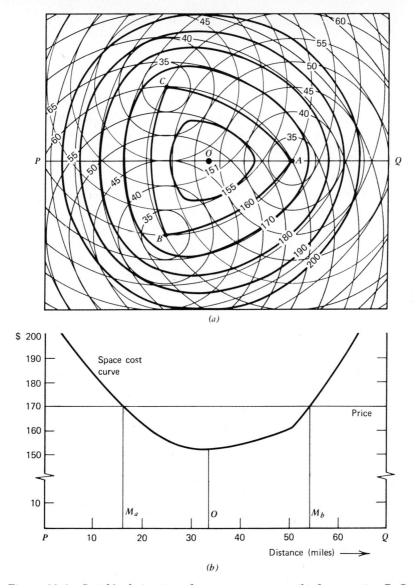

Figure 11.6 Smith's derivation of a space-cost curve (b) from section P–Q *of map (a). Points A, B, and C in (a), representing lowest cost sources of material, labor, and power, are centers of concentric* isotims (isovectures) *(lighter circles) that show the rate at which costs rise from the three points. The thicker lines are* isodapanes (isopleths), *which define a total cost surface having a lowest value at point O. The introduction of a price line in (b) establishes the area of profitability between Ma and Mb. At point O unit revenue is maximized. (Source: David M. Smith,* Industrial Location: An Economic Geographical Analysis, *John Wiley and Sons, New York, 1971, Fig. 11.2, p. 195.)*

procedures based on personal knowledge about their local situation. Although informal, this decision process usually requires the entrepreneurs' knowledge of subtle market, labor, and supply factors. Many small or medium-sized firms ignore location possibilities outside their region, since a major perceived advantage for them is to operate within a familiar area. A study by Hunker and Wright[4] found that a majority of manufacturing plants in Ohio were established in the home communities of their founders. In the United States and a number of other countries, special *industrial districts* or *industrial parks* have been established to attract and assist smaller manufacturing firms. Such districts provide sites, facilities, and vital services for a fee. Examples are Chicago's Clearing Industrial Association, Trinity Industries, Inc. in Dallas, and Teterboro District in Northern New Jersey.

At the other end of the spectrum are the giant, multi-plant firms that sell to a national or international market, and that have cost structures highly sensitive to plant locations. Large meat packing companies are examples. These firms have highly technical plant location procedures carried out by permanent staffs. (Motels, supermarkets, and fast food chains are examples of retail and service industries that also have highly organized location analysis operations and specially staffed departments.)

Companies of all sizes sometimes employ the services of consultants as principal or supplementary location planners. A long-established consulting firm is the Fantus Company of South Orange, New Jersey, with offices in many United States cities.[5] Some real estate firms also specialize in industrial properties.

Every manufacturing plant can be thought of as having its own special combination of location factors. Although we discuss individual factors in this section as though they were independent variables, it should be kept in mind that actual location planning must consider combinations of factors. The discussion that follows relates primarily to industrial plant location practice in the United States. However, much of the material applies more generally to plant location in other countries as well. Even in the Soviet Union, as pointed out by Brenton M. Barr, "Soviet decision makers operate within a behavioural environment which is similar to, but not identical with, that of decision-makers in other industrial societies."[6]

[4] Henry I. Hunker and A. J. Wright, "Factors of Industrial Location in Ohio," Columbus, The Ohio State University Press, 1963.

[5] The following statement is quoted from a Fantus Company brochure: "Fantus specializes *exclusively* in economic geography. We are the oldest and largest organization devoted to location planning and strategy for companies considering expansion, consolidation, or relocation of plant facilities, distribution centers, and corporate headquarters."

[6] "The Changing Impact of Industrial Management and Decision-Making on the Locational Behaviour of the Soviet Firm," in F.E. Ian Hamilton (Editor), *Spatial Perspectives On Industrial Organization and Decision-making*, John Wiley and Sons, New York, 1974, p. 443.

GENERAL CULTURAL AND POLITICAL INFLUENCES

The location of manufacturing activity throughout the world is influenced by a broad set of cultural and political factors that are not usually measurable. Cultural values and attitudes toward work, savings, and materialism are examples. Within some countries racial, religious, or ethnic differences create groups that differ in their acceptance of economic modernization. A large part of the Indian population of Western Guatemala, for example, shuns city life and westernization, preferring to remain apart in their isolated villages. Even within small, highly industrialized countries, such as Belgium, Switzerland, or Northern Ireland, cultural and religious differences find expression in the economic landscape.

The establishment and survival of manufacturing industries within nations is strongly influenced by governmental policies. Protective tariffs, import restrictions, currency controls, trade agreements, and other instruments of national policy obviously can affect industrial activity and location within nations.

Where the state acts as owner of the capital and manager of the operations, factors other than individual plant efficiency may weigh heavily in the location decision, and military defense and regional development can be key considerations. The movement eastward of heavy industry in the USSR to the Ural Mountains and beyond during World War II was based on national security considerations. The Cuban government has restricted manufacturing growth around Havana in order to displace industrial development toward the eastern end of the island.

Within nations having decentralized political authority, such as the United States, Canada, and Australia, state (provincial) and local governments often compete to attract new firms or branch plants of existing firms.

In the United States, certain spatially *footloose*[7] industries associated with national defense have been located at least partly in response to political influence. These include aircraft plants, ordnance depots, and missile factories. In the aircraft industry, Congressional pressures imposed during World War II helped to locate production centers at Wichita, Kansas; Marietta, Georgia; and Fort Worth, Texas, among others. Political influence has always been a factor in the location of naval shipyards.

THE ATTRACTION OF URBAN MARKETS

An advantage for most types of manufacturing is nearness to large and diverse urban markets. This is particularly true for operations considered

---

[7]The term *footloose* is sometimes applied to manufacturing industries that can operate with about the same degree of profitability in many places within a national spatial economy.

market-oriented, that is, ones that turn out products having high distribution costs that can be minimized within an urban market. This applies, for example, to products much more bulky or perishable than the materials from which they are made. Examples of market-oriented products are newspapers, beverages, and bakeries (especially of pastry goods). Firms that supply the construction industry with concrete blocks, bricks, and other bulky building materials have high distribution costs and are also strongly market-oriented.

For market-oriented industries with plants that must be very large to be efficient, the strategy is to locate near the center of a regional market. This is usually the chief commercial city in the region—for example, Seattle for the Northwest, Denver for the High Plains, and Minneapolis-St. Paul for the Upper Midwest. These cities developed as wholesale-market distribution points. Manufacturers shipping through them first established resident salesagents there, then built warehouses, and finally erected assembly or manufacturing plants.

Many manufacturing plants that ship to a national market are attracted to the American Manufacturing Belt. The concentration of both consumer-good and producer-good markets in this region is one of its great economic advantages (see Fig. 11.5). More will be said about the attraction of urban markets for manufacturing in Chapter 13.

LABOR

Where the labor requirement per unit output is large, as in machine tools, glassware, and other labor-intensive industries, spatial variations in the cost of labor exert a strong influence on location. Not only wage levels, but skill, productivity, and reliability are important elements in overall labor costs.

Considerable variations exist in manufacturing wages within the United States (Table 11.4). In fact, there can be spatial variation within the same firm. In the Bell System in 1968, for example, top weekly pay for plant craftsmen ranged from $128.00 in the Southwestern Bell Telephone Company to $167.50 in New York. The pay of switchboard operators ranged from $80.00 a week in Southern Bell to $102.00 in Northern California.[8]

Where large numbers of unskilled or semiskilled labor are necessary, such as for repetitive machine operations in cotton textile mills, new plants and firms will be drawn to regions with large, unskilled labor pools, low wage levels, and weak unions. The concentration of cotton textile mills in states adjacent to southern Appalachia is an example of this orientation.

---

[8] *The New York Times,* May 3, 1968. Reprinted by permission.

Table 11.4   Average Hourly Earnings of Manufacturing Workers for Selected United States Areas, 1979

Area	Average Hourly Earnings
Gary-Hammond-East Chicago, Indiana	$ 10.12
Galveston-Texas City, Texas	9.56
Detroit, Michigan	9.36
Peoria, Illinois	8.76
Baton Rouge, Louisiana	8.66
San Francisco-Oakland, California	8.34
Casper, Wyoming	7.81
Milwaukee, Wisconsin	7.73
Wheeling, West Virginia	7.55
Portland, Oregon	7.46
Birmingham, Alabama	7.09
Denver-Boulder, Colorado	6.67
Phoenix, Arizona	6.44
Boston, Massachusetts	6.38
Atlanta, Georgia	6.18
Binghamton, New York	5.80
New York, New York	5.73
Waterbury, Connecticut	5.45
Jackson, Mississippi	5.16
Miami, Florida	4.82
Austin, Texas	4.74
Asheville, North Carolina	4.63

Source: Adapted from *Employment and Earnings, July, 1979,* U.S. Dept. of Labor, Bureau of Labor Statistics, Vol. 26, No. 7, Table C-13.

World War II accelerated the movement of unskilled labor from the rural south to northern cities. In recent years this flow has abated, and a small but significant reverse flow has been reported by the Bureau of the Census.

Highly skilled workers are not as mobile as unskilled or semiskilled workers. High labor skills have been shown to form the basis for a stable family and social life. Well-paid and respected, the highly skilled worker usually has deep roots in the community. Skilled blue-collar workers are often reluctant to leave their home towns, even for appreciably higher money wages elsewhere. The machine trades exemplify this stability. A skilled machinist is the product of years of apprenticeship. Tool and die makers form the elite of the metal working industries. The existence of clusters of such workers in the small cities of lower New England accounts for the concentration of small metal-working firms there, serving national and even world markets. There are more tool and die makers in the city of Bristol, Connecticut (population 74,000 in 1975), than in many Less Developed Countries.

RAW MATERIALS, FUEL, AND WATER[9]

Certain manufacturing processes require large inputs of bulky or perishable raw materials, extracted from localized sources in the natural environment. Where such processes involve a reduction of bulk, they tend to be located near the material source to minimize transport costs of the product to market. Examples are the concentration of mineral ores, the processing of forest products, and so on. Other processes that reduce perishability, such as frozen food preparation, canning, meat packing, and cheese making, also locate as close as possible to the input, since it is cheaper to ship the product after the process has reduced its perishability.

In some industries production may be oriented to the fuel supply. Processes that make cement, glass, and synthetic nitrates try to locate near fuel sources in order to reduce costs. In the same manner, the need for large quantities of process water will attract the process to reliable, low cost water supplies.

When transportation rates are lowered as the result of mechanization, the cost of moving bulk materials and fuels decreases and the attractive force of the raw material site lessens. Also, as industrial development proceeds, the proportion of total manufacturing based on raw materials decreases. For these reasons, raw material orientation normally tends to lessen over time.

The raw material-oriented process sometimes becomes the supplier for other plants on adjacent sites. Examples of such direct linkages are pulp mill—newsprint mill, and meat packing plant—canning plant.

Raw material- and fuel-oriented processes have formed heavy industrial concentrations in certain parts of the world. The metallurgical industries established in the mineral-rich Ural Mountains region of the Soviet Union is an example. In the United States, the Youngstown-Wheeling-Johnstown region centered in Pittsburgh illustrates an original orientation to coal fields. Some of the best coking coal found anywhere is in the world is still mined in this area. An example of a raw material- and fuel-oriented manufacturing

[9] Discussing markets, raw materials, and transportation as separate factors is customary in plant location literature. However, this leads to considerable redundancy. Markets and raw materials could be subsumed under a general heading of transportation, since minimization of transport costs is an objective in all cases (Chapter 12). For a clear discussion of the role of "transfer costs" in the location of manufacturing, see Edgar M. Hoover, *The Location of Economic Activity,* McGraw-Hill Book Co., New York, 1948.

region in Latin America is the Concepción region of south central Chile (Fig. 11.7).

ELECTRIC POWER

Small water wheels furnished scattered sources of power for primitive manufacturing operations prior to the Industrial Revolution. The advent of the steam engine changed this orientation to coal, and the coal fields of England and other industrializing nations became the centers of growing manufacturing regions. The commercial development of electric power, particularly in the form of high-voltage, alternating current systems early in this century, permitted a far greater spatial availability of energy for manufacturing (Chapter 10).

The irregular distribution of hydroelectric sites, and the variable distances from fossil fuel sources today create wide spatial variations in the cost of electric energy. For most kinds of manufacturing, the cost of electric energy is low relative to other inputs. However, a few manufacturing processes use large amounts of electric energy per unit of output, and these are attracted to low-cost electric power sources. Examples are the electro-metallurgical and electro-chemical groups. As stated earlier, the oldest concentration of such industries, around Niagara Falls, is still the center of a large industrial complex.

The most striking example of electric power orientation is the aluminum refining industry. Plants in this group have been located in parts of the world having the potential to produce large quantities of very low cost (usually hydro) electric power. These include sites in British Columbia and Quebec in Canada, the Pacific Northwest in the United States, and others in Scandinavia, Ghana, and elsewhere.

ENVIRONMENTAL AND SITE FACTORS

For some types of production, such as shipbuilding, climate has a direct effect on the costs of production. Aircraft airframe construction in its early days was attracted to the warm, dry climate of Southern California. Pleasant climate has attracted people and expanded consumer markets in regions such as Florida, Southern California, and the Southwest.

The specific location of a manufacturing plant can be strongly influenced by physical site factors. For plants requiring a large space for their operations and ancillary facilities, such as parking, level topography is essential. Hills and rough topography may limit the location of such plants or confine them to valley floors, which are subject to flooding. Sites are also sought that will minimize drainage problems and eliminate foundation failure.

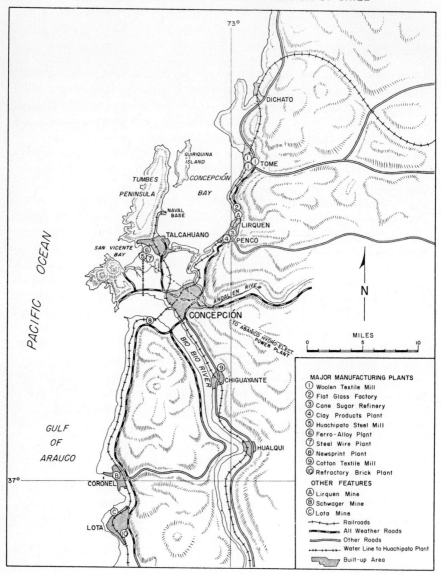

Figure 11.7 On the Coast of Chile 250 miles south of the capital, Santiago, lies a significant concentration of large manufacturing plants. The region has a diversified combination of raw materials and energy resources, and low cost water access to others. An integrated iron and steel mill was established at a

298   INDUSTRIAL REGIONS AND THE LOCATION OF MANUFACTURING

INDUSTRIAL POLLUTION

Environmental pollution has become a major plant location factor for some industries in recent years. In Chapter 5 it was emphasized that all production processes create waste in the form of unwanted matter and/or energy. Since manufacturing industry tends to concentrate spatially, pollution can rise to levels that overload the local waste assimilating capacity of the environment, creating health hazards and other negative externalities.

Industrial water pollution has become a significant factor in the location of food processing, chemical, iron ore, and other processing industries. In many forms of production, heated cooling water is passed back into the environment. Federal legislation in 1972 in the United States established new standards and enforcement procedures for waste water disposal. In the coming decade, the costs of waste water management will increasingly influence industrial activity.

Waste products from some manufacturing processes, such as combustion and metallurgical operations, take the form of soot and other particulate matter, smoke, and gaseous emissions into the atmosphere. All are negative plant location factors. The plume of smoke and other emissions from a factory stack can, depending on atmospheric conditions, extend over many square miles. Dirt, dust, fly ash and other particulate matter fall on people, homes, clothing, and automobiles, creating inconvenience, corrosion and cleaning bills, to say nothing of health hazards. Persons who travel along parts of the New Jersey Turnpike see and smell emissions from the petroleum refineries that border the Turnpike for many miles and many traffic deaths have been caused along that highway by multiple automobile crashes during periods of smog. Serious industrial smog conditions exist in Los Angeles, a number of Gulf Coast cities, and many other places in the country.

Industrial air pollution can often be reduced by expenditures that modify

tidewater site (5) on San Vicente Bay in the 1950s. Here, coal from two of the few large coal mines in South America (B and C) is available, and iron ore and limestone are shipped from deposits near the coast further north in Chile. The large Bio Bio River provides ample water, and electric power is supplied from a hydroelectric plant. In addition to a cluster of steel-using plants around the steel mill, the region also has large ceramic, plate glass, newsprint, and other heavy manufacturing plants. (Source: Joseph H. Butler, Manufacturing in the Concepción Region of Chile: Present Position and Prospects for Future Development, Foreign Field Research Report No. 7, Earth Sciences Division, National Academy of Sciences—National Research Council, 1960, Fig. 3, p. 8.)

DUPONT PLANT LOCATION BASED ON WASTE DISPOSAL FACTOR

The Dupont Company considered 16 locations in the East and Midwest before deciding on a site at Fayetteville, Arkansas, for its new chemical plant. According to a company official, the final determining factor in the decision was waste disposal. The Fayetteville site is suitable for proper disposal of solid wastes, and for treatment facilities and holding tanks or ponds for liquid wastes. "It's [waste disposal] becoming more of a factor all the time . . . safe waste disposal facilities are inherent in the site; you can't move them around."*

* Joseph W. Pochomis, E. I. du Pont de Nemours and Company, Wilmington, Delaware.

manufacturing processes. Where such changes cannot be made economically, the elimination of the offending production or its relocation may be the only alternatives. However, history shows that large industrial complexes can be cleaned up to a very considerable degree. Pollution in heavy manufacturing regions has been greatly reduced without causing economic decline in a number of places, including the Greater Pittsburgh region in the United States, and the Ruhr Valley in West Germany.

RESEARCH, ENTREPRENEURSHIP, AND EXECUTIVE PREFERENCE

One type of locational influence about which little has been formally studied is the spatial distribution of invention, technical innovation, and research facilities. Certain manufacturing industries, such as those producing computers, aircraft, and communications equipment have large research and development costs. For such firms it is advantageous to be near the personnel and facilities of centers of applied science and engineering. The development of an "electronics belt" outside Boston in the postwar period has been stimulated by its proximity to MIT, Harvard, and many other research-oriented institutions and consulting firms. Santa Clara County, California, is another research and development oriented industrial cluster, forming one of the densest concentrations of innovative industries in the world.[10]

There is strong evidence that inventors and innovators tend to attract each other in an atmosphere of mutual creativity. The bar room of the old Pontchartrain Hotel in Detroit was the meeting place of many inventors and engineers who contributed to automotive technology in the early 1900s.

[10] E. Willard Miller, *Manufacturing: A Study of Industrial Location*, The Pennsylvania State University Press, 1977, p. 130.

There is also evidence that business entrepreneurs and managers tend to concentrate in time and space. As the early automotive industry began rapidly to develop around the nucleus of Henry Ford and other technical "wizards" in Detroit, the area attracted risk-takers and business managers anxious to build financial empires. An example was William Durant, whose financial creation was General Motors Corporation.

New firms or branch plants are often located, at least in part, on the basis of preferences of owners or key management personnel and their families. Strong attractions are the presence of good schools, libraries, concert halls, universities and other forms of "cultural capital."

The founder of a company may, as shown above, regard his home community as the best location for his plant or company headquarters. For smaller firms, a hometown location seems obvious considering the entrepreneur's limited information concerning factors operating elsewhere, and his/her willingness to sacrifice possible greater money income for the other benefits of a smaller, less efficient hometown operation. This would be considered an example of *satisficing behavior* as opposed to *maximizing behavior.*

COMPETITION FOR INDUSTRY AND THE ROLE OF PROMOTION

During the postwar period of industrial expansion, a location factor influencing many footloose industries has been the aggressive promotion by many cities, counties, states, and other regional entities. The competition for new industry has been keen, particularly for clean, attractive, nonpolluting forms of light industry that bring payrolls, tax revenues, industrial purchases, and other benefits to the local community.

Thousands of communities of all sizes across the land maintain industrial development programs that employ various incentives to firms seeking a plant location, including special tax concessions. In many places, industrial parks have been established that furnish essential local services and facilities in an attempt to attract light manufacturing firms.

In recent years some states in the Northeast have undertaken vigorous campaigns to attract industry away from other states. New Jersey, starting in 1974, developed a multimillion dollar promotion to pull new business and industry into that state. Connecticut developed a similar program. In 1976 Vermont used radio ads, stressing the absence of big city crime and the "good living" in Vermont. Massachusetts compiled a "hit list" of New York State firms to try and lure. One attracting device has been the use of revenue bonds to raise money to provide tax exemptions for incoming firms. Some states—but not New York because of its own state laws—can directly aid locating companies.

It is difficult to tell how much impact such promotion has had. However, for the five year period 1975-1979, New York State lost a total of 359 manufacturing plants (having a labor force of 25 or more) to other states, while attracting 218 plants from other states.[11]

SUMMARY

Highly Developed Countries are ones that have been transformed into industrial economies supported by manufacturing. Modern manufacturing industries have been established in many parts of the globe; however, industrial production is heavily concentrated in Europe, North America, Japan, and a few other nations. Industrial nations have high incomes but consume disproportionately large amounts of the world's material and energy supplies. Manufacturing industries can be classified into two broad categories, those that process raw materials from primary industries, and those that fabricate or assemble parts and components already manufactured in a prior stage. Manufacturing firms and establishments (plants) have very different sizes and spatial patterns. Since manufacturing is the source of most of its own production inputs, most manufacturing firms find it advantageous, as suppliers or purchasers, to locate within an urban-industrial region. Insights into the complex nature of industrial region formation and growth can be gained by viewing them in terms of the positive feedback model. Most plant location decisions are based on industrial experience and the consideration of a series of time-tested location factors.

Questions

1 Describe in broad terms the distribution of manufacturing in (a) the United States (b) the world.

[11] Source: New York State Department of Commerce.

2 Analyze the development of the great industrial region in Europe in terms of a positive feedback model.

3 Contrast the characteristics and locational patterns in the United States of (a) integrated iron and steel production and (b) beer or soft drink production.

4 Discuss labor as a plant location factor.

5 Explain the growing role of environmental pollution and waste management in industrial location.

6 Choose a small manufacturing plant in a place familiar to you and, from the information available, try to explain why it is located where it is. If possible, check your analysis with officers of the firm and others familiar with its operation.

12

TRANSPORTATION AND COMMUNICATIONS: THE MOVEMENT OF PEOPLE, GOODS, AND INFORMATION

"In her daily foraging [the prehistoric mother] carried or was accompanied by her brood, the older ones learning from her what was good and how to secure it. She discovered the first hard rule of economic geography, the cost of distance."

Carl Sauer*

Within any spatial economy, whether an isolated island or the entire globe, people must interact over space to exchange information and to acquire goods and services necessary for survival. In this process, people strive to minimize the cost of overcoming distance. "Cost" here can refer to money, time, or energy. An objective in planning is to reduce the amount of *circulation* necessary for the conduct of the normal business of living.[1] Man's attempt to minimize the cost of distance is a key factor in the shaping of the economic landscape; this is true whether we speak of primitive societies (Fig. 1.1) or modern, industrialized nations.

In Chapter 5, we saw that transportation and communications create *place utility*. This means that goods and information, such as ton of steel or a purchase order, increase in value by being moved or transmitted electronically from one place to another.

---

* "Seashore—Primitive Home of Man?" Chapter 15 in John Leighly (Editor) *Land and Life,* Univ. of Calif. Press, 1963, p. 308.
[1] Michael Chisholm, *Rural Settlement and Land Use: An Essay in Location,* John Wiley and Sons, Inc., New York, 1967, p. 11. Chisholm's use of the word *circulation* to mean both transportation and communications follows the usage of classical French geography.

Various aspects of circulation are mentioned in other chapters. In this chapter the focus is specifically on people, goods, and information as universal flow phenomena.

ECONOMIC EFFECTS OF LOW-COST CIRCULATION

THE UNEVEN IMPACT OF MECHANIZED TRANSPORT

Various technological responses have been made to the problem of overcoming distance by different cultures throughout history. The domestication of the horse and other draft animals, the invention of boats and wheeled vehicles, the creation of paved road systems, and other innovations all had the effect of lowering the real costs of circulation, thereby compressing the spatial economy. Prior to the Industrial Revolution, however, trade in bulk goods was normally confined to short distances.[2]

During the past century the world has changed from an era of sailing ships to one of jet travel, and from month-long overseas mail delivery to instantaneous transmission of information by radio satellite. Increased transportation efficiencies result in economic benefits, but these benefits have been felt very unevenly throughout the world. The effect of reduced transportation costs, where they occur, is a rise in the real incomes of the people served.

In a pre-industrial community economic activity is largely confined to a limited area, because persons must laboriously lift and move things from place to place by hand, or, if they have them, with the aid of draft animals. This makes the costs of movement, in terms of labor inputs, exceedingly

---

A REMINDER ABOUT DIFFERENT CULTURAL ATTITUDES TOWARD MATERIALISM

While economic doctrine holds that improved transportation and trade bring higher incomes, some people do not necessarily equate material wealth with overall quality of life (Chapter 2). In the remote mountain community of Vilcambamba in Ecuador, life without the stress of modern urban living produces an unusually healthy and long-lived people. The people of Vilcambamba have resisted the building of a road from the outside, precisely because they believe it to be a threat to their way of life.

---

[2] Some exceptions to this existed where water transport by sailing ships had been developed. Athens, in Ancient Greece, was supplied by grain-growing regions elsewhere and, later, the City of Rome came to depend for its wheat on shipments from Egypt and North Africa.

high. Many places exist today in parts of Latin America, Africa, and Asia where people carry heavy loads on their backs or heads. In Asia, human porters are still an important form of overland transport.

Consider for a moment the actual cost of human porterage. If a ton of coal is to be moved one mile by one person, he or she would have to make, say, 20 round trips carrying 100 pounds on each, for a total distance of 40 miles. Even if superbly conditioned, well fed, and able to work continuously, the person would take over 13 hours to complete the move at a regular walking speed of 3 mph. Even assuming very low money wages, such a move would cost the equivalent of many dollars per ton-mile. In contrast to this, coal can be moved by rail, barge, or other bulk carriers for a few pennies per ton-mile.

When mechanized transport is substituted for animal-drawn vehicles in rural areas, the effect on the farmers' costs and incomes are striking. In the 1920s and 1930s motor cars and trucks radically changed the spatial economy in rural America.

In Highly Developed Countries there has been a wholesale substitution of mechanized transport for the original, primitive types. The rapid generation of capital permitted heavy investment in transportation and communication facilities within highly productive environments. As time passed, these networks were extended across less productive regions to reach other productive ones, thus integrating the entire national economy. The United States, Canada, Australia, and USSR are examples of this process. In Highly Developed Countries the economic assumption is approached that every con-

---

THE IMPACT OF MECHANIZED TRANSPORT ON AN IOWA FARMER

A first-hand account of a farmer's experience in Iowa, quoted below from an article by Edward L. Ullman, is instructive:

Years ago to haul hogs to market, I had to get the help of five of my neighbors. In 6 wagons we would carry 30 hogs. We went 5½ miles to the railroad stop in Irwin. I had to buy a meal for the men and myself. Generally it cost me about 50 cents apiece: Those men ate a real meal, not a lunch. That's $3. To put the 6 teams in the livery barn cost $1.20. Because I had the men come and help me, I had to go and help them, which meant 5 days of work off the farm for myself and my team. The cash cost alone was $4.50. Today, I can hire a trucker to take 25 or 30 hogs to Harlan, more than twice as far, for only $2.50. He can get them there and be back in 2 hours. And I don't have to spend any time off the farm.*

*Quoted in E. L. Ullman, "The Role of Transportation and the Bases for Interaction," in W. L. Thomas (Editor), *Man's Role in Changing the Face of the Earth*, Univ. of Chicago Press, 1956, p. 867.

TRANSPORTATION AND COMMUNICATIONS

sumer has access to every good—that is, that every consumer lies within the market area of each good.

The Less Developed Countries, on the other hand, have experienced only a partial transition from primitive to modern forms of transport. As a result, in LDC's, where capital for investments in transport is scarce, it is common to find modern facilities in the capital and other large urban centers, while primitive, high-cost systems still serve the rural hinterlands. In the cities of an LDC, both primitive and modern transport are found together. Where the modern systems end, the costs of transport abruptly jump.

MECHANIZED TRANSPORT, REGIONAL SPECIALIZATION, AND TRADE[3]

The invention and rapid improvement of modern transportation and communications systems since the Industrial Revolution has had two seemingly opposite results. On the one hand, the world has become more uniform, at least superficially, as people and ideas move about more freely. For example, jet airports in countries all over the world bear a striking resemblance to one another, and English has become the common language of most international air service communications.

On the other, major modifications have been made in the spatial economy of the world through the development of specialized regions of production, made possible by a succession of technological advances in bulk transport. The development of refrigeration ships, for example, gave great impetus to the rise of export beef production in Argentina and Uruguay, and to export banana production in the countries of Central America. As rates for bulk

---

CONTRASTING PRIMITIVE AND MODERN TRANSPORT SYSTEMS

Felstehausen provides an example of the extremes that exist where both jet airplanes and pack animals are part of the overall transport system:

A Colombian traveler can have lunch in Bogotá and dinner in New York—the same amount of time it takes his rural neighbor to bring two bundles of fireplace wood by pack burro 10 kilometers to Bogotá's northside residential district and return home again. This paradox is not just a matter of contrasts in time and distance—if the farmer could have loaded his wood on the national airline instead of renting or maintaining the burro, his transportation costs per kilometer would have been less.*

* Herman Felstehausen, "Planning Problems In Improving Colombian Roads and Highways," *Land Economics,* Vol. 47, 1971, p. 1.

---

[3] This section relates to earlier discussions of regional specialization and trade in Chapters 3, 7, and elsewhere.

cargoes such as coal, lumber, and grain dropped, these commodities could be shipped longer distances and still be sold at competitive prices. Investments in port facilities and at strategic places—especially in the form of canals and locks, such as those at Suez, Panama, and on the St. Lawrence River—caused radical contractions in world shipping lanes. This intensified export production from regions around the world specializing in products for which they have comparative advantage.

The emergence of specialized regions of production and trade also took place within nations, especially in large nations with different environmental regions. As shown in Chapter Seven, agriculture in the United States became regionally specialized, with cotton, corn, wheat, rice, cattle, citrus fruit, and so on, all produced in surplus and shipped to other regions throughout the nation, or exported to other countries.

FACTORS AFFECTING TRANSPORT DEVELOPMENT AND UTILIZATION

POSITIVE FEEDBACK INTERACTION

The influences of spatial accessibility and environment show up in an interesting way in Europe (Chapters 7 and 11). As industrialization and economic growth proceeded rapidly in the agriculturally productive core (see Fig. 7.2), the fringe areas, such as western Ireland, northern Scotland, Southern Italy, Southern Spain, and northern Scandinavia, fell relatively behind. In addition to having poorer agricultural and mineral resources, the fringe areas were less accessible to Western Europe's raw materials, growing urban markets, and products. Investment in transport in the fringe areas could not bring the high returns that it did in Southeast England and the North European Plain.

Feedback models help to explain the role of prices in a developing spatial economy. The notion of spatial price equilibrium and its link to transportation[4] assumes that supply and demand are affected by prices, and that prices, in turn, are affected by the levels of supply and demand. The spatial price system provides signals that govern the flow of trade. Theoretically, trade will flow from places of surplus production to places of deficit production as long as price differentials between the places are large enough to cover the transport costs of overcoming distance. In this way, commodity prices and transportation prices (rates) ideally determine both the direction and flow of goods within a transport network, connecting regions of specialized production.

---

[4] Theoretically described by economist Paul Samuelson in 1952, and given geographical expression by geographer William Warntz in 1959 (*Toward a Geography of Price*, Philadelphia: University of Pennsylvania Press).

Transport routes and land use have strong, mutually reinforcing effects. An interesting case is the positive feedback loop linking wheat production and railroad development in the prairie provinces of Canada. Wheat farmers there first located within 10 miles or so of rail heads, since the costs of hauling wheat by wagon beyond this distance was prohibitive. This produced zones of wheat farming along both sides of the rail lines. The shipping of wheat to distant markets, in turn, provided revenue for the railroad. The land beyond the limit for wheat was commonly used for grazing livestock, which could profitably be driven to rail heads over longer distances. (Note the Thünen zonation principle operating here.) Similar land-use patterns developed along rail lines in Australia, Argentina, and the United States. The same principle also operates to link road development and land use throughout the world.

OTHER SPATIAL AND ENVIRONMENTAL CONSIDERATIONS

Certain other environmental and spatial factors affecting transport system design and operation can be singled out for special attention. A fundamental influence on the development of a national transport system is obviously the sheer size of the national territory. A large nation requires massive investments in transport if it is to be integrated into one spatial economy. Scarce capital can be diluted to the point of ineffectiveness if applied to a large region having low population density. This is particularly true for Less Developed Countries, and can lead to policy differences at the highest levels of

---

AN EXAMPLE OF ROADWAY-LAND USE INTERACTION

The following example from Guyana appeared in The Times (London) on November 13, 1959, and was quoted by Michael Chisholm.

Modernisation of the road (from Georgetown) to Atkinson airport is a striking proof of the principle in colonial development, that if you drive a road or railway through a cultivatable [sic] area you automatically stimulate economic development. Ten years ago this was a dismal track 23 miles (37 kilometers) long, running through neglected savannah and flanked by the odd peasant's shack. . . . Today the road has been widened and macadamised.

What is more remarkable, however, is the ribbon development which has followed. There are habitations, many of them prosperous looking, all the way. Alongside the Colonial Development Corporation's sawmill, now a paying concern, have sprung up a beer factory and a margarine factory, and along the road ground is being cultivated which was not cultivated before, and small concerns like chicken farms have taken root.

*Michael Chisholm, *Rural Settlement and Land Use,* John Wiley and Sons, New York, 1962, 1967, p. 85.

---

government. One development strategy is to concentrate transport investment in those parts of the country already developed and productive. The other approach is to use transport investment to exploit new resources in the more remote parts of the national territory.

Inhabitants of Highly Developed Countries with large land masses, such as the United States or Canada, spend a higher proportion of their incomes to overcome space than those living in smaller, compact HDC's, such as the Netherlands, (Table 12.1). To overcome its greater internal distances, the United States devotes about 25 percent of its national energy budget to transportation (Chapter 10). By contrast, in the nations of Western Europe, despite much higher gasoline prices, the comparable figure is typically 10 to 15 percent. These, however, are average national figures. Within the United States, empirical studies confirm that people living in remote areas of low population density, such as Wyoming, expend much more energy in overcoming distance than those living in more accessible, heavily populated areas (Fig. 12.1).

The shape of a national territory is another factor that can influence transportation development and utilization (Chapter 6). The length and configuration of coastlines is another environmental "constant." Europe, or example, has a high ratio of coastline to area and an abundance of good harbors. On the other hand, much of Central Africa and South America have few good harbors for port development.

Topography is critical in transportation development (Chapter 6). A level, unbroken topographic surface, such as the Pampas of Argentina or the Ukraine in the Soviet Union, provides very low-cost overland transport (see Fig. 6.6). On the other hand, steep slopes (see Fig. 7.7) or poorly drained land greatly increase construction, operation, and maintenance costs.

A factor related to topography is the presence and location of navigable

Table 12.1 Expenditures on Personal Transportation and Communication[a] as a Percentage of All Private Consumption, 1955–58, for Selected Nations

Country	Percentage
United States	14.3
Canada	13.4
Sweden	12.1
Italy	7.8
France	7.5
Netherlands	4.3

[a] United Nations definition.

Source: Adapted from Colin Clark, *Population Growth and Land Use,* London: Macmillan, 1967, Table IX.16, p. 369.

TRANSPORTATION AND COMMUNICATIONS

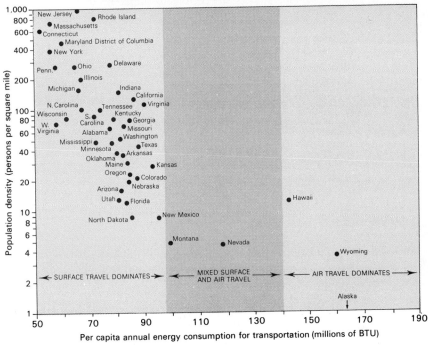

Figure 12.1   Least energy per capita for transportation is used where distances travelled are short, in the small, densely populated states of the Northeast. Air travel dominates in Wyoming. Note the logarithmic scale on the ordinate. (Source: U.S. Department of the Interior, 1973.)

rivers and lakes. Bolivia has no coastline and no river outlet to the Pacific. Switzerland has no coastline, but enjoys a river (Rhine) route to other nations downstream and to the North Sea. In South America the Amazon River system provides a water transport network for half a continent. On the other hand, the rapid descent of the Congo River as it falls from the central African Plateau to the sea creates rapids that block navigation to the interior. In North America the St. Lawrence-Great Lakes system, improved by a system of locks, provides deep water routes into the heart of the continent.

NETWORK CONNECTIVITY AND TRANSPORT SYSTEM EFFECTIVENESS

Overland mechanized transport normally follows established, linear routes within fixed networks. Once established, a physical route, such as a road, railroad, pipeline, or canal, becomes a spatially fixed element within the economic landscape. This makes it possible to apply mathematical techniques such as graph theory to problems of transport system analysis and design.

One concept in graph theory, which has been used in transportation studies by geographers and others, is that of *connectivity*.[5] From the standpoint of topological space, some transport networks are more interconnected than others. (Topology deals with the interconnections among points in a space, without regard to the distance between them.)

In graph theory, a transport network can be modeled as a combination of *edges* (routes) and *vertices* or *nodes* (terminals, cities, etc.). The *coefficient of connectivity* is expressed as the Greek letter *beta,* where:

$$\beta = \frac{e}{v} = \frac{\text{Number of edges}}{\text{Number of vertices}}$$

indicating the degree to which the nodes in the network are interconnected (Fig. 12.2). Looking at it intuitively, connectivity indicates the ability (ne-

DEGREES OF CONNECTIVITY
IN SIMPLE NETWORKS

NETWORK   COEFFICIENT OF
CONNECTIVITY

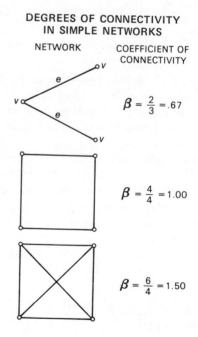

$$\beta = \frac{2}{3} = .67$$

$$\beta = \frac{4}{4} = 1.00$$

$$\beta = \frac{6}{4} = 1.50$$

Figure 12.2 See text for explanation.

[5] See, for example, William L. Garrison, "The Connectivity of the Interstate Highway System," *Papers and Proceedings of the Regional Science Association,* Vol. VI, 1960, pp. 121–137.

glecting distance) with which one can move between random nodes in a network.

Figure 12.3 shows the results of a study of national railroad networks in relation to per capita income for 18 countries. A strong positive correlation can be seen to exist between high levels of connectivity and high per capita incomes. The way in which the coefficient of connectivity tends to increase with economic development is shown in Figure 12.4.

DISTANCE-COST FUNCTIONS AND RATE STRUCTURES

A fundamental relationship in economic geography is the *distance-cost function*. The function can be expressed in various ways, but the underlying idea is a simple one: the cost of moving people, goods, and information increases with distance (Fig. 12.5).

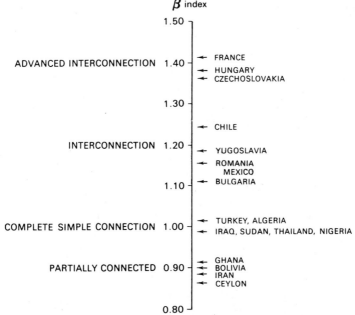

Figure 12.3 *Higher degrees of railroad network interconnection are associated with higher states of economic development.* (Source: *Maurice H. Yeates,* An Introduction to Quantitative Analysis in Economic Geography, *Fig. 8-2, p. 116. Copyright 1968, McGraw-Hill, Inc., New York.)*

THE DEVELOPMENT OF THE ROAD SYSTEM IN GHANA,
1910 – 1959

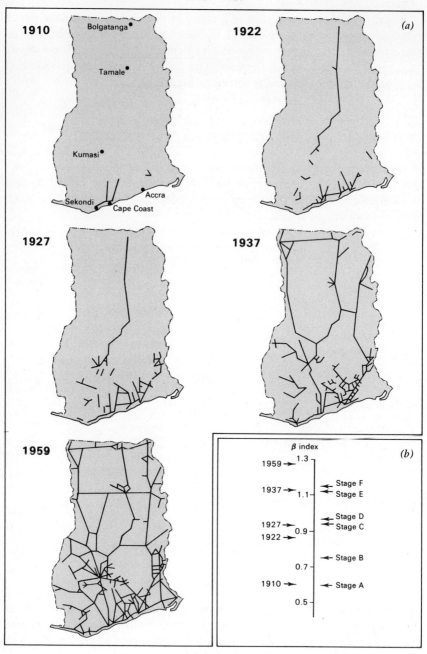

Figure 12.4 (see facing page) Economic development within a country is associated with increasing levels of transport network connectivity. The idealized networks in (a) show the primary and secondary road system in Ghana for five periods. From 1910 to 1959, during a period of rapid economic growth, the calculated beta coefficient for the road system increased from .6 to nearly 1.3 (b). This has important implications for Less Developed Countries, where the start up phase of national transport development is characterized by low levels of system interconnection, and the danger exists of diluting scarce capital in space. (Source: *Maurice H. Yeates,* An Introduction to Quantitative Analysis in Economic Geography, *Fig. 8-5, p. 118 and Fig. 8-6, p. 119. Copyright 1968, McGraw-Hill, Inc., New York.*)

An important distinction must be made between the hypothetical costs of a transport service and the rates (prices) charged the customers for the ser-

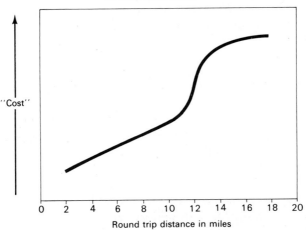

COST CURVE FOR OBTAINING MONGONGO NUTS BY
!KUNG BUSHMEN

"Cost"

Round trip distance in miles

Figure 12.5 The universal nature of the distance-cost function is illustrated by this graph, which measures the real cost to !Kung Bushmen of the Kalahari Desert of Southwestern Africa of travelling from their water sources to gather mongongo nuts. A round trip of up to about 10 miles can be accomplished in a single day, but longer trips require an overnight stop, and this involves the packing of drinking water. The sharp rise in "cost" between 10 and 14 miles reflects this. The graph also illustrates the combined influence of space (distance) and environment in economic activity. (Source: *Richard Lee, "!Kung Bushman Subsistence: An Input-Output Analysis," in Andrew P. Vayda (Ed.),* Environment and Cultural Behavior, *The Natural History Press, Garden City, N.Y., Fig. 2, p. 60.*)

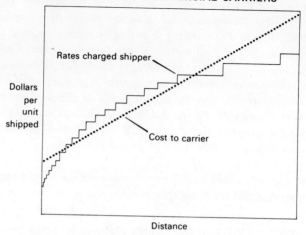

Figure 12.6 The actual unit cost of rail, truck, or water transport includes terminal handling charges and other fixed costs, which are independent of distance moved, and line-haul costs, which can be assumed to increase linearly with distance. The "tapered" stepped rates charged the shipper by the carrier reflect long-haul economies resulting from the spreading of the fixed costs over a greater distance. (Source: Edgar M. Hoover, The Location of Economic Activity, *McGraw-Hill Book Co., New York, 1948, Fig. 2.2, p. 21.)*

vice. It is often impossible to assign costs to individual shipments. Consider, for example, the problem of determining the actual cost to a railroad company of transporting a large machine from Cincinnati to Denver. How much of the fixed costs associated with the many bridges on that run, for example, should be assigned to that particular shipment? For this and other reasons, the rates charged the customer by railroads and other commercial carriers in the United States have often been related to "what the traffic will bear." The stepped rate schedules in common use by railroads and other carriers approximate the costs to the carrier (Fig. 12.6).

Production involving the processing of bulky materials requires low cost shipping facilities. Since waterborne transport is very low cost for bulky hauls, many types of heavy manufacturing operate efficiently on navigable water sites, particularly water sites within urban-industrial regions (Fig. 12.7, 12.8). Examples are steel mills, chemical plants, sugar refineries, and petroleum refineries. Many large port cities destroyed in World War II in Europe were rebuilt and expanded, and have become important heavy manufacturing centers. Rotterdam, Hamburg, and Dunkerque are examples. Navigable river, canal and lake sites also provide low-cost locations for

316

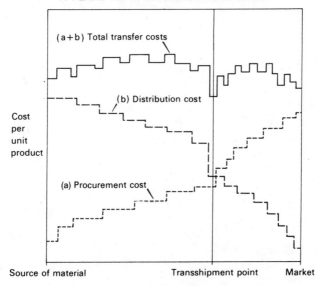

Figure 12.7   Gradients of procurement cost, distribution cost, and total transfer costs for processing locations along a route from a source of material to a market via a transshipment point. By locating a processing plant at a waterland transshipment (bulk-breaking) point, the total transport (transfer) costs can be minimized. The cost of transferring the bulk raw materials from one form of transport to another is eliminated, since the plant receives the raw materials at its dock and after processing, ships the product overland to the market. (Source: *Edgar M. Hoover,* The Location of Economic Activity, *McGraw-Hill Book Co., New York, 1948, Fig. 3.8, p. 39.*)

heavy manufacturing. Lowland river corridors within industrial nations or regions attract not only urban centers, but manufacturing as well. Such corridors permit the development of low-cost barge traffic, as well as railroad and highway traffic.

For many forms of light manufacturing, transport costs are low relative to labor and other costs. These industries do require, however, reliable, efficient transportation facilities to assemble inputs and to market their products. Some plants still require locations directly on a railroad line, however, many plants built in recent decades have been located in open, parklike settings, served by nearby limited-access highways.

In the United States and Canada there are innumerable examples of railroad cargo rate schedules that appear to be inconsistent and often unfair to shippers in certain regions. This has resulted in a long history of court litiga-

Figure 12.8   The economic landscape of Cleveland contains a wide variety of production and transportation activities, as well as the generation of polluting wastes. (Source: Cleveland-Cliffs Iron Company.)

tion and federal regulatory agency actions in the United States. A classic case involved favorable railroad rates given to California shippers in order to get their business when that state became an important supplier of fruits and vegetables to the East Coast urban markets. Similar advantages (lower rates) were not made available to the Florida shippers of these commodities when they became competitive suppliers, and they turned to truckers to move their produce north to the urban markets.

The railroad rate structures in the United States are further complicated by special arrangements that evolved over the years to attract special classes

318   TRANSPORTATION AND COMMUNICATIONS

of customers. Stopover privileges such as *fabrication-in-transit* or *milling-in-transit* allow a customer to ship wheat by rail from Kansas to Minneapolis with a free stop along the way to have the wheat processed into flour. Without this arrangement, the stopover costs (loading and unloading, storage, etc.) might prohibit the customer from shipping, and the railroad would lose the business. *Backhaul rates* are low rates charged when a vessel carrying a bulk cargo from A to B would ordinarily return to A empty. The low backhaul rates encourage shipments that would otherwise not take place from B to A, and gain additional revenue for the carrier. Backhaul rates add to the advantage of certain ports as low-cost assembly points for bulk raw materials; examples are certain Great Lakes ports.

THE VARIOUS FORMS OF TRANSPORT

Each transport form has a special set of technological and economic characteristics. Fluid commodities can be moved efficiently by a continuous flow in pipelines; solid commodities are shipped in batches by motor truck, freight train, ship, or barge. The distribution of electric energy requires a network of copper or aluminum wire conductors. Natural gas cannot be carried by ship, except as a liquid in specially designed, high-pressure tank vessels. The uses of the various transport media vary greatly from nation to nation, and from place to place within nations.

ROADS, HIGHWAYS, AND MOTOR VEHICLES

The first overland routes in pre-history were merely trails that enabled people to transport high-value commodities, such as gemstones, tin, silk, salt, and so on. At its height, the great Roman road system of antiquity, designed for wheeled vehicles, included 50,000 miles and ranged from Britain to Jerusalem. The vast Inca road network was a later, New World counterpart of the Roman system, extending from present day Ecuador to Central Chile. Its paved routes were not used by wheeled vehicles, but by messenger runners, porters, and pack animals, moving over great mountain ranges, and tying together the far-flung Inca Empire.

The speed, cost and volume of flow on roads and highways changed radically with the advent of the motor car around the beginning of the twentieth century. Since then, the passenger car and motor truck have revolutionized ground transport throughout much of the world.

Motor trucks and trailers have certain advantages over rail transport. They are more efficient for handling less-than-carload shipments, for shorter hauls, and for point to point deliveries. They are much more flexible in their routing, since they are not required to be assembled into long trains in switching yards as freight trains are. Motor trucks and trailers are preferred for most types of higher-value, packaged freight. Trucks and trailers can ride

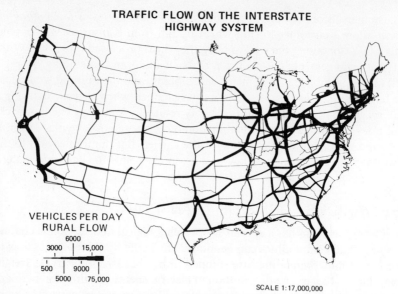

TRAFFIC FLOW ON THE INTERSTATE HIGHWAY SYSTEM

VEHICLES PER DAY
RURAL FLOW

6000
3000 | 15,000
500 | 9000 |
5000 75,000

SCALE 1:17,000,000

Figure 12.9 Note that the thickest line represents a flow of 75,000 vehicles per day—five times greater than the next thinner line. (Source: *Council on Environmental Quality*, Environmental Quality, *Washington, D.C., September, 1976, p. 300.*)

railroad flat cars "piggy back" over long hauls, thus combining the better features of both modes of transport.

In the case of passenger travel in the United States, the automobile has become dominant for intercity traffic as well as for metropolitan transportation (Fig. 12.9).

Many of Man's first trails followed the energy-efficient tracks of animals. Such trails often became the routes of later, more advanced roads and highways. For example, St. Augustine, Florida, was the starting point for the first road built by Europeans in North America. The 40 mile path was cut through dense forests and swamps in 1565 by Spaniards to attack a French settlement. Today, U.S. Highway 1 coincides with that Spanish trail. Interstate 90 in New York State follows the old Iroquois Trail, connecting Albany, Schenectady, Syracuse, Rochester, and Buffalo. The 600 mile Spanish road that linked the 21 Franciscan Missions in early California, *El Camino Real,* today is U.S. Highway 101, connecting San Diego and Los Angeles with San Francisco. Daniel Boone's wilderness road across the mountains from Virginia to Kentucky is the route of Interstate 75 today.

In 1956, Congress passed legislation establishing the Interstate Highway System. This Federal program, whose original rationale was national defense, has had the effect of further integrating the continental spatial econ-

TRANSPORTATION AND COMMUNICATIONS

omy over the past two decades. Together with other federal and state highways, the multibillion dollar Interstate Highway System enables passengers and cargo to move nearly nonstop for hundreds of miles at average speeds of nearly a mile a minute.

Most transportation planners agree that investments in limited-access "super highways" do not necessarily "solve" traffic congestion problems in high use areas. As movement becomes quicker and cheaper, more and more consumers demand the service. In other words, traffic inevitably increases as the service to potential consumers is improved. There are countless examples of this. The New Jersey Turnpike was built to relieve traffic flow on U.S. Highway No. 1. However, within two and a half years it was carrying as much traffic as Highway No. 1, and Highway No. 1 had five percent greater traffic than it had originally. The flow of traffic between Trenton (New Jersey's capital) and New York City doubled because improved service had become available. The Hollywood Freeway, which opened in 1954, was originally designed to carry an ultimate daily volume of 100,000 vehicles. One year after it opened, the daily traffic exceeded 168,000 vehicles. The much-maligned Long Island Expressway was planned to relieve traffic entering and leaving New York City from the east. Since its completion, however, it has been called "the world's longest parking field" because of daily rush-hour delays. In all these cases, the problem of traffic congestion per se was not solved; instead, a much greater traffic flow was made possible by the investment in limited-access highways. Congestion still exists, but at higher levels of traffic flow. This suggests an interesting behavioral problem related to system equilibrium that deserves greater study if our traffic planning is to improve in the future.

HOW AMERICANS GET TO WORK

In July 1972, the United States Bureau of the Census released figures describing how Americans get to work. According to that report, 59.7 million persons drove or rode in a car to their jobs; 5.7 million walked to work; 4.2 million rode buses or streetcars; 1.8 million used commuter trains; 502,000 used railroads; and 296,000 rode cabs to work.

Although the Bureau of the Census Report did not mention bicycles, it is known that they are used by growing numbers for commuting. In recent years, a number of states, including Oregon, Washington, California, Illinois, and Florida, have reserved part of their gasoline tax revenues for biking facilities. The use of bikes for commuting follows a long-established practice in many other countries. Anyone viewing the rush-hour traffic in downtown Dublin, Copenhagen, or Amsterdam will see thousands of people from all walks of life commuting to or from work on bicycles.

In 1950 the first hard evidence was found of automobile engine exhaust emissions as a public health problem. Scientists confirmed that a chemical reaction in still air and strong sunlight converts hydrocarbons and nitrogen oxides from automobile exhausts into photochemical oxidants, with potential health effects far more serious than mere eye irritation. It is difficult, without direct experimental evidence from human subjects, to assess the long-term effects of these toxic substances. However, evidence from heavy dosage experiments on animals shows serious physiological effects. The problem of motor traffic emission pollution is obviously worst in urban areas, especially those prone to natural conditions of atmospheric stagnation.

The United Nations and other international agencies have long recognized the strategic role of roads in the economic development of Less Developed Countries. Within the past decade, the World Bank in Washington has invested over 1.3 billion dollars in Less Developed Countries, involving the construction or improvement of 30,000 kilometers (18,600 miles) of roads.

RAILROADS AND RAIL TRAFFIC

Railroads were established in the industrialized parts of the world well before the advent of motor transportation. The completion of the railroad between New York and Chicago shortened the trip between those two cities from three weeks to less than three days. The first transcontinental rail line across North America was completed in 1869, transforming the United States into an integrated spatial economy from ocean to ocean (Fig. 12.10). Before that, most goods and passengers between the East and West coasts travelled the long and dangerous passage around Cape Horn at the southern tip of South America.

Railroads carry the greatest volume of commodities moved today in the world, and also account for a large share of passenger miles. The relative importance of rail traffic, however, varies greatly from nation to nation. High concentrations of railroad trackage exist in the industrialized nations of the world. An extensive rail network also exists in India, built by the British in the early decades of this century.

Figure 12.10   (see facing page) In 1979, Class I railroads operated 191,000 miles of rail lines in the United States. Influenced by environmental factors and inaccessibility, parts of the nation have relatively low rail densities: the arid and mountainous regions of the Western states, the Appalachian Mountain chain, the Ozark Mountains of Southern Missouri and Northern Arkansas, the Adirondack Mountains in New York State, the Northern Maine woods, and the South Florida everglades. (Source: Association of American Railroads.)

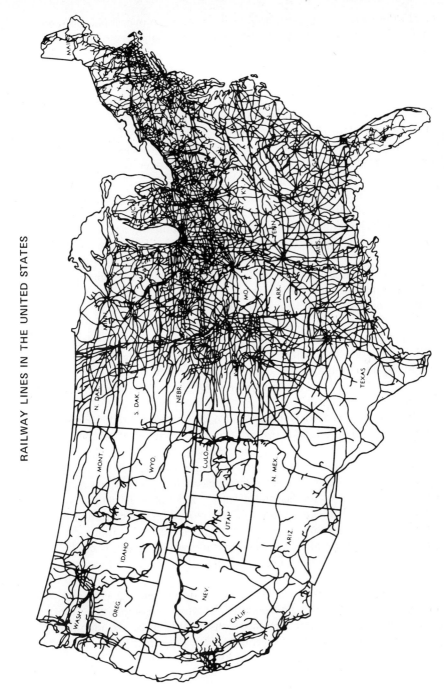

RAILWAY LINES IN THE UNITED STATES

In the United States, motor vehicles have taken over much business from the railroads, particularly since the Interstate Highway Program got underway in the late 1950s. By contrast, it is estimated that 75 percent of all overland freight in the Soviet Union is carried by railroads.

Construction of a railroad network requires extremely large capital investments in rights of way, bridges, and other large structures, and terminal facilities, as well as in rolling stock. Since World War II, diesel locomotives have replaced steam in most parts of the world. Unlike trucks or vessels, trains are made up of linear series of freight cars—often over one hundred in a single train—that must be assembled and broken down at classification yards in junctions or terminals. While this is cost-efficient for long haul operations, it is time consuming and inefficient for shorter ones, especially where delivery time is an important consideration.

A severe limiting constraint on the construction and operation of railroads is that of *grade,* the ratio of vertical rise or fall to distance travelled, usually expressed as a percentage. Engineering design normally limits railroad grades to around one percent. Obviously, in hilly or mountainous terrain severe limitations are placed on route design, and going from one place to another involves much weaving back and forth to keep below the maximum allowable grade. If this isn't done, the design must call for high-cost bridging or tunnelling. In addition to construction costs, railroad operating costs (including energy) and maintenance costs are also very high in areas of uneven topography. (Rough terrain is also a limiting factor in the case of road and highway design; however, maximum grades for these can be considerably higher; see Chapter 6.)

In contrast to motor vehicles, railroads are considered the environmentally preferable mode of transportation for a number of reasons. Railroads are already in place and do not compete with other forms of land use as new or expanded highways do, especially within crowded urban areas. Railroads are efficient in energy use, since they deliver four to six times as much ton-mileage per unit of fuel as motor trucks. Air pollution caused by trains is small compared to other modes of transportation. Precipitation percolates rapidly into the ground water system through permeable railroad beds. Water quality is practically unaffected by rail service; no salt is used to control ice and snow on railroad beds, and the salt pollution of water supplies is avoided.

When, for any reason, traffic demand drops below a certain level, rail freight service becomes uneconomic. Because of competition from motor trucks and trailers, there has been considerable track abandonment in the United States over the past several decades. Passenger service in the United

States, with few exceptions, has operated at a loss for the railroads. AM-TRAK was established to coordinate and improve passenger service. Piggy back operations, containerization, and other shipping innovations have been adopted by many American railroads in an effort to raise efficiencies, lower costs, and gain business through more competitive operations (Figures 12.11 and 12.12).

In contrast to the United States, railroad service in Europe and Japan has flourished, and the Soviet Union railroad trackage has been expanded in recent years. Very limited new railroad construction now goes on in Less Developed Countries, since road construction and air transport are often more appropriate to their needs. In East Africa a few new rail lines have been built to link coastal ports with inland regions producing for the export market.

Figure 12.11   Five locomotives pull over 100 cars, each loaded with 100 tons of coal. Under this unit train *operation, mechanized loading at the mine requires only four hours, and the entire shipment is delivered to one customer at a substantial rate reduction.* (Source: *Norfolk and Western Railway.*)

Figure 12.12   A 40 ton capacity straddle lift crane at the West Oakland, California yards transfers containers from piggyback flatcars fitted with a special mounting device to a truck trailer for shipment to destination. The combination of the best features of both forms of transport results in lower unit transport costs to the shipper. (Source: *Southern Pacific Company.*)

INLAND WATERWAYS

Rivers, lakes, canals, and other inland waterways have been used to move people and cargo since the invention of rafts and boats. The significance of riverine corridors as low-cost transportation routes has been emphasized earlier. Where hydrologic and topographic factors are favorable, capital invested in dredged channels, canals, locks, and port facilities, results in marked improvements in the ability to move bulk cargoes. The Erie Canal in New York State, linking the Hudson-Mohawk River Lowland with the Great Lakes System at Buffalo, altered the course of American economic history after its completion in the 1820s (Chapter 1).

The ideal factors for low-cost, inland waterway development are the presence of interconnected lake or river systems within industrially productive regions. Two of these regions are the Mississippi River-Gulf-Intercoastal waterway system in the United States and the international river and canal system of the North European Plain. In both regions steam- and diesel-fueled tugs, barges, and special purpose vessels move mountains of bulk or liquid commodities, such as coal, iron ore, petroleum, chemicals, lumber, and grain, at extremely low unit costs. This permits low-cost assembly and delivery for heavy processing industries located on the system.

OCEAN SHIPPING AND PORTS

The trans-oceanic or coastal movement of bulk or liquid cargo is performed by large ships driven by fossil-fuel energy. Once the large investment in ships and port facilities is made, very low ton-mile costs are attained. The greatest ocean flow of commodities is between the two great trading regions of the world: North America and Western Europe.

The spatial distribution of natural harbors suitable for deep water port construction is very uneven. In parts of the world some ports have grown very large and act as *entrepots* (master ports) for reshipment to smaller ports along adjacent coasts; London, Rotterdam, Hamburg, New York, Singapore, and Hong Kong are examples.

The role of much ocean shipping in the global economy depends on the canals built to link certain seas or oceans. The Panama Canal and the Suez Canal represent enormous investments in capital structures, and have the effect of radically shortening ocean trade routes, voyage times, and shipping costs for a large share of world trade. The Kiel canal is an example of a man-made structure linking two seas, the North Sea and the Baltic Sea.

A number of innovations in the past two decades have markedly improved the efficiency of bulk shipping and terminal operations, and have thereby considerably lowered unit costs of cargo movement (Fig. 12.13). The trend continues toward using larger vessels and larger-scale, more mechanized terminal operations.

During the 1970s, a frenzy of supertanker construction took place (mainly in the highly automated shipyards of Japan) for the booming world oil trade. This has been called the greatest miscalculation in the history of free enterprise. In 1979, about 750 supertankers were afloat, with business for half that number. Many of the tankers, never used, are slowly rusting at anchor in a Norwegian fjord, representing billions of dollars of unpaid mortgage debt.

In the minds of some observers this glut of supertankers poses an environmental "time bomb." They envision these debt-ridden ships being purchased at bargain prices by marginal international operators who will sail them with minimum safety standards, thereby greatly increasing the dangers of disas-

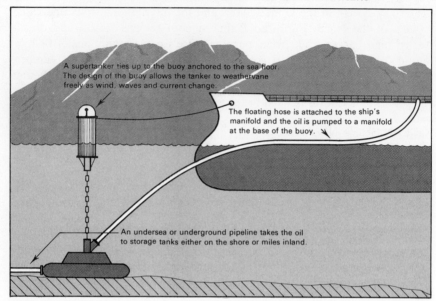

A supertanker ties up to the buoy anchored to the sea floor. The design of the buoy allows the tanker to weathervane freely as wind, waves and current change.

The floating hose is attached to the ship's manifold and the oil is pumped to a manifold at the base of the buoy.

An undersea or underground pipeline takes the oil to storage tanks either on the shore or miles inland.

Figure 12.13   Deepwater terminals, which are located in over 100 sites around the world, enable supertankers to load or unload miles from shore. The United States has no facilities of this kind. Supertankers discharge oil at deepwater terminals in the Caribbean area for transshipment to United States ports in smaller tankers. (Source: Exxon Corporation.)

trous oil spills. The largest marine oil spill on record, on March 16, 1978, occurred when the *Amoco Cadiz* lost steering control as it passed very close to the Brittany coast of France, following an international traffic pattern. If the *Amoco Cadiz,* a model ship run on the highest international standards by a company with a good safety record, could become disabled, resulting in $100 million in damages, the danger from "fly by night" companies operating surplus tankers would be far greater.

Looking ahead several decades, some observers see radical technological changes in ocean shipping. One prediction is the use of nuclear-powered submarines as "locomotives" to pull streamlined "box cars" under water at speeds exceeding 150 miles per hour.

PIPELINES

Under certain conditions fluids, both liquid and gaseous, can be moved efficiently under pressure in pipeline systems. In addition to carrying water, pipelines are now used primarily to transport petroleum and its products and natural gas. They can also be used to carry materials that can be moved in slurry form (liquid suspension) such as powdered coal.

Petroleum and its products are carried in pipes ranging up to four feet or more in diameter. The product is pumped at a velocity of about four miles per hour—a person's fast walk. The interior of the pipe is lined with spiral grooves (rifled) so that petroleum products can be efficiently pumped. A small amount of water is introduced and, as the mass begins to spiral, the water, being heavier, is forced to the outside and lubricates the walls, permitting even relatively viscous (thick) commodities to flow with a minimum expenditure of energy.

Unlike rail movement, pipeline transport does not involve the return of empty cars. Maintenance and labor costs are low. However, remote pipelines and pumping stations are vulnerable to sabotage and are hard to reach for emergency repairs.

In pipeline transport the chief costs are for the pipe and its installation, usually underground. Efficiences of scale encourage the laying of pipe with as large a diameter as possible. The economics of pipeline operations are such that, per barrel mile, the full load cost in a 20-inch diameter line is only 40 percent of that in a 10-inch line.

The highly publicized Trans-Alaskan Pipeline was begun in 1974 only after publication of a six volume environmental impact statement, public hearings, prolonged public debate, and litigation carried through the Supreme Court. The final court decision ruled that the probable potential environmental damages were not great enough to outweigh the national benefits of the project. A set of environmental safeguards for the project was established by the Court and guaranteed by the Department of the Interior.

AIR TRANSPORT

The flow of travellers, mail, and high value cargo on air lines has increased dramatically in the postwar period. However, the limited payloads of even the largest aircraft incur high operating costs, and thereby prohibit the air movement of most bulky or heavy cargoes. The overall economic importance of air cargo should not be implied from tonnage carried alone; much of the air freight is highly valuable cargo, and a critical factor is delivery time.

High fixed costs must be paid by the airline, regardless of flight distance. These include fuel consumed on takeoff and landing, landing fees and other terminal costs, and general operating overhead. As a result, costs per-seat-mile for short flights are considerably higher than for long flights. It is estimated, for example, that the per-seat-mile cost for a 200 mile trip is about twice that for a 900 mile trip. Scale efficiencies also favor long-distance flights over short ones in terms of total trip time. By nonstep jet, the very large Dallas-Fort Worth Airport (Fig. 12.14) is no more than four hours from any large United States mainland city. On the other hand, to fly from the capitals of some states to the capitals of adjacent states may take much more than four hours because of the lack of direct service.

The efficiences of long-distance operation have stimulated the use of air transport in large countries, particularly in free-market economies such as Canada, Australia, and the United States, where air travel has taken over much of the passenger market from railroads. On the other hand, in small nations such as Ireland, Belgium, Israel, or Portugal, air transport is less competitive because of the short distances of domestic flights, and rail and motor transport remain relatively more important modes of domestic transport.

Wherever they are used, large jets must fly with payloads as often as possible to justify their very high cost. The result is a strong tendency toward agglomeration of air departures and arrivals in very large urban jet ports, such as New York's Kennedy Airport or Chicago's O'Hare Field. The concentration of air terminal traffic in the largest cities and the need for longer runways to accommodate larger jets results in airport design so large that it has become difficult to find sites for new air fields or additions to old ones. Fuel emissions, noise, danger from crashes, and environmental disturbance result from the concentration of air service in very large jet airports.

In the late 1960s a mammoth jetport was proposed for the Everglades west of Miami to serve the rapidly growing air transport demands of south Florida. The plan caused a great deal of controversy. In 1969 a report by a special Department of Interior task force concluded: "Regardless of efforts for land use regulation, the result of proceeding with development of the airport will be destruction of the South Florida ecosystem. Estimates of lesser damage are not believed to be realistic." On the basis of this report and other considerations, the U.S. Secretaries of Interior and Transportation, together with the Governor of Florida, jointly decided against development of the airport complex, declaring that an alternative site would have to be found.

This problem is by no means confined to the United States. In Canada the Mirabel International Airport, located 35 miles northwest of Montreal and costing 500 million dollars, surpasses even the Dallas-Fort Worth Airport in overall area. When it was officially opened by the Canadian Prime Minister, police held a crowd of protesting farmers at bay with tear gas. In Japan,

Figure 12.14   (see facing page) The airport serving Dallas-Fort Worth, has an area as large as Manhattan Island. (Source: *North Texas Commission.*)

TRANSPORTATION AND COMMUNICATIONS

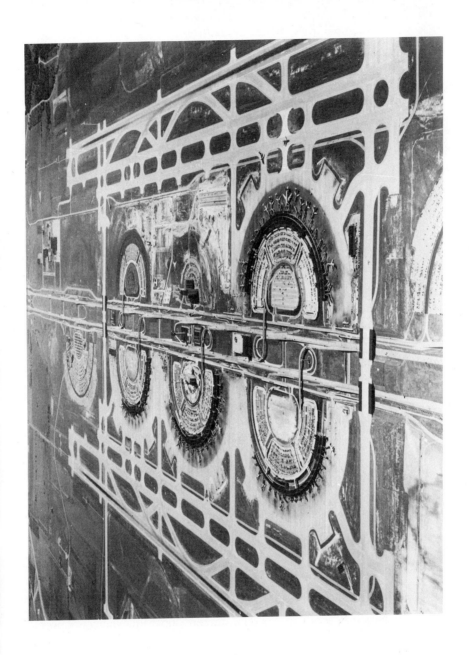

protests against the opening of a new jet airport northeast of Tokyo became so massive and violent that they precipitated a national emergency.

A bizarre example of negative externalities resulting from airport operation involved a tiny community in England. Fernhill was a hamlet of several dozen homes in Surrey, near London. The peaceful serenity of the village was shattered when it found itself barely a mile from the end of a new jet runway at Gatwick Airport. In 1973, jet planes began passing over the village at elevations of a few hundred feet on the average of once every three and a half minutes, night and day. In addition to the incessant noise and vibration, the residents were fearful of the pollution generated overhead by the large jet engines and were, of course, terrified over their vulnerable position in case of an accident. (Ironically, one resident had moved to Fernhill 13 years before to escape the city dangers.) The value of the property in the village plummeted. The residents, having exhausted legal and political remedies, banded together in an effort to sell the entire village. They hoped to interest an industrial buyer, since the property had become virtually worthless for normal patterns of life. One must assume from this that Fernhill was ignored by the planners who designed the Gatwick Airport expansion.

A response to the problem of overcoming distance in Less Developed Countries has been a special interest in air transport. In many parts of the world, air transport (mainly non-jet) has made radical changes in the spatial economy. Brazil and Colombia, for example, which have much mountainous terrain, have developed extensive air service without having gone through a railroad development phase comparable to that in the United States or Europe.

In some ways air service is especially suitable for LDC's. A low budget, far-flung transport system can be started or modified quickly, using older-model planes, small, primitive airfields, and modest maintenance facilities. In such regions, aircraft carry many kinds of freight, in addition to passengers. Airline service, however primitive or erratic, greatly improves the mobility of scarce entrepreneurial and administrative talent—an important consideration within developing economies.

Most airlines outside the United States are nationally owned and are subsidized. Subsidization can have an important influence on domestic as well as international air service.

TRENDS IN INTERNATIONAL TRADE

By far the largest flow of goods and information, or the movement of people to acquire goods and services, takes place within the borders of countries. However, statistical data on intranational flows, even for industrialized

332   TRANSPORTATION AND COMMUNICATIONS

WEBB ON AIR SERVICE SUBSIDIZATION IN BRAZIL

Transportation policies of governments in nations with large, undeveloped areas can have an important economic impact on those areas. An example is the policy of airline service subsidization for the remote interior of Brazil. There, rates are kept low by the central government despite the lack of enough current business to justify them on economic grounds. Geographer Kempton Webb explains:

Let us picture an imaginary line connecting Belem, Brasilia, and Porto Alegre, dividing eastern Brazil from western Brazil. The air traffic east of that line generally pays its own way, whereas the costs of air travel west of that line are not covered by revenues from fares and freight fees. This illustrates how governments can help airlines and thereby subsidize development in those areas. It is hoped that the small interior communities will grow and become sufficiently productive to justify the construction of alternative means of transportation. In the meantime, relatively inexpensive air fares allow those communities to benefit from contacts with the more densely settled areas of the country.*

* Webb, Kempton, *Geography of Latin America: A Regional Analysis,* Prentice-Hall, Englewood Cliffs, N.J., 1972, p. 65.

---

countries, are difficult to compile. On the other hand, international trade—the flow between nations—is well documented, since careful records of exports and imports must be kept by trading nations. International trade has been the subject of theoretical and analytical inquiry ever since the earliest writings in economics.

The classical argument for free trade reviewed in Chapter 3 bears repeating here. If countries raise tariffs or otherwise impede the flow of imports to protect higher-cost home industries, they increase the price of these goods to the consumers. Mutual reduction or elimination of trade barriers ideally encourage countries to specialize in the production of commodities and services for which they have a comparative (not necessarily an absolute) advantage. Trade that enables nations (regions) to specialize in the production of goods making the best use of its scarce factors of production tends to increase the real incomes of all. The benefit of increased international trade, in the words of John Stuart Mill, has been "a more efficient employment of the productive forces of the world."[6]

International trade is also strongly influenced by noneconomic factors. In the world of competitive nations, political and military influences can alter

[6] *Principles of Political Economy.*

trade patterns overnight. The sudden disruption in the international oil market in 1973 was a dramatic example. An important factor influencing the direction and volume of international trade is the existence of formal or informal trading blocs of nations.

Selected data on international trade for important trading nations appears in Table 12.2. Except for the petroleum exporting countries, the important trading nations are, for the most part, also the industrialized countries of the world. The two great trading regions—Europe and North America—are also the leading industrial regions. By contrast, with the exception of Japan, the nations of South and East Asia, with over half of the world's population, generate relatively little foreign trade. In fact, small industrialized nations, such as Holland or Switzerland, have greater volumes of international trade than India or China. The Canadian economy is also heavily dependent on foreign trade. Canada is one of the world's major trading nations and is the largest trading partner of the United States.

WORLD BANK VIEWS ON THE FUTURE OF INTERNATIONAL TRADE

The International community faces a long period of shifting comparative advantage, and it is essential that countries be ready to accept and facilitate the changes in industrial structures that this will involve.

The developing countries, too, face problems in adjusting to changing international trade patterns. The more advanced of them need to step up programs to diversify the product composition and markets of their manufactured exports. To promote trade among developing countries will require changes in industrial incentive structures, relocation of trade barriers, and strengthening of the institutional infrastructure in transport, communications, and credit.

In addition, countries must move jointly to strengthen the international framework governing trade relations so as to assure that the barriers to trade, which exist in both industrialized and developing countries, will be gradually dismantled, and that explicit criteria are established for those barriers which must be imposed to deal with temporary difficulties.*

* *World Development Report 1978,* The World Bank, Washington, D.C., August, 1978, pp. 66, 67.

MODERN INFORMATION TECHNOLOGY

Communications and transportation have been linked from the very earliest times. In any spatial economy, information exchange must be part of the

Table 12.2   Nations with Exports and/or Imports Exceeding Two Billion Dollars in 1976

	Merchandise Trade (Million U.S. Dollars)	
	EXPORTS	IMPORTS
Low Income Countries[a]		
India	5,424	5,515
Pakistan	1,144	2,134
Indonesia	8,547	5,673
Middle Income Countries[a]		
Egypt	1,522	3,808
Nigeria	10,567	8,199
Thailand	2,980	3,572
Philippines	2,433	3,950
Morocco	1,262	2,618
Korea, Republic of	7,716	8,774
Peru	1,365	2,183
Malaysia	5,707	4,245
Algeria	5,061	5,312
Turkey	1,960	4,993
Chile	1,684	2,071
China, Republic of	8,156	1,609
Mexico	3,298	6,030
Brazil	10,128	13,622
Iraq	8,835	3,461
Romania	6,138	6,095
Argentina	3,916	3,033
Yugoslavia	4,878	7,367
Portugal	1,820	4,317
Iran	23,380	12,894
Hong Kong	8,526	8,882
Trinidad and Tobago	2,213	1,976
Venezuela	9,149	6,023
Greece	2,543	6,013
Singapore	6,585	9,070
Spain	8,727	17,463
Israel	2,310	4,052
Industrialized Countries[a]		
South Africa	4,776	6,751
Ireland	3,313	4,192

Table 12.2 Continued

	Merchandise Trade (Million U.S. Dollars)	
	EXPORTS	IMPORTS
Italy	36,969	43,428
United Kingdom	46,271	55,986
New Zealand	2,795	3,254
Japan	67,225	64,799
Austria	8,507	11,523
Finland	6,342	7,393
Australia	12,868	11,084
Netherlands	40,167	39,574
France	55,817	64,404
Belgium	32,847	35,368
Germany, Federal Republic	102,032	87,782
Norway	7,917	11,109
Denmark	9,113	12,419
Canada	38,128	37,910
United States	113,323	128,872
Sweden	18,440	19,334
Switzerland	14,845	14,774
Capital Surplus Oil Exporters[a]		
Saudi Arabia	36,119	11,579
Libya	8,438	3,950
Kuwait	9,843	3,321
Centrally Planned Economies[a]		
China, Peoples Republic	h	b
Korea, Democratic Republic	b	b
Albania	b	b
Cuba	b	b
Mongolia	b	b
Hungary	4,934	5,529
Bulgaria	5,382	5,626
USSR	37,169	38,108
Poland	11,017	13,867
Czechoslovakia	9,035	9,706
German, Democratic Republic	10,087	11,290

[a]World Bank Designations.
[b]Not available.
Source: Adapted from *World Development Report,* The World Bank, Washington, D.C., August, 1978, Table 6, p. 86.

TRANSPORTATION AND COMMUNICATIONS

marketing functions of buying and selling. An example of interaction between transportation and telecommunications was the use of the newly invented telegraph for railroad scheduling.

Prior to World War I, the installation of telegraph and telephone systems had helped to compress the spatial economies of industrializing nations by radically increasing the speed and volume of information flow. The invention of the radio (wireless) and the rapid diffusion of radio broadcasting stations throughout the United States, and later elsewhere, brought instantaneous messages into the homes of millions of families, and thereby influenced their economic behavior as part of a new, mass consumption market. The post-World War II burgeoning television industry created another powerful impact on the spatial economy.

The term *information technology* has evolved to mean the long distance, electronically based, point-to-point or broadcast communications systems, such as telegraph, telephone, radio, and television, together with supporting facilities, such as computers and space satellite systems. As these words are being written, changes continue to take place in information technology, changes given impetus by a succession of advances in basic science, miniaturization technology, and space engineering (Fig. 12.15).

The implications of the Electronics Revolution for the global economy are truly profound. Telecommunications can now be substituted, at least in part, for human contact, and vastly increase the speed of long distance information transmission and processing. A person with access to a telephone has a potential communications link to 250,000,000 other telephones in all parts of the world. Originally a voice communications network, the interstate telephone trunk lines within the United States now carry a higher proportion of nonvoice traffic, such as data, facsimile, and television messages. The American telephone network as a whole is undergoing a significant shift from local to long distance traffic (Table 12.3).

In recent years, new common carrier microwave systems have been established to link up major urban centers within the United States. These systems operate as trunk lines for carrying commercial communication traffic. Access is gained by users through their own telephone, landmobile radio, and so on. It is anticipated that these independent microwave networks will blanket the nation in the future and will compete with the Bell System and Western Union.

At the global level, international communication satellites have been in commercial operation by the International Telecommunications Satellite Corporation (INTELSAT) since 1965, carrying voice, data, and television signals. In 1970 telephone voice transmission accounted for about 80 percent of the total INTELSAT channel capacity and revenues. Satellites can broadcast to a nearly unlimited number of earth receiving stations. Unlike land lines (cable or microwave), satellite systems do not require hardware inter-

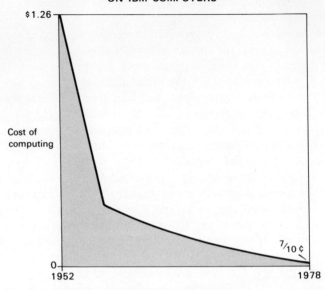

REDUCTION IN THE COST OF CALCULATIONS ON IBM COMPUTERS

Figure 12.15   Despite inflation, the cost of information processing has declined drastically. A set of calculations that cost $1.26 in 1952 could be done for .7 cents in 1978. Compared to the buying power of the 1952 dollar, that is over 400 times less. The computing power of a machine that filled a large room in 1952 is contained in circuits that could be held in one hand in 1978. And computation speeds have increased a thousandfold over this period. (Source: International Business Machines Corporation (IBM).)

Table 12.3   Growth Rates of Mail Delivery and Telephone Service in the United States, 1972

Message Category (per person)	Annual Rate of Increase in Percent
Pieces of mail	3.5
Local telephone calls	5.0
Toll telephone calls	10.0
Overseas telephone calls	25.0

Source: John R. Pierce, "Communication," *Scientific American* 227, no. 2 (September, 1972), p. 37.

TRANSPORTATION AND COMMUNICATIONS

ABELSON AND NOYCE ON THE "ELECTRONICS REVOLUTION"

It is difficult to comprehend the magnitude of the changes taking place before our very eyes today in the field of information technology. Concerning this, Philip H. Abelson, President of the Carnegie Institution of Washington, wrote:

The Industrial Revolution was based on the profligate use of energy (mainly fossil fuels). . . .

In contrast, the electronics revolution represents one of the most noble intellectual achievements of mankind. . . . In many applications electronics requires little energy. Indeed, one factor that guarantees enduring impact for the electronic revolution is that it is sparing of energy and materials.

With electronics one can control the disposition of large amounts of energy and force, but the relationship is much like the use of the brain in directing the effort of muscles. *

Dr. Abelson goes on to quote Robert N. Noyce on the incredible cost reductions for electronic applications over the past decades:

The individual diffused transistor sold for a price of approximately one dollar in 1961, a few years after its introduction. Today, a 1024 bit memory including over six thousand transistors sells for about one dollar a few years after its introduction, representing a cost reduction of about 6,000:1 in 15 years. The resulting effect on equipment costs can be seen in the electronic calculator, which has been reduced in cost by a factor of 500:1 in the last 8 years, creating a substantial new market unforeseen only 10 years ago. *

* "Report of the President, 1975-1976," *Carnegie Institution of Washington Year Book 75,* 1975-1976, pp. 3 and 4.

connection of various receiving sites. This eliminates land distances as a factor in the cost of this type of communication.

The cost of earth stations is expected to decline in the future. As this happens, satellite broadcasting of radio and television to the more remote parts of the globe will become economically more feasible, and will greatly assist the economic development process in the LDC's.

Industries engaged in production related to information technology are mainly based in the United States, Japan, and a few other HDC's. Their rapidly growing markets, however, are worldwide. Large markets and standardization of products bring down the costs of the exported information systems. When International Business Machines Corporation (IBM) is planning the design and marketing of a new computer, the specifications reflect inputs from as many as 20 nations around the world. This enables IBM to meet the needs of virtually every market, whether the currency is decimal or sterling, and with printed output in typefaces for any of 22 different languages.

SUMMARY

The need to overcome distance in human affairs is a universal factor shaping the economic landscape. Drastic reductions in the cost of circulation—the movement of people, goods, and information—have integrated much of the world into a global economy. The economic benefits of improved transportation and communications have not been felt evenly throughout the world. Most people in Less Developed Countries are still served by primitive, high unit cost transport, which confines them locally, limits their incomes, and inhibits economic development. Transport improvement and land-use change have interacting effects. Spatial and environmental factors affect transport development and operating costs, and set economic limits on various transport modes. Low unit cost mechanized transport encourages regional specialization and trade, and this increases the incomes of the trading partners. Political factors also strongly influence international trade. The world is undergoing a continuing revolution in *Information Technology*, which is having profound effects on the spatial economies of all nations, despite its very small energy requirement.

Questions

1 Compute roughly how much you would have to charge to make it worth your while to move one ton of coal one mile (rate per ton mile.) on level, hard packed terrain by:
  (a) moving it in a bag on your back
  (b) moving it in a rented wheelbarrow
  (c) moving it in a rented pickup truck
2 Give examples of environmental factors that influence transport system design and operation.
3 Explain why so many large, process manufacturing plants are located in ports and other transshipment (bulk-breaking) points.
4 Explain the concept of network *connectivity* and how it might be useful in transportation planning.

5 Discuss the term *Information Technology*, and the impact the "electronics revolution" has had on the national and global economies in this century.

6 Ask an elderly member of your family or community about the changes in transportation and communication that have taken place in his or her life, and how it changed their mobility and life style.

13

CITIES AS SPATIAL CONCENTRATIONS OF ECONOMIC ACTIVITY

"Whoever wishes to see all the goods of the world must either journey throughout the world or stay in Rome."

Aelius Aristedes (117–187 A.D.)

After more than 5000 years of evolution, cities have become in the twentieth century the most conspicuous features in the economic landscape. Urban places in the modern world are spatial concentrations of all three forms of economic activity: production, exchange, and consumption. Cities represent the total culture in which they are embedded—the best elements and the worst. Urban centers have been the origin of Man's highest intellectual achievements, and innovations have diffused outward from them to other cities and to the intervening spaces between them.

The space-time process of urbanization has accelerated since the Industrial Revolution, resulting in the increased agglomeration of the growing world population. In 1900 there were about a dozen cities in the world with populations of a million or more. By the end of the 1970s there were nearly 200 such cities.

THE NEED FOR BETTER KNOWLEDGE OF URBAN DYNAMICS

DEFICIENCIES IN URBAN ANALYSIS AND PLANNING

Urban planning in America and elsewhere throughout the world has resulted in many disappointments. New urban problems keep arising, and many older ones continue to get worse. The fundamental difficulty seems to be a lack of understanding of the extremely complex nature of the modern metropolis. According to Professor Jay Forrester of M.I.T., many short-range policies and programs, designed to solve pressing urban problems, actually create new and greater problems over the long run.[1]

Lack of understanding of the modern city is by no means confined to the United States. In Great Britain, where formal urban planning has been emphasized more than in the United States, many results have been the subject of serious criticism. "One is tempted to ask: Which country did worse—Britain with a rather elaborate system of urban planning, which has produced results different from those its sponsors intended, or the United States, where city planning never really promised much, and never delivered much?"[2]

The Western democracies are limited in the sense that they cannot exert the kind of governmental control over urban populations that is possible in totalitarian nations. In the Soviet Union, land is owned by the state, and urban redevelopment is accomplished by government fiat. City size and migration are regulated by the Central Government. In the middle 1960s, the Soviet government established a 68 mile limited-access highway around Moscow as its "permanent outer boundary." Soviet authorities have established many other "closed cities." Anyone wishing to move to a closed city must first obtain an official residence permit.

The Marxist government in Cuba has attempted to redirect the pattern of urbanization there. Havana's port facilities have been allowed to deteriorate, and its population growth has been restricted. A ring of rural village centers,

[1] Jay Forrester, *Urban Dynamics,* M.I.T. Press, Cambridge, Mass., 1969.
[2] Marion Clawson and Peter Hall, *Planning and Urban Growth: An Anglo-American Comparison,* Johns Hopkins University Press, Baltimore, Md., 1973, p. 271.

called the *Cordon de la Havana,* has been built to encircle the city and limit its areal expansion.

The argument is made that only by such forced measures can effective, large-scale urban improvements be accomplished. The counter-argument is that human rights and the democratic process are forfeited when central governments do the planning and force compliance. Another counter-argument is that the possibility exists for blunders on a colossal scale when urban planning is centrally controlled, without provision for critical review. Whatever the political system, it is clear that a deeper understanding of the dynamic nature of the modern city is needed.

THE PROBLEMS OF CLASSIFYING AND DEFINING CITIES

The rapid diffusion of technology around the world has had a culturally homogenizing effect on urban places. The airport serving Nairobi, Kenya, is strikingly similar to those outside Dublin, Ireland, or Quito, Ecuador. A person raised in Toronto or Rio de Janeiro is likely to feel more familiar in the center of any of the world's great cities than in the rural parts of his or her own country. Nevertheless, no two cities are alike; among other things, each city has its own special combination of economic functions. The characterization of Greater Pittsburgh or Jamshedpur, India, or Yawata, Japan, as "heavy manufacturing" centers is not inaccurate. On the other hand, Washington, D.C., Canberra, Australia, or Brasilia, Brazil, are chiefly governmental administrative centers, while Denver, Dallas, and Atlanta are primarily regional commercial and financial centers. Even the functions of "twin cities" can be quite different. Dallas and Fort Worth is an example; Minneapolis and St. Paul is another.

A number of attempts have been made to classify cities according to economic criteria. Such classifications, however, usually do not reveal changing urban functions over time. This is particularly true of older cities, such as Boston, Charleston, or Philadelphia, which have undergone different epochs of growth and change. Boston's preeminence as the "capital" of New England has always been linked to its historic role as a cultural and educational center. Boston's relative decline as a port has been counterbalanced by the postwar growth of space-age industries and its leadership in scientific research and development.

In contrast to Boston, Detroit's position as a regional metropolis grew out of its function as a national center of automotive engineering and production, the original location of which was largely a matter of chance. Detroit's degree of specialization among American cities is very high. Business leaders there made a decision after World War II to deemphasize production of aircraft engines and to specialize in the consumer automobile market. At the same time, Los Angeles and Seattle, without Detroit's opportunity for reconversion to the automobile and truck industry, began to make efforts to expand in the postwar aircraft industry.

Some cities undergo an economic rebirth through a conscious shift in functions planned and carried out by broad community effort. Pittsburgh, after being economically stunned by the postwar steel glut and recession in the late 1940s, decided for survival to broaden its industrial base. Through strong community leadership it managed to greatly abate its air and water pollution problems and to rebuild its central core (Fig. 13.1). The Greater Pittsburgh area is still a world steel and heavy manufacturing center, but its cluster of universities and industrial laboratories also now make it a prominent regional research center.

Geographer Mark Jefferson once observed that urban and rural, city and country, are one thing, not two things. Except where a city has been built within walls, it has always been difficult to establish urban limits with precision. The problem of defining the boundaries of urban areas has become even more difficult as a result of postwar urban sprawl.

Analyses of cities involving such criteria as population density can be misleading. For example, was the population density of Detroit, based on the 1950 Census, greater than that of Chicago? It has been shown that this

Figure 13.1 View of the "Golden Triangle," Pittsburgh's Central Business District. Note the convergence of major transport routes and the intensive land use at the core. Two rivers join here to form the Ohio River.

THE NEED FOR BETTER KNOWLEDGE OF URBAN DYNAMICS   345

FUTTERMAN ON THE DIFFERENCES IN AMERICAN CITIES

Large cities differ greatly in personality and style, even those in the same country. A number of United States cities were described by one urban scholar in 1961. After two decades his perceptions remain valid in many respects.

New York: "While concentrating their efforts on the city itself, the planners might give more than an occasional thought to the mounting problems of the sub-cores, already graphically demonstrated in the collapse of Yonkers (my home town, and for years distinguished by one of the worst and most provincial city administrations in America). Perhaps the greatest threat to the future of New York lies in the area's failure to develop even metropolitan-area political cooperation—let alone a metropolitan government."

Chicago: "Temperamentally, Chicago remains central to America—a baffling and fascinating study in contrasts, very rich and very poor, handsome and hideous, intelligent and idiotic. Perhaps in Chicago we will find the answer to the question of whether America will use its unique resources to create a greater civilization—or will condemn itself to a meaningless, soul-destroying proliferation of goods, comforts and waste."

Los Angeles: "Can a decaying downtown be revitalized to such a degree that it will act as pumping station for so vast a circulatory system? The answer here lies in the solution to the transit problem. Given adequate transit, I think the answer may be, Yes."

Philadelphia: "To compare Philadelphia with the newer cities of mid-continent and the West Coast is a rather discouraging exercise; Dallas, for example, which has done virtually nothing in the line of urban renewal and has openly denounced Federal aid, is in far better condition than Philadelphia after a decade's massive effort."

San Francisco: "More beautiful than Washington, more cosmopolitan than New Orleans . . . wealthier and more civilized than Los Angeles or San Diego. San Francisco offers to the next generation much of what New York offered to the last generation. San Francisco could become the City of the Future."*

* Robert A. Futterman, *The Future of Our Cities,* Doubleday, Garden City, N.Y., 1961.

seemingly simple question can be answered both "yes" and "no," depending on which of several definitions of Detroit and Chicago are used (Table 13.1).

The U.S. Bureau of the Census attempted to meet the problem of urban definition by creating census regions called *Standard Metropolitan Areas* (SMA) for use in the 1950 Census; these were slightly modified and called *Standard Metropolitan Statistical Areas* (SMSA) in the 1960 and 1970 censuses. The SMSA includes one or more cities of 50,000 population, plus

Table 13.1   Population Density Comparisons for Different Definitions of Detroit and Chicago, 1950

Areal Unit	Density of Detroit (Population per Square Mile)	Ratio of Densities (Detroit/Chicago)
City	13,249	0.76
Urbanized Area	6,734	0.87
Metropolitan District	3,375	0.79
Standard Metropolitan Area	1,535	1.01

Source: Otis D. Duncan, Ray P. Cuzzort, and Beverly Duncan, *Statistical Geography: Problems In Analyzing Areal Data,* The Free Press of Glencoe, Ill., 1961, p. 36.

those adjoining counties that have more than 75 percent of their population engaged in nonagricultural activities. Certain other criteria have been met in establishing the national system of SMSA's (Fig. 13.2).

In 1960 the U.S. Bureau of the Census officially used the term *megalopolis* to define the urbanized region extending from Boston to Washington, D.C. along the Eastern Seaboard. The term *megalopolis* had been used by the French geographer, Jean Gottmann, in his classic study of the region.[3] Gottmann also perceived the emergence of other megalopoles in the United States: in Southern California along the Los Angeles-San Diego axis; around Chicago along the shore of Lake Michigan; and, along the Cleveland-Pittsburgh axis. Megalopoli (also called *conurbations*) can be observed in other parts of the world; examples are Greater London and the Ruhr Valley in Europe, and the eastern coastal plains of Honshu in Japan.

THE ECLECTIC STRATEGY FOR URBAN STUDIES

No single urban theory, however important as a partial explanation, can encompass the exceedingly complex metropolis in its totality. For this reason an *eclectic*[4] approach suggests itself in any attempt to better understand the modern city. We saw in Chapter 4 that the models of classical location theory, taken together, furnish a considerable measure of explanation about

[3] Jean Gottmann, *Megalopolis: The Urbanized Northeastern Seaboard of the United States,* A Twentieth Century Fund Study, The M.I.T. Press, Cambridge, Mass., 1961.
[4] *Eclecticism,* or the *eclectic approach* simply means the combined use of all the means available to attain an end. The end in this case is a better comprehension of cities and urban functions.

Figure 13.2 (Source: *U.S. Department of Commerce, Bureau of the Census,* *1979.*)

CITIES AS SPATIAL CONCENTRATIONS OF ECONOMIC ACTIVITY

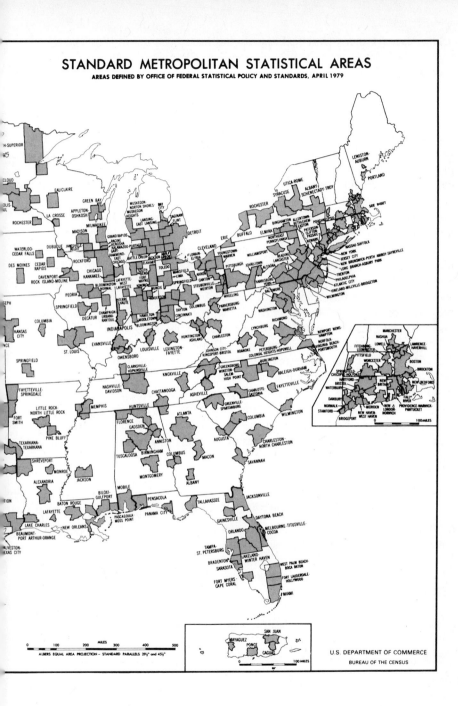

STANDARD METROPOLITAN STATISTICAL AREAS
AREAS DEFINED BY OFFICE OF FEDERAL STATISTICAL POLICY AND STANDARDS, APRIL 1979

U.S. DEPARTMENT OF COMMERCE
BUREAU OF THE CENSUS

THE NEED FOR BETTER KNOWLEDGE OF URBAN DYNAMICS   349

urban places. Other theoretical approaches have been developed. The contribution of *diffusion theory* was discussed in Chapter 2. Still another perspective is gained by viewing the city as an ecological system, which is discussed later in this chapter.

Historical research also contributes knowledge useful to urban scholars. Among other things, history reveals much about certain timeless urban problems. For example, the behavior of street gangs in ancient Rome has been documented, and much is now known about organized crime that plagued the cities of Medieval Europe. Historical evidence shows that cities emerge from small settlements having special spatial and/or environmental advantages. As such favored settlements grow—and this may depend on institutional, chance, and other factors—their advantage is enhanced as size increases.

In many cases, spatial and environmental factors have combined to give a place special transportation advantages. Cincinnati, St. Louis, Kansas City, and Omaha are all located on sites where early rail lines converged to cross rivers. Other cities flourished as strategic rail junctions or terminals; examples are Los Angeles, Denver, Portland, Seattle, Indianapolis, Minneapolis, and Atlanta. Port cities with overland routes to the interior had their positions greatly strengthened as break-of-bulk points (Fig. 12.7). New York, Philadelphia, and Baltimore are examples. The development of motor transport routes and terminals later reinforced the earlier advantages of these older cities, and also led to the rapid growth of newer, "auto-age" cities, such as Phoenix, Miami, Houston, and, of course, Los Angeles.

The history of urban growth in the United States and Canada has been marked by competition between cities in an effort to gain control of transport routes and the business they generate.[5]

THE RIVALRY BETWEEN CHICAGO AND ST. LOUIS

The historic rivalry between Chicago and St. Louis as a gateway to the developing West has been documented by Lewis F. Thomas.* The role of the Mississippi River as an east-west barrier and a north-south transport corridor, plus other, institutional factors, combined to give Chicago an advantage over St. Louis, and ultimately, urban supremacy in the Middle West.

* Lewis F. Thomas, "Decline of St. Louis as Midwest Metropolis," *Economic Geography*, April 1949, pp. 118-127.

---

[5] Factors in the competitive rise of New York City to national supremacy are mentioned in Chapter 1 (see Fig. 1.5).

CITIES AS SPATIAL CONCENTRATIONS OF ECONOMIC ACTIVITY

Empirical studies of cities as elements within a national system of urban places reveal certain regularities in size distribution. A tendency exists for city sizes within some countries to follow, at least roughly, a mathematical regularity. This tendency, formulated by G. K. Zipf[6] in 1949, has been called the *rank-size rule.* The rule holds that if all cities (urban centers) in a country are ranked by size of population, the size of the rth city from the top is $1/r$ times the size of the largest city. That is,

$$P_r = \frac{P_1}{r^q}$$

Where: r = the rank of the city
P_r = population of the city with rank r
P_1 = population of the largest city (rank = 1)
q = an exponent that approximates 1.0

Figure 13.3 shows the rank-size distribution of cities in the United States, which conforms quite closely to the mathematical model.

Another empirical statement had been made earlier by geographer Mark Jefferson, who observed that in many countries one city (in most cases the capital city) had grown much larger than all the others and dominated the economic affairs of the nation. He called these dominant urban centers *primate cities.*[7] A third group of countries has city size distributions that appear to be intermediate between the rank-size pattern and the primate pattern (Table 13.2).

This brief review by no means exhausts the multiple paths that can be followed in attempting to reach a better comprehension of the modern city. The field of urban studies is highly interdisciplinary, and contributions come from a wide variety of academic disciplines and professions.

The eclectic strategy—really a strategy of common sense—calls for the weaving together of as many explanatory strands as possible into a "big picture" view of the city. If this is too formidable an intellectual challenge for the present, the eclectic method nevertheless can serve as an organizing strategy for future efforts toward the ultimate goal. One promising development in urban studies, which attempts to simulate the total function of a city, is that of urban system modelling.

---

[6] *Human Behavior and the Principle of Least Effort,* Addison-Wesley, Reading, Mass., 1949.
[7] Mark Jefferson, "The Law of the Primate City," *The Geographical Review,* Vol. 29 (1939).

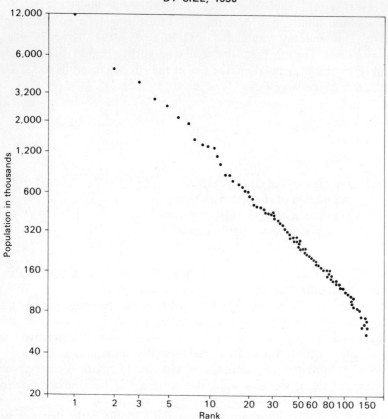

Figure 13.3   The size distribution of United States "Urbanized Areas," as described by the Bureau of the Census in 1950, closely conformed to the hypothetical distribution described by the rank-size equation. For example, Binghamton, New York, with an "urbanized population" of 144,570, ranked 84th of all United States Urbanized Areas in 1950. The Rank-Size Rule predicts a hypothetical population for Binghamton of 1/84 the population of the New York Urbanized Area (12,222,963), or 145, 511. (Source: Rutledge Vining, "A Description of Certain Spatial Aspects of An Economic System," Economic Development and Cultural Change, *Vol. 3, 1954–55, Fig. 1, page 152.)*

ECONOMIC FUNCTIONS OF CITIES

Whatever else they may be, cities are also spatial concentrations of economic activity. As a nation becomes economically developed, the proportion

Table 13.2   Types of City Size Distributions in Selected Countries

Countries with Rank-size Pattern	Countries with Primate Pattern	Countries with Intermediate Patterns
Belgium	Austria	Australia
Brazil	Ceylon	Canada
China	Denmark	Ecuador
El Salvador	Dominican Republic	Malaya
Finland	Greece	New Zealand
India	Guatemala	Nicaragua
Italy	Japan	Norway
Korea	Mexico	Pakistan
Poland	Netherlands	England and Wales
South Africa	Peru	
Switzerland	Portugal	
United States	Spain	
West Germany	Sweden	
	Thailand	
	Uruguay	

Source: Peter E. Lloyd and Peter Dicken, *Location In Space: A Theoretical Approach to Economic Geography,* Harper and Row (2nd edition), New York, 1977, Table 3.4, p. 79.

of its people living in urban places increases. As urbanization proceeds, the cities become more and more dominant in the economic life of the nation. In a Highly Developed Country, such as Australia or Sweden, most of the markets, labor skills, manufacturing capacity, construction activity, and service industries are concentrated in urban places.

However, the urban areas cover only small fraction of the total national space. In the United States, approximately 25 million acres are occupied by the urban (the term *urban,* unless otherwise specified, includes "suburban") population. Highways, railroads, and airports cover roughly 27 million acres. This makes a grand total of built-up area of about 52 million acres, or about 3 percent of the nation's area. By comparison, nearly 500 million acres are devoted to commercial forestry, and about 700 million acres are used as grazing land in the United States.

THE CITY AS A MANUFACTURING CENTER

Pre-industrial cities have been described as "parasitic," in the sense that they were chiefly centers of consumption. The modern city, however, is also a spatial concentration of production. Manufacturing is an important part of the total economic base of urban centers, whether for consumption within

URBAN SYSTEM MODELING

An important advance in the study of cities has been the design of urban models based on the rapidly developing systems science and computer science fields. Research by Jay Forrester* and other investigators involves computer simulation of the long-range activities of cities. The new generation of digital computers, with their greatly expanded capacities and speed, enables researchers to simulate feedback processes analogous to those operating in large cities.

The urban models of Forrester have been challenged by many. However, if the past rate of progress in urban system modelling is maintained, the hope exists for a more sophisticated level of urban analysis and planning by the end of this decade.

*Jay Forrester, *op. cit.*

the city itself, or for export beyond. In most American cities, manufacturing industries employ over 25 percent of the labor force.

The role of manufacturing in the great cities of the world is often underestimated. New York City and London each have over 30,000 manufacturing establishments; most of these are small, but in the aggregate each city has roughly a million manufacturing workers. Paris is thought of as a cultural center, but it also contains by far the greatest concentration of manufacturing in France, including most of the automobile production. Manufacturing is also concentrated in the major cities of the Less Developed Countries.

In general, the larger the urban center, the greater its industrial diversity. Large places, such as Philadelphia or Los Angeles, have very diversified manufacturing structures, similar in many ways to those of small industrial nations.

Manufacturing industries strongly represented in cities are those that must be close to urban activities to be efficient, and those that can pay the high land prices or site rentals for industrial space. Many types of manufacturing attracted to cities are market-oriented, such as newspapers or soft drink bottling plants, which must minimize high distribution costs. Other types, such as apparel industries and publishing, depend on external economies *(urbanization economies)* provided by the concentrations of suppliers, special services, and labor skills. The availability of space in vacant buildings, the level of taxes, zoning restrictions, transport facilities, and other factors also affect the attraction of manufacturing to urban centers.

The fashion garment industry is one that operates efficiently in the center of certain large metropolitan centers and the concentration in mid-town

Manhattan is the largest in the world (Fig. 13.4). A more recent development, the garment district in Los Angeles, has taken on the same pattern of intensive concentration near the city center, confirming that this is a spatial tendency for efficiency.

The attraction of states with dense, highly urbanized populations for manufacturing industry is clearly revealed in Figure 13.5, created by Australian economist Colin Clark and based on work done in association with geographer Chauncy Harris at the University of Chicago in the 1950s. Using the concept of *economic potential*—similar to the concept of market potential (Fig. 11.5) except that regional incomes and not populations are the variable—Clark shows a conspicuous positive correlation between the proportion of manufacturing to primary incomes and economic potential in the United States. Note that the ordinate is a log scale, covering a five hundred fold range, indicating the very different status of manufacturing in Wyoming and the Dakotas as contrasted to the densely populated, highly urbanized states of New Jersey and Connecticut.

Many manufacturing industries cannot operate profitably in central cities. Examples are firms that have large-scale, pollution generating operations, or those requiring much ground or floor space. These types must seek locations outside urban centers, where land costs are lower, and where negative externalities resulting from their operations are less of a problem.

In the older cities, heavy manufacturing was often located along lakes, rivers, bays, or other navigable waterways, or next to railroad tracks, where bulk shipment costs could be minimized (see Figures 12.7 and 12.8). Many cities with such transport advantages still support process-type manufacturing. However, much heavy manufacturing has tended to become dispersed to outer parts of the metropolitan areas, to satellite cities, or, in some cases, to rural sites within easy reach of major highways (Table 13.3).

Rapidly rising urban real estate prices, more stringent environmental regulations, and the change from rail to truck transport have all combined to accentuate the move of many other forms of manufacturing from the city center. Part of the problem, also, is the obsolescence in the inner city of the older, multistoried factory buildings. Modern requirements for most types of manufacturing call for plant layout all on one floor to facilitate work flow. This requires a spacious, one-story building, to permit straight assembly-line operations—an arrangement not feasible in the centers of large cities.

Some smaller cities and towns not near large urban centers have become the home sites of large-scale manufacturing operations. In certain cases, the community is economically dominated by one company, which, for some special set of reasons, has successfully functioned and expanded there. In the case of some firms, the original location in a small city or town was a matter of the personal preference of the founder, or of some chance occurrence.

MIDTOWN MANHATTAN GARMENT CENTER

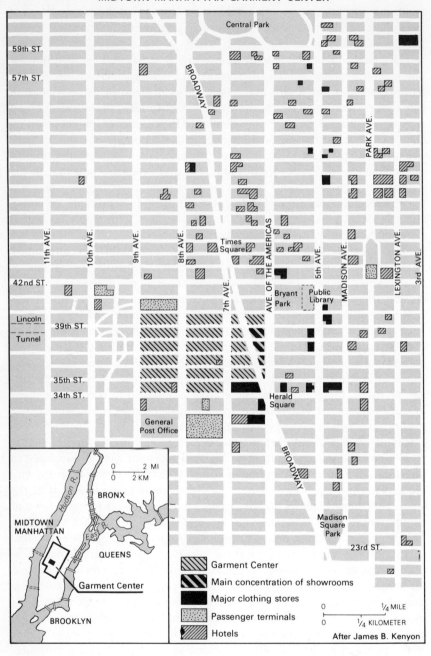

Central Park

59th ST.

57th ST.

BROADWAY

42nd ST.

Times Square

11th AVE.
10th AVE.
9th AVE.
8th AVE.
7th AVE.
AVE. OF THE AMERICAS
5th AVE.
MADISON AVE.
PARK AVE.
LEXINGTON AVE.
3rd AVE.

Bryant Park

Public Library

Lincoln Tunnel

39th ST.

35th ST.
34th ST.

Herald Square

General Post Office

Madison Square Park

23rd ST.

BROADWAY

0   2 MI
0   2 KM

Hudson R.

East R.

BRONX

MIDTOWN MANHATTAN

QUEENS

Garment Center

BROOKLYN

Garment Center

Main concentration of showrooms

Major clothing stores

Passenger terminals

Hotels

0   ¼ MILE
0   ¼ KILOMETER

After James B. Kenyon

356   CITIES AS SPATIAL CONCENTRATIONS OF ECONOMIC ACTIVITY

Figure 13.4 (see facing page) Note the proximity of the Garment Center to major clothing stores, showrooms, hotels, and railroad terminals. Not shown is the intricate pattern of subway lines that serve the district. What appears to be an almost paralyzing congestion in the streets of the Garment District during working hours is not enough of a disadvantage to the myriad small firms operating there to overcome the advantages of agglomeration and accessibility. (Source: After James B. Kenyon, "The Industrial Structure of the New York Garment Center," in R.S. Thoman and D.J. Patton (Eds.), Focus on Geographic Activity: A Collection of Original Studies, *McGraw-Hill Book Co., New York, 1964, p. 160.)*

In the United States and elsewhere, groupings exist of two or more small cities that, taken together with their surrounding suburban areas, provide the agglomeration advantages of a larger city for manufacturing. An example is the "Triple Cities" of Binghamton, Johnson City, and Endicott in New

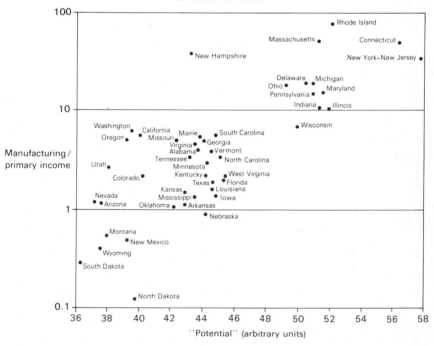

INDUSTRIAL LOCATION AND ECONOMIC POTENTIAL
UNITED STATES

Figure 13.5 See text for explanation. (Source: Colin Clark, Population Growth and Land Use, *Macmillan, New York, 1967, Diagram VIII. D, p. 296.)*

Table 13.3   Selected Data on the Deconcentration of Intrametropolitan Economic Activity in the Fifteen Largest Standard Metropolitan Statistical Areas (SMSA's)

SMSA	Percent Suburban Share Total Jobs		Percent Suburban Share Total SMSA Retail Sales		Percent Suburban Share Total SMSA Manufacturing Employment	
	1960	1970	1963	1972	1963	1972
New York	28.8	35.9	32.9	N.A.	19.1	53.4
Los Angeles[a]	47.8	54.3	58.7	60.0	63.9	64.0
Chicago	32.2	47.5	43.1	56.8	41.0	57.4
Philadelphia	37.0	51.8	56.6	66.7	50.5	59.3
Detroit	43.3	61.4	57.3	74.1	59.3	67.6
San Francisco	44.9	50.0	52.0	63.3	53.3	62.3
Washington DC	36.2	54.9	57.9	76.3	55.8	64.7
Boston	55.5	62.2	68.8	76.3	71.8	78.2
Pittsburgh	64.0	63.7	65.9	77.0	70.0	76.1
St. Louis	39.3	58.0	62.5	77.2	50.3	62.0
Baltimore	34.1	49.9	41.9	61.5	45.4	68.3
Cleveland	28.3	46.0	45.2	69.0	39.7	51.3
Houston[a]	15.7	24.4	17.6	29.0	28.8	34.3
Minneapolis-St. Paul	23.6	41.1	38.5	62.9	32.7	45.3
Dallas[a]	24.4	29.0	28.8	58.6	21.2	53.6
Average	37.0	47.6	48.5	64.9	46.8	59.9

[a] Annexation of suburban territory since 1960.

Source: Peter O. Muller, *The Outer City: Geographical Consequences of the Urbanization of the Suburbs* (Washington, D.C.: Association of American Geographers, Resource Papers for College Geography, No. 75-2), 1976, p. 30, Table 3. Reprinted by permission.

York State. These places, together with surrounding communities and suburbs, have a total population of about 200,000. Within this complex, which makes up the urban part of the Binghamton SMSA (Standard Metropolitan Statistical Area), are a number of large manufacturing plants. Other examples of urban combinations are the Chapel Hill-Durham-Raleigh Triangle in North Carolina, the Saginaw-Bay City-Midland Complex in Michigan, and the Albany-Troy-Schenectady cluster in New York.

Like manufacturing, construction is a form of *secondary production,* and

Figure 13.6   Trading on the New York Mercantile Exchange.

also represents a large part of a city's total economic activity. However, while a substantial share of a city's manufacturing output is exported beyond the city itself, the construction of buildings, bridges, streets, port facilities, and other civil engineering structures is uniquely "market oriented."

TERTIARY ACTIVITY: THE ROLE OF SERVICE INDUSTRIES

Although many forms of manufacturing have been drawn away from urban centers, the central city remains attractive to the diverse group of activities called *service* or *tertiary industries*. Very large cities continue to attract those tertiary activities classified as *high order functions* in Central Place Theory (Chapter 4).

Service industries are often labor-intensive, many of which require face-to-face transactions (Fig. 13.6). The U.S. Bureau of the Budget classifies service industries into four main groupings:

1. Wholesale and retail trade.
2. Banking, financial, and real estate services.
3. Government activities at all levels.
4. The diverse class of personal services that includes medical services, entertainment, lodging, and so on.

Within Highly Developed Countries, the tertiaries[8] represent a preponderant share of the Gross National Product. In the United States and Canada, the proportion of the labor force in tertiary activities is among the highest in the world—about two-thirds.

Cities have always been centers of administration.[9] The great urban centers of the modern world have become huge depositories of information in the form of libraries, archives, business records, computer data banks, government files, and so on. Processing information and making decisions based on it are functions that make the large city a center of economic control.[10]

All nations with modern economies have retail and other service functions hierarchically structured in central places (Chapter 4). Modern cities evolve as elements within national and world systems of cities, mutually influencing each other through global transportation and communication links.

Modern jet travel and telecommunications have greatly increased the flow of people and information throughout the world, and have given certain cities increased dominance within the world economic system. New York and London, for example, are the locations of the two great stock exchanges and currency markets that serve much of the Free World.

Settlements of all kinds—from hamlets to great cities—are marketplaces where the travel and communication necessary for exchange is minimized by nucleating activities. A key feature of retail, personal service, and other tertiary business establishments is their tendency to cluster in these market centers (Chapter 1).

Anyone attempting to analyze the changing economic functions of American cities during the 1970s was faced with confusing, often contradictory trends. In no place were seeming paradoxes greater than in New York City. While large sections of the Bronx and Brooklyn ghettos were becoming nightmarish landscapes as landlords abandoned buildings (in December 1978 Mayor Edward Koch announced that New York City would own 55,000 abandoned dwelling units in 1979, making it the nation's largest landlord), parts of Manhattan were undergoing a construction boom of office buildings and hotels.

The growth of office space in Manhattan has been uneven since World War II. From 1946 to 1965, 64 million square feet of office space were built, giving Manhattan Island a total of 150 million square feet. From 1965 to

---

[8] The term *quaternaries* is used by some writers in referring to research and development, or certain other service industries.

[9] Law school graduates of 1977 in the United States are reported to have taken jobs in the following cities in the numbers shown: New York City, 1275; Washington, 1227; Chicago, 610; Los Angeles, 475; San Francisco, 454; Philadelphia, 389; Boston, 364; Atlanta 268; Dallas, 241; Denver, 240. (*The New York Times*, August 4, 1978.)

[10] John R. Borchert, "Major Control Points in American Economic Geography," *Annals of The Association of American Geographers*, Vol. 68, No. 2, June 1978.

CITIES AS SPATIAL CONCENTRATIONS OF ECONOMIC ACTIVITY

TOWNS AND CITIES AS MARKET CENTERS

Many geographers have analyzed the universal function of towns and cities as market centers. Glenn Trewartha, for example, wrote about the relationship between people, settlement, and commerce in the smallest of all settlements: hamlets.*

From the economist's viewpoint, the city, whether ancient Rome or modern Miami, is first and foremost an economic entity. Although every city has its own unique "mix" of functions, Wolfgang Stolper wrote, "The only function all cities appear to have in common seems to be to reduce or minimize transport cost and to lead to the establishment of an efficient system of market areas."†

---

*Glenn T. Trewartha, "Unincorporated Hamlet," *Annals of the AAG,* 33 (1943), 32-81.
†Wolfgang Stolper, "Spatial Order and Economic Growth of Cities: A Comment on Eric Landpard's Paper," *Economic Development and Cultural Change,* Vol. 3, 1954-55, p. 140.

1975, another 80 million were added, but by 1975 there was great concern about overgrowth, since 18 percent of Manhattan office space was vacant— the highest percentage since 1939. By 1979, however, a complete turnaround had occurred. The glut of office space had disappeared, and a new construction boom was underway.

A paradoxical aspect of this is that many corporate headquarters have moved out of Manhattan in recent years. In 1965, there were 125 major industrial corporations with home offices in New York City. However, by 1971 two dozen of these firms had relocated their headquarters in the surrounding countryside, primarily in the adjoining states of Connecticut and New Jersey. This exodus from the nation's largest city was the result of a number of factors, among which was the need for better quality life for headquarters personnel. This was illustrated on March 19, 1976, when the Union Carbide Company, the nation's second largest chemical producer, announced it was moving its headquarters from Manhattan to a spacious, 144 acre site near Danbury in southwestern Connecticut, about 30 miles away. The move, involving 3600 head office personnel, was explained by a company executive: "The long-term quality of life needs of our headquarters employees were the overriding factors in arriving at this conclusion."

However, in 1978, as American Airlines was preparing to move its corporate headquarters to Dallas-Fort Worth, IBM and AT and T announced plans to build office towers of 43 and 37 stories in Manhattan. Similar kinds of inconsistent patterns can be observed in other large cities.

The function of governmental administration reinforces the economic position of some urban places. As capitals, and therefore national centers of political influence and authority, the economic roles of London, Paris, Tokyo, Moscow, Rome, Stockholm, and Copenhagen are reinforced. (Washington, D.C., Canberra, Australia, Ottawa, Canada, and Brasilia, Brazil, are capital cities with specialized governmental functions, but are not the largest cities in their countries.)

At the state level in the United States, capitals are often not the largest city, but specialize as political-administrative-university centers; examples are Sacramento, Madison, Trenton, Albany, Austin, Montpelier, and Tallahassee.

At the county level in the United States, the county seat holds a special position of economic influence and stability as a fountainhead of local, state, and federal services and funding. Where there is no town or city larger than the county seat, the economic dominance of the county seat within the county is virtually assured.

THE PHYSICAL ENVIRONMENT AND METABOLISM OF CITIES

ENVIRONMENTAL SITE FACTORS

Modern urban land-use theory recognizes environmental as well as spatial aspects of comparative advantage for cities. One advantage is location on or near a navigable waterway. Of the 50 largest U.S. cities, 34 lie below 1000 feet, and 6 have maximum elevations of less than 100 feet. Location on navigable water at lower elevations gives a city accessibility by means of low-cost water transport. Some cities, such as Montreal, were strategically situated at the head of navigation on rivers. The "Fall Line" cities along the Eastern Seaboard of the United States are other examples: Philadelphia, Baltimore, Washington, Richmond, Augusta, and Charleston. Some cities are advantageously situated on or near river deltas, such as Alexandria, Egypt, and New Orleans. The cost advantages of land-water "bulk-breaking" sites for heavy industries were discussed in Chapters 11 and 12.

Urban locations on rivers or river deltas are not, of course, always an unmixed blessing. Recurrent flooding can be a potential problem. The cost of elaborate flood protection systems, such as those at Kansas City, must be considered in any assessment of a city's overall advantages and disadvantages. Buenos Aires, Argentina, is an example of a great city plagued by dangerous and costly river silting, which results in chronic port congestion. River or delta sites can also pose foundation problems for large buildings and heavy structures.

The topographic (landform) factor is another environmental influence that can affect urban places (Table 13.4). Level, well drained land is a de-

Table 13.4   Examples of Urban Sites with Special Environmental Characteristics

Environmental Characteristic	Examples
River Confluence	Koblenz (Rhine-Moselle)
	Khartoum (White Nile-Blue Nile)
Gap	Toulouse
	Belfort
River gorge exit	Bonn (Rhine)
	Turnu Severin (Danube)
River bend	Volgograd (Volga)
	Magdeburg (Elbe)
Bridgepoint	London (Thames)
	Gloucester (Severn)
Fall Line	Richmond, Virginia
	Augusta, Georgia
Lake-River point	Chicago
	Rostov (Soviet Union)
Mountain-Plain contact	Denver
	Verona (Italy)
River Promontory	Durham (England)
	Toledo (Spain)
Isthmus	Tunis (Tunisia)
	Detroit
Corridor	Innsbruck (Alps)
	Kabul (Himalayas)
Rocky outcrop	Edinburgh
	Salzburg
Outport	Bremerhaven (Bremen)
	Cuxhaven (Hamburg)

Source: Dean S. Rugg, *Spatial Foundations of Urbanism,* Wm. C. Brown Co., Dubuque, Iowa, 1972, Table 3.1, p. 86.

cided advantage, since it minimizes grading operations, allows low-cost construction of urban structures, and permits the efficient intraurban flow of people and goods. It is true that hillside locations are often sought as premium residential sites for their views and scenic value, but such sites are costly and can be enjoyed by very few urban dwellers. The existence of a good groundwater supply, especially in arid regions, is a great advantage for a city or town. The presence of a stream, river, lake, estuary, or bay as an assimilating body for urban waste water effluent is a critical environmental requirement.

THE CITY AS AN ECOLOGICAL SYSTEM

An important insight is gained when the city is viewed as an ecological system. The city is an *open system* because its metabolic functions depend on matter and energy from outside the system itself. In order to support its thousands, or millions, of inhabitants, a city must provide them daily with the ecological necessities of life: space, breathable air, potable (drinking) water, food, energy, and shelter.

The provision of a city's massive daily needs for solid, liquid, and gaseous substances requires great concentrations of capital investment in life support systems and other civil engineering structures. These include transportation and communications systems, water supply systems, waste water disposal systems, fuel delivery systems, electric energy systems, and others.

The concentration of physical capital in large metropolitan cities approaches staggering proportions. For example, in New York City (not the entire metropolitan area, but the five boroughs of the city) the water distribution system contains no fewer than 105,000 hydrants.

To pay for the daily inflow of water, food, energy and other resources it receives, the city must, in turn, produce wealth in the form of goods and services to be distributed outside, or to be consumed within the city by customers from outside. The large urban region, in this sense, is very much like a small, industrially advanced nation. Both Los Angeles and Belgium must "export" enough to pay for their "imports," or they will fail both as ecological and economic systems.

URBAN METABOLIC WASTES[11]

As ecological systems, cities require not only inputs of materials and energy, but also the removal of waste products. Where this removal is inadequate, urban processes and growth are inhibited. This general principle holds for ecological systems at all scales. For example, studies have shown that algae growing in streams have a critical dependence on the diffusion of wastes by the water current.

The metropolitan region is extremely efficient in collecting the material and energy resources it needs to survive, but the problems of waste removal grow year by year. Cities pass their growing loads of waste into the environment in a highly concentrated form. If the environment becomes overloaded at a given place, it cannot assimilate and neutralize the waste products through natural processes. This affects not only the city itself, but creates negative externalities over large areas outside the city as well. The need for removal of polluted waste water from a community is critical. An American city of one million inhabitants must get rid of about 150 million gallons of polluted waste water each day. In all but a very few cities, this is accomplished by discharging the waste effluent into a nearby body of water. The effluent is usually the outflow from a sewage treatment plant, but in some cases is raw sewage.

The discharge of untreated or partly treated waste water from cities along the coasts has had an adverse effect on some marine activities. Many of the world's great fisheries are located in shallow banks not far from urban-industrial regions, and are vulnerable to wastes flowing from these regions. It was estimated in 1978 that more than a tenth of the 10.7 million square miles of shellfish-producing waters bordering the United States were unusable because of pollution. There were indications, however, that urban waste-

[11] This relates in part to the section on wastes in Chapter 5.

water programs were beginning to result in a reversal of the trend. For example, some of the waters around Long Island had been improved to the point where shellfish production could be resumed.

Air, in economic terms, has traditionally been treated as a *free good*. This concept is undergoing a fundamental change. Reasonably clean air can be maintained over cities only if air pollution is eliminated or minimized (Fig. 5.5). Air pollution resulting from urban activities covers cities with gaseous and particulate wastes, including layers of fine soot that corrodes metals and other materials, damages natural vegetation, increases cleaning bills of all kinds, and generally lowers tax revenue bases through reductions in property values. The estimated costs of air pollution in the United States have reached the level of $16 billion annually. The most pernicious harm of all results from air pollution's effects on human health. Several major disasters in the past have been directly attributable to polluted air. The Meuse Valley of Belgium in 1930; Donora, Pennsylvania, in 1948; London, England, in 1953—all were scenes of death and sickness resulting from severe episodes of air pollution (Table 13.5).

Although it is not the kind of problem that often makes headlines, the problem of solid waste management for cities is becoming formidable (Table 13.6). In industrial nations, solid waste generation is rising sharply. Every day millions of tons of materials are shipped into cities, and a large proportion of the resulting waste must be handled by solid waste removal systems. Burning in incinerators and burying in land fill operations have been able to meet most disposal needs thus far, but year by year these methods become more inadequate. The emphasis in planning for the future is to develop systems that will recycle as much of the wastes as is economically feasible (Chapter 5).

Table 13.5   Relative Air Quality by Size of Population in United States Metropolitan Areas

	Relative Air Pollution Levels		
Population	Particulates	Sulfur Dioxide	Nitrogen Dioxide
100	1.0	1.0	1.0
2,000	1.4	2.3	1.3
10,000	1.6	3.2	1.5

Source: Allen V. Kneese, *Economics and the Environment,* Penguin Books, New York, 1977, Table 2, p. 40.

CITIES AS SPATIAL CONCENTRATIONS OF ECONOMIC ACTIVITY

Table 13.6   Solid Waste Collection Costs in 166 American Cities

City Size	Average Cost per Ton
10,000–100,000	$ 9.50
100,000–500,000	10.20
Over 500,000	24.05

Source: U.S. Bureau of Solid Waste Management, 1969.

OTHER NEGATIVE EXTERNALITIES LIMITING URBAN GROWTH

The history of modern urban development suggests that once a city reaches a certain threshold size, roughly 250,000 people, it then enjoys a set of advantages that give it an ecologically dominant position among smaller cities and towns in the region. The viability and dominance grow much more if the city becomes very large. The ability of great urban centers to rebuild after nearly total destruction attests to their survival powers. The wartime devastation of cities such as Warsaw, Hamburg, and Stalingrad proved only a temporary disruption of their economic functions.

This raises an interesting question: if increased size creates scale economies and other advantages, why does a city stop growing? The answer is that not all the effects of increased size are advantageous; beyond certain sizes, various costs begin to rise and act as limiting factors to continued growth. This is seen graphically in Figure 13.7.

The unit costs of private urban transport tend to rise rapidly as a city in the United States reaches a few hundred thousand inhabitants. This results from rising congestion, which begins to choke off the flow of cars and trucks. Significantly, rapid transit systems are efficient at much higher levels of urban population.

Urban life support systems also become less efficient when certain city sizes are reached. Rarely is a large city able to get along without water from outside its own boundaries. A large city's needs can preempt the natural water supply over a large region (Chapter 6).

Some cities have special environmental problems that increase with their growth. An example is the lowering of the water table under some cities that results from high-discharge pumping of the underlying aquifers. Parts of Mexico City have sunk many feet, due to removal of water from the ground (a former lake bed) on which it rests. The heavy pumping of ground water in Houston (over 100 billion gallons each year) has caused the downtown part of that city to sink over four feet in the past 30 years, with total damages

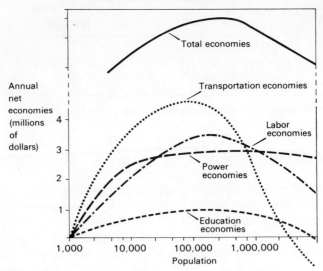

HYPOTHETICAL ECONOMIES OF SCALE
RELATED TO URBAN SIZE

Total economies

Annual
net
economies
(millions
of
dollars)

Transportation economies

4

Labor
economies

3

Power
economies

2

1

Education
economies

1,000   10,000   100,000   1,000,000
Population

Figure 13.7   The net economies (economies minus diseconomies) of various municipal functions generally increase with city size (scale economies) up to some level, and then decrease. (Source: Walter Isard, Location and Space Economy, MIT Press, Cambridge, Mass., 1956, Figure 35, p. 187.)

estimated at $250 million. One of the most serious negative externalities associated with urban growth is traffic congestion.

LAND USE WITHIN URBAN AREAS

A plot of land within a city, as elsewhere, has two economic attributes: site qualities and site location. Certain site qualities, such as good foundation material, can increase the value of the plot of land, while others, such as susceptibility to flooding, can decrease its value. In most cases, however, it is the attribute of site location that most affects the value of a plot of urban land.

While the dominant force shaping the urban economic landscape is economic, the pattern of land use is also influenced by administrative policies and decisions based on other criteria. Examples would be the special zoning restrictions around hospitals and schools, or the location of public facilities for handicapped persons.

TRANSPORTATION, ACCESSIBILITY, AND LAND USE

A key to understanding the economic functions of cities, and the distribution of land uses within cities, whether old or new, large or small, is to recognize their chief characteristic—accessibility. The proximity of people to people by means of transportation and communication systems within cities facilitates all types of human interaction.

Changes in transportation technology have had profound effects on city size, shape, and land-use patterns. The state of urban transport affects the city's size and form. Cities in ancient times were designed as "walking cities," and had small physical dimensions. It was possible, for example, to walk from one end of Athens to the other in less than an hour. In modern times the railroad, the motorized street car, and the subway greatly expanded cities and gave them a "star" shape. Later, the automobile and motor truck filled in the undeveloped areas and created still larger cities, roughly circular in shape (Fig. 13.8).

The location of streets, highways, and railway and subway lines all determine urban accessibility, and therefore influence land use. At the same time, as noted in Chapter 12, land use has a reciprocal effect on the demand for transport services and the location of transport facilities.

The main transport routes converge on a city, creating corridors of intense development leading into the urban core, giving it an extremely high degree of accessibility. (Nearly a dozen large railroad terminals are located in downtown Chicago.) The central, most accessible core of a city or town is called the Central Business District (CBD). It is here that land values peak up sharply (Fig. 3.5, 13.9). In the CBD's of certain large cities, land prices reach millions of dollars an acre.

Moving away from the Central Business District (CBD), the competition for space is reduced, land prices drop rapidly, and land uses are sorted out on the basis of location rent capabilities per acre (Fig. 13.10).

In reality, the decline in land values outward from the downtown area is not a smooth one. At mass transit stations and intersections of principal streets, minor peaks of accessibility and traffic flow occur. At such places retail establishments locate, pushing up land values to local peaks. Thus, in addition to a main CBD, larger cities have subsidiary commercial districts serving various parts of the urban region. Throughout the residential districts, small neighborhood retail clusters, having "Ma and Pa" groceries and other low order functions with small market ranges, serve local residents with convenience shopping items.

A view of CBD's and subsidiary commercial districts at the micro level reveals that land values, reflecting accessibility to potential retail customers, can vary greatly over short distances (Fig. 13.11). (See Box, p. 374.)

THREE-DIMENSIONAL RESPONSES TO URBAN GROWTH

Around the beginning of this century the first skyscrapers were built, made possible by the development of steel-framed buildings and high-speed eleva-

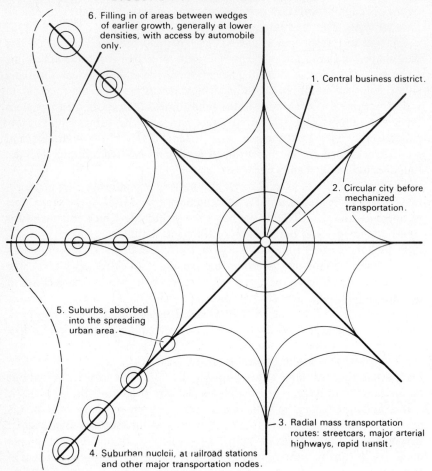

6. Filling in of areas between wedges of earlier growth, generally at lower densities, with access by automobile only.

1. Central business district.

2. Circular city before mechanized transportation.

5. Suburbs, absorbed into the spreading urban area.

3. Radial mass transportation routes: streetcars, major arterial highways, rapid transit.

4. Suburban nuclei, at railroad stations and other major transportation nodes.

Figure 13.8 A generalized picture of the sequence of development of cities. The evolution of the urban pattern is closely interrelated with the changing forms of internal transport. (Source: Harold M. Mayer, "A Spatial Expression of Urban Growth," Association of American Geographers, Resource Paper No. 7 (1969), Figure 9, p. 40.)

tors. Increasingly since then, three-dimensional development has been a major response to the growing competition for space, especially in city cores. As land prices rose, it was judged profitable to invest in the construction of very tall buildings. Since the late 1940s, a building boom of high rise buildings has taken place in the CBD's of large American cities. The same phenom-

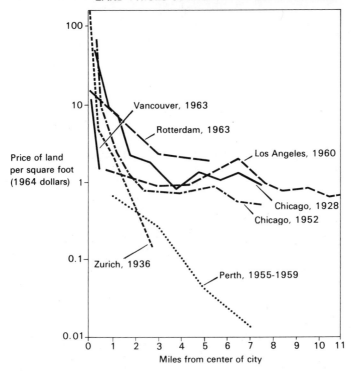

LAND PRICES SURROUNDING CITY CENTERS

Figure 13.9   The peaking of land prices at the city centers would appear much more dramatic if the ordinate scale were arithmetic instead of logarithmic. (Source: *Colin Clark,* Population Growth and Land Use, *Macmillan, New York, 1967, Diagram IX. 0, p. 384.*)

enon has been repeated in many other countries. Billions of dollars have been invested in skyscrapers in Mexico City, Toronto, Moscow, Frankfurt, Tokyo, and other large cities around the globe. In every case, the three-dimensional organization of urban space requires an extensive vertical transportation system of high-speed elevators. In New York, for example, there are 30,000 elevators that daily carry passengers a total of 125,000 vertical miles.

Some of the modern skyscrapers have been designed to provide all the services of a self-contained community. Chicago's 100 floor John Hancock Center, for example, contains apartments, office space, restaurants, seven floors of parking space, and a five-story department store.

Within cities, particularly in the center of large ones, there is an intensive

LOCATION RENT AND THE SPATIAL ORGANIZATION
OF URBAN LAND USE

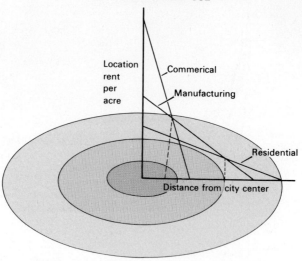

Figure 13.10   As in the case of agricultural land use based on the Thünen model (Chapter 4), urban land uses are sorted out competitively on the basis of location rents, ideally forming concentric zones about the center of the city.

use of subterranean space for water, sewer, electric power, gas, and other utility lines, for subbasements and foundations, and for subways. In recent years there has been added emphasis on other uses, such as underground pedestrian malls, parking areas, and tunnels.

A number of extensive underground structures have served several North American cities for many decades. A large system underlies part of downtown Montreal; this complex will eventually connect 100 acres of space beneath downtown buildings.

The utilization of underground space for urban and other uses is far more common in some other countries. It has been estimated that in 100 cities in U.S.S.R., 35 percent or more of investment in structures is underground. Sweden also has extensive underground urban development, including sewage treatment plants and other facilities.

Another device for employing high-value urban land more intensively is the use of transportation rights-of-way on one level, covered by a platform on which high-rise buildings can be erected. In the CBD's of large cities the cost of platforming over transportation rights-of-way is low compared to the value of the "new land" produced. Such *air rights* have long been used over railroad terminals and tracks.

THE RELATIONSHIP BETWEEN LAND VALUES AND PEDESTRIAN TRAFFIC ALONG ASHLAND AVENUE, CHICAGO

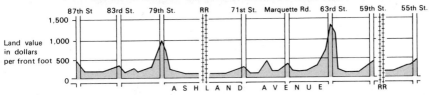

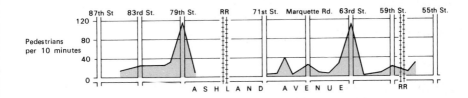

Figure 13.11   Differences in pedestrian traffic can cause sharp changes in land values over very short distances along city streets. On Ashland Avenue in Chicago there are main business intersections at 63rd Street and 79th Street. The pedestrian traffic drops off sharply from these intersections. Retail business proprietors compete for sites where pedestrian flow is highest. As a result, the graph of land values along Ashland Avenue closely replicates the level of pedestrian traffic. (Source: *Brian J.L. Berry,* Geography of Market Centers and Retail Distribution, *Prentice-Hall, Inc., Englewood, N.J., 1967, Fig. 2.21, p. 49.*)

THE DYNAMICS OF URBAN SPRAWL

There is another way, in addition to vertical development, in which a city responds to growth, and that is by spilling over its political boundaries into the surrounding countryside (Fig. 1.3). This process, called *suburbanization,* is also referred to as *urban sprawl.*

Nearly all metropolitan population growth in the United States during the two decades, 1950–1970, took place outside central city boundaries. By the mid 1970s, fully a third of the United States population lived in what can be described as suburban places. Since the majority of home owners carry mortgages, the new suburbs have been characterized as a giant "credit bubble." In addition to population, there has been an outward expansion of manufacturing, construction, retail trade, new capital investment, taxable wealth, and political power.

Geographer Kathryn A. Zeimetz and three colleagues in the U.S. Department of Agriculture studied the nature of major land-use shifts in 53 urban-

CONSUMER BEHAVIOR AND DEPARTMENT STORE LOCATION

The behavioral aspects of consumer purchasing habits make fascinating research studies. One day the author was standing on the corner of a busy intersection in the Borough of Queens, New York City, talking to the manager of a large department store. The manager estimated that his sales volume was 25 percent greater than that of a competitor directly across the avenue, because, he reasoned, a subway entrance on the sidewalk outside his store brought many more "impulse buyers" past his store windows. Here is a case where market accessibility (the flow of potential buyers), and therefore location rent and land prices, all vary considerably from one side of the avenue to the other.

izing counties during the period 1961–1970. The major land use changes are shown graphically in Figure 13.12.

A number of factors, in addition to the general population increase, have stimulated postwar suburbanization in the United States. One factor has been the "ghettoization" of sections of the large, northern cities. Since blacks and other minorities began migrating in great numbers to them in the 1940s, the more affluent whites have moved to the suburbs (Fig. 13.13). The rapid growth of the ghettos, along with the attendant social and economic problems it raised, has transformed the central cities. As the more prosperous families moved to the suburbs, the taxable base of the cities eroded. This problem has been compounded by the sharply increased needs for services from the remaining, poorer residents. The series of urban crises in the 1960s and early 1970s was caused in considerable part by problems related to the changing economic and social character of the central cities (Fig. 13.14).

Significantly, Bureau of Census studies made since 1970 indicate that some blacks as well as whites have been leaving the poverty areas of American inner cities. A significant migration of middle- and upper-income blacks has taken place to the suburbs.

A related factor contributing to suburbanization has been the impact of federally funded urban renewal programs. These programs result in the decentralization of residential housing and retail functions and a radical transformation of the Central Business District. Urban renewal strategy has been to replace older residential structures in the central city core with office buildings, government centers, high-rise apartments, and public housing, all of which result in the outward displacement of population.

A third factor stimulating suburban expansion has been the improvement of transportation facilities, especially the increase in high-speed automobile and truck access between the city core and the suburbs. In the 35 years since

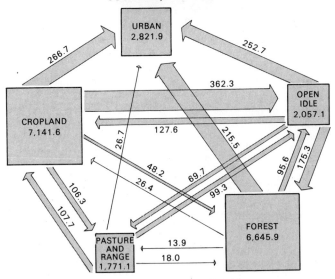

MAJOR LAND—USE SHIFTS IN 53 URBANIZING
COUNTIES, 1961—1970

Figures indicate thousands of acres   Box sizes are proportional to 1961 acreages

*Figure 13.12   Changes interpreted from aerial photography for 53 counties in
which 20 percent of the 1960 to 1970 U.S. population increase occurred. Urban
land uses occupied 16.4 percent of total land area in 1970, up from about 13.0
percent in 1961. About 770,000 acres were converted to urban uses in the 53
counties during the 9 year period. For all the counties, .173 acres of rural land
were urbanized for each person increase in population. (Source: Kathryn A.
Zeimetz, Elizabeth Dillon, Ernest E. Hardy, and Robert C. Otte, "Dynamics
of Land Use in Fast Growth Areas," Economic Research Service, U.S. Dept. of
Agriculture, Agricultural Economic Report No. 325, April, 1976, Fig. 1.)*

the end of World War II, motor transport has altered the urban landscape in
all Highly Developed Countries, particularly in the United States and Canada. Fully a fourth of the Interstate Highway Program mileage constructed
between 1956 and 1980 has been built within the boundaries of metropolitan
areas.

The development of mass transit systems before World War II tended to
concentrate urban activities in the central cores, with subsidiary nodes at the
surrounding stations. However, the limited access highway (also called freeway, expressway, quickway, etc.) tends to decentralize population and economic activities. Commuters, shoppers, and others who live in the outer city

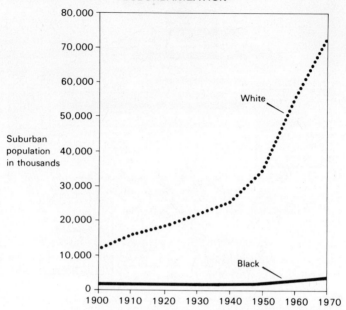

RACIAL SEGREGATION RELATED TO
SUBURBANIZATION

Figure 13.13   Postwar trends in the United States show a rapid divergence of whites and blacks related to the growth of the suburbs. (Source: Peter O. Muller, "The Outer City: Geographical Consequences of the Urbanization of the Suburbs," Resource Paper No. 75-2, Association of American Geographers, Washington, D.C., Fig. 8(b), p. 18.)

or beyond now have fast highway access to the CBD or to other parts of the metropolitan area. In 1972 the Bureau of the Census reported that one-fourth of all American job holders traveled to a different county to get from their homes to their jobs. Since so many commuting workers live in outer residential sections, the otherwise bustling downtown areas of many cities seem deserted at night and on weekends.

A fourth factor stimulating urban sprawl has been the extension of relatively low-priced utility services, particularly water and sewer lines, to outlying areas. Decisions relating to the location of these critical facilities establish the patterns of land use in the suburbanizing areas. Since the extension of utilities allows development of lower-cost land, house plots in the outer suburbs can be very spacious. Large house plots are, however, an inefficient use of the land because they increase the costs for schools, roads, fire prevention, postal service, garbage disposal, and other municipal services.

Beyond the existing networks of water and sewage lines, but often still

CITIES AS SPATIAL CONCENTRATIONS OF ECONOMIC ACTIVITY

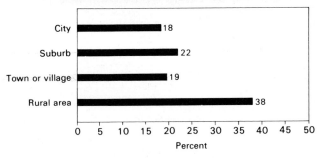

PREFERRED PLACE OF RESIDENCE ACCORDING
TO A NATIONAL SURVEY IN 1972

*Figure 13.14   Results of a national survey conducted by the Gallup Organiza-
tion in June, 1972.* (Source: Environmental Quality, *Council on Environmental Quality, Washington, D.C., Sept., 1976, p. 297.*)

within the county or counties making up a Standard Metropolitan Statistical
Area (SMSA), a transitional zone exists, where rural land is gradually converted into residential property. House plots are even larger here; tax rates
are lower, but the owners must provide many of their own services, such as
wells, septic tanks, fire protection, and so on. Residential land use in these
outer zones is spotty, with development characterized as a "leap-frog" process. Very often land is bought on speculation and held, unused, for an
anticipated price rise.

JUNG AND HALL ON THE PATHOLOGY OF URBAN CROWDING

The problem of human disorders caused or aggravated by life in large cities has
been studied by a number of behavioral and social scientists. Anthropologist Edward
Hall concluded from research carried out over many years that urban overcrowding
causes stress that contributes to violence and crime, delinquency, sexual deviation,
drug addiction, mental illness, hypertension and other serious malfunctions.* The
findings of Hall and other contemporary researchers confirm the earlier insights of
the renowned Swiss psychiatrist, Carl Gustav Jung:

*Life in a small city is better than life in a large city. . . . The large cities are responsible
for our rootlessness. . . . With all my heart and thought, I believe in the human need for
roots.*†

*Edward T. Hall, *The Hidden Dimension,* Doubleday and Co., New York, 1966.
†*Modern Man in Search of a Soul* (Trans. W. S. Dell & C. F. Baynes), New York: Harcourt,
Brace & World, 1957.

Geographer Robert Sinclair[12] has argued that urban encroachment on surrounding rural land causes, paradoxically, a reverse type of agricultural zoning than in the Thünen model. According to Sinclair's model, land closest to expanding urban areas has the highest future *anticipated* value, and owners there tend to hold the land in unintensive uses or even unused in the expectation of future sales. Conversely, the outer zones will have less future anticipated value, and here farmers are likely to make the long range investments necessary for intensive farming to serve the growing urban market. Sinclair and others have accumulated empirical evidence from a number of places that supports the hypothesis.

Because of tightening energy supplies and inflation, reaction against the extravagant use of land for residential purposes has increased in recent years. More and more, community planning and design reflect an interest in greater spatial efficiency.

RECENT POPULATION TRENDS IN AMERICA

The postwar "baby boom," which began in 1946, had a profound impact on the population geography of the United States. In the 1950s and 1960s the cities swelled and the nation doubled the use of land for urban purposes. A demographic turning-point occurred in the mid-1960s, when the birth rate began to fall. By 1977, the birth rate had dropped to an all-time low of 15

[12] Robert Sinclair, "Von Thünen and Urban Sprawl," *Annals of the Association of American Geographers* Vol. 57, 1967, pp. 72-87.

per thousand (1.5 per cent) per year, roughly the same as in the Highly Developed Countries of Europe. The population growth rate fell to 0.8 percent in 1976, but the total population will probably continue to grow until the end of the century, even assuming the lowest reasonable projections.

Despite dropping birth and population growth rates, population mobility in the United States has remained very high. The U.S. Bureau of the Census estimated in 1972 that the average American changes residence 14 times in his or her lifetime. This means that about 40 million Americans change their home address each year. Although population mobility remained high, the direction of flow by the 1970s had changed. By 1974, for the first time since the Civil War, more blacks were migrating into the South than were moving North.

Another important geographic trend in the United States is the migration of people and economic activity from "Snowbelt" cities in the North to "Sunbelt" cities in the South and West. The Bicentennial of 1976 marked the first year that more Americans lived in the South and West, taken together, than in the North. On July 1, 1978, the estimated U.S. population was 218,000,000. See Figures 13.15 and 13.16.

The increased mobility of older, retired people is resulting in a move away from the severe winters of the North to sunny retirement areas. Also, many younger workers are moving with their families from older, declining, industries in the North to more dynamic, space-age industries in the South and West (Chapter 11). For the years 1971 through 1975, 82 percent of the new manufacturing jobs were gained by cities in the South or West.

In general, it is expected that metropolitan areas in the South and West will continue to grow rapidly relative to those in the North, whereas the

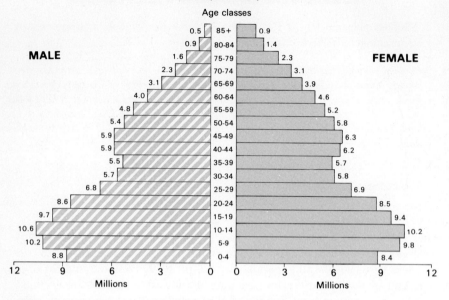

POPULATION OF THE UNITED STATES BY AGE AND SEX, 1970 (ACTUAL)

Age classes

MALE

FEMALE

MALE		Age classes		FEMALE
0.5		85+		0.9
0.9		80-84		1.4
1.6		75-79		2.3
2.3		70-74		3.1
3.1		65-69		3.9
4.0		60-64		4.6
4.8		55-59		5.2
5.4		50-54		5.8
5.9		45-49		6.3
5.9		40-44		6.2
5.5		35-39		5.7
5.7		30-34		5.8
6.8		25-29		6.9
8.6		20-24		8.5
9.7		15-19		9.4
10.6		10-14		10.2
10.2		5-9		9.8
8.8		0-4		8.4

Millions   Millions

Figure 13.15 (Source: *U.S. Department of Commerce, Bureau of the Census, January, 1978.*)

growth of such places as metropolitan Philadelphia, Chicago, and New York will be slow or stabilized. Economic growth in the South has been sparked, not only by new manufacturing, but also by increases in agricultural, forest product, and oil and gas industries. The relative price rises for these commodities in recent years has given the South's economy an additional thrust. Many cities, such as Dallas, Houston, Jackson (Mississippi), Tampa, St. Petersburg, and Greenville (South Carolina), are expected to continue to grow substantially for at least another decade. As expected, the operations of the federal government will continue to make Washington, D.C. a growth center.

The West has been less successful in attracting manufacturing because of its distance from markets in the Northeast; however, it has a special attraction for white collar and professional jobs. Office employment is growing, particularly in San Francisco, Los Angeles, and Denver. Phoenix, Salt Lake City, Portland, Oregon, Seattle, and other western cities are expected to continue growing through the 1980s. A threat to longer range urban growth in many parts of the West is its water limitation.

CITIES AS SPATIAL CONCENTRATIONS OF ECONOMIC ACTIVITY

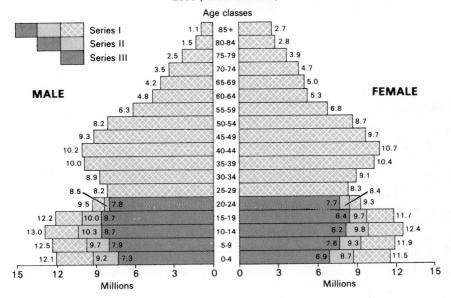

POPULATION OF THE UNITED STATES BY AGE AND SEX, 2000 (PROJECTIONS)

Figure 13.16   Three projections for the year 2000 were made in 1978, based on three assumptions for Average Number of Lifetime Births. The three series are shown in the graph. Projections for Series I, II, and III are 282,837,000, 260,378,000, and 245,876,000. (Source: U.S. Department of Commerce, Bureau of the Census, January, 1978.)

URBAN DEVELOPMENT IN THE THIRD WORLD

SPECIAL FEATURES AND PROBLEMS

Throughout most of the Third World, a large proportion of the total population remains agriculturalists who continue to live in rural villages. Large cities contain a much smaller share of the population than in the Highly Developed Countries. However, the rate of urbanization is high in the LDC's, higher than the population growth rate in general. Unless an unforeseen change occurs, by the end of the century a greatly expanded urban population will exist in the Third World, living under poverty conditions (see Fig. 2.8).

The great cities of the Third World tend to be located on or near the coasts, where they are accessible to ocean shipping and to world export markets. The coastal cities of West Africa, such as Dakar, Abidjan, Accra, and Lagos, are examples; they are transshipment points for the export of commodities produced in the interior and moved down the rivers to the coast. These ports also act as gateways for goods from overseas destined for inland markets. In South Asia, coastal cities such as Bombay, Calcutta, Singapore, and Bangkok serve similar gateway functions. In South America, the largest cities, with few exceptions, are also located on or near the coast. In most LDC's one city, usually the capital, is the dominant center of economic power.

Industrialization in the HDC's provided economic opportunities in the growing cities that drained off the surplus rural labor, thereby keeping farm incomes from falling. However, the situation is very different in the LDC's. By the time industrialization began to have an impact in such LDC's as India, Egypt, and Brazil, their population growth rates were so high that the cities could not absorb the fast-growing rural population surplus. Cities in the LDC's do not act as economic "safety valves" for relieving rural poverty as they did in the HDC's. The result is that unemployment, underemployment, low incomes, and economic distress in general prevail in the rural sector, while another set of problems has emerged in the teeming cities.

To persons who have always lived in HDC's, the problems that beset the great mass of poor urban dwellers in the LDC's seem nothing short of incredible. The list of acute problems includes not only lack of housing, transportation, schooling, and sewage and garbage disposal, but even the lack of sanitary drinking water facilities. The World Health Organization (WHO) reported in 1963, after an extensive study of 75 LDC's, that only 33 percent of the urban population had piped water on the premises, and that 41 percent had no access to piped water, either on the premises or from public outlets. Over the intervening years, discouragingly little improvement has been made as the urban populations continue to grow.

THE WORLDWIDE GROWTH OF SQUATTER SETTLEMENTS

The growth of *squatter settlements* (*uncontrolled settlements*) in cities of the Less Developed World is a subject that has not received adequate attention. The global extent of the phenomenon and the number of people involved often astound otherwise informed people in the HDC's.

The dictionary definition of a *squatter* is one who settles on land, especially new or unsettled land, without title or right.[13]

---

[13] Many expressive local terms are used around the world in referring to squatters or squatter settlements. Some examples are: "shanty towns," "ranchitos" (Venezuela), "paracaidistas" or "parachutists" (Mexico), "gecekondu" (Turkey), "barriadas" (Peru), "callampas" or "mushrooms" (Chile), "favelas" (Brazil), "bidonvilles" (North Africa), and "bustees" (South Asia).

The process of squatting has accelerated over the past few decades. Roughly a third of the population of metropolitan Lima, Peru, lives in "barriadas."

Although variations occur in squatter settlements from country to country, certain generalizations about them can be made. They appear, sometimes literally overnight, on vacant, government-owned land. Squatter settlements exist in tropical or sub-tropical realms, where the mild climate does not require space heating. The typical squatter's home, at least when first erected, is a primitive structure of one or two rooms made of scrap lumber, sheet metal, stone, or even straw mats. The normal urban utilities, thought to be indispensable in the HDC's, are usually nonexistent. The settlements are therefore vulnerable to waterborne diseases and other dangers that have been virtually eliminated in the cities of Highly Developed Countries.

The total array of public health, economic, social, and other problems associated with life in the squatter settlements thoughout the world would require a separate volume for adequate description. However, despite their

---

SOME POSITIVE ASPECTS OF SQUATTER SETTLEMENTS

A number of investigators from various disciplines who have studied the squatting phenomenon in Peru, Chile, Jamaica, and elsewhere report certain favorable features of the process. Emrys Jones of the London School of Economics, writing about Venezuela, says, "Most 'ranchos' were built by those who live in them. They are not expressions of despair, but of hope and activity and courage; whereas society in a Western slum is often fragmented and disintegrating, all the evidence points to a high degree of organization and consciousness of neighborhood in the barrios."*

Anthropologist William Mangin wrote that at least 250,000 of Lima's squatters had built their own community and organized themselves politically and socially, almost without outside intervention. After a decade of research in Lima, he believes that the squatter settlements there succeeded because of, not in spite of, the lack of government intervention.†

Geographer Brian Berry suggests that squatter communities be viewed as *transitional urban settlements,* because the people in them "demonstrate remarkable vigour and ingenuity in improving their living conditions."‡

---

* Quoted in Charles Abrams, "Squatter Settlements: The Problem and the Opportunity," Office of International Affairs, Department of HUD, Washington, D.C., April, 1966. (Preface).
†William Mangin, 1967, "Latin American Squatter Settlements: A Problem and a Solution," *Latin American Research Review,* Vol. 2, pp. 65–98.
‡Brian J. L. Berry, *The Human Consequences of Urbanisation,* St. Martin's Press, New York, 1973, p. 88.

problems the squatter settlements have certain positive aspects that should interest urban planners in the United States and other industrialized nations.

SUMMARY

Cities are spatial concentrations of production, exchange, and consumption. A better understanding of the complex nature of modern cities is needed. A major influence on the growth of cities during the nineteenth and early twentieth centuries was the development of manufacturing. A more recent impetus has been the growth of service industries. Where the city is also a government center, its economic position is enhanced. Large cities become ecological dominants, ranging over wide areas for their material and energy needs, and generating metabolic wastes that pollute the city and its surroundings. Urban growth follows a feedback model in which advantages reinforce each other in an upward spiral until sizes are reached where constraints inhibit further growth. The value of urban land is determined chiefly by location and accessibility, although environmental site characteristics can also be factors. City commercial cores, called *Central Business Districts* (CBD's), are places of transportation convergence with very high accessibility. Land in the CBD is bid up to very high prices, which fall off rapidly outward, creating an ordered pattern of urban land uses. Urban land use and transportation service are mutually interacting influences. Two responses to rapid urban growth have been: (1) the use of three-dimensional space, and (2) suburbanization, resulting in urban sprawl. Shifting population and economic patterns in the United States include a migration from "Snowbelt" to "Sunbelt" cities. Urbanization in the Less Developed Countries has special features and problems. Squatter settlements, which are a dynamic part of urban development in many LDC's, have certain positive features that should interest urban planners in the United States and other Highly Developed Countries.

Questions

1 Analyze the city as an ecological system, with reference to its metabolic requirements and waste products.
2 Show graphically how the pattern of land use within a city can be hypothetically explained in terms of location rent.
3 Make an analysis of the economic base of your home community. Predict how it is likely to change over the next two decades.

4 How do you explain the extreme differences in land values within an urban area?
5 Discuss the dynamics of urban sprawl. What changes appear to have taken place in the process during the decade of the 1970s?
6 What are the reasons behind the migration of people and economic activity from the "Snowbelt" to the "Sunbelt"?

EPILOGUE

TRENDS
IN
THE
WORLD
ECONOMY—
LOOKING
AHEAD
TO
2000 A.D.

"A general description of what is happening in the modern industrial world can be given in one sentence, vast though its consequences may be. The macro-location of industry and population tends towards an ever-increasing concentration in a limited number of areas; their micro-location, on the other hand, towards an ever-increasing diffusion, or 'sprawl'."

Colin Clark*

The twenty-first century will arrive before most readers of this book reach their middle forties. The future, of course, holds many imponderables, yet certain trends can be identified that—barring unforeseen catastrophes—are likely to affect the world economy over the coming two decades. These trends are significant because they help reduce planning from a consideration of limitless futures to a more manageable set of possibilities. Although we view them individually, the trends act interdependently in influencing the location and character of economic activity.

The population of the world can be projected with reasonable assurance to about 6 billion by 2000 A.D., double the number it was in 1960. Significantly, the LDCs will account for 90 percent of this increase. It is highly probable that the higher latitude, arid, mountainous, and many tropical parts of the earth will remain sparsely populated. The global process of urbanization will continue to accompany population growth. By the end of the century an estimated 75 percent of the people in the HDCs will be urban

* *Population Growth and Land Use*, London: Macmillan, 1967, p. 280.

386

dwellers, while in the United States 9 out of 10 persons will reside in large cities or their suburbs. As urban sprawl expands, however, the densities of the inner city cores will continue to decline.

It is anticipated that the nations of the world will function within an increasingly interdependent global economy, a result more of technological advances than political or cultural affinities. World travel and trade, television connections via INTELSAT, overseas telephone messages, computer hook-ups, and other forms of international exchange will continue to increase at very high rates. Because of low energy requirements and a dynamic technology, telecommunication systems will have the dual effect of integrating distant regions and of dispersing population and industry within core areas. The problems of food supply, resource depletion, ocean exploitation, energy supply, and environmental pollution will become increasingly global in character.

A trend to larger scale operations will persist in most sectors of the modernized economies—manufacturing, agriculture, mining, and energy production, among others. The growing size and complexity of many production systems, such as electrical distribution, telecommunications, computer-controlled services of all kinds, and others will make them more vulnerable to accidental failure or to sabotage.

With growing economies of scale and agglomeration, high levels of productivity, high incomes, and growing mass markets, the industrial regions of the HDCs will continue to be sustained by natural and human resources pouring in from many corners of the earth. The economic gulf between the HDCs and many LDCs will continue to grow. The debate over economic growth versus environmental quality will continue, with low income nations fearful of being locked in at low levels of development in a no-growth world economy.

A trend that may grow acute within a few years is the mounting foreign debt of many LDCs, resulting in large measure from high oil prices. In contrast, the massive flow of capital funds to the oil-exporting OPEC nations is creating a different kind of problem. No one at this point can foretell what effects the accumulation of oil revenues will have on the monetary and political stability of the world.

The future ability of world agriculture to feed the growing population cannot now be determined because of a number of uncertainties. Most of heavily populated South and East Asia will remain engaged in labor intensive, low income agriculture. In direct contrast, the United States will be able to expand its agricultural output and exports substantially. America's role as a supplier of food to deficit nations is very likely to increase in the coming two decades.

High oil prices, among other things, will cause increasing deforestation and erosion in many LDCs, as low income groups scour the landscape for desperately needed firewood. On the positive side, the accessible forest regions of the tropical world hold promise for greatly increased output of wood products, including the production of alcohol as a substitute fuel. The United States is fortunate in having a large forest resource, which, despite high production, will continue to grow over the years under good forest management.

The serious events in Iran and Afghanistan during the winter of 1979-1980 highlighted the critical role Middle East oil plays in the global economy. Even if the world petroleum market is not disrupted by political or military events, the rising costs of oil supplies will adversely affect the economy of virtually every nation on earth. The United States and other nations with options will shift to other forms of energy, but at much higher prices than the pre-1973 levels. A four year study of American energy options released by the National Academy of Sciences in January 1980 concluded that: (1) conservation offers the greatest potential for mitigating the future energy supply problem, (2) coal and nuclear fission are the only practical, large scale replacements for oil and gas on the horizon, and (3) unless an unexpected breakthrough takes place, solar energy will not make a major contribution before the end of the century. The report acknowledged an array of environmental and other problems related to expanded use of coal and nuclear power, but believed that they could be overcome.

Mineral consumption by the HDCs will create some serious depletion problems. For many minerals, future price increases are expected to increase lower grade supplies to adequate levels. Certain critical metals, such as some of the nonferrous additives used in steel making, will continue to be imported by the industrialized nations from LDCs. The possibility exists of OPEC-type cartels rising among unstable or unfriendly mineral exporting governments in Latin America, Africa, and Asia.

Although the ocean floor contains enormous quantities of minerals such as copper, nickel, iron, manganese and cobalt, it will probably not become a major source of these minerals during the next two decades. Unless and until international agreement is reached regarding the cooperative operation of ocean fisheries, the full resource potential of the world's oceans will not be realized.

None of the problems looming on the horizon appear to be insurmountable for creative science and technology. Instead, the great challenge for the remainder of the century will be to work out peaceful political and institutional solutions to these problems. Not only our economic well-being and quality of life, but our very planetary survival depends on our ability to meet this challenge.

388

BIBLIOGRAPHY*

Airov, Joseph (1959), *The Location of the Synthetic Fiber Industry: A Study in Regional Analysis.* New York: John Wiley and Sons.

Alexander, J.W., and L.J. Gibson (1979), *Economic Geography,* 2nd ed., Englewood Cliffs, N.J.: Prentice-Hall.

Alexandersson, Gunnar (1967), *Geography of Manufacturing.* Englewood Cliffs, N.J.: Prentice-Hall.

Alonso, W. (1964), *Location and Land Use: Toward a General Theory of Land Rent.* Cambridge, Mass.: Harvard University Press.

Bain, J.S. (1968), *Industrial Organization,* 2nd ed., New York: John Wiley and Sons.

Beckmann, Martin (1968), *Location Theory.* New York: Random House.

Berry, B.J.L. (1973), *The Human Consequences of Urbanization.* London: The Macmillan Press.

Berry, B.J.L., et al. (1976), *The Geography of Economic Systems.* Englewood Cliffs, N.J.: Prentice-Hall.

Berry, B.J.L., and Quentin Gillard (1977), *The Changing Shape of Metropolitan America.* Cambridge, Mass.: Ballinger Publishing Co.

Berry, B.J.L., and John D. Kasarda (1977), *Contemporary Urban Ecology.* New York: Macmillan.

*This listing includes representative books, but does not attempt to cover the growing and diverse periodical literature relating to economic geography.

Bohi, D.R., and Milton Russell (1978), *Limiting Oil Imports* (Resources for the Future Publication). Baltimore, Md.: The Johns Hopkins University Press.

Bunge, William (1966), *Theoretical Geography*. Lund Studies in Geography.

Burton, Ian, et al. (1978), *The Environment As Hazard.* New York: Oxford University Press.

Carter, H. (1976), *The Study of Urban Geography,* 2nd ed. London: Edward Arnold.

Cecelski, Elizabeth, et al. (1979), *Energy and the Poor in the Third World* (Resources for the Future Publication). Baltimore, Md.: The Johns Hopkins University Press.

Chenery, H.B., and P.G. Clark (1959), *Interindustry Economics.* New York: John Wiley and Sons.

Chisholm, M. (1962), *Rural Settlement and Land Use.* London: Hutchinson.

Chisholm, M. (1966), *Geography and Economics.* London: Bell.

Chorley, R.J., and P. Haggett (1967), *Models in Geography.* London: Methuen.

Christaller, Walter (1966), *Central Places in Southern Germany,* translated by C.W. Baskin. Englewood Cliffs, N.J.: Prentice-Hall.

Clawson, Marion (1971), *Surburban Land Conversion in the United States* (Resources for the Future Publication). Baltimore, Md.: The Johns Hopkins University Press.

Clawson, Marion (1973), *Modernizing Urban Land Policy* (Resources for the Future Publication). Baltimore, Md.: The Johns Hopkins University Press.

Clawson, Marion (1975), *Forests For Whom and For What?* (Resources for the Future Publication). Baltimore, Md.: The Johns Hopkins University Press.

Conkling, E.C., and M. Yeates (1976), *Man's Economic Environment.* New York: McGraw-Hill.

Cooper, M.J.M. (1975), *The Industrial Location Decision Making Process.* Birmingham, U.K.: Centre for Urban and Regional Studies, The University of Birmingham.

Dales, J.H. (1968), *Pollution, Property and Prices.* Toronto, Canada: University of Toronto Press.

Darmstadter, Joel, et al. (1978), *How Industrial Societies Use Energy* (Resources for the Future Publication). Baltimore, Md.: The Johns Hopkins University Press.

Darmstadter, Joel, et al. (1979), *Energy in America's Future* (Resources for the Future Publication). Baltimore, Md.: The Johns Hopkins University Press.

Duncan, O.D., R.P. Cuzzort and B. Duncan (1961), *Statistical Geography: Problems of Analyzing Areal Data.* New York: The Free Press of Glencoe.

Dunn, E.S. (1954), *The Location of Agricultural Production.* Gainesville, Fla.: University of Florida Press.

Eliot Hurst, M.E. (1972), *A Geography of Economic Behavior.* North Scituate, Mass.: Duxbury.

Estall, R.C., and R.O. Buchanan (1973), *Industrial Activity and Economic Geography,* 3rd ed. London: Hutchinson.

Forrester, J.W. (1969), *Urban Dynamics.* Cambridge, Mass.: M.I.T. Press.

Forrester, J.W. (1973), *World Dynamics,* 2nd ed. Wright Allen Press.

Foust, J.B., and A.R. de Souza (1978), *The Economic Landscape: A Theoretical Introduction.* Columbus, Ohio: Charles E. Merrill.

Freeman, A. Myrick, III (1979), *The Benefits of Environmental Improvement* (Resources for the Future Publication). Baltimore, Md.: The Johns Hopkins University Press.

Friedmann, J. (1973), *Urbanization, Planning and National Development.* Beverly Hills, Calif.: Sage Press.

Friedrich, C.J. (1929), *Alfred Weber's Theory of the Location of Industries.* Chicago: University of Chicago Press.

Fuchs, V.R. (1962), *Changes in the Location of Manufacturing in the United States Since 1929.* New Haven, Conn.: Yale University Press.

Glikson, Artur (1971), *The Ecological Basis of Planning.* The Hague: Martinus Nijhoff.

Goddard, J.B. (1975), *Office Location in Urban and Regional Development.* London: Oxford University Press.

Gottmann, Jean (1961), *Megalopolis.* Cambridge, Mass.: M.I.T. Press.

Gottmann, Jean, and R.A. Harper (1967) (eds.), *Metropolis on the Move: Geographers Look at Urban Sprawl.* New York: John Wiley and Sons.

Greenhut, M.L. (1956), *Plant Location in Theory and Practice.* Chapel Hill: University of North Carolina Press.

Hägerstrand, T. (1967), *Innovation Diffusion as a Spatial Process,* translated by A. Pred. Chicago: University of Chicago Press.

Haggett, P. (1965), *Locational Analysis in Human Geography.* London: Edward Arnold.

Haggett, P., and R.J. Chorley (1969), *Network Analysis in Geography.* London: Edward Arnold.

Hall, P. (1966) (ed.), *Von Thünen's Isolated State.* London: Pergamon.

Hamilton, F.E.I. (1974) (ed.), *Spatial Perspectives on Industrial Organization and Decision Making.* New York: John Wiley and Sons.

Hamilton, F.E.I. (1978) (ed.), *Contemporary Industrialization: Spatial Analysis and Regional Development.* New York: Longman.

Hance, William A. (1977), *Black Africa Develops.* Crossroads Press.

Hay, A.M. (1973), *Transport for the Space Economy: A Geographical Study.* London: Macmillan.

Healy, R.G., and John S. Rosenberg (1976), *Land Use and the States* (Resources for the Future Publication). Baltimore, Md.: The Johns Hopkins University Press.

Hitch, Charles J. (1978) (ed.), *Resources for An Uncertain Future* (Resources for the Future Publication). Baltimore, Md.: The Johns Hopkins University Press.

Hoover, E.M. (1948), *The Location of Economic Activity.* New York: McGraw-Hill.

Hoover, E.M. (1975), *An Introduction to Regional Economics,* 2nd ed., New York: Knopf.

Isard, Walter (1960), *Methods of Regional Analysis.* Cambridge, Mass.: M.I.T. Press.

Isard, Walter (1969), *General Theory: Social, Political, Economic, and Regional.* Cambridge, Mass.: M.I.T. Press.

Kansky, K.J. (1963), *Structure of Transportation Networks.* Chicago: University of Chicago, Department of Geography Research Paper No. 84.

Karaska, G.J., and D.F. Bramhall (1969) (eds.), *Locational Analysis for Manufacturing: A Selection of Readings.* Cambridge, Mass.: M.I.T. Press.

King, L.J. (1969), *Statistical Analysis in Geography.* Englewood Cliffs, N.J.: Prentice-Hall.

Kneese, Allen V. (1977), *Economics and the Environment.* New York: Penguin Books.

Kneese, Allen V., and Blair T. Bower (1979), *Integrated Environmental Quality Management* (Resources for the Future Publication). Baltimore, Md.: The Johns Hopkins University Press.

Knos, D.W. (1962), *Distribution of Land Values in Topeka, Kansas.* University of Kansas Press.

Krutilla, John V., and Anthony C. Fisher (1975), *The Economics of Natural Environments* (Resources for the Future Publication). Baltimore, Md.: The Johns Hopkins University Press.

Krutilla, John V., et al. (1978), *Economic and Fiscal Impacts of Coal Development* (Resources for the Future Publication). Baltimore, Md.: The Johns Hopkins University Press.

Lloyd, P.E., and Peter Dicken (1977), *Location in Space,* 2nd ed. New York: Harper and Row.

Lösch, August (1954), *The Economics of Location.* New Haven, Conn.: Yale University Press. (Originally published by Gustav Fischer, Verlag).

Lowe, J., and Moryadas, S. (1975), *The Geography of Movement.* Boston: Houghton Mifflin.

Manthy, Robert S. (1978), *Natural Resource Commodities* (Resources for the Future Publication). Baltimore, Md.: The Johns Hopkins University Press.

Marsh, G.P. (1864), *Man and Nature,* edited by D. Lowenthal in 1965. Cambridge, Mass.: The Belknap Press of Harvard University Press.

Mayer, Harold M., and R.C. Wade (1969), *Chicago: Growth of a Metropolis.* Chicago: University of Chicago Press.

McCarty, H.H., and J.B. Lindberg (1966), *A Preface to Economic Geography.* Englewood Cliffs, N.J.: Prentice-Hall.

McDivitt, J.F., and Gerald Manners (1974), *Minerals and Men,* 2nd ed. (Resources for the Future Publication). Baltimore, Md.: The Johns Hopkins University Press.

Meinig, D.W. (1962), *On the Margins of the Good Earth.* Chicago: Rand McNally.

Mikesell, Raymond F. (1979), *The World Copper Industry* (Resources for the Future Publication). Baltimore, Md.: The Johns Hopkins University Press.

Miller, E. Willard (1977), *Manufacturing: A Study of Industrial Location.* University Park: The Pennsylvania State University Press.

Moore, G.T., and R.G. Golledge (1976) (eds.), *Environmental Knowing: Theories, Research and Methods.* Stroudsburg, Pa.: Dowden, Hutchinson & Ross.

Morrill, R.L. (1974), *The Spatial Organization of Society,* 2nd ed. North Scituate, Mass.: Duxbury Press.

Myrdal, Gunnar (1957), *Economic Theory and Under-Developed Regions.* London: Duckworth.

Page, Talbot (1977), *Conservation and Economic Efficiency* (Resources for the Future Publication). Baltimore, Md.: The Johns Hopkins University Press.

Pearce, D.W. (1976), *Environmental Economics.* New York: Longman.

Pelzer, Karl J. (1945), *Pioneer Settlement in the Asiatic Tropics.* American Geographical Society.

Perloff, H.S. (1969) (ed.), *The Quality of the Urban Environment* (Resources for the Future Publication). Baltimore, Md.: The Johns Hopkins University Press.

Pratten, C.F. (1971), *Economies of Scale in Manufacturing Industry.* New York: Cambridge University Press.

Pred, A.R. (1966), *The Spatial Dynamics of U.S. Urban-Industrial Growth, 1800-1914.* Cambridge, Mass.: M.I.T. Press.

Repetto, Robert G. (1979), *Economic Equality and Fertility in Developing Countries* (Resources for the Future Publication). Baltimore, Md.: The Johns Hopkins University Press.

Riley, R.C. (1973), *Industrial Geography.* London: Chatto and Windus.

Roepke, H.G., (1967) (ed.), *Readings in Economic Geography.* New York: John Wiley and Sons.

Rugg, Dean S. (1972), *Spatial Foundations of Urbanism.* Dubuque, Iowa: Wm. C. Brown.

Samuelson, Paul A. (1976), *Economics,* 10th ed. New York: McGraw-Hill.

Sauer, Carl O. (1969), *Agricultural Origins and Dispersals,* 2nd ed. Cambridge, Mass.: M.I.T. Press.

Smith, D.M. (1971), *Industrial Location.* New York: John Wiley and Sons.

Smith, R.H.T., E.J. Taaffe, and L.J. King (1968) (eds.), *Readings in Economic Geography.* Chicago: Rand McNally.

Smith, V. Kerry (1979), *Scarcity and Growth Reconsidered* (Resources for the Future Publication). Baltimore, Md.: The Johns Hopkins University Press.

Spencer, J.E. (1966), *Shifting Cultivation in Southeastern Asia.* Berkeley: University of California Press.

Taaffe, E.J., and H. Gauthier (1973), *Geography of Transportation.* Englewood Cliffs, N.J.: Prentice-Hall.

394

Thoman, R.S., and P. Corbin (1974), *The Geography of Economic Activity.* New York: McGraw-Hill.

Thomas, W.L. Jr. (1956) (ed), *Man's Role in Changing the Face of the Earth.* Chicago: University of Chicago Press.

Thompson, W.R. (1968), *A Preface to Urban Economics* (Resources for the Future Publication). Baltimore, Md.: The Johns Hopkins University Press.

Toyne, Peter (1974), *Organization, Location and Behavior: Decision-Making in Economic Geography.* New York: John Wiley and Sons.

Van Valkenburg, S., and C.C. Held (1952), *Europe.* New York: John Wiley and Sons.

Vance, J.E. Jr. (1970), *The Merchant's World: The Geography of Wholesaling.* Englewood Cliffs, N.J.: Prentice-Hall.

Warntz, William (1959), *Toward A Geography of Price.* University Park: University of Pennsylvania Press.

Warren, K. (1973), *American Steel Industry, 1850-1970: A Geographical Interpretation.* New York: Clarendon Press.

Webber, M.J. (1972), *The Impact of Uncertainty on Location.* Cambridge, Mass.: M.I.T. Press.

Weber, Alfred (1909), *Theory of the Location of Industries.* Chicago: University of Chicago Press.

White, Gilbert F. (1969), *Strategies of American Water Management.* Ann Arbor: The University of Michigan Press.

White, Gilbert F. (1974) (ed), *Natural Hazards.* New York: Oxford University Press.

Wiener, Norbert (1954), *Cybernetics and Society.* New York: Doubleday and Co.

Wingo, Lowdon (1963), *Cities and Space* (Resources for the Future Publication). Baltimore, Md.: The Johns Hopkins University Press.

Yeates, M.H. (1968), *An Introduction to Quantitative Analysis in Economic Geography.* New York: McGraw-Hill.

Zimmermann, Erich W. (1972), *World Resources and Industries,* 3rd ed. New York: Harper & Row.

Zipf, G.K. (1949), *Human Behavior and the Principle of Least Effort.* Reading, Mass.: Addison-Wesley.

Index

Common property resource, 109
Comparative advantage, 65-70, 106, 200
Conklin, Harold C., 8
Conkling, Edgar C., 203
Conservation, 110, 255
Consumer behavior and store location, 374
Consumption, 4, 5, 114, 276
Coon, Carleton, 35, 151
Copper, production, 135
 production stages and environmental
  impacts, 232
Cornbelt, 154
Cost substitutions based on environmental
 variations, 58-59
Cost surfaces and space-cost curves, 291
Counter production, 12, 16, 117
Cox, Kevin R., 138
Crusoe, Robinson, as economic decision
 maker, 58
Cybernetic models applied to economic
 development, 48, 50-51

Deductive modelling, 72-104
Demand: curve, 94-97
 threshold, 94-99
Depletion, concept of, 110
Dicken, Peter, 353
Diffusion, of innovation, 21, 42
Distance: cost of, 304
 as key variable in location
  theory, 56-58, 73-75, 85
 and rent, 132
Distance-cost functions and rate structures,
 313, 315-319
Doehring, Donald O., 139
Dual spatial-environmental approach to
 economic activity, advantages of, viii
Dunn, Edgar S., Jr., 77, 132
Dust Bowl disaster, 127

Earth moved on construction projects, 126
Ecological consequences of water regulation,
 147-148
Ecology, interaction with economics, 58,
 124-129
Economic change, spatial diffusion of, 20-52
Economic decision making, 9, 58
Economic development, 45-51
 arguments for and against, 49
 as feedback process, 48, 50-51
 and productivity, 51

Economic doctrine of substitutability, 110
Economic effects of low-cost circulation,
 305-308
Economic functions of cities, 352-362
Economic geographers, 21
Economic geography, 131, 162, 292, 304
 relevance of, to contemporary problems, viii
 typical questions in, 3
 usefulness of, in private sector, vii
Economic growth, process of, 51
Economic landscape, 9-16, 69, 85, 92, 94, 98,
  109, 111, 114-115, 117, 123, 132, 318
Economic man, 36, 73, 75-76, 94
Economic potential, and industrial location,
 355, 357
Economic production: definition of, 113-114
 intermediate stages of, 114
 model of, 106-108
 spatial character of, 114
Economic rent, 59-63, 69-70, 221, 225
Economics, link with ecology, 58
Economics and economic geography as
 complementary fields, 16-18
Electric power grids, 248-249
Electronics revolution, 337-339
Energy: as Achilles' Heel of U.S., 254
 alternatives for U.S., 255-271
 changing patterns of production and
  consumption of, 246-272
 conservation of, need for, 255
 global crisis over, 249-255
 impacts of higher prices, 252
 prodigious use of, in U.S. and Canada, 248
 and spatial economy, 247-249, 311
Environment, as an intellectual frontier, vii
Environment, waste-assimilating limitations
 of, 121
Environmental approaches to economic
 location and land-use, 53-70
Environmental Determinism, intellectual
 error of, vii-viii
Environmental factors influencing economic
 activity, 131-154
Environmental impact, 15-16, 117-118, 123,
 237-240, 262-263, 365-366
Environmental pollution, 118, 365-366
European economic development,
 environmental and spatial influences in,
 287, 308
Exchange, 4
Exchange economies, 9

398